Old Order Mennonites of Ontario: Gelassenheit, Discipleship, Brotherhood

Old Order Mennonites of Ontario: Gelassenheit, Discipleship, Brotherhood

By Donald Martin

Published by Pandora Press
Co-published with Herald Press
2003

National Library of Canada Cataloguing in Publication

Martin, Donald, 1944-
Old Order Mennonites of Ontario : gelassenheit, discipleship, brotherhood / Donald Martin.

Includes bibliographical references and index.
ISBN 1-894710-33-9

1. Old Order Mennonites—Ontario—History. I. Title.

BX8129.O43M37 2003 289.7'713 C2003-901901-2

Old Order Mennonites of Ontario: Gelassenheit, Discipleship, Brotherhood

33 Kent Avenue
Kitchener, Ontario N2G 3R2
www.pandorapress.com

Co-published with Herald Press
Scottdale, Pennsylvania / Waterloo, Ontario

International Standard Book Number: 1-894710-33-9
Book design by Julia Stark
Cover design by Greg Heipel

13 12 11 10 09 08 07 06 05 04 03 12 11 10 9 8 7 6 5 4 3 2 1

Table of Contents

Acknowledgments

"The lines have fallen upon me in pleasant places: yea, I have a goodly heritage" (Psalms 16:6).

Those born into the Old Order Mennonite community indeed have a goodly heritage, but it took me years to learn to appreciate this blessing. The Old Order Mennonite community has been a social haven for me, and the church was like a lighthouse that led me towards the Lord and Saviour Jesus Christ. These blessings are truly a gift from God.

As I entered the years of adulthood and began reading books of Mennonite history and theology, I began to appreciate my heritage. I am indebted to the historian John L. Ruth who, through personal conversation and his many historical writings, gave me a better understanding of my Mennonite birthright. Walter Klaassen's book, *Anabaptism: Neither Catholic nor Protestant*, showed me that there were some significant theological differences between Anabaptism and the other mainline Christian churches. Robert Friedmann's *Mennonite Piety Through the Ages* gave me a thirst to further study Pietism and the Anabaptist theme of *Gelassenheit.* There were many writings regarding Pietism and Gelassenheit written from a perspective outside of the Old Order Mennonite community, but no attempt had been made to deal with Gelassenheit from an Old Order viewpoint. Having received some encouragement to pursue this challenge, I prayerfully considered the question at hand and then decided to write my personal views on the values of my special birthright—Anabaptism—and how its underlying theme, Gelassenheit, shaped the Old Order

Mennonite communities of Ontario. Gelassenheit is a word for which there is no English equivalent. It refers to an attitude that is ready to yield, abandon, or surrender personal desires before God and the community. Not only does Gelassenheit shape the Old Order understanding of salvation, it shapes everyday life in the community. The attitude of Gelassenheit can be called "non-assertive humility," as will be noted in more detail later. This book is an attempt to present an accurate account of the Old Order Mennonites by neither glorifying the strength of the people nor hiding their weaknesses; nevertheless, I acknowledge my humanity and ask for forbearance if I err or offend any person.

I am indebted to many individuals who assisted in the making of this book. The first and most important is my wife, Irene, who for years patiently endured the cluttered mess on my desk which, to me, was very importantly arranged. She accepted that at times her husband was so involved with his project that she had to wait for him to respond to her. Such patience was an invaluable asset to the making of this book. Samuel Steiner, the archivist at Conrad Grebel University College, also gave much-needed guidance and encouragement as the project unfolded. I am grateful towards Julia Stark for editing the manuscript. Without the layout expertise of Pandora Press there would be only a manuscript and no book. I am thankful to Arnold Snyder and his staff for publishing this book. Last but not least my gratitude goes to the many brethren and friends within the various Old Order Mennonite communities who spent countless hours reading the manuscript and making the much needed, and highly appreciated, critical comments. Without these comments this book would have been the voice of one person, but it now includes the opinions of others from within the Old Order communities.

Though this book has been critically read by those from within, it is not a church-sponsored project but an individual's endeavour to present a story from within the Old Order Mennonite circles of their goodly heritage.

Foreword

Donald Martin has provided insights into the history of the varied "Old Order" Mennonite groups in Ontario from a perspective that is at once both uniquely Old Order and a valuable contribution to the literature on this group. *Old Order Mennonites of Ontario* is virtually alone in its attempt to describe and analyze, in a comprehensive way, Old Order history from within the conservative Mennonite community.

Martin is a member of the Markham-Waterloo Conference - a group that separated 60 years ago from the Old over use of automobiles, electricity and gasoline-powered farm equipment. However The Markham-Waterloo Mennonites share some meetinghouses with the Old Order Mennonites, and administer Mennonite parochial grade schools together with the Old Order. Although Old Orders still travel by horse and buggy, in recent decades they have accepted telephones and electricity in their homes, and some use of mechanized equipment in the fields.

Although a farmer all his life, Donald Martin developed a passion for the history of his Mennonite community. This was reflected in his earlier involvement in the preparation of two history texts for use in the Old Order / Markham Mennonite parochial schools. Although not a formally trained historian, Donald Martin has read widely in Anabaptist-Mennonite literature, as his bibliography attests. He thinks like a historian, and tries to identify the important theological cords that bind together a cohesive Old Order Mennonite theology.

This is an important effort because the history of conservative groups has usually been written by assimilated Mennonites who speak from a perspective that has "moved beyond" a "narrow" Old Order theology. Donald Martin, however, describes a "Gelassenheit" theology founded on community that becomes a remarkably coherent apologetic for an Old Order theology.

Old Order Mennonites of Ontario is not only a uniquely "insider" account, it is a valuable addition to the growing shelf of Ontario "Old Order Mennonite" literature that has emerged in recent years - ranging from Carl Hiebert's beautiful photographic essays to John F. Peter's sociological snapshot of the "Plain People" to Isaac R. Horst's numerous reflective works on Old Order Mennonite life and culture.

But none of these other works, valuable in their own right, provide the detail and analysis of Martin's work that allows the reader to delineate the strands of the Old Order Mennonite community so clearly - the Stauffer Mennonites, the Old Order, the Dave Martins, the "Orthodox" Mennonites, the Hoover group, etc. This is detail and analysis that only an informed insider could provide.

The importance of *Old Order Mennonites of Ontario* is underscored by the financial assistance toward publication it received from the Mennonite Historical Society of Ontario, and the Institute of Anabaptist Mennonite Studies at Conrad Grebel University College in Waterloo, Ontario.

Sam Steiner, Librarian & Archivist
Conrad Grebel University College

Introduction

Chapter One

"And Jesus said unto him, No man, having put his hand to the plough, and looking back, is fit for the kingdom of God" (Luke 9:62 AV). In this passage Jesus implies that his followers need to devote all unto Him if they want to be His disciples. In St Matthew's gospel Jesus makes clear what it takes to be His disciple. "Then said Jesus unto his disciples, If any man will come after me, let him deny himself, and take up his cross, and follow me" (Matthew 16:24). God's love for the sinful human race draws individuals to make a voluntary commitment to serve Him. This commitment to God's service is one of the basic Christian attributes that yields the peaceful fruits of holiness, virtues that are also displayed by many of the Old Testament characters.

Noah, for example, labored many years to construct the Ark that God asked him to build. The ridicule he faced as he patiently worked to build the Ark on dry ground we'll never understand. Abraham also demonstrated servitude when, at God's command, he offered his son Isaac on the altar. This episode is hard to comprehend, but God evidently blessed Abraham because he was willing to surrender unto God that which was most dear to him. Another example of yielding personal feelings in exchange for God's commands can be seen in the life of King David. Even though Samuel the prophet had anointed David to be king of Israel, David elected not to kill King Saul when the opportune time came, but only cut off a piece of Saul's skirt. David knew it was not his right to remove Saul from the throne and he was willing to wait until God had removed Saul from the throne before he took it. Many other examples could be taken from the Bible to show that people were willing to leave all for God and serve him. Servitude or discipleship is a virtue that has been displayed throughout the whole Bible and has continued throughout the Christian era. Discipleship did not necessarily distinguish the Anabaptists, or today the Old Order Mennonites, from the mainline Christian Churches.

The Anabaptists differed from the other Christian Churches in several ways.

1. The Anabaptists received their nickname because they considered infant baptism only as a "Romish Bath," as Conrad Grebel put it, and refused to accept it as a baptism. The Anabaptists believed that before baptism a person must have faith in God, a recognition of Jesus as Saviour, and express repentance and sorrow for one's sins. There had to be some understanding and a faith in God and salvation before a person was ready to be baptized.

2. The Anabaptists believed that the Word of God was supreme and the ultimate guide for the church and her people. They encouraged their members to study the Word and those who could not read memorized large portions of the Bible. Conversely the Catholic Church discouraged her people from reading the Bible, and held that only the priests were able to interpret the Word. Nevertheless, when almost a hundred thousand copies of Martin Luther's German Bible spread across Europe during the Reformation, it became impossible for the Pope to control the literature the people would read. The introduction of the Bible in the vernacular gave the people the opportunity to study the Bible, but it would be over a hundred years before the Protestant Churches encouraged their people to study the Bible.

3. The Anabaptists' view of the church also set them apart from the mainline churches which held that the church and the state were two institutions that were interwoven to the point where they were one. The Anabaptists ... "believed and confessed in a visible Church of God, consisting of those...who have truly repented, rightly believed, are rightly baptized, are united with God in heaven, and incorporated with the communion of the saints on earth."[1] The Anabaptists believed that the church was separate from the state. The church was subject to the state, but only if the laws of the land did not conflict with the Anabaptists' understanding of the Bible. The Anabaptists were persecuted for this belief because during the Reformation era the rulers thought anarchy

would surely develop if the church were not controlled by the state. The concept that Catholics, Protestants and Anabaptists could all co-exist peacefully developed first in the Netherlands and then in Pennsylvania during the 1700s.

4. The Anabaptists' belief that the church is separate from the state brought them into conflict with the state when they refused to swear the oath of allegiance. Their strict adherence to their word "yes" or "no" also distinquished them from the other churches of their day.

5. The Anabaptists' interpretation of the Word led them to a non-resistant faith. They were ready to suffer the spoiling of their goods and to flee to another country rather than defend themselves. This ultimate yieldedness to God—*Gelassenheit* (see chapter three) is the foundation of the Anabaptist faith that separated them from other Protestant churches. The Old Order Amish and Mennonites have retained this spirit of Gelassenheit in varied forms in their groups, and as we study the Old Order Mennonites of Ontario we find that theme of Gelassenheit still separates them from their Protestant neighbours.

John Driver notes, "The Anabaptists also had a solid sense of their collective identity. They were God's people. They stood in contrast to the world. They suffered the birth pangs of the new order, which was being born. They anticipated the advent of God's Kingdom. They thought of themselves as a people living in solidarity with the Messianic community of the first century."[2] The Old Order Mennonites' sense of identity traces back to Anabaptism, but they do not share the evangelistic fervour of sixteenth-century Anabaptists. Radical Anabaptism has, over the centuries, quietly evolved to the Old Order Mennonite concept of being the "Stillen in dem Lande" (the quiet in the land). The Old Order Mennonites, like their Anabaptist forefathers, stand in contrast to the world, but the plot has changed. The persecution and martyrdom the Anabaptists endured has ended, while today the Old Order Mennonites are challenged by prosperity, cultural pressures and Protestant religious literature. Only on rare occasions are books printed that hold the Anabaptist ethos of Gelassenheit, discipleship and brotherhood.

To suggest that these Christian values are unique to Old Order Mennonitism is wrong, but the emphasis the Anabaptists had placed on Gelassenheit, discipleship, and brotherhood is particularly Anabaptist and has been adopted by the Old Order communities. Their emphasis on discipleship reflects the voluntary commitment of being obedient to God's Word and the brotherhood of believers. The molding of Gelassenheit into a brotherhood of believers and the church sets the Old Order people apart from other Christian churches. Even though they are weak in theology, the Old Order Mennonites have for centuries passed down the values of Gelassenheit as a distinct faith—a remarkable feat.

In simple terms, the Anabaptists thought of Jesus as *Lord* while the Protestants look upon Jesus as their *Saviour*. The Anabaptists' emphasis on Jesus as Lord created a *responsibility* towards God and how they could worship and serve Him. The Protestant focus on Saviour reflected more a *gift* or grace and what God *had done* for the human family. Salvation truly was a gift from God through the blood of Jesus. It is certain that Anabaptists and Protestants both understood that Jesus was both Lord and Saviour. Nevertheless, as the Protestant focus on *gift* began to seep into the Mennonite Church and the theme of worship or Gelassenheit diminished, there were individuals who felt and resisted the change. In this story of the Old Order Mennonites of Ontario we will endeavour to explain how the theme of worship or Gelassenheit resulted in the birth of the Old Order Mennonite Church.

The Anabaptist Heritage

The Old Order Mennonite heritage is Anabaptism. The formation of the Swiss Brethren fellowship in 1525 is truly a milestone in their history, but there were also other religious pressures affecting Europe at that time. In Spain small Bible study groups sprang up as early as 1511, clearly preceding the Reformation in German lands. Their teaching was similar to the Anabaptists', but the Inquisition extinguished the tiny flame and completely destroyed the movement. The Swiss Brethren were just one of many religious groups during the Reformation era.

In Switzerland the Anabaptist movement was driven by persecution into the remote areas of the Alps Mountains. For over a hundred years the Anabaptists, or Brethren as they preferred to call themselves, were intermittently hunted like mad dogs. By 1639 Zurich lords had had enough and were determined to eradicate the Brethren. In November of that year an order went out that all Brethren be arrested, their goods confiscated, their marriages annulled, and their children declared illegitimate. In the harshest conditions they were crowded into the prisons which had been emptied of criminals. Their children were forcefully taken from them; there was no mercy. The general population strongly disapproved so the attempts to sell their properties found few buyers.

News of these atrocities drifted down the Rhine. The Dutch Mennonites were aghast at the tidings. They secretly sent relief to their Brethren in distress, but all their pleas for mercy on behalf of the Brethren were rebuffed. Imprisonments of up to three years were the lot of many steadfast Brethren; others wasted away and died martyrs' deaths in prison. The common people were sympathetic towards the Brethren, therefore the authorities avoided open confrontations with them

The Palatinate had been devastated during the Thirty Years War (1618-1648) and beckoned these ragged and often homeless saints. Many Brethren quietly moved from Zurich to the Palatinate. Ultimately, the might of Zurich succeeded in driving the peace-loving Brethren from their homes nestled on the mountain slopes. Several anecdotes about Old Order Mennonite names that are found in the archives tell of how Zurich went about driving them out.

In 1641 Hans Rudolf Bauman, a minister, was kept in prison for over sixty weeks. He escaped but his home was sold and his wife and children were exiled. Peter Brubach and Hans Landis were arrested in 1637 and kept in confinement for sixty weeks. While they were in bonds their property was sold to the benefit of the state. Hans Huber was fettered and chained with no prospect of release, and his wife and three other women were driven into exile. In 1639 Ulli Schneider, a minister of the Brethren, was apprehended and died as a result of his mistreatment. George Weber became severely ill after a fare of bread and water for seventy weeks, and also had his property confiscated. Even after enduring such persecution, the Swiss Brethren were reluctant to leave their homeland. Since the Eby, Good, Miller, and Nissley families were steadfast in their faith, their descendants can trace their heritage to the beautiful valleys of Zurich.

Anabaptism was also deeply rooted in the canton of Bern. Imprisonments, confiscation of their goods, and banishment were all tactics the Bernese officials used to free their land of these unwanted people. The high point of the Bernese persecution came in 1570. The ministers were flogged, branded, and sent over the border. The Brethren's homes were confiscated and they were given fourteen days to leave the country. Those who refused to comply were scourged and led across the border; if they returned they could expect more severe measures to be taken. Such orders created untold hardships for the Brethren, especially when there were other family members in prison or when some of the family were still part of the Reformed Church.

The Dutch intervention of 1660 was to no avail, even though documents were submitted which explained the Mennonite freedom in Holland. Bern nevertheless felt justified in ridding itself of the Brethren and in 1671 decided to deport the healthiest Brethren as galley slaves. Public and foreign political pressure forced Bern to abandon this cruel act. In the Emmental Valley (the home of the Old Order Martins) the populace opposed these "hunters," and would issue warnings that the hunters were coming by shouting, blowing horns, and similar signs. In 1714 the Sumiswald hunters had captured some Brethren, but a mob surrounded them and forcibly released the Brethren.

The Baumans, Brubachers, Erbs, Lichtys, Martins, and Sherks were among these despised and hated outcasts who left Bern and wandered down the Rhine to the Palatinate seeking new homes. They put into practice the words of their Lord: "But when they persecute you in this city, flee ye into another . . . " (Matthew 10:23 AV).

Reluctantly Tolerated

Religious toleration, the Anabaptist dream, was first achieved in Holland. Although the Reformed clergy adamantly sought to suppress Anabaptism, William of Orange, the leader of the Dutch revolt, wanted toleration. The Union of Utrecht in 1579 decreed that no one was to be persecuted for his faith. With the magistrates favouring the Anabaptists, the Reformed clergy could only harass them, which they did. However, the Mennonites in Holland generally worshipped and lived in peace.

The devastated Palatinate was the next district to beckon these religious refugees. The Elector Karl Ludwig of the Palatinate desperately needed experienced farmers, and the fugitive Brethren of Switzerland easily fitted this role; however, as soon as these renegades became known, the Reformed clergy began their clamouring—away with these "Mennists," as the Swiss

Brethren called themselves after they had moved into the Palatinate. Being a Mennist was not as dangerous as being a *Taufer* (the "Taufer" or "baptizers" were a hated sect in Switzerland while the Mennists were a tolerated group in Holland). The Mennonites presented a petition to the elector in 1653 to obtain permission to meet for worship. After a decade of negotiations the elector finally granted them limited religious toleration for a fee of six guilders which was called "Mennist Recognition Money." This concession was considered a great privilege in that day. It was the norm for the dominating Reformed Church to levy special taxes on all other religious groups for the privilege of working and living in the country. Therefore the Catholics also paid fees for baptism, marriage and death rites, as did the local Jews. The religious concessions had to be renewed by each elector. Charles Philip (1716–42) doubled the Mennonite Recognition money, and as a result many Mennonites emigrated to Pennsylvania during his rule.

The story of the Dutch Mennonite's generosity has often failed to reach the people who were the beneficiaries of this benevolence. In 1672 no less than 787 pitiful Bernese Mennonites received 15,466 guilders from the Dutch Mennonites. For sixty years appeal after appeal was sent down the Rhine to the prosperous Dutch Mennonites. Their increasing resistance towards paying ocean fares must be appreciated, but the basic needs of the refugees were met with brotherly compassion.[3]

Suffering was the main theme of the Anabaptist religion, a theme that gave the Anabaptists much patience and an absolute trust in God "But I am poor and needy: make haste unto me, O God: thou art my help and my deliverer; O LORD, make no tarrying" (Psalms 70:1-5 AV). However, they were people who had feelings, families, and loved ones, and who needed food and shelter.

For centuries religious toleration was not understood in Europe: "Religion was not thought of as a private matter between God and a man's conscience, but was inextricably bound up with society and politics. It kept the king's subjects in obedience, and because it did so it became the direct concern of the state."[4] In this the Anabaptists differed. Their religion was a private matter between God and their conscience, and furthermore, their loyalty was directed towards what they considered the Church of Christ.

For these reasons the Swiss Brethren endured persecution in Switzerland, and from about 1650-1725 the majority of the Brethren fled from Switzerland. They first re-established in the Palatinate, but when they again experienced religious suppression, they moved on to Pennsylvania. The story of how these people were painfully uprooted from their homeland and then transplanted in the New World is effectively covered in Ruth's book, *The Earth is the Lord's*,[5] and other writings.

Notes

1 Dortrecht Confession Article Eight

2 John Driver, *Radical Faith: An Alternative History of the Christian Church* (Kitchener, Ontario: Pandora Press, 1999), 210.

3 John L. Ruth, *Maintaining the Right Fellowship* (Scottdale, PA: Herald Press, 1984), 42, 95.

4 Neville Williams, *Milestones of History* (New York: Newsweek Books, 1974), 492.

5 John L. Ruth, *The Earth is the Lord's* (Lancaster, PA: Lancaster Mennonite Historical Society, 2001).

The Sojourn in Pennsylvania

Chapter Two

The Indians left a legend in Skippack, Pennsylvania. It's a memory of sadness—a story of an Indian and a white man sitting on a log. Without comment the Indian slid along the log towards the white man. The Indian's quiet gestures continued until the white man no longer had room on the log and was forced to sit on the ground beside the log. The perplexed white man asked the Indian what he meant by his peculiar behaviour. The Indian replied that in like manner the white man had crowded the Indian off his land. The sad story of the ethnic cleansing of the North American Natives is also part of the Mennonite heritage because after the natives were driven away, the Mennonites were active buyers of the purloined native lands.

The Quest for Freedom

Although many different religious groups came to the new world, they each brought with them the notion of religious uniformity. The Quaker's rule of religious freedom in Pennsylvania failed, but it became the prototype for religious freedom as the United States became a nation.[1]

Religious freedom and the freedom of one's conscience are two distinct issues. An example of religious freedom is a Catholic community and a Protestant community living side-by-side under one political government. Freedom of conscience occurs when people can worship according to the dictates of their consciences without interference from the civil authorities, and especially when minority groups hold values contrary to the general public such as the Mennonite doctrine of non-resistance. Freedom of conscience, especially the exemption from military service, has been a continual struggle for the Peace Churches in Canada and the United States.[2] Medieval European warfare had been little more than a risky game, but when French soldiers crossed the Alps in 1494 and entered Italy to fight and kill, a new age was born.[3] The old international loyalties to the Catholic Church had given way to patriotic nationalism. The religious strife of the sixteenth and seventeenth centuries brought elements of cruelty and revenge which were not present in the earlier mercenary warfare. With patriotism there arose a new concept—that military service is one of the essential elements of good citizenship.[4] For the peace-loving Mennonites of North America, these new values violated their non-resistant faith. The French-Indian War and the American Revolution illustrated for American Mennonites the difficulties of maintaining such a faith.

Religious Freedom—The Anabaptist Utopia

In 1688, William III of Orange stepped across the English Channel as the invited monarch of the English throne; he brought with him the more tolerant religious values of Holland. The following year the English parliament passed the Toleration Act which gave Quakers legal exemption from the militia.[5] In America, on the other hand, most colonies were quick to impose heavy fines on those who neglected to attend militia-training exercises.

The Quaker's rule of religious freedom in Pennsylvania is an interesting part of the Old Order Mennonite story because it helped shape them as a people. Pennsylvania became politically divided as the Peace Churches actively supported the Quakers in voting. However, as England became more involved in her quarrel with Spain, the Quakers came under heavy pressure to give England military support. In 1742 the Quakers passed a law that made it easier for members of the Peace Churches to receive citizenship. This strengthened the political allegiance between the immigrant Germans from Europe, the Peace Churches, and the Quakers. This voting block kept the Quakers in power until 1770, but it also sharply divided the Pennsylvania colony. When the political block disintegrated during the American Revolutionary War, the Peace Churches were in a difficult position because they had been politically involved with the Quaker party that gave way to the militant Scotch-Irish bloc.

At that time the Mennonite community was also concerned about its public image. In 1742, Martin Mylin was reprimanded by the church for building "a sandstone palace" because "the appearance of it might strengthen their enemies in prejudicing the government against them."[6] A Lancaster Catholic priest observed that "the thrifty Mennonites became the wealthiest of the Germans. Some of them possessed a thousand acres."[7]

> (1) *Christian Eby built a barn ninety-nine feet long in the 1750s. It was built only so long so he would not offend his neighbour who had built a barn a full hundred feet long. Even though Christian held the tenets of the Mennonite brotherhood, his large barn could not be hidden from the public.*[8]

"Sandstone palaces" and large barns could not be hidden—Mennonites were no longer just "the quiet in the land."(1) This concern was warranted, as during the American Revolution many Patriots resented the "rich Mennonites of Lancaster County."

The French-Indian War (Seven Years War) broke out in 1755 and brought unnerving and deadly Indian raids. As the paranoid frontiersmen were flushed out of the foothills by the Indians, the pressure for organized militia increased. The procrastination of the Quaker Assembly which was supported by the Peace Churches only fed the anger of the frustrated Scotch-Irish.[9]

While the Mennonites resisted militia drills, they responded positively to the appeal for wagons and teams for the disastrous Braddock campaign against Fort Pitt in 1755. Peter Bricker would later tell his son, Samuel, the popular hero in the *Trail of the Conestoga*, about his adventure with Braddock's army.[10]

Again in 1759 the Mennonites not only supplied wagons and produce for the army, but also were willing to "mention it at their meetings next Sunday."[11] As the call for frontier defence through militia raged, the Mennonites saw even more clearly the tension between their obligation to support the civil government and their lives as followers of Christ within a disciplined brotherhood.[12] (The twentieth century Old Order Mennonites would resist such army contacts.) When the Patriotic pressure

(3) *The difference in monetary values renders it almost impossible to demonstrate the harshness of fines the Peace Churches paid during the war. For the duration of the war the total fines were equivalent to the value of a farm.*[13]

Abraham Boehm, a miller and brother to Martin Boehm, was fined eight hundred pounds in one year during the Revolution because he would not take up arms. This was between one-third to one-half of the value of a farm. Boehm became the first Mennonite to settle at Niagara in 1787. In 1778 over one-third of Washington County's revenue came from these fines. A British officer observed that the people were grievously oppressed and pay more taxes in one year now than in twenty-one years before.[14] *Even though only a minority of the Americans welcomed independence in 1776, the fines and the Test Act rapidly separated those who had convictions against war and those who had no interest in the war. Those who would not take the oath (Test Act) could not vote, engage in trades such as law and medicine, take part in legal administration, make a will, and would have to pay double taxes.*

to support the Revolutionary War increased, some Mennonites again assisted the revolutionaries to escape the censure of the military. The famous Conestoga wagons drawn by the durable Conestoga horses were necessary to move the army's powder and flour.

The Peace Churches endured many trials during the war. Some of these misfortunes were self-inflicted because the simple Mennonites were naive of their grave situation. For example: farmers were forbidden to carry produce across enemy lines, but Matthias Tyson disregarded the order and was arrested for trying to sneak eggs and butter across the line. He was tied to a tree. The soldiers used him as a target and his eggs for ammunition. One John Roberts was not so fortunate. He was convicted for treason and hanged.

The Peace Churches gave lodging to anybody without distinction. It did not matter if the soldier was American or British, but they would help those in need. The Patriots engaged in deliberate entrapments. American soldiers would pose as ragged, needy, escaped British prisoners of war and after receiving aid would charge their benefactor for helping the enemy. Susanna Longacre, an elderly saint, gave a meal to such villains and was sentenced to a 150-pound fine or to receive 117 lashes on her bare back at the public post. Some of these outlandish charges were appealed in court, but some people suffered untold hardships.[15]

Mennonite gunsmiths met a different challenge. To sell a rifle to a frontiersman who *might* use it to kill an Indian was one thing, but to accept a contract from the army was to the Mennonite a violation of conscience. John Newcomer, a Mennonite, was summoned to court because he refused to manufacture guns for the army. The court ordered him to discontinue his trade and dismissed him. For as much as the Peace Churches had dabbled in assisting the army, the heavy fines (3) imposed upon them dampened their enthusiasm for the Patriot cause, and it is safe to conclude that "there were few waverers": "Non-resistance was a deeply ingrained and 'popular' doctrine among" the Peace Churches.[16] Their experiences during the American Revolution brought the Mennonites back to an understanding of the suffering church.[17] At the end of the Revolutionary War in 1783, the Mennonites held the same vision they had embraced when they approached the Philadelphia harbour a century earlier in 1683, but before the war there was already a new breeze that was gently blowing along the Atlantic coast which also drifted into the Pennsylvanian valleys. It would be this breeze, Pietism, which would in time change the course of the Mennonite church.

Notes

[1] Richard K. MacMaster, *Land, Piety, Peoplehood* (Scottdale, PA: Herald Press, 1985), 138.

[2] See Glossary regarding Peace Churches.

[3] Richard A. Preston, Sydney F. Wise, and Herman O. Werner, *Men in Arms* (New York, Washington: Frederick A. Praeger, Publishers, 1962), 95.

[4] MacMaster, Horst and Ulle, *Conscience in Crisis* (Scottdale, PA: Herald Press, 1979), 30, 535.

[5] *Ibid.*, 62.

[6] *Ibid.*, 33.

[7] *Ibid.*, 46.

[8] Eldon D. Weber, *A Historical History of Waterloo Township by Ezra E. Eby* (Kitchener: Self Published, 1984), 135.

[9] See Glossary regarding the Scotch-Irish.

[10] I. C. Bricker, *The History of Waterloo Township up to 1825* (Kitchener: Waterloo Historical Society, 1934), 88.

[11] MacMaster, *Conscience in Crisis*, 99.

[12] *Ibid.*, 215.

[13] Conversation between John Ruth and the Author, ca. 1992.

[14] MacMaster, *Conscience in Crisis*, 503.

[15] John L. Ruth, *Maintaining the Right Fellowship* (Scottdale, PA: Herald Press, 1984), 191.

[16] MacMaster, *Conscience in Crisis*, 525.

[17] *Ibid.*, 55.

Gelassenheit Challenged

Chapter Three

Before we enter the sensitive discussion of Gelassenheit, Pietism, and other related Biblical issues, the author desires to clarify his position. The intent of this book is to portray the Old Order Mennonites. The complexity of the task at hand is to present to those outside of the Old Order circles a non-compromising view of the Old Orders' beliefs in a non-offensive way. Frequently differences are nominal, but a shift in emphasis has directed the Old Orders on another course of life. The author begs patience and forbearance from the reader if he or she finds it challenging to grasp the Old Order story as the author attempts to put into words how the Old Order "feel" their religion. The author will deviate from standard literary rules and not footnote the quotations of Old Orders living today, as the Old Order culture would find this offensive.

Anabaptism or Old Order Mennonitism Defined

At the time of the Reformation the various churches differed in understanding what it meant to be a Christian. "The Catholic answer to the question was essentially sacramental, and the Protestant response was essentially doctrinal."[1] For the Anabaptist, to be a Christian was to live in discipleship and obedience to God. How the people lived and responded to their faith demonstrated what it meant to be a Christian.

Catholicism had over the centuries adopted a form of worship where the priests had a controlling power over the people. The priests were the essential mediators between God and man; furthermore, there were many rites for the priests and the laity to perform, but the study of the Bible was discouraged and the Pope had the final say in regards to the interpretation of the Word.

Protestantism placed a strong emphasis on biblical theology that in turn affected Europe. The learned men made the Bible a study manual for the universities. The union of church and state meant that the interpretation of theologians was universally applied to all people, whether they were sincere or just nominal Christians. For several centuries the people had united to build massive and magnificent cathedrals. This was how they "lived" their religion, but as the times changed the focus of religious life shifted from age-old traditions to new theological interpretations enforced by the state. The Anabaptists emphasised discipleship and a believer's church, which separated them from general society. By denying the state any right to govern their brotherhood, the Anabaptists effectively rejected the absolute claims of the Pope and the Protestant state.

The Anabaptists also differed from both the Catholic and Protestant churches in their interpretation of the way of salvation. The Anabaptists' path to salvation is to first acknowledge the sinfulness of human beings and to become dead to sin (Romans 6:2). "Our old man (our nature) is crucified with him, that the body of sin might be destroyed, that henceforth we should not serve sin" (Romans 6:6). This emphasis on crucifying our carnal nature with Christ leaves a tone of soberness and yieldedness within the believer. The heart is prepared for the Anabaptist mind-set of Gelassenheit, but the faith is not without hope. "Therefore we are buried with him by baptism into death: that like Christ was raised up from the dead by the glory of the Father, even so we also should walk in newness of life. For if we have been planted together in the likeness of his death, we shall be also in the likeness of his resurrection" (Romans 6:4-5). This confidence in Christ is found in 1 John 1:7: "But if we walk in the light, as he is in the light, we have fellowship one with another, and the blood of Jesus Christ his Son cleanseth us from all sin." The cleansing power of the blood of Christ is a gift from God (Ephesians 2:8).

The Anabaptists believed that salvation grew out of a personal choice. "...whosoever will, let him take of the water of life freely" (Revelation 22:17). Even though they experience sorrow when one departs from their fellowship, their only recourse is to admonish the wayward soul. They will not use force to keep an individual within the fellowship against his or her will. They believe that, firstly, a Christian voluntarily surrenders all unto Christ at the cross; secondly, by faith the Christian is resurrected unto Christ by the cleansing power of his blood; and thirdly, through the Spirit the Christian leads a holy life unto Christ.

To be sure, all Christians believe that sin is sin, that we are raised by Christ through the power of his blood, but the emphasis or the order of importance of these beliefs varies among Christians. At the time of the Reformation, the Catholic Church maintained that all had sinned and it was necessary to work out salvation through penitence and prayers to the saints. Belief in the resurrecting or cleansing power of the blood of Christ was not effectively taught.

For the Protestant reformers, belief in the resurrecting power of the blood of Christ was the foundation of salvation. They emphasized, "For by grace are you saved through faith; and that not of yourselves: it is the gift of God" (Ephesians 2:8). But what were the people to think when Martin Luther wrote, "Sin bravely"?[2] Luther's personal experience as a Catholic monk had made him adverse to any suggestion of the law of Christ. For Luther salvation was by grace alone through faith. The Epistle of James' theme of works of faith clashed with Luther and he referred to it as the "strawy epistle."

Through infant baptism, the doctrine that all men are Christian, and therefore part of the state church, brought the sins of unconverted people into the church. Through infant baptism, salvation was not a voluntary commitment, but a forgone conclusion. This toleration of sin within the church made it difficult to effectively teach the sinfulness of sin as the Anabaptists believed. For them a believer must become "dead to sin" (Romans 6:2). Since the Protestant state churches tolerated sin, the corruption that had been within the Catholic Church remained also within the Protestant churches. This corruption within the church gave rise to Pietism.

Pietism also emphasized the resurrecting power of the blood of Christ over and above the need to become dead unto sin. Pietism's evangelistic thrust must be admired, but the dying to self with Christ on the cross was not part of salvation in Pietism. The foundation of Pietism was to rise with Him in newness of life through the power of the blood. Though the Anabaptists also claimed the above promise, their foundation was first to be dead to sin and then no longer to live therein (Romans 6:2). The Anabaptists believed that one must die unto self *before* Christ can resurrect him through the power of his blood as a newborn child of God. As a child of God one has access to the unlimited power of the Holy Spirit which God gives to his people. Everything is a gift from God.

Since all Christians believe in the above three points, what is the issue? Those whose foundation for salvation is the resurrection with Christ have a joyous vision of their salvation; however, those whose foundation is crucifying self with Christ on the cross have a more reverential view of salvation. To the latter, "It is a fearful thing to fall into the hands of the living God" (Hebrews 10:31).

In the *Biblical Concordance of the Swiss Brethren* the first topic listed is the "Fear of God."[3] This emphasis on the fear of God has been carried down into the Old Order Mennonite churches. Such an emphasis discourages boldness and frivolity within the group. Conversely it promotes an air of sacredness and a high level of respect for their faith and God. Even though the Old Order Mennonites recognize that the Holy Spirit is required to live a pure and holy life, they firmly hold that there needs to be a personal commitment to abolish sin. With this voluntary commitment comes a yieldedness to God. These are the virtues required to build a brotherhood, or the visible Church of God, as taught in the eighth article of the Dortrecht Confession of faith. Being resurrected unto a new life through the blood of Christ is a gift from God. To understand Old Order theology the above shift of emphasis must be considered. Their lifestyle at times suggests that the Old Orders work to earn their salvation. It is, however, a work of God when new life is seen.

The Old Order's interpretation concerning salvation to some degree, limits their evangelistic efforts to a daily testimony of life within the communities where they live. They are content to "Let (their) light so shine before men, that they may see your good works, and glorify your Father which is in heaven" (Matthew 5:16). Even though they are not very enthusiastic towards outside missionary work, they are very committed to helping their neighbours outside the fellowship at a time of loss by fire or other natural disasters. The Old Order view of salvation is: first Good Friday—surrendering all upon the cross; secondly Easter—being resurrected with Christ unto newness of life; thirdly Pentecost—the pouring out of the Spirit.

Anabaptists' interpretation of Romans 13 restricted the state's power to civil administration only. To medieval Europe this teaching meant outright anarchy. The Anabaptists' belief in a pure church separate from society was the basic cause of the ensuing persecution. The Anabaptists' belief in non-resistance and their refusal to swear the oath also brought them into direct conflict with the state (1). When Michael Sattler said he would not fight against the Turks, most people considered him to be saying, "let the infidels conquer Europe." The Turks were indeed threatening Europe from the East, and in 1683 had invaded Austria, which was the gateway to Western Europe. In spite of that threat and persecution, the Anabaptists did not waver. A generation later, Hans van Overdam of Holland would write in prison:

> (1) *The city of Strassburg had a day called* Schwortag *(Day of the oath). Her citizens were required to swear an oath of allegiance in front of the Cathedral. Records from 1531-1534 indicate that the Anabaptists refused to take this oath, which undermined the foundation of the state. Their conscience against violence appeared to the authorities as suspect of sedition. Their rejection of infant baptism was a violation of civil law.*[4]

> Hence we would rather, through the grace of God, suffer our temporal bodies to be burned, drowned, beheaded, racked or tortured, as it may seem good to you (the lords), or to be scourged, banished, or driven away, and robbed of our goods, than show you any obedience contrary to the Word of God, and we will be patient herein, committing vengeance to God; for we know Him that hath said, Vengeance belongeth unto me, I will recompense, saith the Lord.[5]

Menno Simons asked a very challenging question: "Tell me, how can a Christian defend scripturally retaliation, rebellion, war, striking, slaying, torturing, stealing, robbing and plundering and burning cities, and conquering countries?"[6]

Anabaptist theology was simple. It was based on a voluntary commitment to God, and that meant to be a disciple of Christ in life. When Conrad Grebel fled from Zurich leaving his family behind, one can fairly assume the following passage encouraged his soul: "And every one that hath forsaken houses, or brethren, or sisters, or father, or mother, or wife, or children, or lands, for my name's sake, shall receive an hundredfold, and shall inherit everlasting life" (Matthew 19:29). The Anabaptists testified that sacredness or holiness do not apply to special words, objects, places, persons, or days, yet their followers, the Old Order Mennonites, embrace their brotherhoods, their *Ordnung*,[7] with an air of sacredness.[8] The brotherhood to them is a disciplined community in which each member finds fulfilment. The key to the right fellowship, as John Ruth puts it, was non-self-assertive humility and faithfulness.[9]

The Anabaptists, unlike adherents of other churches of the day, had little to say about their inherited sin through Adam, while those who believed in infant baptism were concerned that the inherited sin be washed away through baptism. The adherents of infant baptism tended to blame Adam for their sinful nature and often continued to live reckless lives, while the Anabaptists assumed the responsibility for their behaviour, their personal sins, and by God's grace sought to live holy lives. There have always been people who lived righteously throughout all ages, but the emphasis on holy living only became widespread after Pietism spread across Europe.

Beginnings of Pietism

For centuries Europeans did not doubt the existence of God, but the different interpretations of the Bible fuelled heated debates during the Reformation. The reformers focused on theology with considerable emphasis on the Old Testament. They also utilized the traditional scholastic method of logically disputing the doctrines of the Bible. In time Protestant scholasticism became increasingly sterile. To combat religious stagnation Philipp Jakob Spener, a Lutheran pastor, organized circles for prayer and Bible study in 1670. Spener and his friends were not interested in forming new congregations, but simply created cell groups within the congregation, emphasizing a personal spiritual experience and moral purity. This movement became known as Pietism and rapidly spread across the Protestant world.

Not all Pietists were merely content with good morals and a personal experience of salvation in Jesus; some also sought to establish a community of believers' fellowship. These radicals, who called themselves "Brethren" (German Baptists, also known as the Church of the Brethren), formed a believer's church in 1708. The civil authorities, who considered the group to be a manifestation of the infamous kingdom of Münster, immediately repressed these brethren for illegal evangelism. The imprisonments, fines, confiscation of goods, forced labour, and exile did not influence the German Baptists, who were ready to sacrifice everything, even their lives.[10] Intense persecution forced the German Baptists to flee to America between 1719 and 1740. These German-speaking people became neighbours to the Mennonites, and since the German Baptists also embraced the non-resistant faith, there was inter-marriage between the two groups. The German Baptists' more charismatic expression of faith also attracted a few Mennonites, consequently the German Baptists introduced Pietism into the North American Mennonite community.

Pietism Defined

Pietists were deeply concerned about morality, and helped to create a deeper awareness of sin. However, Pietists did not separate from the state church because such a move invited persecution. Instead Pietists took passages like John 14:20 which says, "At that day ye shall know that I am in my Father, and ye in me, and I in you." They emphasised the in-dwelling of Christ, that is, the relationship between God and the individual, but the idea of a church comprised solely of believers was not part of Pietism. The Pietists' individualistic outlook explains why they did not share the same concern about the relationship with their fellowmen as the Anabaptists, who believed that the church was to be a body made up only of sincere, born-again believers.

In a state-church society everybody, both sinner and believer, was part of the "national" church. Pietists laboured and took communion within the established churches. They emphasised an emotional, personal experience of salvation. It was an inner experience where the joy of salvation and the resurrecting power of the blood were stressed. In contrast to the Pietists, the Anabaptists had left the established churches. They stressed the concept of a brotherhood of believers. Although faith was definitely personal, the emphasis remained on being a disciple of Christ and crucifying self with Christ at the cross.

About 1534 Hans Haffner wrote, "The world truly accepts Christ as a gift, but does not know him at all from the point of view of suffering." Hans Denck wrote, "When we truly realize the love of God, we will be ready to give up for love's sake even what God has given us." It was by Gelassenheit that the Anabaptists recognized a true disciple. A community of love was possible only by overcoming all selfishness.[11] The voluntary acceptance of the cross of suffering separated the Anabaptists from the Pietists. There is no English word equal to the meaning that the Anabaptists drew from Gelassenheit, but since the Old Order ethos is so bound up with the spirit of Gelassenheit we should attempt to summarize what Gelassenheit meant to the Anabaptists and what it continues to mean to present-day Old Order communities.

Learned men have suggested fifteen possible English words to express the meaning of Gelassenheit, but none seize the Anabaptists' theme of suffering and discipleship. The following phrases will give an idea of what the Anabaptists meant when they used the term: Self-surrender, self-abandonment, resignation in God's will, the readiness to suffer for the sake of God, and also peace and calmness of mind. The idea of martyrdom only becomes bearable on such a basis of self-surrender and joyous acceptance of God's will. Michael Sattler wrote, "In this peril I completely surrender myself unto the will of the Lord, and prepare myself even for death for His testimony."[12] Once the persecutions and executions had stifled the Anabaptists' evangelistic fires and they accepted the more passive role of the *Stillen im Lande* (quiet in the land), the theme of Gelassenheit was changed. The Stillen im Lande left the world to itself and all its activities. The Old Order Mennonite community appreciates the Anabaptist value of Gelassenheit by gently fanning the remaining embers of a complete surrender to God—a voluntary commitment of submission, obedience to the brotherhood of believers.

Pietists sought to avoid the cross of suffering by a compromise, which was to live a pious life within the state church without persecution. The early Anabaptists didn't identify with such a compromise, even though over time the Anabaptists became more and more comfortable with making a compromise. The Anabaptists' original emphasis was to apply the teaching

> (2) *The Swiss Anabaptists compiled a topical concordance that had fifteen different editions from ca. 1540-1710. This booklet was arranged under sixty-six different topics such as Fear of God, Faith, Persecution, Humility, Greed, and Child Rearing. The verses in the Bible that the Anabaptists deemed important for a given topic were printed in full and therefore gave the reader a valuable scriptural reference for each topic listed in the concordance. Fifty-three percent of the references in the Swiss Concordance were from the Old Testament and thirty-seven percent of the references were from the New Testament. The remaining ten percent were taken from the Apocrypha. The references from the Gospels and Epistles are about equal. The Book of Proverbs was the most popular with 426 references while the Gospel of Matthew was quoted 405 times. This is no surprise when one considers the practical and literal way the Anabaptists interpreted the Bible.*[13]

of the word to their lives. They had a high regard for both the Old and New Testaments and even considered the Apocrypha to be Scripture. (2)

The Anabaptists' interpretation of the cross of Christ also differed from that of the Pietists. In the illustration below, the heart of man is considered the centre of love. The Anabaptist's heart is at the centre of the cross. The vertical bar of the cross demonstrates love and peace between God and man while the horizontal bar symbolizes love and peace between brother and brother. Pietism does not acknowledge the horizontal bar. It looks toward God in search of inner peace and joy, but the horizontal bar, the reason for the Anabaptists' discipleship and brotherhood, is taken away. The disciplined brotherhood of believers, the pure church, was replaced in Pietism by a personal, emotional experience in Christ. The difference between Anabaptism and Pietism is a shift in the emphasis on community, since both movements stressed that the Bible be the only guide.

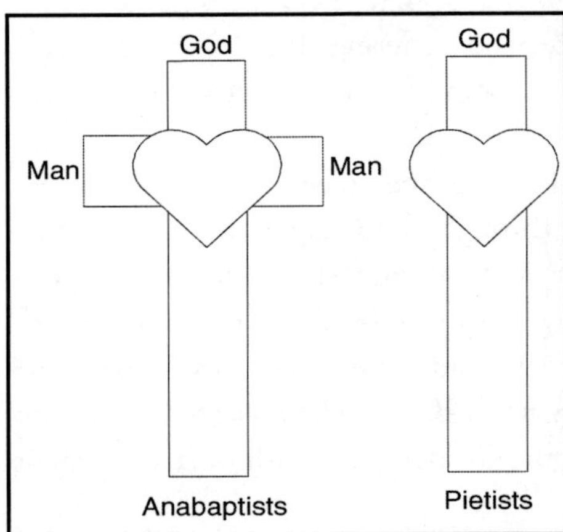

The Anabaptists had a very straightforward interpretation of the Word. The Pietist quoted Ephesians 2:8-9, "For by grace are ye saved through faith; and that not of yourselves; it is the gift of God: Not of the works, lest any man should boast." The Anabaptists continued with verse 10 "For we are his workmanship, created in Christ Jesus unto good works, which God hath before ordained that we should walk in them."

The Anabaptists' emphasis on the church being a brotherhood of believers resulted in a belief that it is more important to know that one is *converted* than to know that one is *saved.* A change of heart was, to the Anabaptists, the answer of a good conscience towards God: "Being then made free from sin, ye became the servants of righteousness" (Romans 6:18). Their emphasis on servitude for Christ, that is serving or working for Christ in righteousness and true holiness, definitely outweighed their concern for being saved. Working for Christ was a voluntary commitment they had made at their conversion; being saved was an act of God they accepted by faith.

The Pietists' emphasis on the joy of salvation was derived from the Pauline Epistles. Pietists sought personal salvation and godliness, while the Anabaptists sought the pure church as a portion of the kingdom of God. Furthermore, the Pietists believed in an *invisible* church of Christ while the Anabaptists believed in a *visible* church of Christ.[14] Pilgram Marpeck (an Anabaptist leader of South Germany 1530-56) in his writings "formulates the basic antithesis between Anabaptism and its theological opponents. Marpeck uses the contrasts 'halo' and 'crown of thorns,' or the 'sweet' and the 'bitter' Saviour. These pairs of expressions represent two contrasting ways of faith."[15] The persecuted Anabaptists viewed their Saviour as one who had a "crown of thorns" in view of the "bitter" sufferings they had to endure, while the non-persecuted Christians could readily view Christ as a "sweet" Saviour with a "halo" over his head. Theron Schlabach commented, "Anabaptists had invited people to follow the 'bitter Jesus' of cross, obedience, and suffering; Pietists called people mainly to a 'sweet Jesus' of personal salvation, inner victory, and warm embrace."[16]

Robert Friedmann's question "Is the Gospel to be understood through Paul, or is Paul to be understood through the Gospel" may sound like theological jargon, but Friedmann explains further.[17] "He who seeks to secure a total understanding of Holy Scripture from the point of view of Paul starts with the experience of sin, and experiences salvation in the consciousness of the freely bestowed grace. But he who seeks to understand the Holy Scripture from the view of the Gospel, starts with the requirement of discipleship (*Nachfolge*), that is, he starts from the point of view of concrete love and the cross, and takes from them his sense of commission."[18]

In the above quotations Friedmann captured the key difference between Pietism and Anabaptism. To be sure, the Anabaptists understood that salvation is possible only through the grace of God and one should never think they minimized God's grace. Rather, they exalted the Gospel of Jesus Christ, the Sermon on the Mount, and the cross of Christ or the dying of self. This exaltation of the Gospel of Christ led the Anabaptists to view Paul's writings from a gospel perspective that emphasized *discipleship*. Furthermore, the Pietist's emphasis on the resurrecting power of the blood of Christ generates an inner joy of salvation and through this focus he accepts the Gospel. The Pietist also truly appreciates the Gospel of Christ and the need to be a follower of Christ, but the reality of the Cross of Christ was not foremost in his thinking, which was rather the *joy of his salvation*. Even though the Anabaptist and Pietist both believe in the whole Bible, their understandings of the Gospel differ. The Anabaptist's primary focus is Christ's words "follow me" while the Pietist's focal point is "For by grace are ye saved" (Ephesians, 2:8).

The understanding of the Kingdom of God and the commission of the Church also differ between Pietism and Anabaptism. The Pietists believed that by preaching the Gospel, Christianity would spread all over the globe until the whole world became Christian. After the evangelistic fires were stifled, the Anabaptists understood their brotherhood as well as their work abroad as a mere leaven in and among the world—"Ye are the salt of the earth…the light of the world" (Matthew 5:13-14). Friedeman notes, "Their conception from the very outset was to build up a nucleus of the Kingdom to which men were to be invited and which was open for everybody. By this, it was hoped, that the brotherhood of the regenerated would grow until the last days and thus eventually overcome the Prince of the World."[19] Eberhard Arnold wrote that, "the Pietist feels satisfied when he experiences the personal sense of salvation and the presence of a personal God."[20] However, "the uniqueness of Anabaptism lies in its conviction that Christ is more than a divine being to be worshipped, more than a Saviour who brings forgiveness through the cross and deliverance from the penalty and power of sin; He is the *Lord* to be followed and obeyed, and with whom the Christian enters into a covenant that controls his whole life."[21]

Although there is a difference in emphasis between the Pietists' and Anabaptists' emphasis, it must be remembered that followers of Anabaptism, including the Old Order Mennonite Churches, have borrowed much from Pietism. Within a century of their beginnings, the Anabaptists began to shift from their original theme of *Gottesfurcht* (the fear of God) to a more Pietistsic theme of *Gottseligkeit* (godliness). Gottseligkeit was seldom used by the early Anabaptists. The sixteenth-century hymnal, the *Ausbund*, still used by the Old Order Amish, maintains a strong emphasis on suffering for the cause of Christ. Pietistic English hymns were written by sincere believers in God, but they rarely refer to suffering with Jesus.

An Old Order Mennonite minister stated that the surrender of self bears the fruits of humility. Christians have traditionally considered pride to be the most basic of human sins, and humility an essential attitude for persons to come to a proper relationship with God. The early Anabaptists felt that disobedience to God was the most central sin. When they defined obedience they did not make humility the central theme: they emphasized Gelassenheit. Henry Funk, who immigrated to America in 1717 and died in 1760, still considered suffering as primary. Funk lamented that Christians avoided persecution by disregarding humility and adopting the ways of this world. There was also too much love of the world and too little faith in God.[22] After the Mennonites had seen several generations of prosperity, the suffering theme was discarded and gave way to the more pietistic theme of humility. By 1800 the Mennonites "had given up the ancient Anabaptist emphasis on confronting the world and accepting suffering."[23] The author's desire is to respect both Pietism and Anabaptism, but it is crucial to identify the differences of the two before we unfold the origins of Old Order Mennonitism.

Pietism in America

In England John Wesley was not satisfied with the Church of England's emphasis on traditional rituals and its neglect of the poor. He and other like-minded men formed a Bible study group, nicknamed the "Holy Club," "Bible Moths," and "the Methodists," because of their methodical approach to life. The Methodist name continued. Wesley engaged in open-air meetings, with a vision that the poor preach to the poor. Wesley was harshly criticized by the established church but he continued to labour with the poor. To Wesley the poor were also Christians.[24]

George Whitefield, Wesley's colleague at Oxford University, travelled to the Atlantic Colonies where he preached in 1738. He continued the labours of Jonathan Edwards and others. The frontier life conflicted with the established churches' tradition that all clergy be trained, thus the colonists' spiritual condition deteriorated. As late as 1760 only eight to ten per cent of the population in the American colonies were church members. With crude lifestyles and a lack of educated leaders only a powerful emotionalized, personal religion could bring a revival into such society.[25]

Under the leadership of George Whitefield, a series of revival movements known as the "Great Awakening" brought religion to the common people. Leaders of the established church opposed the movement because "revivalism" emphasized the individual religious experience rather than particular denominational doctrines. Even though the church order, such as keeping the Sabbath, was strictly enforced by the courts, the people had no difficulty separating religion and secular concerns.[27] The established churches, unlike the Peace Churches, had never committed themselves to serve Christ seven days of the week. Nevertheless, the Great Awakening prevailed. Lay participation in the worship service was part of this awakening. Itinerant lay preachers roamed over the land with the message of a loving Saviour and emphasized personal salvation. (4)

(4) *During the 1740s the Moravians attempted to arouse the people from their spiritual slumber. The Mennonites coolly received these Moravians, as did others. Since almost all Old Order Mennonites are descendants of the Martin family we will include comments of Hantsch, a Moravian missionary, who visited the Martin homes. The July 12, 1748 entry states that "we visited David Martin. With him was his brother, Heinrich who lives about two miles from David. Also still living with David was their father, an old man of seventy-nine years. Things really went well for us with these people. They responded warmly to us and understood us well. That was especially true of the old man and his son David, as they were loving towards us. Henrich, on the other hand, was only out for a good argument." This jewel from history reveals the age of the immigrant Christian Martin who was the progenitor of the numerous Old Order Martins.*[26]

Wesleyan "holiness" or the second work of grace also formed part of Methodist theology. Nevertheless, the success of the Great Awakening did not mean there was religious freedom throughout the colonies. The established churches' practice of shunning those of other denominations continued. Virginia retained an official state church until 1787, while Puritans in Massachusetts remained intolerant of other denominations until the U.S. Supreme Court ordered religious freedom in 1844.

William Penn's Charter of Privileges gave his "holy experiment" broad religious freedom.[28] Under this umbrella the Peace Churches had found refuge. In 1768 a resident of Berks County wrote to Europe stating, "We are all going to and fro like fish in water." "You can hardly imagine how many denominations gather together for a funeral," wrote a pioneer to his relatives in Europe.[29] Some historians suggest that the eastern counties of colonial Pennsylvania became a prototype of what would later be a live-and-let-live pattern among the churches in the United States.[30] This discarding of denominational barriers would in time affect the Mennonites also, as

> (5) *Non-theologically-minded Mennonites found the "holiness" movement difficult to decipher, but they certainly felt it. Wesleyan "holiness" or Christian perfection did not blend with Mennonite humility. "It was in the mutual yielding to Christ within a disciplined covenant that the Mennonites 'felt' their religion. It hardly occurred to them to discuss the emotional states that accompanied this yielding and mutuality, as subjects in themselves."[31] Martin Boehm and Solomon Eby both claimed to have experienced that inner renewal of the Holy Spirit.*
>
> *"Holiness" advocates taught that by God's grace and the power of the Holy Spirit it was possible to attain such a degree of holiness that one no longer had to struggle with one's carnal nature. However, this presented a very confident, even boastful, attitude that was contrary to traditional Mennonite thought. The River Brethren, or Tunkers, and the "New" Mennonites accepted the "holiness" doctrine. (on "New" Mennonites see chapter six.)*

they began to absorb the pietistic breezes saturated with "holiness" that gently drifted across the Pennsylvanian valleys.(5)

Pietism of the 1700s absorbed much from Wesleyan "holiness." One could say that Pietism was the foundation on which the "holiness" theology was built. The blend of these two movements affected the Mennonites of the 1800s. Wesleyan theology and Pietism will be termed "holiness" in the remainder of this document.

The Mennonite church had successfully resisted the revivalism of the Great Awakening until the War of Independence. The persecution the Peace Churches endured during that war increased their separation from the general public and strengthened the bond of their closed community.[32] Nevertheless, the appealing aspects of "holiness" began to attract some Mennonites. Martin Boehm, a Lancaster County Mennonite bishop, came into contact with the great revivalist, George Whitefield, in 1761. He was drawn into the revivalistic stream and took part in a famous revival meeting in Isaac Long's barn in 1767. Three years later the River Brethren (Brethren in Christ) were organized and drew many Mennonites into their fold. Boehm's revivalistic practices were tolerated by the Mennonite church until 1777, when he was excommunicated. The "holiness" fervour became irresistible for some Mennonites who would testify with Christian Newcomer, "I withdrew myself from the Mennonite Society on account of want of the life and power of religion among them."[33] Newcomer was seeking personal revival. MacMaster, Horst, and Ulle concluded, "This was the crux of the problem presented by the Great Awakening to the Mennonite community. Emphasis on personal conversion, the new birth, and repentance could be readily absorbed into the life of the congregation, but a community based on nonconformity, non-resistance, and daily discipleship could not accept religious experience as the only basis of Christian fellowship."[34]

"Holiness," with its shift of emphasis, caused disunity among the Mennonites. In about 1790 John Neidig, a Mennonite minister of Dauphin County, Pennsylvania, was rejected by his congregation because of his new "holiness" doctrine. A century later a man would write that Neidig's "new experience gave him a message which he in turn preached to his church, that they might be born again and have a change of heart to please God and get to heaven at last." A Lancaster County minister, Christian Burkholder, also wrote that the new birth, a conversion, was necessary for salvation, though he downplayed the testimony of personal experience and insisted that the true evidence of conversion was a changed life.[35] Although the Mennonites were concerned about repentance, new birth, faith, and grace, their emphasis differed from that of the "holiness" movement.

During the nineteenth century the Mennonite community slowly began to accept more of modern Protestantism, until two Mennonite preachers, John. F. Funk and Jacob Wisler, clashed at the Yellow Creek congregation in Indiana in 1871. Wisler and his colleagues retained the traditional Mennonite values of the eighteenth century, while Funk was influenced by Dwight L. Moody's evangelism. The similarities of Pietism and traditional Mennonitism made it easy for many to leave the Mennonite community. For example, in Ontario's Markham District fifty per cent of the second generation left for other churches.[36] The loss of members threatened the Mennonite church and the attempts to reverse the situation resulted in many schisms.

Christian Newcomer's accusation that the Mennonite church had "want of life" has haunted the Old Order churches for over two centuries. The Old Order Mennonites must confess that at times this accusation was all too true, but they reject the charge that they are legalistic. For them discipline and order are necessary guardrails to protect their people. This is not legalism, but rather evidence of a bond of love.

A member steeped in Gelassenheit is not just *sensitive* to what the community tolerates or condones, but also *willingly abides by the community's values*. In an Old Order brotherhood, where the individual stops and the brotherhood begins is a blurred distinction. A brotherhood cannot function without the spirit of Gelassenheit. Martin Boehm's dismissal from the Mennonite Church marked the beginnings of the disharmony which "holiness" created within the Mennonite Church. Boehm's expulsion by the Lancaster Bench also presumably marks the conception of the Old Order movement marked by the clash between Anabaptist and pietistic values.

Notes

[1] John Driver, *Radical Faith: An Alternative History of the Christian Church* (Kitchener, Ontario: Pandora Press, 1999), 218.

[2] Walter Klaassen, *Anabaptism: Neither Catholic nor Protestant* (Waterloo, Ontario: Conrad Press, 1973), 29.

[3] Gilbert Fast and Galen A. Peters trans., *Biblical Concordance of the Swiss Brethren* (Kitchener: Pandora Press, 2001).

[4] Klaassen, *Anabaptism*, 53.

[5] Thielman J. van Braght, *Martyrs Mirror: The Story of Seventeen Centuries of Christian Martyrdom, From the Time of Christ to A.D. 1660.* Joseph F. Strohm trans. (Scottdale, PA: Herald Press, 1950), 492.

[6] Menno Simons, *The Complete Writings of Menno Simons*, (Scottdale, PA: Herald Press, 1966), 555.

[7] See Glossary re: Ordnung.

[8] Klaassen, *Anabaptism*, 11.

[9] John L. Ruth, *Conrad Grebel Son of Zurich* (Scottdale, PA: Herald Press, 1975), 11.

[10] Driver, *Radical Faith*, 236.

[11] Mennonite Encyclopedia (hereafter ME), II (Scottdale, PA: The Mennonite Publishing House, 1955), 449.

[12] *Ibid.*, 448.

[13] See Fast and Peters, *Biblical Concordance.*

[14] See article eight Dortrecht Confession.

[15] Robert Friedmann, *Mennonite Piety Through the Centuries: Its Genius and Its Literature* (Scottdale, PA: Herald Press, 1980), 86.

[16] Theron F. Schlabach, *Gospel Versus Gospel* (Scottdale, PA: Herald Press, 1988), 88.

[17] Friedmann, *Mennonite Piety*, 86.

[18] *Ibid.*

[19] *Ibid.*, 88.

[20] Quoted in *ibid.*

[21] ME, IV, 1076.

[22] Henry Funk, *Restitution or an Explanation of Several Principal Points of the Law* (Elkhart, Indiana: Mennonite Publishing Company, 1980), 268-69.

[23] *Ibid.*, 269-70.

[24] Richard K. MacMaster, *Land, Piety, Peoplehood* (Scottdale, PA: Herald Press, 1985), 181.

[25] Driver, *Radical Faith*, 250.

[26] ME., IV, 309.

[27] Jason Martin, "Christian and Ells Martin: Immigrant Patriarch and Matriarch." *Pennsylvania Mennonite Heritage* (July 1987): 16.

[28] MacMaster, Horst, and Ulle, *Conscience in Crisis* (Scottdale, PA: Herald Press, 1979), 26.

[29] See Glossary: Penn's "holy experiment" was the Quaker administration where the Quakers tried to govern the state by Biblical values and tried to avoid the use of the militia and was the first state to advocate religious freedom to other denominations

[30] MacMaster, *Land Piety*, 138

[31] *Ibid.*

[32] John L. Ruth, *Maintaining the Right Fellowship* (Scottdale, PA: Herald Press, 1984), 221.

[33] MacMaster, Horst, Ulle, *Conscience in Crisis*, 525.

[34] *Ibid.*, 527.

[35] MacMaster, *Land Piety*, 211.

[36] Frank H. Epp, *Mennonites in Canada* I. (Toronto: Macmillan of Canada, 1974), 234.

Mennonite Migration to Ontario

Chapter Four

Into The Wilds

"The wind goeth toward the south, and turneth about unto the north; it whirleth about continually, and the wind returneth again according to his circuits" (Ecclesiastes 1:6 AV). So are the Mennonite migrations.

The unavailability of land plagued the agrarian Mennonites of Pennsylvania by 1780. The best land in eastern Pennsylvania was claimed, and the slighted Indians beyond the Appalachian Mountains were a deterrent to settling in the Ohio Valley until after the War of 1812-14. Crossing the Appalachian Mountains was a forbidding task that a few Mennonites undertook in 1799, after the Whiskey Rebellion of 1794 made western Pennsylvania a more desirable haven for the peace-loving Mennonites. Land, land, where was the good, cheap land?

German Influence in America

The Swiss Mennonites seldom, if ever, relocated by themselves. They generally moved with their neighbours: they were pioneers not explorers. When they fled from Switzerland, they moved with their neighbours.[1] When Germantown was settled in 1683, there were a few Mennonites amongst the Quakers who emigrated from Krefeld in North Germany. It would be several decades before the large Mennonite migrations to Pennsylvania occurred.[2]

Queen Ann of England, because of her German husband, was kindly disposed towards the Germans. The Queen's kind gestures sent the landless

Palatines swarming down the Rhine River in 1709, and by fall some thirteen thousand Germans had crowded into the Rotterdam harbour. The Dutch shipped them over to England, and sent two men up the Rhine to stop this uncontrolled influx. Both the Dutch and English became annoyed and began returning the Catholics first, and then all others. An English royal declaration stated that any who intended to go to America should be prepared to support themselves. Enough of these penniless Palatines! How many Mennonites were found in this chaos? About a dozen families and a few single persons were among these thirteen thousand vagabonds.[3]

Did the Germans stop immigrating to America? Despite the royal edict, like an artesian well the Germans swelled into America, filling both Berks and Lebanon counties in Pennsylvania and parts of New York State. By 1770, about a hundred thousand Germans had found homes in the New World. Of these only three to five thousand were Mennonites.

The Germans had a large impact on the politics of Pennsylvania. Before 1776 they voted with the Quakers and kept the Quakers in power, much to the annoyance of the Scotch-Irish. In 1776, ironically, these despised Germans held the deciding vote whether the Thirteen Colonies would fight for independence. With six colonies voting for independence and six colonies against it, Pennsylvania held the deciding vote and at this time the Germans voted with the Scotch-Irish and chose for independence; however, in New York State some of the Germans supported the British, and it is these Germans that fit into our story of the early settlement of the Niagara Peninsula in Canada.

The Niagara Settlement

During the American Revolution, a British battalion of mostly Germans was formed in New York called the Butlers Rangers.[4] The Butlers Rangers made telling raids against the Revolutionaries, and at the end of the war had to flee from America. They made their base at Fort George on the Niagara River. The first stragglers came to the fort in 1776 as the fugitive families of the Rangers sought refuge.[5] By 1783 the settlement consisted of forty-six families and had cleared 713 acres. For another nine years it would be chaotic as more Loyalists flowed into the unsurveyed wilderness. This remote settlement was still administrated from distant Montreal.

After the war ended in 1783 the British concentrated on supporting those who had fought with them during the Revolutionary War. Thousands of Loyalists had fled to Canada and founded new homes in the Maritimes, along the St. Lawrence River, and at Niagara. Our story focuses on the Niagara settlement.

At that time Quebec included all of Ontario, but the French laws were not acceptable to the Loyalists, so they complained to the British. The compromise was the Constitutional Act of 1791, which divided Quebec and formed two new provinces—Lower and Upper Canada. (Upper Canada became known as Ontario after 1867.) Upper Canada was divided into four districts—Lunenburg, Mecklenburg, Nassau, and Hesse in honour of England's German King George III and the many German settlers. This Act also granted to the Church of England certain rights, including free possession of one-seventh of the land (the clergy reserves) and made her the pre-eminent religious institution in Upper Canada with the sole right to solemnize marriages. These discriminatory laws would only be effectively addressed after the 1837 insurrection.

Governor John Graves Simcoe came to Upper Canada in 1792 to oversee British rule in this new province. Simcoe, an ardent Englishman, renamed the districts giving them English names. He did much to encourage the new settlement. He chose the present-day site of Toronto for the capital city of the province and had the army build several roads. His request that the land be surveyed and laid out in townships brought order and ended the chaotic squatter's era. A point of interest is Simcoe's November 6, 1794 proclamation that any immigrant who could show that he was in a position to cultivate and improve land would be granted two hundred acres of free land. The grantee was obliged to clear five acres of land, to build a house, and to open a road across the front of his land, a quarter of a mile in length.[6] Simcoe advertised these attractive terms in the Philadelphia papers.

Militia Exemption in Canada

The Militia Act of 1793 exempted the Quakers, Mennonists, and Tunkers (River Brethren) from personal militia duties for a fine, which was a very favourable gesture to the Peace Churches (1). This does not suggest that

(1) *"And it be further enacted, that the persons called Quakers, Mennonists, and Tunkers, who from certain scruples of conscience, decline bearing arms, shall not be compelled to serve in the said Militia, but every person professing that he is one of the people called Quakers, Mennonists, or Tunkers, and producing a certificate of his being a Quaker, Mennonist, or Tunker, signed by any three or more of the people (who are or shall be by them authorized to grant certificates for this or any other purpose of which a pastor, minister, or preacher shall be one) shall be excused and exempted from serving in the said Militia, and instead of such service, all and every such person and persons, that shall or may be of the people called Quakers, Mennonists, or Tunkers, shall pay to the lieutenant of the county or riding, or in his absence to the deputy lieutenant, the sum of twenty shillings per annum in time of peace, and five pounds per annum in a time of actual invasion or insurrection."*[7] *Twenty shillings is equal to $2.50 and five pounds to about ten dollars. This meant that during a time of peace a labourer would have to work half a week to pay his dues and during a war it would take two weeks wages to pay his fine. The Waterloo Mennonites paid the equivalent, if not more, of the purchase price of the German Company Tract in Militia fines from 1813-1826.*[8]

Simcoe supported the Peace Churches' non-resistant views; he wanted a strong militia. Simcoe wanted to preserve British North America, a very difficult task indeed with so few people inhabiting Upper Canada. He welcomed the Peace Churches not because he favoured them, but because he wanted to attract experienced settlers. In passing the Militia Act in 1793, Simcoe abided by the precedent set by the Motherland.

In 1688, five years after the budding of Germantown, the dissenters in England had received their first reprieve from the Church of England. William of Orange, a Dutch ruler, laid claim to the English throne and ousted his Catholic father-in-law, King James II, from the English throne. William and Mary's accession to the English throne ensured Protestant rule in England. The Dutch had already begun to practice partial religious toleration, and with William and Mary on the throne, England also began to exempt dissenters from penalties for certain crimes, such as failure to baptize their infants. By 1761 in England, exemption from the militia was also allowed if a substitute was found. Exemption from the militia, for a fee, was adopted by Pennsylvania in 1789 and in Maryland in 1793. Thus Simcoe only followed the precedent of other governments. Mennonite historian Frank Epp drew the conclusion that although it cannot be documented, it may be assumed that the favourable clauses in the 1793 Militia Act were inspired by precisely the kind of Mennonite petitioning frequently referred to in the first fifty years of the *Journal of the Legislative Assembly* of Upper Canada.[10]

Violating the Militia Act had consequences in Upper Canada. The Quakers, unlike the Mennonites, did not readily consent to the payment of exemption fines and at times had their goods confiscated. Neither was it a small issue to report to the militia to pay one's fines. The patriotic fervour and the rowdy social activities of the militia drills, such as horse racing, was not a congenial environment for non-resistant Mennonites. A notice appeared in the *Niagara Herald* May 23, 1801, ". . . that the militia will meet at the Chippawa Bridge (Welland River, Niagara) on June the fourth and that all Quakers, Mennonists, and Tunkers must attend, bring certificates and pay the exemption fee, or expect to be proceeded against as the law in such cases directs."[11] After 1809, the law provided for jail sentences lasting until the exemption fine was paid. Boys from sixteen until the age of their baptism were excluded from the exemption. This caused the Peace Churches to lobby the government to have these young men also included in the Militia exemption, and they also sought to have these heavy exemption fines reduced. The Mennonites believed in the separation of church and state, but that did not mean they had nothing to say to, or ask from, the state. In 1810 a petition was granted in "an Act for the Relief of Minors of the Society of Mennonists and Tunkers." However, the Peace Churches' request to have the exemption fine lowered was denied. The twenty-shilling per annum fine during a time of peace and a five-pound fine per year during a time of actual war was a burden for the early settlers. The War of 1812-14 suspended further lobbying of the government concerning the Militia Act until 1829. However, during the next twenty years fifteen different Mennonite petitions reached the government and the persistent lobbying achieved success in 1849, when Royal assent was given to a bill which rejected the principle of fines as a substitute for militia service. In 1867, after confederation, the new Dominion passed a Militia Act which again gave the Mennonites their cherished exemption.[13] (3) However, after fifty years of exemption from military service the Mennonites were ill-prepared for the War of 1914-19.

(3) *The 1868 militia exemption states that "any person bearing a certificate from the Society of Quakers, Mennonists, or Tunkers, or any inhabitant of Canada, of any religious denomination, otherwise subject to military duty, but who, from the doctrines of his religion, is averse to bearing arms and refuses personal military service shall be exempt from such service when balloted in time of peace, or war, upon such conditions and under such regulations as the Governor in Council may, from time to time, prescribe."*[12] *The last phrase created concerns during the World Wars.*

The Loyalist Mennonites in Ontario

During the American Revolution the revolutionaries needed arms. They usually confiscated (with compensation) the "non-associators" guns, but a feisty Bucks County Mennonite miller, John Fretz, challenged this. When the Patriots asked for his gun he took it from its usual place and said to the soldiers, "You can have my gun, but I'll keep hold of the butt end." Tradition is silent about how the argument ended. The Deep Run area in Bucks County where Fretz lived was along the Delaware River, a pocket of Loyalist sympathy. John Overholt, another Mennonite miller, had his mill confiscated by the Patriots. He fled across the river to the British where he died; however, his son, Abraham, elected to join the Butler's Rangers. After the war had ended someone reported that 185 Bucks Countians were emigrating to Niagara in 1786. Within this group we find five families of Mennonite background: Staats Overholt and his wife Susan Hunsberger, John Han (Hahn), Franklin Albrecht, Jacob Kulp, and his brother Tilman who was married to John Fretz's sister Molly. These Mennonites made successful appeals for land as United Empire Loyalists and received a total of 2168 acres in the vicinity of "the Twenty" or Vineland (Vineland is located at the creek twenty miles from Niagara Falls). These people of Mennonite origin made no attempt to retain the Mennonite faith, but were assimilated by Tunkers, Baptists, and Methodists.[14]

The following year Abraham Boehm arrived at Niagara. He was a miller and a brother to Bishop Martin Boehm whose "holiness" views had cost him his fellowship in the Mennonite Church. Abraham Boehm had been convicted of advising two Revolutionary soldiers to defect to the British and was fined 750 pounds by the Lancaster Court in 1781. Boehm always declared his innocence, and in his claim for land he testified he had lost everything except his life and integrity. Later, Abraham's son Martin would donate the land for the first Mennonite Church at Stevensville in 1838.[15] Another disgruntled Mennonite, Casper Sherk, arrived at Niagara in 1796 and bought a clearing from John Rowe, a Butlers Ranger. The revolutionaries had burnt down Sherk's house because he had sympathized with the British and harboured British officers. Sherk had appeared as a witness for the defence at Boehm's trial in 1781.[16]

Peace Churches in Welland County

Welland County lies in the southwest portion of the Niagara peninsula along the north shore of Lake Erie and west of the Niagara River (see map on page 49). Quakers began to settle in Welland County and by 1792 there were two Quaker communities, at Black Creek and in the short hills in Pelham Township. In 1788 a Tunkers group also arrived and made their homes in the short hills of Pelham and Thorold Townships. From this group Hans Winger became the first Tunker bishop in Canada. The Tunkers were aggressive evangelists and had an impact on the Mennonites in the area. The Tunkers believed in non-resistance and baptism by immersion, from whence they received their name. In Ontario "Tunkers" was the official name until about World War I when they adopted "Brethren in Christ." They have also historically been known as River Brethren because the movement began along the Susquehanna River. The Brethren in Christ should not be confused with the Church of the Brethren (German Baptist) group. Very few of the Church of the Brethren came to Ontario. It is evident that in Welland County the Tunkers were blessed with continual strong leadership because in Welland the Tunkers won over the Mennonites, but in Waterloo and Lincoln Counties the reverse was true.[17] The once-prosperous Mennonite Church at Sherkston was sold to the Tunkers in 1931.

The first Mennonites to settle in Welland County arrived in 1788 and made their homes along the north shore of Lake Erie, about fifteen miles west of Fort Erie at Sugar Loaf. Jacob Sevitz came with several other families, and two years later Abraham Neaff also arrived at Sugar Loaf with another company of immigrants. In 1789 two Amish men, John and Christian Troyer, continued on one hundred miles west to Long Point. In John's petition for land he stated that it was "against the Tenets of his Profession to bear arms."[18]

As early as 1793 Welland County had a hundred families adhering to the Peace Churches; moreover, others were on the way. Simcoe's generous land grant was effective and there was heavy immigration to the Niagara peninsula from 1796-98.

This flourishing community had at least three places of worship: at Sherkston, Black Creek, and Stevensville. However, the community was soon challenged by discord. In 1825 John Herr organized two Reformed Mennonite congregations which drew about half of the members away from the "Old" Mennonites. ("Old" Mennonites is a historical term to identify the main body of Swiss Mennonites. In this writing this group will be called the Conference Mennonites.) The 1841 census records indicated there were approximately 860 Mennonites and two hundred Tunkers in Welland County. It cannot be determined who were the Reformed or Conference Mennonites.

The Welland congregations accepted English preaching at an early date. Bishop John Zavitz's (1798-1872) wife did not understand German, therefore he preached in English. When Waterloo preachers came to Black Creek, Michael Sherk became annoyed: "Why don't they realize that we're living in a country which uses English?"[19] Interesting that in 1824 the Black Creek congregation participated in an interdenominational Sunday school. Of the thirty-five families contributing money and materials for the school, sixty per cent were Mennonite. The first books were purchased in Buffalo on September 8, 1826. Later, Navy Island in the Niagara River became a favourite location for the annual Sunday-school picnic. The Mennonites in Welland were evidently assimilated into wider society at an early date.

There were no Welland County appointments in the Meeting Calendar before 1873, even though Bishop Moyer recognized two ministers there in 1831. Cayuga, just west of the Grand River, was listed as early as 1854 and meetings across at the "Falls" in New York were held in 1865.[20] One might suggest that worshipping only every four weeks was inadequate for a Mennonite community so interwoven in society, and who also were challenged by aggressive revival movements from the Tunkers and other churches. Was the Mennonite leadership not strong enough to stop the decline? Why did Peter Sherk (1814-1889) decline to serve as a minister in the Sherkston meetinghouse? Why did Martin

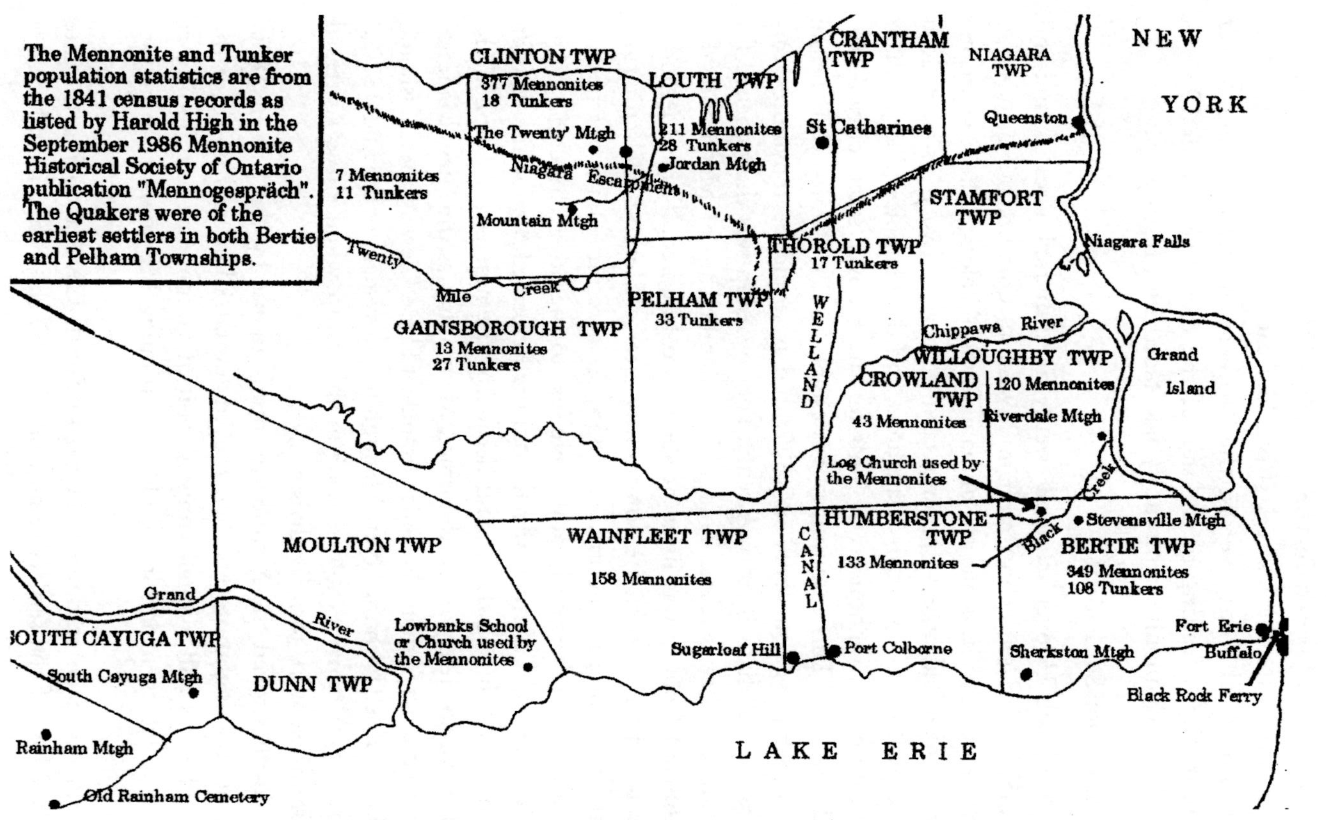

Map data from Harold Nigh, "The lost tribes of the Niagara Plain Folk," in Mennogesprach *4.2 (Sept., 1986).*

Weaver (1814-1887) not preach at the Black Creek church when he was "a man well informed in the Scriptures?"[21] He was one of the last Mennonites in the Black Creek (Riverside) community. At Sherkston the Mennonites all went over to the Tunkers, Methodists and other denominations, leading to the sale of the meetinghouse in 1931. A flourishing Mennonite community had faded into history.

The Rainham Settlement

In 1791 Jacob Hoover acquired twenty-five hundred acres of land and became the first settler in Rainham Township, Ontario. His acquisition of the first two concessions of Rainham Township along Lake Erie became symbolic of other large Mennonite land purchases. Two years later Jacob arrived with his six sons, three daughters, and their families. The Rainham Mennonite meetinghouse was built on the Hoover tract, circa 1810, beside the lake. This community was established over thirty years before the township was surveyed in 1829, and it would be ten more years before the Rainham Road was built. The township was then opened for the influx of new settlers. The greatest membership of Mennonites for Haldimand County was listed at about two hundred. Three Methodist churches sprang up in the community after a Methodist circuit rider spent some time in the area in 1835. As a result, many prospective Mennonite members and youth were lost to the other churches.

Haldimand County suffered from the Reformed Mennonite division that occurred during the second decade of the nineteenth century. The local historians refer to the Reformed Mennonites as the "new Maneese" who were stricter than the older branch. (These "new Maneese" should not be confused with the "New Mennonite" movement of the mid-1870s.) There was a considerable loss of membership when these scattered communities were torn by divisions.

Fire destroyed the Mennonite meetinghouse by the lake in 1870, and the meetinghouse was then moved several kilometres north of the lake. There is still a small congregation of Conference Mennonites at Rainham, which makes it the oldest continuing Mennonite community in Ontario.

An outreach settlement began in South Cayuga during the late 1830s. Most of the settlers came from "the Twenty," but included were several families from the nearby Welland community. In 1850 a log meetinghouse was built about seven miles west of Dunnville on the Rainham road at Fry's Corners. Twenty years later a new meetinghouse was erected which was used until 1965 when the congregation amalgamated with the Rainham fellowship, leaving the old cemetery as the sole reminder of another former Mennonite congregation.

Jacob Hoover arrived in 1791 in Rainham Township. He was one of the first Mennonite settlers in Ontario that did not have Loyalist connections. The original cabin had been incorporated into a house and was preserved. When that house was torn down the old cabin was discovered inside of the other building. The Hoover cabin was then moved to another location. Very few of these early pioneer cabins remain to reveal how small they were.

The Vineland Settlement

The early settlers of Mennonite heritage at Niagara had extensive Loyalist involvement, but the next wave of settlers would flow into Upper Canada after Pennsylvania had repealed the Test Act in 1789. The Peace Churches in Pennsylvania now had an alternative to the bearing of arms, and the migrations to Upper Canada took on a different character. Moreover, before 1793 there were no clear legal exemptions from military service in Upper Canada. To reside with recently discharged soldiers who had lost their homes during the Revolutionary War was not the most appealing setting for non-resistant Mennonites. After a number of years, the Mennonites' ready cash would become more acceptable as the ex-soldiers sought to dispose of their large land holdings. Some historians state that the desire to live under British rule was a major pull for the Canadian Mennonites. This factor is convincing, but the behaviour of the Mennonite migrations back and forth across the border suggests other considerations. Why did some Mennonites from Ontario move on to Ohio, Indiana, and Michigan? Did the devastation of the Niagara Peninsula during the War

Rainham Cemetery: The original meetinghouse was built adjacent to Lake Erie. The old meetinghouse stood on the far distant right in this photo.

of 1812-14 strengthen the pro-British sentiment? Did the war make the Mennonites more anti-American, or was it *land*?

In 1798 Abraham Hunsberger and his two sons went to investigate "the Twenty" and visit his sister, Mrs. Staats Overholt. Hunsberger chose land adjacent to Overholts and Kulps. Early in the following year another prospecting party arrived at "the Twenty." Amos Albrecht (doubtless a relative of Franklin Albrecht) and Abraham and Jacob Moyer were so well pleased that they left a deposit of forty dollars for eleven-hundred acres of land before they walked back to Bucks County. This was still an era when riding in a wagon was considered an unnecessary convenience.[22] That fall a wagon train from Bucks County undertook the demanding twelve-week trek to Upper Canada. Every able person walked. Children walked unless their feet were sore, even Sarah Hipple, age twenty-eight, baby in arms, walked all the way. Even though there was a ferry from Black Rock to Fort Erie as early as 1783, the children remembered getting their feet wet as the water seeped into the wagon boxes, and the cattle and oxen had to swim as they crossed the Niagara River.[23]

In 1800 another party arrived at "the Twenty." John Fretz (who held to his gun) would join his sister, Molly Kulp, who had arrived in 1786. There were about sixty persons in Fretz's party. The colony at "the Twenty" had, in a few short years, attracted about thirty families and there were more on the way.

On behalf of the group, Samuel Moyer wrote back to bishop Jacob

Gross, of the Deep Run district, asking that some Pennsylvania bishops come to oversee the ordinations of ministers and deacons. In September 1801, Bishop Gross replied to "our little brotherhood in Upper Canada." He had written to "Conestoga" (Lancaster County) and they wrote that they had enough work with their outreach settlements. Now there was no one among the elderly bishops in Pennsylvania who felt "armed with courage and strength" to walk those five hundred miles of muddy trails. Gross considered the group's request in order and advised them to proceed by themselves. After a time spent in prayer they were to nominate the candidates, and if more than one be nominated they were to cast the lot to see whom God had chosen. The elderly bishop wrote that, "as long as it is of the Lord, it will have good consequences, unless the one called does not remain true and in humility (note "in humility"), which is what the Lord demands of all his servants."[24]

The community at "the Twenty" accepted the required advice and permission from the home community. An ordination within a Mennonite community was no trivial affair, as it was a call from God. In the fall of 1801, the community at "the Twenty" chose the forty-year-old Valentine Kratz as their minister and the seventy-year-old John Fretz for their deacon. They had also built a log meetinghouse that year on Samuel Moyer's farm, which also served as a schoolhouse. Samuel Moyer was the schoolmaster. The following year Jacob Moyer was ordained as a minister. In 1807 he was ordained as the first Mennonite bishop in Upper Canada. There were other scattered Mennonite groups in the Niagara Peninsula, but it was at "the Twenty" where ties with the leadership in Pennsylvania were nurtured. In 1810 a frame building was erected on the east side of the cemetery; the log church had been on the west side. In 1833 this cemetery was enclosed by a stone wall at a cost of ninety silver dollars.

The Waterloo Community

The first white men to look across the beautiful Grand River valley were two French missionaries, Brebeuf and Chaumonot. In 1640 these men traversed the Grand River valley and made a fairly accurate sketch of the river.[25] The valley was granted to the Six Nations Indians by Governor Haldimand in 1784 for their services during the American Revolutionary War. This tract of land was six miles on each side of the river from its mouth on Lake Erie to where the town of Fergus stands today. The part that interests us is "Block Two," which became known as Waterloo Township. This home for the early settlers would, in time, be swallowed by the cities of Kitchener and Waterloo. The Indians had desired to lease part of the tract, but the government denied this request. After several years of wrangling, the government relented and gave the Indians the right to sell their land. The land north of Paris, or the Governor's Road (Highway 99), was divided into five large tracts and sold.

On May 10, 1798, Block Two was sold to Richard Beasley, James Wilson and John Rousseau, who was a son-in-law of Chief Joseph Brant. Beasley's partners soon withdrew and he became the sole owner of the tract. Beasley, a German Loyalist from the Mohawk River in New York State, lived near Dundas. Amongst his neighbours were individuals who had emigrated from Pennsylvania. Peter Horning, a man of Mennonite heritage, was the first man to receive a deed for a thousand-acre tract of land known as Horning's Tract. Beasley's neighbours also knew of the Mennonites who were on a quest for land.

Beasley surveyed the lower third of Block Two so he could market his holdings. In 1799 Jacob Bechtel accompanied the group who settled at "the Twenty." He heard about Beasley's holdings and continued to Dundas where Beasley provided him with an Indian guide and a surveyor. Bechtel spent almost two months exploring Block Two. As Bechtel was returning back to Pennsylvania, he encountered Joseph Sherk and Samuel Betzner who were from another prospective party from Franklin County, Pennsylvania. Bechtel recommended the Grand River valley to the Franklin County group.[26]

The following year, 1800, Beasley's tract flourished. George Bechtel bought 3150 acres and John Biehn, who had sold his mill and farm in Montgomery County, Pennsylvania, bought thiry-six hundred acres. (5) Not only the Mennonites but also the Tunkers and Moravians from all over Pennsylvania were on the migration trail. Almost fourteen thousand acres of Beasley's land sold in the first year and more settlers were on the way, but a dark, uncertain shadow loomed. In December 1802 Samuel Bricker went to register a farm he had bought from George Bechtel and discovered that Beasley's tract was held by a mortgage. Beasley has been defamed by many for the mortgage scandal that ensued. However, "no

(5) *These large land purchases are evidence that land was the primary reason for the Mennonite migrations to Upper Canada. Tradition is not silent with regard to the Mennonites desiring British rule, especially in the stories of those who suffered bad experiences with the new American government. Being pressed into military transport service during the American-instigated War of 1812-14 only strengthened this tradition. From the Canadian Mennonites viewpoint, the destruction from this needless war reinforces this folklore, but their migration patterns do not.*

primary evidence exists to indicate that Beasley concealed the situation from the purchasers in Block No. 2," but Benjamin Eby wrote in 1841: "they had not known…that the whole township was mortgaged."[27] Beasley's efforts with Captain William Claus, Superintendent of Indian Affairs, to have a separate mortgage for the surveyed portion of his tract was denied, even though Joseph Brant, the spokesmen for Indians, urged Claus upon the matter. In February 1803, Beasley petitioned the Parliament of Upper Canada, in co-operation with the Indians, requesting relief that would meet both his needs as well as those of the Indians. In June the Council responded, stating that since Beasley was in arrears with his interest payments the Trustees of the Six Nations were to enter legal action against him for payment.[28] It has been suggested that Beasley was the victim of a continuing dispute with the Executive Council over the disposition and control of Indian lands. The earliest documentation of Beasley's troubles is recorded in *Canada Museum*, 23 February 1837: "[Beasley] was not in a position to make the promised payment by his own means. For that reason he called on his Pennsylvania friends for assistance."[29] What was the Mennonite community's response to such legal wrangling? The evidence suggests those not involved steered clear of the trouble and travelled on to Markham.

In 1803 Henry Wideman and Peter Musselman continued on to Markham Township and settled there. The next year the Christian Reesor and Martin Hoover families also arrived at Markham and formed the nucleus of the Markham community. It is apparent that the Mennonite community was uneasy concerning the outcome of the Beasley fiasco because the immigrating settlers of 1803 and 1804 continued on to Markham. Furthermore, in June 1803, ten men from Block Two also took land grants for 2150 acres in Whitchurch Township north of Toronto. Only one settled in Whitchurch, the rest forfeited their grants.[30]

The story of the Waterloo settlement focuses on the Bricker families. Both Samuel and John Bricker's wives' families were on the migration trail looking for a large tract to accommodate group settlement. Samuel had married into the wealthy Christian Eby family and John had married into the even wealthier Christian Erb family. Daniel Erb, a scout for the Erb family, arrived in 1803 and had authorization to negotiate with Beasley and acquire land. On November 28,1803, a legal contract was drawn by a lawyer, William Dickson, between Richard Beasley and Daniel Erb and Samuel Bricker, providing for the sale of sixty thousand acres for ten thousand British pounds (approximately twenty thousand dollars). The following May Daniel Erb appeared before the Trustees for the Indians with £4,602.10 with the intent of receiving a mortgage for the balance. After three days of negotiations, Claus again refused to yield. Claus required that Beasley's entire mortgage be liquidated. Claus accepted the £4,602.10 as an instalment and required that Erb pay the balance of £10,795 by May 23, 1805. This amount included six per cent interest on the balance owing. (6)

> (6) *Abraham Sherk (1853-1945) had a quarrel with the predominant tradition. To transport ten-thousand British pounds in a light wagon was to him nonsense. Ten-thousand pounds would have been about half a ton of silver. A four-horse Conestoga wagon only carried four barrels of flour, or 784 lbs, over the rough and muddy trails through the bush. How could they have packed their food, camp gear and horse feed into a light* weggalie. *Sherk thought that they brought the money over in a four-horse wagon along with a heavily armed guard. He also was adamant that nobody ever came through the Beverly Swamp before it was drained. It was still bear-infested in his younger days. Folklore has many versions and there may be a crumb of truth in all of them, but one fact has never been disputed and that is that money was brought over from Pennsylvania to pay for Waterloo Township.*[31]

The conveyance of such large amounts of cash was a high risk. The initial payment was carried to Upper Canada in saddlebags, but this Beasley affair was becoming more and more common knowledge to the people. The transportation of the final payment must have been extremely risky. According to tradition, the money was packed into an oaken keg that was fastened to a light wagon with Sam Bricker as the driver. John Bricker, Daniel, Jacob and John Erb completed the convoy. They were mounted on horseback and armed with heavy muzzle-loaders. At night three men slept while one man guarded the keg by sitting on it with his gun on his knees.[32] Although these manoeuvres deviate from the traditional Mennonite values, these men ultimately responded to the circumstance at hand and they were instrumental in forming a Mennonite community in Ontario.

On June 29, 1805, the Erbs paid for the tract in full and received clear title to the Upper Block henceforth known as the German Company Tract, but the Indians never received their payment. Since the government refused to take charge of so large an amount of money, Claus was forced to personally accompany it to England, but no record of the £10,795 could be traced in 1830. Remember that story in which the Indian forced a white man off the end of a log? Here again the Indian was defrauded.

The new syndicate, the German Company Tract, had been formed largely by the extended families of the Ebys and Erbs. The Erbs held almost one-half of the shares and the Eby's investment consisted of over one-quarter. Only one-quarter of the shares remained for the other shareholders to buy. The Weavers and the Hersheys were an inter-married clan who purchased another twelve per cent of the remaining shares. With the value of farms in Pennsylvania being about twenty-five hundred dollars at the time, it appears that several wealthy families were on the migration trail (Mennonites were moving to Ohio as well as Ontario) and could gather sufficient funds to alleviate Beasley's embarrassment. There was definitely co-operation within the Mennonite community in forming the German Company Tract, but this was not a full-scale effort of the brotherhood. The purchase of Block Three or Woolwich Township in 1807 clearly suggests that the buying of Block Two had been a success.

The German Company Tract drew in large numbers of settlers from Lancaster County and with them came the traditional Swiss culture that would be mixed in Waterloo with the "Skippack," or Dutch Mennonite culture. Their community spirit, the brotherhood, brought the Mennonites from all the districts together in one place where the two cultures would harmonize and form one community—a Mennonite brotherhood.

Notes

1 ME, IV, 1047.

2 John L Ruth, *Maintaining the Right Fellowship* (Scottdale, PA: Herald Press, 1984), 69.

3 *Ibid.*, 84-89.

4 G. Elmore Reaman, *The Trail of the Black Walnut* (Scottdale, PA: Herald Press, 1957), 23.

5 *Ibid.*, 45.

6 *Ibid.*, 84. See also L. J. Burkholder, *A Brief History of the Mennonites in Ontario* (Altona MB: Friesen Printers, 1986), 48.

7 Frank H. Epp, *Mennonites in Canada* I (Toronto: Macmillan of Canada, 1974), 101.

8 *Ibid.*, 105.

9 Neville Williams, *Milestones of History* (New York: Newsweek Books, 1974), 539.

10 Epp, *Mennonites,* 102.

11 Edwin C. Guillet, *Early Life in Upper Canada* (Toronto: University of Toronto Press Toronto, 1963), 346.

12 William Janzen, *Limits on Liberty* (Toronto: University of Toronto Press, 1990), 164.

13 Epp, *Mennonites*, 93-108.

14 Ruth, *Maintaining*, 161-62.

15 M. S. Boehm, *History of the Boehm Family.* (Kitchener, ON: Waterloo Historical Society, 1936), 221.

16 Ontario Historical Society (hereafter OHS), 25, 423.

17 Harold Nigh, *The Lost Tribes of the Niagara Plain Folk* (Kitchener: Mennonite Historical Society, 1986), 18.

18 J. C. Fretz, "The Early History of the Mennonites in Welland County ON." *Mennonite Quarterly Review* (January 1953): 58.

19 Nigh, *The Lost Tribes*, 17.

20 Burkholder, *A Brief History* , 52.

21 Fretz, "The Early History," 70.

22 Ruth, *Maintaining*, 164.

23 Burkholder, *A Brief History*, 26.

24 Ruth, *Maintaining*, 172-74.

25 I. C. Bricker, *The History of Waterloo Township up to 1825* (Kitchener: Waterloo Historical Society, 1934), 92.

26 Elizabeth Bloomfield, *Waterloo Township Through Two Centuries* (Kitchener: Waterloo Historical Society, 1995), 34.

27 Benjamin Eby, "Origin and Doctrine of the Mennonites," (Markham-Waterloo Mennonite

Conference, 1999), 100.

28 Reginald E. Good, *Frontier Community to Urban Congregation: First Mennonite Church, Kitchener 1813-1988* (Kitchener: First Mennonite Church, 1988), 18.

29 *Ibid.*

30 Bricker, *The History*, 88.

31 Abraham Sherk, Letters (Kitchener : Waterloo Historical Society, 1959), 42-43.

32 Bricker, *The History*, 92.

The Transition

Chapter Five

In the nineteenth century, the different values Mennonites held drew them into controversy. Where there is too narrow a vision, the peoplehood polarizes, and each wing then retains only part of the original vision.[1] For the Old Order Mennonites the changes that were taking place became more than their conscience could allow. The traditional Anabaptist ethos was subtly being exchanged for gentle Protestant breezes, and one may question if any in that day understood the forces that were rupturing Mennonite peoplehood.

A Time of Diversion

At the beginning of the nineteenth century the hardy settlers began to hew their clearings out of the majestic forests in Waterloo Township. Thirty years later the woods still encompassed their farms. It would take the settlers fifty years to bring one half of the township into cultivation. In 1831 there were only 12,566 acres cultivated from Waterloo township's total of 94,012. However, by 1851, the cultivated acreage had increased to 41,067 acres. The remaining bush lands in the township did not hinder the development of this thriving community.[2] From their secluded dwellings nestled in the woods their only evidence of neighbours was to hear shouts to oxen or a barking dog.[3] For the first twenty years the Mennonite church was the only governing body in Waterloo Township. Furthermore, even the local Justice of the Peace was none other than the Mennonite miller, John Erb, of Preston. Then in 1822 a new era began when the first council meeting was held in Waterloo Township and civil government, rather than church order, controlled the community.

Transportation remained difficult for many years. Many roads resembled a sugar-bush trail, which for six months a year were so bad that the only way to travel was by foot or on horseback. William "Tiger" Dunlop, agent for the Canada Company, said that for four months of the year you were up to the neck in mud; for four more you were either burned up by the heat or stung to death by mosquitoes; and for the other four, if you managed to get your nose above the snow, it was only to have it bitten by the frost.

On Sundays the young men may have gone to visit friends while the maidens passed their time cross-stitching their show towels, but what do they hear? The shrill cry of the train whistle was beckoning a different era. After the Grand Trunk rolled into Berlin in 1856, it became possible to market their products and to travel with greater ease to their American friends. The subsistence agricultural community was slowly evolving into an industrial society.

This towel was cross-stitched by Mary Biehn. She was a grand-daughter of John Biehn who came to Waterloo in 1800. In 1849 she married Benjamin Martin whose son Moses took a firm Old Order position. From 1835-1840 Mary laboured painstakingly in her spare time to complete this towel.

Before 1835 the inhabitants of Waterloo Township were largely Mennonite. The total population in 1835 was 2791, and the Mennonites numbered about two thousand, or seventy per cent. Twenty years later, in 1851, the population had risen to 7,698, but the Mennonite total remained static. By 1851 there were more German Lutherans in the township than Mennonites.[4] There are several reasons for this phenomenon. After the 1837 Rebellion, the political climate became more stable in Upper Canada and thousands of

European immigrants flowed into Canada. The German-speaking Mennonites in Waterloo Township attracted hundreds of German Lutherans and Catholics so that by mid-century there were almost twice as many continental Germans as there were Mennonites. These continental Germans came with little means and were obliged to occupy the more marginal land of Waterloo township or take residence in the villages where they began to practice their trades. Meanwhile, the agrarian Mennonites moved into both Wilmot and Woolwich townships, or even to the shores of Lake Huron, in their quest for large, cheap acreage. The Mennonite migrations contributed to the static Mennonite population in Waterloo.

The Mennonites were widely scattered in Markham and especially the Niagara Peninsula. From their isolated environs the Mennonite youth sought friendships and there was some intermarriage outside of the Mennonite fellowship, as was the case of John Erb's daughter.[5] Since marriage outside their fellowship was taboo, these couples left the Mennonite brotherhood. Such gravitation of their youth to other denominations weakened the Mennonite fellowship. Even the grave markers of the earliest settlers are engraved in English at the Vineland cemetery. A few German tombstones are found there, but it is evident that some assimilation began at an early date.

Mennonites made no direct effort to remain separate from the general society. The hard and difficult times of the early pioneer days had demanded that everybody work together. Pluralism of religion strengthened as people learned to live and let live, or to dwell amongst their neighbours like "fish in water." This concept agreed with the Christian "golden rule" of doing to others as we would have them do to us. Their non-resistant faith differentiated the Mennonites from the mainline churches, but during peaceful times non-resistance was neglected. In 1858 Deacon John C. Shantz, contrary to the Mennonite rule of faith, began a lawsuit with several tradesmen. This caused quite a stir amongst the brotherhood and he was called before the church.[6] The problem persisted. Fifty years later a Mennonite sued a Mennonite contractor because the water levels at the Floradale Dam were alleged to be above the expected levels. The case came before the courts, but the matter was evidently dropped because no further records have been found.

The September 1864 conference resolved "that according to our understanding of God's Word, campaigning and voting for candidates to serve in public office does not conform to our non-resistant Christian confession of faith." (2) Mennonite involvement in public office must

(2) *Each Mennonite community held a semi-annual conference every spring and fall after the Council Meetings had been held. On the fourth Friday in May they held the Annual Conference where the three districts came together to discuss the issues as one fellowship. The Annual conference was held alternately in the three districts at "the Twenty," Markham, and Waterloo. For this reason reference may be made of a conference held in various places even though it was the same conference held in another district.*

have continued to haunt the Mennonite Church for in an April, 1883 conference another resolution was made: "According to the Gospel of Matt. 6:24, 'No one can serve two masters,' etc. and 2 John 'whosoever transgresseth . . . ' when brethren accept the office of councillor, they cannot be considered as brethren until they reconcile themselves through admission and confession in front of the church and have been taken up by the bishop with hand and kiss [of peace]." Later, Peter Shirk's involvement in politics as an Old Order, reveals that the problem continued to haunt the Old Order church until the beginning of the twentieth century. Shirk served twenty-six years at the Berlin High School [1878-1904] and from 1892-1912 he served as township treasurer.[7] The Mennonites had an unofficial scheme by which such an office was accepted: they would only accept a political position if appointed by acclamation. They would never enter a political campaign because a Mennonite esteems his fellow man better than himself.[8]

The fact that going to shows (farm fairs) was forbidden in 1842, and that hoop skirts and trimmed beards were deemed unacceptable in 1861, indicates that the Mennonites were keeping track of the times. Temperance Associations in 1842, attending livestock shows in 1844, and secret societies in 1875, were all issues over the years that confronted the conference body and were viewed as opposing to the teachings of Christ. These issues were not part of the back-woods times, but those of a developing and a prosperous society. The Mennonite community in Waterloo was evolving from being a traditional, rural Mennonite community into being a "Waterloo" community—a community flirting with the modern world.

In his diary Elias Eby expressed no objection to his son Tobias' prospect of working in Montreal. When his son Elias Jr. left for California in 1873, his well-written diary leaves no note of concern for his son's spiritual future. It had been the pioneering spirit that drove the settlers into Waterloo County and it was the same spirit that motivated others to make their homes on the endless prairies and the cities afar. The pioneering spirit had not been wrong, but when it became a subtle form of prodigality, the Mennonite church lost many of her prospective members. John Funk's return from his business enterprise in Chicago to labour in the Mennonite Church was not the norm, but a rare event. Persecution had separated the Mennonites from the world, but pioneer life drew them towards society as a whole; therefore, to remain a separate people within the realm of a general public was a new experience for the Mennonite community and they were not prepared. The organization of the Mennonite Aid, or brotherhood fire coverage, in 1864 was one of the first attempts by Mennonites to formally separate themselves from society as a whole.[9]

Revivalism

In Europe, where religious pluralism was not known until after the Napoleonic Wars, the movement between two different faiths was restricted because the controlling state church took advantage of all other churches. During the 1600s the Catholics in Krefeld, Germany had to pay the ruling Reformed Church fees for baptism, marriage and death rites.[10] During such times the chances for a Catholic youth to become familiar with an elite Reformed youth were remote. In neighbouring Belgium, the reverse power balance was true during the same era. The state churches diligently sought to frustrate all other sects so that their "true" religion would be maintained. It was the mainline churches that devised all kinds of inventions which hindered gravitation from church to church.

In the United States the separation of church and state led the way to a distinctive form of church life. The abuse of political power, ever-prevalent in the traditional state church setting, gave way to American

Protestant pluralism or denominationalism where the Christian churches tolerated, and in time respected, each other. The revival movement that gripped the New England colonies also compelled the mainline churches to accept laymen's involvement in the church's administration. Consequently, the evangelistic laymen's frontier revival meetings became part of the New World's religious life. The emotional sensation generated by these lively revival meetings was the medium that snared many Mennonites who were disillusioned by the lackadaisical nature of the Mennonite Church during the nineteenth century. This new personal religion was free from the "restrictions" of the so-called "static" Mennonite Church (3). The boundaries of the brotherhood were cast away. The

(3) *Ruth N. Smith felt the "restrictions" of the dress code of her father's church (Old Order) and resented them while some of her contemporaries were content with those regulations. Ruth felt her "wedding ceremony left little room for individuality."*[11] *Once the church regulations are deemed as "restrictions" the emphasis shifts from the brotherhood to individual. The orders of the church to those who are at peace are considered guidelines, whereas to those who are discontent the guidelines become restrictions. To those who are at peace, guidelines are as guardrails along the highway to protect the traveller from harm. To the others guardrails are restrictions that prevent them from their off-road excursions.*

liberty to boldly testify of one's conversion drove the movement to the remotest cabin on the frontier. Furthermore, it could be stated that revivalism laid the foundation for the Protestant churches of America and Canada, but it also shook the very foundations of the Mennonite Church.

For the Mennonites it was their commitment, their yieldedness to the brotherhood and their ethos of non-resistance and nonconformity that separated them from the mainline churches. If individuals expressed interest in their fellowship and proved faithful, they were accepted into the brotherhood, and if one of their number became disillusioned, he was allowed to depart. The present-day Old Order Mennonite emphasis on the separation of the church from general society was part of their Swiss Brethren heritage. The Anabaptists always demanded purity within the group, and we find by the 1690s they also were stressing distinctive clothing as a means to separate themselves from the world.[12] One could wonder, had not persecution effectively separated them from the world? Nevertheless, once the sword was put into its sheath and the Mennonites were allowed to swim to and fro like fish in the water, they were ill prepared to combat the new forces such freedom allowed.

Times of change began to trouble their waters. *Der mach-nichts geisht* (the doesn't-matter spirit) was the aspiration of many a youth. The popular slogan, "As long as the heart is right then all is well," echoed over mountains and plains. Isaac R. Horst said, "The cross of Christ is too heavy for many; they do not wish to bear it, and say it matters not how we go in and out."[13] Christian Horst held a different view: "Some say it is not in the coat nor in the hat (that is to say) if the heart is right all is right. My opinion is if the heart is right, the coat and hat will soon get right."[14] Horst's thought was along the lines of Gelassenheit and brotherhood where what is expected is a change of life and a yieldedness to the fellowship. Der mach-nichts geisht went counter to the traditional Mennonite ethos.

Economic liberties and religious freedom were tearing the simple Mennonite communities apart. Their values, their non-resistant faith, and their brotherhood were challenged not only by the "gentle Protestant breezes" and the love of mammon, but also by the fiery Methodist preachers. These Methodist revival meetings could at times become rather rowdy affairs. In 1839 a three-day camp meeting in Berlin attracted eight-hundred people from all denominations including Mennonites, Tunkers, and Catholics. The Justice of the Peace was present because he expected some unruly behaviour, but later commented that that was one of the most orderly camp meetings he had ever heard about. The result of that meeting was the formation of the Evangelical Association in Berlin. The Evangelical Church was the German wing of the Methodist Church. A Methodist evening house meeting during the early 1860s became so loud that it was heard four miles away.[15] When rumours sped across the Mennonite community that some girls had rolled around on the floor of their meetinghouse, the staunch members were sure that nothing good could come from such absurd nonsense. Nevertheless, after several generations the Methodists also mellowed and such stories would remain part of frontier revivalism.(4)

(4) ***A New Mennonite Revival Meeting at Blair, 1890***
Naturally, at that tender age, I was easily impressed with all I saw and heard. . . The house was crowded with . . . people from miles around. They came in cutters and double-sleigh loads, bells jingling as the trotting horses hurried them towards that meetinghouse. The evangelist, Rev. Ruth, was a fiery, jumping, shouting preacher. He had been an acrobat in a circus before his conversion, we were told. Anyway, he rushed back and forth behind the pulpit, proclaiming the Gospel. He fairly screamed as he said, "You must not only be saved—but you must be sanctified. I preach entire sanctification as a second work of Grace." Then jumping up and down behind the pulpit, almost leaping over it at times, he preached about the awfulness of sin and its consequences. He pictured Hell in its most terrifying aspects. I fairly trembled as he spoke of the damnation of the wicked. . . . After the sermon, Mr Ruth asked the believers to come to the altar—and the unsaved to do likewise. . . . Then began such shouting, singing, clapping of hands, crying and praying, all at the same time, that it seemed bedlam was let loose! It lasted for several hours. . . . The evangelist came tearing down the aisle and asked a young man . . . near me: "Are you saved? . . . are you not afraid of the lake of burning fire and brimstone?" . . . The evangelist preached against styles and "wearing of gold" (and) girls and women laid aside their jewelry, pulled plumes and feathers from their hats, and removed "frills" and lace from their dresses, and became "plain." All the converts were baptized by immersion and joined that church. . . .
When I spoke to father about this, and how disturbed I had felt, he said, "I just don't have any use for all that excitement. They work themselves up into that state by shouting and clapping, and getting almost beside themselves. I tell you, I'd rather see my children join the United Brethren any day than these shouting New Mennonites."[16]
"I just don't have any use for all that excitement" captures the view of the Old Order about any charismatic meeting.

Social Pressures

Two issues beyond its control perplexed the Mennonite Church during this era. First, there was a conflict between its teaching of humility and the popular aggressive American individualism. Secondly, it was accused of losing its testimony to the world, a change that would continue to haunt it for decades. Let us first consider the impact of American individualism. (5)

The victory of the New England colonies over Great Britain resulted in the birth of a new nation. They were now "individuals" separate from Great Britain, and they were a people who would aggressively build a

(5) *During the 1840s Jacob Stauffer wrote that the Mennonites "needed less of* Freiheits-Geist, *that is, the spirit of liberty." (He might as well have said the American spirit of liberty.) This "liberty was the national rhetoric, and the law favored unhumble eighteenth-century ideas of individualism, enterprise, and emergent, aggressive nationalism." For as much as the "Mennonites and Amish appreciated the new American nation, they also retained a strong sense of being called-out people of God. And their humility outlook was a odds with much of American religion, individualism, and nationalism."*[17]

great nation; furthermore, the revivalistic fervour also generated a spiritual individualism as the *personal* conversion in Christ was emphasised. Although this was the American scenario, the Canadian situation was very similar after the 1837 Rebellion. The Canadian grievances were not the heavy taxation which triggered the American revolt, but the overbearing power of the Anglican Church which shackled all other denominations. Once the grip of the Anglican Church was loosened after the 1837 Rebellion, the Canadians, to a lesser degree, also hoisted the banner of individualism. The Mennonite Church's teaching of unassuming and agrarian humility was not sufficient for those who had tasted of this popular individualism that embraced both revivalism and industrialization. James Juhnke has written,

> Since the sixteenth century, Anabaptists-Mennonite teachings and the Mennonite reading of the Bible had defined a charter of community values that were genuinely in tension with the ways of American individualism, materialism, and upward mobility. Intentionally limiting themselves to primary school education, the traditionalists were not as articulate as the progressive denominational-builders. But in their holding to the ways of humility, simplicity, and obedience, they pressed an important question: whether the acclaimed denomination blooming was not in fact a loss of an original and authentic Mennonite vision.[18]

American individualism and Gelassenheit did not mix well.

What is, or should be, the Old Order Mennonite testimony to the world? Was there truly a "want" of life and power of religion as Newcomer (an ex-Mennonite who turned out to be a leader of the United Brethren movement) thought, or was the aged minister's observation correct when he observed an aggressive revivalist and stated, "Ich vil kein dahl mitt so frech ein Krist" (I want no part with such a bold Christian)? For the era in question both views are correct. The fact that the first industry in Waterloo district was a distillery is a down-played, hush-hush matter, and so is the fact that the Mennonites at "the Twenty" considered liquor part of the building expense when they erected their simple Mennonite meetinghouse. A century later a person wrote that, "My dad built a straw-shed to the barn, they had a raising and served beer for the men as was the order of the day."[19] Such issues were fuel for the fire of controversy that the revivalists used to wedge their way into the Mennonite community.

By mid-century the impact of the temperance movement challenged the Mennonites in Waterloo. The 1842 conference report includes the following: "While the participation with Temperance Societies and their work was discouraged yet drinking and drunkenness are most strongly condemned. The use of intoxicating liquors in the home, with guests, at public sales and among workmen, was declared to be improper."[20] Serving liquor to the men at harvest time was so entrenched in the community as a whole that when a Mennonite, Jacob Y. Shantz, and several others elected to go against the tradition, they were warned that it would be impossible to retain men without serving liquor. The workmen accepted the challenge against tradition and as a result the serving of liquor at harvest time declined.[21] It was a disgrace to the Mennonite community that it took outside pressure from the Temperance Societies to bring about a necessary change. However, a community that is able to successfully resist assimilation is most likely steeped in tradition. The use of tobacco and its elimination within the Mennonite community had the same problems as the liquor issue did a century earlier. For a time the Mennonites condoned frivolous behaviour. During the first decades of the twentieth century, local Evangelical youths observed the Sabbath more strictly than their Old Order Mennonite counterparts. On the east side of St. Jacobs on a pleasant Sunday afternoon one could find some Mennonite boys engaged in a jovial baseball game, while on the west side of town the Evangelical boys spent the Sunday afternoon quietly in their parents' parlour. Mennonite girls also would have found it quite out of the ordinary to follow the rule of the children in Alma who were to sit quietly on wooden benches on Sunday afternoons. Only quiet conversations were acceptable, giggling was not allowed. Yet, it would be the Evangelical boys who enlisted in the armed forces during World War II, while the Mennonite boys went off to Alternative Service camps.[22] Another account indicates that the young Mennonites spent the Sunday afternoon dancing on the lawn with the adults as their audience. One would not expect this to have been the norm, but the evidence suggests that the Mennonites were far more frivolous than the present generation would like to believe. The mainline churches before the world wars had high Christian values. In the 1860s the older people in Fergus frowned on skating. D. N. Panabaker would remember being reprimanded by his grandfather for whistling on a Sunday. The Puritans had considered it sin to whistle on Sunday.[23] After the initial disorder on the frontier, society had become religious and law-abiding. The many small old churches that dot the countryside are the evidence.

In summary, the Old Order Mennonites' testimony to the general public the decades before and after the turn of the twentieth century was weak. There were those who felt the traditional ethos of Gelassenheit and lived lives that commanded the respect of their neighbours, but there were those who were being swept away by the beckoning sirens of American individualism.

Industrialization

The rumbling and thundering of steel on steel vibrating through the quiet land beckoned another era—industrialization. Even before the trains thundered across the fields, the lowly spinning wheel had given way to the woollen mills, and soon the cradle lay idle in the shed while the reaper cut down the grain. The thrashing machine was welcomed, but the horses and oxen had no more grain to tread. Next the binder came and the maidens had no more sheaves to tie. Change, change and more change: the passion for wealth would soon invite the use of mechanical power. In 1831 Cyrus McCormick demonstrated the first successful reaper; however, the early equipment was frequently more novel than practical.[24] A story goes that the immigrant Peter Martin was present when some new equipment was demonstrated. His sons were interested in the contraption; however, the old man rebuked them and told them to get back to work. The old immigrant clearly displayed the Old Order work ethic. Nevertheless, the binder entered the Old Order Community without a ruckus. Paul Martin, the son of Deacon David Martin, purchased the first binder in the church before he was ordained preacher in 1888.[25] The conservative character of the Old Order Mennonites has generally resisted change.

The present Old Order mentality could be defined as "waiting until a new thing is proven for some time before endorsement."[26] Maybe a literal interpretation of Luke 16:15 would yet best capture the mood: " . . . for that which is highly esteemed among men is abomination in the sight of God." The popular trend of the world and brotherhood humility are difficult to reconcile peacefully.

The labour force went through a dramatic change as its major employer, the farmer, began to replace manual labour with mechanical power. Jacob Y. Shantz once had to appease his labourers when he bought a reaper. The workers feared their job security, but Shantz explained to the men that though the reaper would reduce handwork, it gave opportunity to the skilled labourers.[27] Furthermore, not everybody found it acceptable when women began to enter the work force. Peter Moyer, editor of the Berlin *Daily News*, observed that:

> There is a large number of these girls who at from ten to twelve years of age enter the factories and remain there until in the usual order of things they get married. After working from eight to a dozen years at making buttons, what fitness it may well be asked, have they to take charge of a household? It is not to be wondered at that there are many unhappy and unhomelike homes, for in the very nature of things it is entirely impossible that happiness can exist where slovenliness, tastelessness and uncleanliness are found in the house or at the table. . . . In a matter of morals too, it is much safer—though it may be quite as pleasant—to be in the quiet of a family than to be day after day crowded in the same shop with from fifty to one hundred other girls, some of whom to say the least are not above suspicion.

He suggested instead that parents who had daughters "whom they no longer needed at home should consult the interest and welfare of their children by encouraging them to accept good situations as domestic elements (working as hired maids) in preference to going to the factories."[28]

There were also Mennonite women working in the factories, such as Jacob Y. Shantz's button factory, and Moyer's concerns of 1879 are ever shared by the Old Order Mennonites. New doors had also opened for young women. Tying the sheaves in harvest and spending endless hours by the spinning wheel were exchanged for time to go to school, and time to adorn themselves with costly array. There was also time to read novels which the editor of the *Berlin Telegraph* questioned: "Novel reading is not only dangerous and acts on the mind as ardent spirits do on the body, but it is also a waste of precious time for which God will require a strict account."[29] There were many changes as the Mennonite community in Waterloo witnessed the transition from subsistence pioneering to an industrial society.

Conclusion

For centuries persecution had been instrumental in separating the Mennonites from the world. The guilds had denied their participation in the trades in Europe, but in America these barriers were removed and the Mennonite Church wrestled to keep itself separate from the world. The Anabaptists' purity and holiness had in part separated them from the churches in previous centuries. By the last quarter of the eighteenth century this barrier had been subtly removed as Pietist revivalism had transformed society. Personal purity and holiness were no longer just a Peace Churches' motto, but also became the banner of the outspoken Methodists. In some aspects of life the Methodists even surpassed the traditional Mennonites' vision. In the temperance issue the Methodists called for total abstinence while the Mennonites stubbornly clung to their traditional order of moderation. With her traditional values challenged, the Mennonite Church was ill-prepared to face the charismatic fervour of Methodism and other revivalistic movements.

The Mennonite emphasis on humility clashed with the individualism that was molding the industrialized American nation. This individualism, the freedom to venture into the greater society and achieve one's dreams, drew many Mennonites, especially the youth, from the Mennonite church. The spirit of Gelassenheit weakened as Mennonites reaped the world's wealth and fell under Protestant influence. Subtle changes in emphasis modified priorities within the Mennonite Church. Those who drew from Pietism and later from Protestantism embraced a sweet Jesus who offered them personal salvation through the resurrecting power of Christ. Those who effectively resisted the new ways embraced Gelassenheit. They maintained a strong emphasis on submission and obedience to their Lord and the brotherhood. Their salvation was based on crucifying ones carnal nature with Christ and repentance and amendment of life. When one boasted about his salvation, one quietly waited to see if his walk of life agreed with the Word. When Christian Huber boasted much of his piety and great salvation, Elias Eby wrote in his diary that this may be true, but we only have his word for it. The audacity of revivalism definitely clashed with the quiet and meekness of traditional Mennonitism. These trivial differences, history reveals, could not reside within the confines of a brotherhood. What made the issue so complex was that the Pietist also believed in crucifying one's carnal nature and the repentance and amendment of life; likewise the Anabaptist also believed in the resurrecting power of Christ. It was the difference in emphasis that changed the outlook on life.

Notes

[1] John L. Ruth, *Maintaining the Right Fellowship*, (Scottdale, PA: Herald Press, 1984), 535.

[2] Elizabeth Bloomfield, *Waterloo Township Through Two Centuries*, (Kitchener, Ontario: Waterloo Historical Society, 1995), 68.

[3] A. B. Sherk, "Recollections of Early Waterloo." (Kitchener: Waterloo Historical Society, 1915), 15.

[4] Elizabeth Anna Haldane, *The Historical Geography of Waterloo Township, 1800-1835* (M.A. Thesis, McMaster University, 1963), 58, 114.

[5] Bloomfield, *Waterloo Township*, 79.

[6] Isaac Horst, Mennonite Conference Reports (April 23, 1858), 5.

[7] Peter Shirk, *Family History of Peter Shirk* (N.p., 1984), 7.

[8] Lorna Bergy, Conversation with Author, 1998.

[9] Isaac Horst, Mennonite Conference reports (Sept. 9, 1864), 7.

[10] Ruth, *Maintaining*, 31.

[11] Loralyn Smith, "Ruth Nighswander Smith," *Ontario Mennonite History* (March, 1994): 7.

[12] John L. Ruth, *The Earth is the Lord's* (Scottdale, PA: Herald Press, 2001), 128.

[13] Isaac R. Horst, *Close Ups of the Great Awakening*. (Mount Forest, ON: Isaac R. Horst, 1985), 150.

[14] *Ibid.*, 136.

[15] Isaac Bean, *Three Generations Tell of Bethel Church* (Kitchener: Waterloo Historical Society, 1983), 93.

[16] Bloomfield, *Waterloo Township*, 231.

[17] Theron F. Schlabach, *Peace, Faith, Nation* (Scottdale, PA: Herald Press, 1988), 30, 32, 207.

[18] James C. Juhnke, *Vision, Doctrine, War* (Scottdale, PA: Herald Press, 1989), 30.

[19] Private Conversation.

[20] Conference Reports and L. J. Burkholder, *A Brief History of the Mennonites in Ontario* (Altona MB: Friesen Printers, 1986), 141.

[21] Samuel J. Steiner, *Vicarious Pioneer: The Life of Jacob Y. Shantz* (Winnipeg, MB: Hyperion Press Limited, 1988), 34.

[22] Noah Martin, Conversation with Author, 1980.

[23] D. N. Panabaker, *Historical Sketch of the Clemens Family*. (Kitchener: Waterloo Historical Society, 1921), 170.

[24] D. N. Panabaker, *Glimpses of the Industrial Activities of Waterloo County About Fifty Years Ago* (Kitchener: Waterloo Historical Society, 1933), 32.

25 Private Conversation.

26 Private Conversation.

27 Menno Shantz, "Adventures in Colonization." Unpublished manuscript written by J. Y. Shantz's son. (Grace Schmidt Local History Room of the Kitchener Public Library, Kitchener, Ontario), 14-15.

28 Kenneth McLaughlin, *Cows and Town Life: Berlin in the 1870s* (Kitchener: Waterloo Historical Society, 1987), 145.

29 Gerald Noonan, *The Local Mentality: A History beyond Words* (Kitchener: Waterloo Historical Society, 1980), 46.

Difficult Separations

Chapter Six

The Hoch Dissension

The oldest Mennonite community was in the Niagara peninsula and was extensively exposed to aggressive Methodist revivalism during the first half of the nineteenth century. The adoption of the English language hastened Mennonite assimilation into general society. Preacher Daniel Hoch of Jordan (Vineland District) was greatly concerned about the problems in the church. His concerns for the church were sincere, but his uncharitable attitude irritated even some who were like-minded to the point that they could not support him. Hoch's emphasis on religion was acceptable, but he was very severe with those who differed from him.[1] His values were similar to those of John Funk several decades later, but Hoch's personality was against him.

Hoch was ordained in the summer of 1831. He laboured effectively with his bishop, Jacob Gross, for over fifteen years. In 1842 two brothers, Dilman and Abraham Moyer, were also ordained as ministers of God's Word. Moreover, at this time there were some strong pietistic breezes drifting along the lakes. This "holiness," or Methodist movement brought disharmony into the Mennonite church so that in May 1847 at the conference in Markham the following resolution was made:

> It was resolved and permitted to hold prayer meetings for all true worshippers, who worship the Father in spirit and truth, as long as it is done in an evangelical order, especially with the

> weak and sick, who cannot attend the regular church; but it shall not be required of any minister to act contrary to his feeling, or his view of the Word, where prayer meetings are asked to be held in cases where there are no weak and sick persons.
>
> The evangelical order requires that those who believe in prayer meetings bear with those who believe otherwise, in love, meekness, and patience; and on the other hand, that those who do not believe in such meetings shall bear with those who do, in love, meekness and patience. Where this is not done it is contrary to the scriptural order. Let all things be done in charity.[2]

The last paragraph implies that there were different views concerning prayer meetings and this manifested itself as time went on. There was an immediate misunderstanding in Markham concerning the above resolution, whereupon the Markham ministry sought a copy of the resolution and evidently peace was restored.[3] At "the Twenty" in 1848, the new privileges of prayer meetings were introduced by Bishop Jacob Gross and Dilman and Abraham Moyer without informing their fellow minister, Daniel Hoch.[4] This strained the atmosphere from the first hour, but when the Methodists also took part in this innovation, confusion and disunity resulted.

Samuel Bauman, a Hoch supporter, wrote:

> The Methodists cast a watchful eye their way, and when Gross, Hoch and others began to hold prayer meetings, Methodists were found among them; and from what I saw and heard from the beginning, I am forced to believe that these evening meetings, not everything proceeded as I would have preferred it. . . . What I am forced to believe is what must shine forth in the whole matter, namely: that Hoch and others began these prayer meetings from their own sense of duty, and that the results, unexpected by Hoch (them), caused no one more regret than Hoch himself.[5]

Samuel Bauman blamed the Methodists for using these prayer meetings to lure the Mennonites into their church. They saturated these meetings with their emotionalism and marred the relations even further within the Mennonite church. The unrest caused by these innovative meetings forced them to close, but peace and harmony would evade the community for several years. The ministry became divided: Bishop Jacob Gross, Minister Daniel Hoch, and Deacon Jacob Albrect were those who supported the principle of extra prayer meetings, while Abraham and Dilman Moyer and Deacon Abraham Kraft opposed the innovation. The accusations and counter-charges confused the congregation. By 1849 Gross had enough of the opposition "Waterlooers" (those from Waterloo County). He and his followers became so saturated with Methodism's emotional and holiness teachings that they forsook the church of their fathers and joined the Methodist Church.[6]

Hoch's involvement with the church's first attempt at holding evening meetings led many to brand him a Methodist. At the conference in September 1849, many accusations rose against Hoch so that Bishop Benjamin Eby said: "It reminds me of Menno, when he was accused that he was a Münsterite, defend himself against it as he would, they still insisted he was."[7] Eby was in a very difficult spot. He had a letter from the church at "the Twenty" stating that they would no longer accept Hoch as their preacher. Hoch's fate was that he was a better lawyer than a meek Mennonite servant of God. In doctrine he was unblamable. Minister Joseph Hagey confessed to one of Hoch's trusted friends that Hoch conducted himself so that no one could get a hold of him according to the Gospel.[8]

Daniel Hoch was expelled from the Mennonite Church in 1849. His followers felt envy was the reason for his excommunication, but the church's true reason may be found in Hoch's own writings.

> Herewith I will close about the many incidents which happened during the last few years in Canada, especially in the church at "the Twenty" and commit the whole work to the leading and prevailing hand of God, praying to Him, that He might accompany it with His spirit, so that it might afford all truth-loving readers comfort, and many, yes, all erring ones a disclosure, awakening, and prospering of their temporal and eternal welfare, since we have not left our precious doctrine, given to us by Christ and his apostles, and our confession

> writings as we are falsely accused by our adversaries, and cannot be persuaded by any means to leave it, as long as our faithful God supports us—to Him be glory in eternity, Amen. But because of this *departure and fall of the Canadian Mennonite Church it has such deep roots that practically nothing is left but an outward form, and satisfy themselves with an outward mouth and lip confession, without seeking after the life which is of God.* (The innocent are free—the Lord knows His own) "*Therefore we separated ourselves from their disunity and disorderly conduct, to serve our God and our heart's conviction, in spirit and truth, faithfully and earnestly.*"[9] (author's emphasis)

In 1873 this conference built the first Mennonite church with a basement for Sunday school, and in the following year on Nov. 7, 1874 they dedicated their first organ that had cost the church $450.00.[10]

It is clear that Hoch had lost all confidence in the Mennonite Church when he writes that "practically nothing is left." Such bold comments are not part of a brotherhood of believers and no doubt his rivals were offended that Hoch supported his wife when she discarded the traditional prayer veil and were sure that Hoch's prayer-minded people had lost focus on their traditional faith. Daniel Hoch and his followers then associated with John Oberholtzer (1) who had led a group out of the Franconia Conference in 1847. In eastern Pennsylvania the quarrel had been the same, only the issues were different.

(1) *John Oberholtzer was ordained minister in 1842. He defied church order and refused to wear the regulation coat as required by all ministers. In May 1844 the conference silenced him. Although there were open issues, the root of the dissension was Oberholtzer's democratic procedures and his different definition of piety versus Gelassenheit and brotherhood. When the unity of the conference snapped, Oberholtzer and fifteen of his colleagues walked out of the conference on October 7, 1847. These progressive leaders then formed the General Conference Mennonites.*

Two models of church order were contending for the future of the Mennonite community. The newer one had rationality, democracy, and clarity on its side, as well as a different definition of piety. The traditional one represented the submission of the individual initiative to the authority of the larger brotherhood, even when personal views might appear more enlightening. That mutual surrender was a key to their self-understanding. In the midst of a rapid flexing in the cultural framework, the traditional leaders were unable or unready to speak of their precious "old non-resistant ground" of Gelassenheit in accents that would charm the imaginations and emotions of those eager for reform, progress, and positive change. For the traditionalists, too, it was a question of conscience. The conservative leaders seemed to value inaction or a kind of ignoring of issues precipitated by changes in the surrounding culture. John Oberholtzer (and Daniel Hoch) were de-emphasizing the covenantal dimension of the Christian fellowship, formerly a central motif in their Mennonite heritage. "Their reaction to an intolerable cultural stagnation had modified their vision and sympathies."[11]

Over four hundred miles of primitive roads and an international boundary separated Oberholtzer and Hoch, but their visions and goals were surprisingly similar. Ruth's summary of the Oberholtzer drama also captures the controversy at "the Twenty." In both cases there was a definite want of submission and yieldedness. Parliamentary rights versus traditional Gelassenheit were the core issues. Had Hoch been willing to step down from the bench as Bishop Eby had suggested, the reprieve may well have secured the required space so that peace could be restored, but Hoch stood by his parliamentary rights and denied Eby the room to work.[12] Although Hoch's sincerity may not be questioned, the pietistic values had clouded his understanding of Gelassenheit—the glue that binds a brotherhood together.

Oberholtzer was the founder of the General Conference Mennonites in Pennsylvania and Hoch worked with that group for a number of years, but when the Mennonite Brethren in Christ movement (to be discussed in following chapter) swept across Ontario, Hoch's followers associated with them. Hoch had already withdrawn from the General Conference in 1866 and stood alone until his death in 1878.

Mennonite Brethren in Christ

The removal of Hoch and Oberholtzer did not assure peace within the Mennonite Church. The rapid progress of settlement in the West kept the individualistic spirit alive. The American Civil War (1861-1865) swept a patriotic spirit across the United States and further undermined traditional Gelassenheit. Numerous small Mennonite communities had more relations with general society as the trains made transportation a pleasure. Individuals hastened to the charms of cities. The American Sunday School Union was formed in 1824, and its mandate was to organize Sunday schools across the whole United States. These interdenominational Sunday schools further blurred the Mennonites' vision as they absorbed Protestant ideologies. The "off" Sunday (2) was a convenient time to attend the union Sunday schools. The spirit of individualistic Protestantism challenged the ethos of Anabaptism in the Mennonite community. One of these communities was at Port Elgin. There was more than just clean air rolling off the lake, as the Evangelicals' camp meetings attracted many people.

(2) *The Mennonites held bi-weekly or once a month services in their meetinghouse. The "off" Sunday was designed to give the people opportunity to fellowship in a neighbouring congregation or to go visiting friends and brethren in the church. With horse-drawn transportation it was not possible to go visiting and attend worship services on the same day. As a result of this custom there were numerous Sundays whenthe backwoods communities had no church services close to home. Irregular attendance at church services was all too common during the 1800s and by mid-century the youth frequently attended Methodist or other Protestant churches. The union Sunday Schools opened a door of opportunity and many Mennonites attended and many youth gravitated to the neighbouring Protestant churches.*[13]

Solomon Eby lived in Port Elgin, Ontario and was ordained minister in 1858. (3) According to his testimony, he preached for eleven years before he was converted. After his conversion he became very zealous for a definite religious experience. He defied the traditional Anabaptist motif of yieldedness—Gelassenheit—and challenged the church of his youth by stating he would follow his convictions regardless of the church or her officials.[15] Although Eby drew a following from the Waterloo District, a majority of the people did not trust him. In the Spring 1872 conference at Berlin, Solomon Eby was told not to encroach on the bishop's work. Eby evidently went home and continued to baptize and serve communion as he desired. On Sunday, November 24, 1872, Eby and Daniel Wismer, one of his supporters, held services at the Ben Eby's meetinghouse. Not all were impressed. Elias Eby commented in his diary:

> I think. . . . Solomon Eby should first obey the church rules and regulations before he takes liberty to preach in our meetinghouses. It is well known to him that it is not allowed for a preacher to baptize or serve communion when a bishop is available, but he, paying no attention to this, went home to Port Elgin, and did according to his own judgment baptizing and administered communion. Here, truly a great disobedience is apparent. Now this young man stands up in his justification in our meetinghouse and tells us much about his conversion, and out of love he would give his life for his Lord. If he were to resign his own will and his obstinacy, I might possibly believe the above, but the way he conducts himself now, I can truly grant him little trust.[16]

Clearly, not all were impressed.

Just over a year later Elias Eby again made notes in his diary concerning the Sunday morning services at Eby's meetinghouse. Daniel Brenneman of Indiana had arrived on January 23, 1874 for a series of evangelistic meetings. Elias laments the discord in the church. Brenneman held meetings in private homes, meetinghouses, and schools and had no regard for the traditional Mennonite community values. He spoke to any person who would listen—which was well and good—but Elias' complaint was that "he communes with men who despise our non-resistant faith. Is this not being unequally yoked together?" Brenneman evidently handed out posters proclaiming "Peace! Peace!" Elias closed the day with, "Too bad

(3) *The agrarian Mennonites' quest for land inspired a group of Mennonites to begin a community at Port Elgin, Bruce County in 1854. Amongst this group we find Martin Eby with his family of ten children and Samuel Bricker Jr. who brought in a heavy steam engine overland to run his sawmill. On August 8, 1858 Martin Eby was ordained deacon and his twenty-four-year-old son, Solomon, was ordained minister. Three years later a meetinghouse was erected on Lot 11, Samuel Bricker had donated Concession 9 C, a three-acre parcel. The location of this meetinghouse had long been forgotten until in 1997 Isaac Horst and Ed Bearinger sought to find the old location. Horst was content that he found the remains of the old meetinghouse when he stood in a depressed hollow about thirty feet across behind the present Port Elgin cemetery.*[14]

that this self-styled peace messenger did not begin at home."[17] Brenneman had little regard for his colleague's values. Without the welcome of the home minister, he threw himself into the presence of a congregation and promoted his new ideas. In this manner Brenneman gathered a following from within the Mennonites churches in Ohio and Indiana. His obstinate behaviour and complete disregard for his cohorts created ill feelings within the Mennonite church.

Brenneman and Eby's aggressive and defiant behaviour against the conference resulted in their excommunication from the fellowship in 1874. These men became a law unto themselves.[19] Their principles no longer reflected the yieldedness and submissiveness of the traditional Mennonite faith. Even though the "Old" Mennonite church was experimenting with the Sunday school, (4) the radical reformers wanted more. Those in

(4) *The nineteenth-century Sunday school and prayer meetings held different connotations from those of today. The earliest Sunday school amongst the Mennonites in Ontario was advertised in April 1841, but there are no records regarding this school. Nevertheless, by 1847 Benjamin Eby had conducted Sunday schools on the church grounds at Berlin. These early Sunday Schools generally taught the German language with Biblical literature (the Bible) on the "off" Sunday, but the Union Sunday schools and their interdenominational nature were a concern, if not an offence, to the conservative wing of the Mennonite Church. Lesson helps of a Protestant type were not introduced until 1866. By 1872 the American Sunday School Union was a thoroughly established and powerful national institution. It was this organization and such episodes as at "the Twenty" which the conservative element of the church feared. The prayer meetings likewise were not as they appear today. Extemporaneous prayer by persons other than preachers was still uncommon (not just with Mennonites). Prayer and edification meetings fostered more overt religious expression by laypersons; indeed the role of ordained persons tended to be minimized in these settings. Prayer meetings also diverted attention from the preaching of the word as the core of religious life, and could be seen as tending toward spiritual pride. As with Pietism, prayer meetings also tended to be ecumenical; they detracted from the authority of the church community.*

The second issue that made these above meetings unacceptable for the Mennonites was the infiltration of the holiness doctrine or the second work of grace.[18]

authority, sobered by responsibility, invariably and wisely moved cautiously towards changes, but the reformers, free from cares of administration, rushed impulsively into action. The Brenneman-Eby movement resulted in the formation of the "New" Mennonite group. The "New" Mennonite division affected the southern part of Waterloo Township and Bloomingdale-Breslau area the most. The United Brethren (German Methodists) had held bush meetings at Breslau where the Mennonites became acquainted with the "holiness" teaching. From 1875 to 1880 the Snyders congregation was not listed in the Calendar of Appointments, indicating that for those years the congregation was not in fellowship with the conference. The "New" Mennonites founded many small congregations. A small church was built in Conestogo at 1022 Sawmill Road. This congregation eventually folded and the building was used as the township hall and for other public uses. The "New" Mennonites adopted the name of Mennonite Brethren in Christ and later, in1947, became known as the Missionary Church.

Stauffer Controversy of 1845

The Mennonite Church in Lancaster County, Pennsylvania was faced with several controversial issues in 1845. An orphan girl had been bound to a Mennonite couple until she was eighteen. Apparently this girl suffered mistreatment at the hands of her foster parents such that in time those outside the church reported it to the law. The courts found the couple guilty and ordered $380.00 in damages be paid to the girl. The offending couple ignored the court order and the case again came before the law before payment was made. The second case developed out of a marriage gone sour. A Mennonite girl had married outside the church and when she feared her husband's behaviour, she returned home to her father. The father went to the Justice of the Peace to swear out a warrant for his son-in-law's arrest (he meant to protect his daughter's life). Further violating the non-resistant faith, the father took a constable and went to his son-in-law's house to take his daughter's belongings. He entered the locked house and took the possessions. An out-of-court settlement ended this dispute between the father and daughter and the rejected son-in-law.

After all these legal manoeuverings, the conservative element led by Jacob Stauffer felt a ban should be applied.[20]

> In the face of this dilemma, progressives and conservatives reacted in two different ways. Progressive leaders decided to

> preserve the outward tranquility of the community by tolerating more deviance from the rites of powerlessness (non-resistance). Conservatives, on the other hand, felt that true peace could not be founded on the search for justice and the use of legal means of coercion. When they recognized that the main body of the church members would not withstand the new methods of interaction as strongly as the conservatives wished (i.e., the ban), the conservatives decided to preserve the traditional ritual process in their own separate communities.[21]

Stauffer called the ban "the deepest digging up through God's love." In short the ban was to him an act of love to make the sinner realize that he had separated himself from God. The love of the brotherhood was to convict the offender and then draw him back into the fold. However, the progressives could no longer see that the aim of the ban was spiritual rebirth and recommitment. An individual who had been excommunicated commented, "Once the ban is just a form of punishment its purpose is as good as lost because those in the ban can feel the difference if one considers the ban an act of punishment or an act of love to separate sin from the church."[22] For the progressivists the rite had become merely the church's own form of coercive punishment.[23]

The Stauffer division appeared to be a local affair, but this deviation (the above legal action) from the church's traditional non-resistant approach displays leniency in church discipline. Stauffer's more conservative values were not localized. David Metzler, from Ohio, wrote to the Lancaster bishops and expressed sympathy toward Stauffer because they wished to punish the "outstanding transgressors" and to purify the church. Metzler also frowned on the Lancaster position that permitted the laity to vote in public elections. In closing his letter Metzler included a list of his ordained men. Amongst them we find a young man named Jacob Wisler who would later relocate in Elkhart, Indiana.[24] (Wisler also had conservative leanings because several decades later he would lead the Old Order movement in Indiana.)

Although this conflict remained local, the effects of the weak discipline of the church continued to smoulder until the smoke of the divisions afflicted the church. The Stauffer (Pike) division can be considered a cry to the Mennonite church for more discipline. During an era of individualism, discipline was not popular. Even the above mentioned Old Order bishop, Jacob Wisler of Elkhart, Indiana, was criticized by Deacon Joseph Holdeman for being too lenient. Evidently it was common for the unbaptized girls to wear the stylish hoop skirts which Holdeman insisted that Wisler forbid and discipline the parents of the disobedient girls, but Wisler thought that it was enough to preach against such worldly fashions.[25] The varied acceptance of acculturation was to set the Mennonites at odds with each other. Some accepted prayer meetings and the "holiness" doctrine while others did not. They clashed with the traditional temperance status and the popular total-alcohol-abstinence-movement. The more outlying areas adopted the English language with its Protestant emphasis, while concentrated core settlements clung more to the traditional German. Was the glue, the yieldedness, Gelassenheit, the bond that held brotherhood together failing to serve its purpose?

The Stauffer and the following Iowa movements were not caused by the controversy between Gelassenheit and "holiness." In these cases as well as the later David Martin group, the issue was Ordnung (order or discipline of the brotherhood). These ultra-conservative groups feared the laxness of the main body and arose in protest on the current issues of their concern. Being rebuffed, the conservatives saw no other option than to leave the main body, which they did. Both parties did not always display the most charitable spirit; however, the conservatives were not inconsistent, insincere, or radical, but they lived according to the dictates of their consciences. We of a later date cannot comprehend the setting of the church of that time nor "feel" their convictions.

Iowa, 1882-1915

In the early 1880s resistance towards acculturation began to manifest itself throughout the Mennonite communities in North America. A group of thirty-year-old men from Waterloo were convinced that the Mennonite church in Canada was becoming too worldly. With them was Jacob S. Brubacher, who had moved to Canada from Pennsylvania to escape the civil war. Brubacher knew of the Pennsylvania Stauffer Mennonites and several of these men visited the Stauffers in 1883. All but one man came back favourably inclined. As a result of this adventure, Bishop David Stauffer came from Pennsylvania in February 1884 to receive into his fellowship seventeen members from the Woolwich area who were interested in becoming members of the Stauffer church.[26] Jesse Bauman and Josiah Martin were ordained ministers for this new Stauffer church in Waterloo in the spring of 1884. That fall Bishop Stauffer came again to Waterloo and ordained Jesse Bauman as bishop.

It is understandable that the Mennonite ministers in Waterloo were not favourably impressed with the coming of the Stauffer group to their district. For Bishop Abraham Martin the challenge of holding the opposing extremes together proved to be a formidable task. (Daniel Brubacher, minister of the Conestogo congregation was also out of fellowship with the main body in 1884, but he and those with him united with the church in 1885. Brubacher and several families had been a separate group from the Stauffer movement.[27]) The ultra-conservatives (Stauffers) were separating to form a church after their utopian order. "The goal behind the entire movement was to have 'a glorious church not having spot nor wrinkle'(Eph. 5:27)."[28] On the other hand the progressive Mennonites were far more acculturated and demanded Sunday schools, English preaching and other more modern Protestant teachings.

The Canadian Stauffers of Waterloo held services in their homes and agreed to adhere to the Stauffer church regulations, a requirement the Canadians never fully met. A very strict and plain dress code was stressed and pride in any area of life was not to be tolerated. Furthermore, the wearing of the beard was optional. The Canadians mostly had beards, but the Pennsylvanians did not. Evidently some women would not tolerate a bearded husband.

The newly organized church feared further acculturation and became interested in settling elsewhere. A real estate agent, Fritz Moyer, knew of some open prairie available in Osceola County, Iowa, close to May City in the northwest corner of Iowa. In the summer of 1886, Bishop Jesse Bauman investigated the possibility of locating in Iowa. He was favourably influenced and bought 640 acres for eight dollars an acre. The following year Bishop Jesse Bauman, with two other families, moved to Iowa. They experienced a long, lonely summer and wrote to Canada encouraging their friends to follow them. On March 6, 1888, a group of seven families, with a total of about fifty persons, departed from the Berlin (Kitchener) station bound for Iowa. They were not without hardships as they erected their houses and barns, but the loss of five children due to a measles epidemic was the most disheartening of all. The newly-founded cemetery claimed the bodies of five children before the settlers had homes to live in.[29]

To their neighbours, these Mennonites were hard-working people and very religious. Their mode of dress was very plain. The men and boys donned brown denim clothing while the women and girls wore dark print that was black, blue, or grey with very little design. Bishop Jesse Bauman set the pattern for buildings so that they were all alike. Barns were of a "bank barn" design and the houses were generally very roomy. All buildings were painted a brownish red; even their meetinghouse was painted red, much to the displeasure of the neighbours who would have donated both time and paint if they could have painted the meetinghouse white. The community prospered financially, but spiritual disunity frequently plagued the brotherhood so that communion was not held for some years.

The new colony struggled for stability from the beginning. The settlers had gathered together from Indiana, Michigan, Snyder, Ontario and from Snyder and Lancaster Counties of Pennsylvania. They all brought with them personal baggage of customs and opinions. Although they agreed on the fundamental biblical doctrines, they could not agree on personal issues. With the strong emphasis placed on pride, there was little leeway for difference of opinion. The differences in customs and practices could so easily be given the broad label of pride. A survivor of the group said that "they failed to apply the Word of God beginning with self and to cultivate an attitude toward the other person as they would have others express toward them."[30] The church leaders were not able to establish unity amongst the laity and neither was the ministry always in harmony. Minister Josiah Martin evidently could not adjust to Iowa and was the first person to leave the community in 1896. His departure revealed the undercurrents of the settlement. John Lehman had applied for membership but was denied fellowship because he refused to surrender his light-weight, one-horse wagon, which was considered too worldly. After Josiah Martin had moved to Michigan the light-weight, one-horse wagon was no longer an issue in Iowa, and neither was it an issue for Josiah any more because he also obtained one.[31]

Josiah Martin's departure left a vacancy in the ministry, and the next year Amos Bauman was ordained as minister and Elias Bauman as deacon. The following winter Amos Bauman visited Ontario friends. While Amos was in the Waterloo district, Peter Shirk made an interesting observation:

> Amos Bauman is here on a visit, and to everyone's amazement he is preaching to the lower churches—the very ones whom he and his people had so harshly accused for being too proud, and their evening meetings as well as the Sunday school. Now since that church has made such progress, he comes and preaches to them. Naturally they accepted him quite graciously. But I believe that when he gets home there will be strife in that church.[32]

In about 1900 the community had reached it zenith with about forty members; however, Peter Shirk's observation was correct. In 1903, Minister Amos Bauman and Abram Wideman left Iowa and moved to Alberta where Amos transferred his membership to the Conference Mennonites. By 1906 the Conference Mennonites expelled him for errors in his teaching and then Amos joined the Pentecostal church. In 1907 Bishop Jesse Bauman was silenced and by 1911 he had moved to Pennsylvania.[33] Jesse had offended the people with his business dealings and by installing telephones in his barns. With her ranks broken this fledgling brotherhood began to wither away so that by 1915 the Mennonite meetinghouse was abandoned. Only the memories and the twenty-six graves in the cemetery remain as a testimonial to the many marred relations.

The community had been drawn together from many areas and they also dispersed to various places. The entire group did not remain within the Stauffer fellowship. Some joined the Conference Mennonites while others, like Milo Lehman, gained fellowship in the Weaverland Conference in Pennsylvania. Their utopian visions had little in common with reality or Gelassenheit. When unity in a brotherhood fails, the people are scattered. The Stauffer movement was a radical protest against the indifference that prevailed in the Mennonite church at that time. It was a tangent in the west, and then a painful scattering of the people. Other than the disruption in the beginnings, the Stauffer movement had little impact on the Old Order community in Ontario.

Barbara Brubacher, the daughter of Jacob B. Brubacher, who moved to Iowa in 1901, experienced this scattering. Elias Bauman took in the Brubacher family for several weeks until a place was found for them. Six-year-old Barbara attended school from this residence and had to change schools when they moved. By the time Barbara was twelve she had moved four times and attended just as many different schools. Barbara drifted between Michigan, Ontario, and Pennsylvania during the years from 1913 to 1925. She had lived in thirteen different places during those years. At forty-two years of age she married Enos Martin of Ontario and her life became settled. The extreme hardships that splintering groups generate are illustrated in Barbara's story.[34]

Notes

1 L. J. Burkholder, *A Brief History of the Mennonites in Ontario* (Altona MB: Friesen Printers, 1986), 179.

2 Isaac Horst trans. Mennonite Conference Reports, CGUC, N.p., May 1847, 5.

3 Isaac R. Horst trans. "Persecution Against Daniel Hoch," (Author's collection, CGUC, 1984), 14.

4 *Ibid.*, 3.

5 *Ibid.*, 26.

6 *Ibid.*, 33.

7 *Ibid.*, 7.

8 *Ibid.*, 3.

9 *Ibid.*, 16.

10 *Mennonite Life* (1947): 33-37.

11 John L. Ruth, *Maintaining the Right Fellowship* (Scottdale, PA: Herald Press, 1984), 272.

12 Horst, "Persecution," 8-9.

13 For further comments see Chapter Eighteen "Meeting Calendars."

14 *Mennonite Historical Society* I, 2; XV, 1-3.

15 Burkholder, *A Brief History*,190.

16 Elias Eby, diary, November 1872, CGUC.

17 Eby, Elias, diary, Feb. 1874, CGUC.

18 Samuel J. Steiner, "Effects of the 1870s New Mennonite Division on Bloomingdale Mennonite Church." *Mennonite Historical Society*, XV vol 1 (Apr. 1997): 29, ME IV, 658.

19 Burkholder, *A Brief History*, 191.

20 Sandra Cronk, "Gelassenheit: The Rites of the Redemptive Progress in Old Order Amish and Old Order Mennonite Communities" *Mennonite Quarterly Review* (1981): 26-27.

21 *Ibid.*, 28.

22 Anonymous quotation.

23 Cronk, *"Gelassenheit,"* 27.

24 Cronk, "Gelassenheit," 28.

25 Amos B. Hoover, *The Jonas Martin Era* (Denver PA: Muddy Creek Library, 1982), 868.

26 Isaac R. Horst, *Close Ups of the Great Awakening* (Mount Forest, ON: Isaac R. Horst, 1985), 154.

27 *Ibid.*, 148, 164.

28 Ezra Martin, "Mennonite Settlement 1887-1915 May City, Iowa" (Waterloo, ON: N.p., Author's collection, 1983), 1.

29 *Ibid.*, 2.

30 *Ibid.*, 11.

31 *Ibid.*, 9.

32 Peter Shirk, Letters to Jacob Mensch in Skippack, PA, 1893-1904. Author's collection. Jan.1, 1898.

33 Isaac Martin, Letters, Conference Reports and Diary Extracts. Translated from the German. Author's collection, 1962, 14.

34 Elizabeth Rudy, "History of the Brubacher church." Waterloo, ON: N.p, Jan 1958.

The Old Order Division

Chapter Seven

To understand the Old Order Mennonite division we need to clarify or identify each group. The main body of Mennonites in this work will be referred to as the Conference Mennonites (historically they are at times called "Old" Mennonites). Old Order Mennonite (OOM) will define the various groups of Old Order Mennonites. Old Order defines the main body of Old Order Mennonites from which all other Old Order Mennonites derive, and OOM relates to all Old Order groups.

Individualism versus Gelassenheit

The malady that afflicted the Dutch Mennonites during the sixteenth century was to trouble the Ontario Mennonites two centuries later. Because of their strong emphasis on having peace within the church, differences of opinion meant disunity for the Mennonites. They had not yet learned that diverse views could strengthen the brotherhood.[1] The nineteenth-century Mennonites struggled with how to control the tensions between a yieldedness to God and the fellowship, and one's personal belief. If there is no yieldedness to God and the Ordnung then there is no Mennonite Brotherhood, and if there is no faith how can there be a brotherhood? It was a new concept to have complete confidence in one's brotherhood and still respect the neighbouring fellowship. The late-nineteenth-century Mennonites scarcely understood that their communities could differ in values and still remain tolerant toward each other. It would have been a great witness if members of the Mennonite Church could have learned to live together in the former bonds of Gelassenheit.

In some divisions the issues are apparent or tangible and such divisions may not be as bitter, but the Old Order division was exceedingly complex. The issues reached down into the very depth of their faith. There were three basic issues that troubled the Brotherhood:

1) The pressure of acculturation: The Mennonites living in the old established communities faced different cultural pressures than did their counterparts living in newly established districts. The scattered communities usually felt more outside pressures, such as the use of the English language, the adoption of Sunday schools, business adventures, and such. The conservative wing, however, was by and large rural and part of the tight-knit fellowship. They were therefore more separate from general society and found it easier to resist acculturation. Nevertheless, there were also many small Mennonite settlements that were weakened by acculturation.

2) The infiltration of American Revivalism: D. L. Moody's influence on John Funk was a major source through which American Revivalism seeped into the Mennonite Church during the last decades of the 1800s. The new religious current embraced many strands of the American religious past: Pietism, revivalism, historic Methodism with its "holiness" bent and also the rather new doctrine of dispensationalism.[2] This blend of Protestant thought clashed with the Mennonites' traditional concept of Gelassenheit. To have Jesus as a personal Saviour was not much different than to have Jesus as Lord over your life, but there was a difference on the emphasis on discipleship.

3) American individualism weakened the theme of Gelassenheit within the brotherhood: The conflict that the Old Orders experienced between individualism and Gelassenheit was constantly aggravated by the "quickened" Mennonites' own version of yieldedness. (The word "quickened," an historical term, describes the Conference Mennonites of the late 1800s.) This yieldedness did not have quite the same meaning as Gelassenheit. There was a difference from the earlier self-effacing American Mennonitism and "the culturally self-confident, sometimes rather cocky,

'Onward Christian Soldiers' mood of the modern Protestant missionary movement" the Mennonites were drawing from.[3]

Mennonite values became more and more varied. All proclaimed that faith, hope, charity, works, forgiveness, discipline, judgment and certainly non-resistance would be part of their lives, but how these attributes were interpreted was changing as the varied effects of "holiness," individuality, and acculturation entered each community. The varied blend of what constituted Mennonitism and the weakening role of Gelassenheit inevitably brought troubled times to the Mennonite Church.

The Wisler Calamity

The first Mennonite settlers arrived in Elkhart County, Indiana in 1843. Three years later Bishop Jacob Wisler from Columbiana County, Ohio, made his home in this fledgling settlement and was joined in 1864, by preacher Daniel Brenneman from Fairfield County, Ohio.[4] Brenneman had already been accustomed to English preaching and four-part singing. Brenneman's English preaching so offended some that they left when he preached in English; furthermore, one can be sure when Daniel Brenneman's group advocated the participation of women in preaching that this became a bone of contention for the conservative faction.[5] The ultra-conservative Wisler forced Brenneman to stop the English preaching. The submission to such orders was a "crushing ordeal" to Brenneman. The disunity continued until the "quickened" Mennonites put Wisler and his followers out of fellowship in 1872. Within two years Brenneman's aggressiveness and unyieldedness cost him the fellowship of the Conference Mennonite Church.

John Funk, a bishop in Indiana and the founder of the *Herald of the Truth* church paper, was an ardent promoter of Sunday schools and protracted meetings. Funk's progressive vision led the Conference Mennonites for many years, but in 1902 he also was censured for similar attitudes that had placed both Wisler and Brenneman out of the church. Three leaders from three different Mennonite fellowships were all censured because their vision of yieldedness no longer harmonized with that of the "congregation."

The chief player in the Indiana Old Order division was Bishop Jacob Wisler. Wisler was a man of quiet disposition who had moved to Elkhart County before the first Mennonite meetinghouse in Indiana was built in

1849. Fifteen years later there were six meetinghouses in Wisler's district. He had in his district a quarrelsome and ultra-conservative deacon, Joseph Holdeman, and an able and popular preacher, Daniel Brenneman, who never had true intentions to yield to Wisler's conservative administration. In 1867 another influential player, John F. Funk, entered the district. Bishop John Brenneman, from Ohio, advised Funk to respect Wisler even if Wisler did not appreciate Funk's publication, the *Herald of the Truth*. He also stated that too many of Wisler's ministers were doing things behind their bishop's back. On June 28, 1867, at a minister's meeting, because of the many accusations heaped upon him, Wisler agreed to desist from preaching until the church should again call him. A congregational vote on August 17, 1867 was only marginally in favour of Wisler's silence.

Wisler had invited Bishop Hoffer from Ohio to oversee the vote. Hoffer, not being pleased with the results of the vote, reinstated Wisler the next day after worship service, without conference approval, to his former office without an agreement of the congregation and suspended Daniel Brenneman and his followers.[6] At this time Hoffer lost the focus of his calling and used the power of his office as a bishop to act on his personal desires. By this time both parties had lost their vision of Gelassenheit. There was no question that the church could any longer go on in peace. Out-of-state ministers attempted to restore peace, but it was to no avail as Brenneman and his followers clashed with the Holdeman group and the battered Wisler stood in between. On March 7, 1869, Wisler and his followers gathered together on the "off" Sunday at the Yellow Creek Meetinghouse and held their first independent service. Numerous attempts to reconcile the two parties continued until January 6, 1872, when the division became final. Wisler declined any further attempts at reconciliation, always stating that he and his people were at peace with each other and desired to be left alone. Wisler drew about one-third of the membership (approximately one hundred members) with him. This group experienced another division in 1907 when the telephone issue rent the fellowship apart.

The key reason for the tense atmosphere was that it truly was a division. On May 11, 1869, nine deeply-concerned leaders from the Ontario Mennonites wrote to the Indiana brethren. For them the thought of division was wrong: "But dear brethren, do consider, as in the presence of

God, that divisions are still more human. Paul calls them, in short, carnal: and the Spirit of Christ has never been the cause of any. He, if we follow Him aright, always leads us together, and unites us with God and with one another in brotherly love."[7] The feeling that division was sin compelled those involved to strive for peace at all cost, which was commendable. Ultimately both sides considered themselves to be right and the other party out of order.

The Old Orders, those who desired to maintain the former housekeeping traditions, deemed that they had been in an impossible situation, or so Minister John Weaver, one of Wisler's chief supporters, wrote to his cousin Samuel Weber in Ontario:

> Bishop George Weaver (Pennsylvania) wrote us a letter wherein he advises us to patience, to forbear in patience, and if we think we are being treated unjustly, then we shall remember the Apostle's advice where he says we shall rather let ourselves be disadvantaged than to recompense or to dispute with each other. That is well and good, which we are willing to do with God's help, for it is better to suffer unrightfully than to do unrightly. But dear brother how can we free ourselves if we always bear with patience and continue to go with the stream of the world? How will we excuse ourselves on the day of judgement, must we not then become speechless, as the one who had no wedding garment?[8]

Lloyd Weiler notes that, "Bishop Weaver could not prevent the conference from officially approving the Sunday school in 1871, but he successfully kept it out of his home district for another twenty years."[9]

This Wisler division dragged painfully on for over five years and obviously resulted in many discouragements. No doubt Wisler and his followers also felt what J. C. Wenger, Goshen College, noted eighty years later: "They [Funk and his colleagues] were winning the Sunday school battle."[10] Wisler's group chose to go separate ways rather than to accept the values of the "quickened" Mennonites.

Sorrow in Waterloo

The most controversial "surface" issue was the Union Sunday school. It was the chief avenue through which the progressive innovations entered into the brotherhood and opened the way for a more democratic church government. Ervin Shantz (1913-1999), an Old Order minister, still remembered that the chief reason the Sunday school was rejected in Woolwich was that the leadership feared the young people would gain control of the church. Another problematic issue of the Sunday school was the use of interdenominational teaching material. This was another avenue that introduced Protestant values into the Mennonite church, and those with an Old Order bent found this unacceptable. The Mennonite Church did not print their Sunday school books until after the division of 1889. When the Moyer ("the Twenty") Sunday school opened again in 1868, they purchased their teaching material from the Methodist Book Room in Toronto.[11]

The flamboyance of the nineteenth-century interdenominational Sunday schools disturbed the traditional Mennonite. There had been Sunday schools in the Waterloo district since about 1840, but the traditionalists distinguished between the earlier German language schools and the contemporary forms of evangelical Sunday school.[12] Theron Schlabach has noted that "The 1871 Sunday schools were in fashion amongst the highest, the proudest, and the dressiest classes of our country; and their study material was partly tales by societies not opposed to war, bloodshed, and lawsuits. Moreover, by using competitive rewards . . . Sunday schools fostered a spirit of pride and exaltedness."[13] The American Sunday School Union's efforts were being felt by the Mennonite community.

An Old Order point of view of the nineteenth-century Union Sunday school would include the following points: The Sunday school was an interdenominational affair which fostered a spirit of pride and exaltedness. It was a medium to introduce non-Mennonite literature into the church and especially to the ears of the youth. It encouraged women to enter the administration work of the church, which according to the Old Order interpretation of 1 Cor 14:34 was not acceptable.

What did those of the conservative mind do to combat the rapid gravitation of their youth to the more modern churches which were luring the Mennonites away from their traditional teachings? (1) The conservative element was so preoccupied with resisting change that few resources were left to contest the aggressive movements of the day. Holding services in more meetinghouses came later, as did their parochial schools. As we open the

(1) *There was a genuine concern for the church by mid-century. In Waterloo Township alone there were about two thousand Mennonites in 1851. When we look at Bishop Henry Shantz's baptismal records for the era, there were alarmingly few united into the Mennonite Church. In 1842 four married couples and one single man were baptized. In 1846 three couples were accepted into the fellowship, but in 1848, '52, and '55 there was only one married woman baptized each of those years, and no record of any single persons. In 1860 seven married couples and eight single persons were taken into the fellowship. By 1871 the currents of revivalism had drifted into the church and twenty married people and thirty-one single persons were baptized. One can suggest that revivalism awoke a slumbering Mennonite Church, but when consideration is given to the total Mennonite population, there were hundreds of would-be members lost to other churches or to the world.*[14]

For Mennonite couples to marry before baptism was all too common during the 1800s. Bishop Isaac Eby of Lancaster County was twenty-six years old and married before he was baptized in 1860. It is interesting to note that twenty years later, when marrying non-members became an issue, couples would go from Bishop Jonas Martin to Bishop Eby to be married.[15]

pages that expose that troubled era, one may never doubt the sincerity of all the participants. The following incident magnifies the sorrow and frustration as conscience became pitted against conscience.

Bishop Abraham Martin of Woolwich went to his brother-in-law's, Bishop Amos Cressman's residence, just outside New Hamburg to persuade him to follow the Old Order. Cressman refused to comply. He knew that the congregations around New Dundee had no sympathies for Martin's anti-Sunday school beliefs. At noon Mrs. Cressman said to her brother, "Komm mal, es ist Zeit zu esse" (Come now, it is time to eat). Martin's reply was, "Nay, wenn sie nett mit mir komme, dann kann ich nett mit euch esse." (No, if you cannot come with me, I cannot eat with you.)[16] Cressman interpreted the word "kann" as "will." The Woolwich Mennonites would interpret "kann" as "can." The dynamics of the brotherhood abound in the above discourse, and their feelings are beyond one's imagination. The marred relations that grieved these men were not fuelled by anger or revenge, but it was agony of the soul. These men were separating on issues of conscience, not doctrine. Schlabach notes, "The newer party [Conference Mennonites] was indeed aware of changes. But were they aware of the sources of many of the changes, particularly the extent to which they might have been absorbing the language and style of the American Protestantism around them? Quite likely the traditionalists were more aware on that particular point than were the innovators."[17]

The 1889 Division

The Mennonite Brethren in Christ movement had drawn away much of the "holiness" factor from the Mennonite church, but the revival, or quickening, sentiment was becoming stronger. The Mennonite community had progressed from the isolation of pioneer days and her people were considering new ways. There were also ultra-conservatives such as the Stauffer Mennonites primarily in Woolwich, who had resisted all changes, and those who became the Old Order Mennonites.

Being torn between two extremes, Bishop Abraham Martin moved cautiously. At a special meeting he proposed that the traditionalists would

> (2) *In the Mennonite circles the switch to the English language was more than a shift to another language. The theme of Gelassenheit was woven through many of the old German writings and hymns. With the acceptance of the English language pietistic values were subtly introduced into the Mennonite Church. I would question that Bishop Martin or any of his peers understood that with the introduction of the English language came Protestant teachings, but Anabaptist theology was primarily written in German and it became lost during the transition to English. In the Markham Mennonite Church some of the founding members claimed that the German language was more meaningful to them than English. No doubt these older members had a yearning for the traditional Anabaptist theology not found in the English writings and songs.*

withdraw their protests to evening meetings and English preaching (2) if the Sunday schools were abolished. The main body made an attempt to honour this request. The Sunday school at Christian Ebys was discontinued for the winter of 1875-76. The closure of Christian Ebys Sunday school led to Deacon Jacob Z. Kolb's opening of the Natchez schoolhouse Sunday school on November 22, 1875. Bishop Martin was not successful in closing the Natchez "Union" Sunday school, because it was out of his district. On September 12, 1879, another compromise was reached at the conference. It was resolved to formally divide the Waterloo District

(3) The Ontario Mennonites had three districts: Waterloo, Markham and the Niagara Peninsula ("the Twenty"). Each of these districts held their own spring and fall conferences. In the spring (the fourth Friday in May, however in the early years this varied) there was an annual conference that rotated over the three districts. After 1879 the Waterloo district was divided into three separate bishop districts, but there was only one local conference.

Conference into three well-defined bishop districts. (3) This resolution allowed Bishop Martin to prohibit his members from participating in Union Sunday schools.[18]

Bishop Abraham Martin's view on what was Mennonite was different from that of Preacher Noah Stauffer of Strasburg and Bishop Elias Weber of Breslau. Abraham Groff had become mentally disturbed and his death caused much concern in the neighbourhood. Noah Stauffer had delivered a powerful evangelistic sermon in the Martin's meetinghouse to about nine-hundred people at Groff's funeral. Noah Stauffer was later asked by those like-minded to hold evening meetings north of Waterloo in Bishop Martin's district. The converts from these meetings were not prepared to submit to Bishop Martin's Ordnung; therefore, Martin declined to baptize them.

Some of these converts were not of Mennonite background, and did not or could not comprehend Martin's Ordnung nor the spirit of the Mennonite "brotherhood." These converts then applied to Bishop Elias Weber for baptism. Weber agreed to instruct and baptize them in the usual manner. This was done against Bishop Martin's wishes.

At the conference of April 1886 the question of musical instruments was addressed, and it was resolved: "We are unanimous that musical instruments have no room in the gospel, and we agreed to testify against them, and exercise our influence to foster awareness that the church members put them away. Each preacher and deacon shall take time to deal with the members in his church who have them, according to Matt. 18."

This affirmation of the 1879 conference resolution was certainly stimulated by the actions of Noah Stauffer's converts who were spending time singing to the accompaniment of an organ in the home of Deacon Jacob Kolb. Bishop Weber, according to his calling, visited Kolb with regards to this thorny organ question. Since the organ belonged to Kolb's unbaptized son, it remained in Kolb's home. Weber stated that the issue was outside of his jurisdiction, but was it? This so-called loophole in church discipline is an obvious disregard for the Ordnung and the spirit of yieldedness was lost; furthermore, at the September 1886 conference it was resolved: "Unanimously, that the resolutions of the conference shall be obeyed and kept." According to Ordnung and Anabaptist Gelassenheit, Kolb had a responsibility and that would have been to remove the offensive item from his house, but was Kolb's love for music greater than his love for unity in the church?[19] No doubt Kolb sensed that the majority was in his favour and therefore was comfortable to act as an individual, and so he disregarded the conference resolutions. Stauffer's converts continued to visit the Kolb home and sing to the accompaniment of the organ. This deliberate disrespect of the Conference did not cause Martin to withdraw, for a resolution was passed at the conference in 1886 "that there be no division in the church."

The spring conference of 1888 appears to have been the watershed. The following resolutions were passed:

> Resolved: No more to discuss or consider the difficulties at the regular conferences.
> Resolved: To hold fast to the resolution of 1886, and not divide the church.
> Resolved: That there be an opportunity to discuss difficulties at a special conference.
> Resolved: That Sunday schools conform to a standard, as nearly as possible, and to use the Sunday school books of the Pennsylvania Committee until the pupils are capable to read the Testament. The Sunday school leaders shall be members of the church in good standing, and be chosen by church members.

Yieldedness one to each other keeps unity within a brotherhood. The evidence suggests that the conservatives sought fair dealing through the conference by having the issue of forbidding musical instruments reaffirmed and also by the declaration that all members be obedient to conference resolutions. But it became more and more clear that the main body no longer supported the old conference resolutions. There was little doubt that Bishop Abraham Martin felt as John Weaver from Indiana did, that "the new order is introduced by force and we must keep silent to it."[20]

It is interesting to note that the spring 1888 conference made no mention of an ordination at the Martins meetinghouse. Paul Martin, who was later ordained bishop, was ordained minister on July 14, 1888. (Samuel Weber had died from an accident in 1885.) Had the division already occurred as Isaac Martin, an Old Order historian, thought, or was it impending? His view was that at the September 1887 conference, the conservative minded brethren were so dissatisfied that they concluded their conference elsewhere. The division became official when the two groups held their annual conferences on two different Fridays at the Widemans meetinghouse in the spring of 1889.

As the evidence suggests, this division was a long, drawn-out affair. During these years Bishop Martin confided in his brother-in-law Bishop Amos Cressman. Cressman would convince Martin to accept the innovations, but when Martin came home to his wife she directed him to his uncle Deacon David Martin who would in turn persuade him to remain in the traditional ways. After several visits of this nature, old David told Bishop Martin, "It's time you stand on your own feet." These were very difficult times.

As the last quarter of the nineteenth century approached, the Mennonites were still under one umbrella, but had two distinct visions. The acceptance of Protestantism by the Mennonites had continued ever since Martin Boehm was put out of the fellowship in ca. 1777. The Anabaptist ethos had also continued through the troubled century. When the Mennonites began to polarize, they focused on the tangible things of Protestantism. Nevertheless, the intangible values such as Ordnung and Gelassenheit versus a modified version of "holiness" and American individualism were the issues that separated the Mennonite brotherhood. Furthermore, it is fair to suggest that the Protestant emphasis on the resurrecting power of Christ, rather than the Anabaptist vision of first dying with Christ, gave the Mennonite Church a slightly different focus and this was felt, but not necessarily understood, by the conservative element.

In retrospect, it is clear that these festering wounds needed time to heal. The sincerity of these people is evident; the one part had embraced more of Protestantism and were more acculturated, while the other side had isolated themselves to a greater degree from general society and held to their Ordnung and the traditional teaching of Gelassenheit. Both sides lost their much-needed counterpart. The progressives, having lost the restraining conservatives, dashed off in all directions, but by the turn of the century the steadiness of Daniel Kauffman and others "reigned in" the Conference Mennonites and gave them direction. Our story will reveal that the conservatives, being deprived of the drive of the progressives, experienced several generations of indifference as they struggled to find a vision of their own.

The Conference Mennonites of Woolwich

At the time of the 1889 division, most of the conservative members lived in Woolwich Township, while the innovators resided in the lower part of the county. Therefore those dwelling in the southern portion of the county were called *die Unera* (the lower) in the Pennsylvania Dutch dialect and those in Woolwich were referred to as the *die Overa* (the upper) or *die Woolwichers*. The official name for the die Unera was the Mennonite Conference of Ontario. After the division the Conference Mennonites in Woolwich included about thirty families. They began to hold worship services in an old house by the road on the David Koch farm just north of Conestogo (1094 Northfield Dr. E). They soon found this building too small and inconvenient and asked permission to use the Conestogo meetinghouse. The Old Orders were opposed to this idea and declined. They had no desire to share the meetinghouse in partnership.

The Old Order Mennonites printed their first Calendar of Appointments in 1891. They added the prefix *Alt* to the traditional *Mennoniten Gemeinde* (Old Mennonite Church), which would in the end cost them the Conestogo meetinghouse. A local legal representative brought it to the attention of the Conference Mennonites that the Alt Mennonite Church had no legal rights to property deeded to The Mennonite Church. Abner Good noted in a letter, "This is rather noteworthy, that even though these Mennonites shied away from 'use of the Law' and especially on matters pertaining to the Church, all at once or suddenly an 'Exception Clause' became very important to them."[21] In any event, old Deacon Levi P. Martin gave the key of the Conestogo meetinghouse to someone and later commented, "*G'nungk g'tsarft*" (enough quarrelling). In January 1892, the ownership of the meetinghouse was transferred to the Ontario Conference

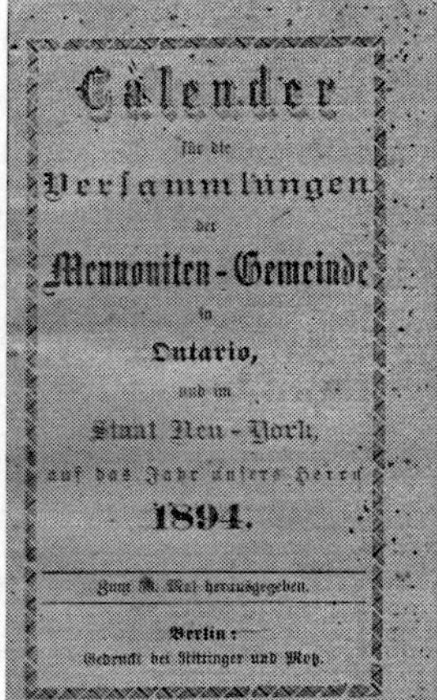

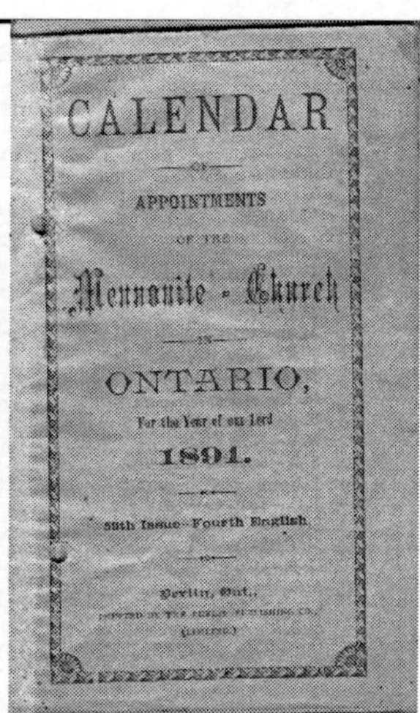

At the first glance the title pages of these Meeting Calendars appear identical. The 1889 calendar is the format that the Mennonite church had used for years. Even though they were officially divided in the spring of 1889, the 1890 calendar still listed all the ministry and meeting places. In 1891 the Conference Mennonites printed their first calendar after the division in English, but reverted to German in the following years. The 1891 Old Order Mennonite calendar is the point in question. Note "der Alt" on the title page of the Old Order 1891 calendar. The following year the Old Orders were still more explicit and included "Alt" before Mennoniten Gemeinde ; however they did not include the following phrase: Zum 56 Mal herausgegeben. (fifty-sixth Year of Publication). By 1894 both groups printed their meeting calendars in German, both named themselves the Mennoniten Gemeinde, and both stated "Zum 59 Mal herausgegeben." This last phrase is significant since the first two years the Old Orders did not include a year of publication, but by 1894 they borrowed the year of publication from the Conference Mennonites and have ever since included it as their own so that the year 2000 was the 165th edition. Title page of 1892, 1894, Old Order and 1894 Conference Mennonite.

Mennonites and, interestingly enough, by 1894 the Old Order Mennonites had changed the title page of their Calendar to the previous Mennoniten Gemeinde. In the same year the Old Orders built their new Conestogo meetinghouse about half a mile south of the Conference Mennonites' property on Three Bridges Road.

After the division there was a small, almost forgotten, group of Conference Mennonites at Floradale. By 1893 Floradale was listed in the Calendar of Appointments, and three years later this group of ten families built a new meetinghouse north of Floradale. The Conestogo congregation also prospered. In 1915 Conference Mennonites built a new church in St Jacobs to replace the old Conestogo meetinghouse. By 1924 the

Conference Mennonites around Elmira began another congregation. They built their church beside the Old Order cemetery in Elmira.

The Conference Mennonites later opened further missions. In July 1947 the Bethel Methodist Church was closed in Pilkington Township and the Mennonites in that area decided to purchase the church. On December 21, 1947, twenty-six members united and formed the Bethel Mennonite congregation. A similar situation developed in Hawkesville where a dwindling United Church closed in 1946. The St Jacobs Mennonite congregation was out-growing its facilities and decided to begin an out-reach at Hawkesville. The old United Church was purchased for one hundred dollars and the dedication services were held on January 1, 1950.

Several Mennonite families settled around Glen Allen during the time it was common for the Mennonites to move beyond the home community. Occasional services were held in homes from 1880-1907. The 1907 services were always in the evening. Evidently, David Ernst lived east of Glen Allen in 1900, because on November 4, 1900 a carriage load of Old Order youth visited the Ernst family. This was a long drive for Isaac Martin who lived close to St. Jacobs. Although he had seen his first automobile only six weeks before, it was very unlikely that their horses were spooked by the "rich man's toys" as the cars were called in those days while on their trip to Glen Allen.[22]

The Floradale Mennonite congregation began holding summer Bible schools in Glen Allen in 1944. This mission prospered and on November 8, 1953, a new congregation held the dedication service for their new church. For decades the congregation flourished and served the community. However, on August 29, 1999, the congregation, with mixed feelings, held their last service at Glen Allen and the members sought fellowship in various local churches.

In 1941 a mission was started at the Parker School by the Conference Mennonites. By 1952 the congregation had grown to about sixty people and they decided to build a church. A two-acre lot was cleared in the bush beside the Parker road and the Berea church was built. The congregation had thirty-eight charter members. The Conference Mennonites were very active in mission work during these years.

The Conservative Mennonite Movement

After World War II the Mennonite Church was faced with more rapid change. The former rural communities were challenged with urban pressures as their people left the farms for occupations in the surrounding cities. High school education became the norm for the Conference Mennonite church. First they supported the Rockway Mennonite School, but later many also attended public high schools. Furthermore, there was a shift in focus when the Mennonite church colleges began to influence the church, rather than the church controlling the colleges. Higher education encouraged the ordination of college graduates and the use of the lot was discontinued. Higher education and more interactions with the general public brought other values into the Conference Mennonite church. During the late 1950s some progressive members were questioning old church standards. The wedding ring, the devotional head covering, cutting of the women's hair, the acceptance of television and the question of divorce and remarriage were the foremost issues. The situation climaxed in 1959 when six ordained men in Wilmot Township withdrew from the conference and began holding separate services on November 22, 1959.

The next year a congregation was formed at Heidelberg in Woolwich Township led by Bishop Moses Roth, formerly of Wilmot. Eleven families had withdrawn from the Conference Mennonite church and another five families from the Markham Waterloo Mennonites joined them when they began services on August 7, 1960. Within several decades more congregations were formed. The Calvary congregation north of Elmira began in 1969. The Otter Lake outreach at Parry Sound began in 1971 and Hesson (Carthage) congregation was formed in 1974. In 1989 Woodlawn church at Dorking began, and in 2000 the Moorefield congregation was formed. Many discontented Old Orders, who had lost the feel of Gelassenheit and desired a more individualistic and revivalistic religion, joined fellowship with the Conservative Churches surrounding the Old Order community.

The Conservative Mennonites have divided into several different fellowships but the details of these developments are beyond the scope of this writing. The reason we have included the Conservative and Fellowship Mennonites is because many members of the Markham Mennonites, and also those from the Old Order Mennonites, gravitated to the Conservative

Churches. It is noteworthy that some of the Conservative Mennonite congregations have a majority of members who trace their roots to the Markham and Old Order Mennonites.

Notes

[1] Theron F. Schlabach, *Peace, Faith, Nation* (Scottdale, PA: Herald Press, 1988), 104.

[2] ME, V, 318.

[3] Theron F. Schlabach, "Reveille for die stillen im lande: A Stir Among Mennonites in the late Nineteenth Century" *Mennonite Quarterly Review* (1977): 221.

[4] ME, IV, 965.

[5] J. C. Wenger, "Documents on the Daniel Brenneman Division" *Mennonite Quarterly Review* (January, 1960): 52.

[6] Amos B. Hoover, *The Jonas Martin Era* (Denver PA: Muddy Creek Library, 1982), 871.

[7] *Ibid.*, 876.

[8] English translation of the John Weaver letter dated Dec. 5, 1871.

[9] Lloyd M. Weiler, "An Introduction to Old Order Mennonite Origins in Lancaster County, Pennsylvania: 1893 to 1993," *Pennsylvania Mennonite Heritage* (Oct., 1993): 3.

[10] Hoover, *The Jonas Martin Era*, 881.

[11] Carson Moyer, The Mountain Church at Campden (Kitchener, ON: Mennonite Historical Society, March 1986), 2.

[12] Elizabeth Bloomfield, *Waterloo Township Through two Centuries* (Kitchener, ON: Waterloo Historical Society, 1995), 231.

[13] Schlabach, "Reveille," 217.

[14] Isaac R. Horst, *Close Ups of the Great Awakening* (Mount Forest, Ontario: Isaac R. Horst, 1985), 128.

[15] *Ibid.*, 159.

[16] Kenneth Cressman, "The Development of the Conservative Mennonite Church of Ontario." (Unpublished essay, no date. Manuscript #70113845 at CGUC), 5.

[17] Schlabach, "Reveille," 214.

[18] Reginald E. Good, *Frontier Community To Urban Congregation: First Mennonite Church, Kitchener 1813-1988* (Kitchener, ON: First Mennonite Church, 1988),89-97.

[19] Brent Bauman, *Forged Anew* (Floradale, Ontario: Floradale Mennonite Church, 1996), 23.

[20] Samuel Weber, Letter, Dec. 5, 1871, CGUC.

[21] Abner Good. Letter to Frank H. Epp, Apr. 23, 1925.

[22] Isaac Martin, Diary, 1900-1901, CGUC.

Old Order Mennonites

Chapter Eight

Introduction

In our story we have now very briefly covered the Mennonite migrations from Switzerland, down the Rhine Valley, over the Atlantic into Pennsylvania and then on to Ontario. We have also touched on how the Anabaptists differed from the other state churches and how Pietism had filtered into the Mennonite community. By the time of the American Civil War, the Mennonite community was scattered as far west as Iowa and many Mennonites had absorbed the inner emotional pulses of "holiness" quite heavily from their neighbouring churches. Those driven by these emotions wanted to express their religion through the resurrecting power of Christ, as did their church-going neighbours, but there were also others within the brotherhood who saw such passions as a deviation from the traditional past of first crucifying self with Christ at the cross. To them the fruits of Christian living were full evidence of resurrection into newness of life. They were satisfied to live their religion as they felt it. The new outward expressions of religion were simply too bold for their traditional values of simplicity and humility.

The community began to polarize as these differences continued to manifest themselves within the brotherhood. The Old Order who were satisfied to "feel" their religion had a "distaste for disputing doctrinal points" as had the Anabaptists in Bern, Switzerland.[1] This distaste for disputing may well have resulted from their inability to dispute since they were untrained men, but one could suggest there was a deeper reason they declined being involved in religious disputes. Old Order Minister Urias Martin declared, "the Word of God is sharper than any two-edged sword but we may not smite with it." Obedience to the Word, as they understood it, carried far more weight than spiritual arguments.

The Old Order stood apart on another issue—the studying of Scripture collectively. They received a lot of criticism because of this stance. Is it possible to study a subject collectively without getting into a debate? Did the Old Orders sense that debating the Scriptures would shift their focus from believing to knowing the Word of God? There are several ways which one can study the Scriptures. One might study the Scriptures with an open mind and then break off a crumb of the Word here and there and by faith believe what is revealed. This describes the traditional Old Order minister's approach to preparing himself for a sermon. The second manner is to set a hypothesis and then use the Scriptures to support that view. This is the scholarly way of interpreting the Scripture. This approach to understanding Scriptures goes against the Old Orders' simplistic satisfaction with what God will reveal from time to time. Collective studying of the Scriptures gives power to the study group and never blends well with the Old Orders' interpretation of brotherhood—a voluntary commitment to Christ, being submissive and obedient to the brotherhood.

Another point on which the Old Order stand apart is the emphasis on obedience. At a time when modern inventions were polarizing the Old Order community, an Old Order minister commented that he must now preach only the grace of God. To be sure, he never intended to stop preaching the grace of God, for the Apostle Paul wrote "but by the grace of God I am what I am . . . " (1 Cor. 15:10). What troubled the minister was the mutiny of certain members within the brotherhood. Political or democratic manoeuvres were being used to undermine the order of the church. Those members were no longer willing to be obedient to the former order and were forcing change upon those who did not desire change.

For the above minister, it was pointless to preach obedience to God and the church to members who were rebelling against the brotherhood and the order of the church. Therefore, he felt forced to go a step closer to Luther's ideology of salvation by grace of God alone. This subtle deviation from the Anabaptist ethos of Gelassenheit towards Luther's dogma of grace alone continues to threaten Old Order communities. Old Orders believe "but by the grace of God I am what I am . . . " but they also believe in obedience to the Word in a very non-compromising way.

Although Old Order Mennonitism has adopted much from Pietism, the brotherhood of believers concept is definitely an Anabaptist vision. Without the Anabaptists' Gelassenheit, the brotherhood of believers cannot function. Also at the core of the brotherhood of believers is the principle of a pure church. The pietistic themes of a pure heart and an individual personal experience of salvation are not adequate for those who appreciate the values of a brotherhood. Personal salvation is essential to the Old Orders, as it is for all Christians, but purity and unity within the church are also believed by the Old Order to be commanded by God. Those who unite in the same faith and who try to have a pure conscience before God and man, form a brotherhood. Members of a brotherhood do not readily distinguish between the group and the individual. The spirit of Gelassenheit welds the two together. The Old Order community and the brotherhood are inseparable. The brotherhood binds an Old Order community together. To appreciate the Old Order community, we will define what the brotherhood means to them.

The Brotherhood

In the traditional German, *Gemeinde* means brotherhood. One meaning of the English word "church" is synonymous with the German word *"Kirche,"* which the Old Orders identify as the place of worship of the mainline churches, and refer to the people as *Kircheleut*. Because of this, the second English definition of church, meaning the congregation, has mixed connotations for the Old Order people. To them brotherhood connotes more the traditional German Gemeinde.

An assertive and sincere young man was involved in a slightly controversial work within the brotherhood. An aged minister told him that within a brotherhood you place your ideas on the table and you leave them there. If the brotherhood picks up on the idea, then give God the glory; if they tear it apart and use a few crumbs, you must accept that and be content; if your idea is pushed into the garbage pail leave it there because within a brotherhood of believers there is no place for politics. The aged minister's advice alluded to a yieldedness or submissiveness to the brotherhood—Gelassenheit.

An aged deacon observed an individual who had difficulty maintaining peace within the brotherhood. The level-headed deacon commented, "Er denkt zu viel von sein ayah denkes" (He thinks too highly of his own thinking). The spirit of Gelassenheit was absent. The capital "I" suppressed submissiveness to the brotherhood. Individualism dominated his views and caused a clash within the brotherhood. The original offence soon became secondary and the prime stumbling block was his selfish views, which opposed the brotherhood's values. Within a brotherhood the pronoun values change. "I" becomes "i" and "we" becomes "WE." When *Gelassenheit* dominates an individual's life the "I" in that person's life diminishes so that the individual becomes "one" of the brotherhood.

In a democratic society individuals promote their personal views through political channels. A politician's chief interest is to convince the electorate that his views excel above all others. This contrasts with meekly presenting an opinion and allowing the brotherhood to discern its real value. Stirring up trouble within a brotherhood is like one who sows discord among brethren, which the Lord hates (Proverbs 6:19).

At the communion service, while the bishop is passing out the bread, he stresses unity by repeatedly reciting the following: "Take eat: this is my body, which is broken for you: this do in remembrance of me" (1 Cor. 11:24). Comments are also made stating that as the wheat ground into flour is inseparable and becomes as one in bread, likewise the brotherhood, being many members, is also to be one body, like the bread. While the wine is passed out the bishop quotes Matt. 26:27-28 or Luke 22:20 (This cup is the new testament in my blood, which is shed for you.) The brotherhood is to be a body of believers who are inseparable one from another. Such perfection is utopian.

Our humanity determines that there are always imperfect human relations rather than utopian harmony; therefore, forgiveness and forbearance are vital elements in the brotherhood. For those with deep religious conviction, tolerance is seldom the primary virtue. To keep the balance between forbearing one another in love, and being true to one's deep personal conviction has always challenged the Anabaptists. Jan van Ophoorn, a

Dutch Mennonite minister in Emden, became lost in his own convictions and banned everybody in his congregation except himself and his wife.[2] In retrospect one could suggest he valued his own thinking to the extreme. During the next four hundred years this sad story of division has continued to repeat itself when members valued their own feelings more than the consensus of the brotherhood.

Christian Funk, a Mennonite bishop of the Franconia district, supported the view that the people should pay the war taxes during the American Revolution. The main body declined because they had given their word that they would be loyal subjects to the King of England and did not want to break that promise. Because Funk refused to support the conference, he lost the confidence of his people on this question. Although the war tax was the visible issue, the underlying cause may well have been the "formidable ego" of Bishop Funk as he defied the social norms of his congregation.[3] As the hammer came down on the anvil, Funk viewed himself as a prophet with an unpopular message, and because he continued to resist the values of the brotherhood and justified his behaviour, Funk was excommunicated and became a victim of the ultimate human vice—gossip.[4] This bane is human and is characteristic of social norms, but not becoming for a Christian within the bonds of a brotherhood.

Funk's treatment by the brotherhood may well appear harsh and even unjust to those outside the community, but what were Funk's baptismal vows? A clause of the Old Order Mennonite's baptismal vows in Ontario for close to two centuries is "to renounce your own will and all dark Satanic deeds."[5] (1) All those who are part of the Old Order Mennonite community of Ontario made this voluntary promise—a promise of yieldedness and submission to God and the brotherhood which is a token from Anabaptism. For this reason a member who stubbornly resists the order and wishes of the brotherhood ultimately violates his or her baptismal vows and incurs the censure of the congregation.

> (1) *At the time of baptism this is the second question each convert is asked by the bishop administering baptism — "Secondly, I ask you if you are sincerely sorry for your sins you have committed; and if you renounce your own will and all dark Satanic deeds? If this is so, answer 'yes.'"*

When Bishop Martin Boehm fell into disapproval of the Lancaster

Conference, he joined fellowship with his "holiness" friends. There was pain in the parting of ways, but there is little evidence of a heated dispute at the time; however, when Funk's resistance towards the Franconia Conference persisted, a ruckus evolved and bitter feelings developed. There was considerable dialogue between Funk and his colleagues, but Funk being totally engrossed "in his own thinking" failed to sense the gravity of his position until all confidence and respect for him was lost by his colleagues and the headache ended on a bitter note. In our story of the Old Order, the nastiness of the above episode will repeat all too often as the "formidable ego" of individuals persuades them to value their "own thinking" more than that of the brotherhood. They lose the vision of their calling as being servants of Christ. They begin to dictate their messages, rather than to present them as a shepherd would. This subtle shift away from the most valued Mennonite ethic of humility erodes the confidence and respect the congregation has for its leader.

The Ordnung and "Hope" Defined

The Old Order Mennonite Ordnung frequently causes misunderstandings when people from other walks of life try to relate to the Old Order communities. All Christians hold that God is the Supreme Being to be worshipped—that is God is the pre-eminence of our life. It is the Old Order emphasis on the Ordnung, or church regulations, that creates the confusion. The Old Orders, except the David Martin and Orthodox, will accept individuals from other denominations for functions, such as pallbearers at their funerals, as long as they are in good standing within their own churches; however, the Old Orders will exclude individuals from having active part in their church functions if their lifestyle is too far removed from the Old Orders' understanding of the Bible. Such discrimination has offended others who don't understand that the Old Orders are not necessarily passing judgment on such individuals, but are only attempting to maintain their church order according to the dictates of their consciences.

Within the confines of the Old Order churches it can also be a challenge for those belonging to a more a cultured group to modestly accept the Ordnung of the more traditional churches. It is easy to become judgmental as one said, "We all know that the Christian must follow the straight and narrow way, but do we have to go off the narrow path and deliberately walk where it is rough and stony?" A case in point could be the Orthodoxs', or David Martins', order of their weddings. Since a wedding is a sacred church ordinance, they do not invite anybody outside of their circles—be it parents, a brother, sister, or grandparents. To them a wedding is a function of the church that pertains only to those of their fellowship. Even though it is generally understood by all people that a person does not attend a wedding unless he or she is invited, the exclusion of family members at a wedding may appear to an outsider as "walking where it is rough and stony." However, when we consider the Orthodox Mennonites' willingness to do so, this clearly shows the Anabaptist spirit of Gelassenheit and how the Old Order put the Brotherhood before family: "He that loveth father or mother more than me is not worthy of me: and he that loveth son or daughter more than me is not worthy of me" (Matthew 10:37).Their dedication to the Brotherhood is stronger than family ties.

It is this strong emphasis on the Brotherhood that creates misunderstandings for those on the outside trying to understand the Old Order groups. In a sense the individual does not exist—it is the group that exists. Such closeness can easily be interpreted by those outside as a holier-than-thou attitude when in reality they are relating to one another within the confines of the brotherhood. Nevertheless, the Old Order community is naive to believe that they are immune to smugness. They are a people like the children of Israel who were human and subject to error, even though their desire is to serve their Creator.

Newcomer's accusation that the Mennonite Society was wanting of life and the power of religion has continued to plague the Old Order community until this day. They are accused of believing "that a Christian cannot know, but only hopes he is right with God."[6] Since theological expression is not an Old Order virtue, silence is frequently their defence when challenged by an outsider, especially if such a one comes with an air of aggression. A spiritual argument has little value to an Old Order.

The Old Orders' confidence in Christ is very clear during funerals within their circles. They shun all ado, but an air of sacred mourning envelops the home. God has called home one of His own. They are taught that they should never question God's ways at the time of death. The spirit of resignation is a prized virtue and the foundation on which to restructure their life after the loss of a loved one. In their circles they openly confess that to die without hope in God would be very sad and grave indeed. The word "hope" is the culprit of confusion for those outside the Old Order community. "If in this life only we have hope in Christ, we are of all men most miserable" (1Cor. 15:19). "And now abideth faith, hope, charity, these three; but the greatest of these is charity" (1Cor 13:13). Even though the Old Order relate only to hope, they have a faith that so completely embraces their hope that the two combined result in a full confidence in Christ their Lord.

The Counsel of the Brotherhood

The third article of the Schleitheim Confession (1527) concludes with these words: "Therefore it is and must be thus: Whosoever has not been called by one God to one faith, to one baptism, to one Spirit, to one body, with all the children of God's church, cannot be made one bread with them, as indeed must be done if one is truly to break bread according to the command of Christ."[7]

God did not leave his bride, the church, without guidelines on how to conduct herself. The Anabaptist reformers bluntly renounced the hierarchical manner of the mainline churches. The 1527 Schleitheim Confession of Faith (2) in the third article clearly stated that unity in the congregation was necessary before communion could be held. In the mid 1700s Hans Tschantz of Lancaster County designated Matt. 18 and 1

(2) *Third Article of the Schleitheim Confession: In the breaking of bread we are of one mind and are agreed [as follows]: All those who wish to break one bread in remembrance of the broken body of Christ, and all who wish to drink of one drink as a remembrance of the shed blood of Christ, shall be united beforehand by baptism in one body of Christ which is the church of God and whose Head is Christ. For as Paul points out, we cannot at the same time be partakers of the Lord's table and the tables of devils; we cannot at the same time drink the cup of the Lord and the cup of the devil. That is, all those who have fellowship with the dead works of darkness have no part in the light. Therefore all those who follow the devil and the world have no part with those who are called unto God out of the world. All who lie in evil have no part in the good.*[8]

Cor. 5 as passages for council meeting services.[9] This emphasis on 1 Cor 5:11-13 as a text for council meetings has been lost by the Old Order Mennonites in Ontario. When the Markham Waterloo Conference revised Benjamin Eby's 1841 "Origin and Doctrine of the Mennonites" in 1999, they recorded 1 Cor. 5:11-13 as a reference. The emphasis in this text is purity within the church: "I have written unto you not to keep company if any man that is called a brother be a . . . sinner . . . with such an one no not to eat." Though the Old Order Mennonites have not lost these teachings, it is not customary to hear sermons on the topic at a council meeting service. The emphasis rests on the importance and procedure to maintain peace within the brotherhood.

An elderly deacon once observed that the power within the Old Order community rests with the congregation and council meeting is the medium by which the congregation speaks its voice to the ordained body and to one another. Counsel meeting has been criticized as an opportunity for members to vent their complaints. This should never be the case. Individual differences should be addressed before council meeting according to the principles taught in Matt. 18.The first step is go and speak with the offending brother on a one-on-one basis. If an understanding cannot be found, the second step is to ask several neutral brethren to mediate the matter and seek peace. To "tell it unto the church" (Matt. 18:17) is serious business and is not part of the council meeting. Such issues then become deacons' work, who must consider the severity of the offence and what action should be taken.

Counsel meeting is for acknowledging peace with oneself and God, and also to express it to the congregation. Readiness to have Matt. 18 applied to oneself is often expressed in council meeting and a voluntary acceptance of church order is understood as part of the profession of peace. An acknowledgement of the minister's preaching, and encouragement for him to continue to preach the word in the truth without fear of man's opinions, are some of the common voices expressed in council. Expressing concern about church order and values within the brotherhood is acceptable and encouraged. The voice of the council is then brought before the conference body where decisions are made. Voting is not an acceptable way to determine church policies in the Old Order Mennonite community. (4) The experience and wisdom gained by the aged

(4) *Samuel Moyer of the Vineland district complained in a letter about Bishop John Lapp's view of going by the majority (Lapp was from Clarence, New York). Moyer told Lapp that if he went by majority then he would reject the old Mennonite teaching and take part with the free-thinkers. Also Bishop Abraham Rohrer of Ohio once presented to his conference the results of majority rule: "When the Gospel agrees with the majority, a blessing will follow. When the Gospel contradicts the majority, and the majority goes ahead contrary to the Gospel, a curse follows and no blessing, and serves to the downfall of our non-resistant church."*[10]

brethren over many years is far more significant to them than the sheer numbers of the group.

The Old Order community is *not* a democracy. It is a patriarchal brotherhood where everybody's voice is encouraged, and where the young people's comprehension of an issue is valued. But since younger people do not have the counsel and wisdom of experience, decisions are generally made by the older people. A brotherhood should not stifle the conscience of the individual or the individuals become like dead wood. Furthermore, the stability of a group conscience guards against radical opinions of individuals. This is arguably the best insurance policy anybody can have. If a person remains sensitive to the criticism of others he or she will never go far astray. The brotherhood needs a balance of members of all ages, "for we being many are one bread and one body" (1 Cor. 10:17).

The Old Order and Communion

"The cup of blessing which we bless, is it not the communion of the blood of Christ? The bread which we break, is it not the communion of the body of Christ? For we being many are one bread and one body: for we are all partakers of that one bread" (1 Cor. 10:16-17).

In John 6:35 Jesus said unto them, "I am the bread of life: he that cometh to me shall never hunger; and he that believeth in me shall never thirst." The unity of Christ and the believers, or his bride, is symbolized by the grinding of the wheat into flour. This is understood by all Christians, but the Anabaptists' definition includes "For we [meaning the brotherhood] being many are one bread and one *body*." There should be no distinction or partiality within the brotherhood (1 Ti. 5:21; Ja. 3:17) and according to Anabaptist theology, the believers are separate from the world and the unbeliever has no part in the communion of the saints. Furthermore, the

Old Order belief is that within a brotherhood one needs to be willing to make a sacrifice for the brotherhood and to blend one's individual conscience to that of the group. This fact amplifies the significance placed on unity and peace within the congregation. Having so strong an emphasis on unity, the Old Orders hold closed communion.

An outsider is welcome to worship at an Old Order communion service as a visitor, but the visitor would be denied the emblems. Neither would an Old Order accept communion from another fellowship, be it a mainline church or even another fellowship under the Old Order umbrella, unless there are formal relations and pulpits are shared between the two groups. Only on very rare occasions are pulpits shared at funerals, and only if the deceased was not a member of the Old Order fellowship. In short, an Old Order minister may preach at a non-member's funeral if asked, but the Old Order would not ask one outside the fellowship to minister unto their people. For the Old Order, a brotherhood is like a family: just as a family has things in common so does a brotherhood, and as a family respects other families so a brotherhood respects other fellowships. If one member is absent at communion there is a concern why that member is absent—one part is missing. The family is not complete. This emphasis of being a "family" of believers sets the Old Order apart from most other churches at the time of communion.

The Role of Leadership

"Let this mind be in you, which was also in Christ Jesus: Who . . . made himself of no reputation, and took upon him the form of a servant . . . " (Phil. 2:5-7).

"For whether is greater, he that sitteth at meat, or he that serveth? Is not he that sitteth at meat? But I am among you as he that serveth" (Luke 22:27).

Leadership and service are synonymous among the Old Order Mennonites as the aged bishop Gross had informed the fledgling congregation at "the Twenty": "As long as it is of the Lord, it will have good consequences, unless the one called does not remain true and in humility, which is what the Lord demands of all his servants.[11] The ordained men frequently address themselves to the congregation as a servant or the servant of God. The apostles Paul, James, Peter and Jude, in their opening salutations, reflected upon themselves as servants of God. The leadership is a position of servitude as well as one of esteem and respect: "How beautiful are the feet of them that preach the gospel of peace, and bring glad tidings of good things!" (Romans 10:15). Christians are reminded that they are "to know them which labour among you… and to esteem them very highly in love for their work's sake" (1 Thess. 5:12-13). This role of the Old Order leadership appears to be paradoxical. It is one of servitude, but also one of power. The Old Order ordained men hold power that belongs to the office God has given them; the power belongs to the office, not to the individual.

Within the Old Order communities, the leaders consider themselves to be called by God in a very formal way. The office of the ministry is not something a man covets. The ultimate emphasis on humility gives no

Order of an Ordination: *After it has been established that there is a need for an ordination, the congregation is admonished to pray for the great work. A special council meeting is held to see if the congregation is at peace. On a set day after the service, with 1 Tim. 3 as the text, the nominations are taken. The ministry retires into the lobby and only the brethren, in turn as they are led, go out to the lobby and give their nominations. The ministry comes before the congregation and announces the names of the candidates. The following day the candidates gather with the ministry for the inquiry service where the candidates are encouraged and questioned in regards to their willingness to accept the call and conform to the church.*

On the day of the ordination the candidates are seated before the pulpit in a well-filled meetinghouse. After a lengthy service with Acts 1 as a text, the bishop hands the same number of books as there are candidates to several deacons who retire to the lobby. There, in privacy, the lot is placed in one book (all the books are secured by elastic bands or the books have a flap) and each of the deacons then take turns to shuffle the books while the others turn their backs and pray. The books are then brought into the auditorium and placed on the pulpit.

The bishop rearranges them as he is led and then asks each of the candidates to take a book. The bishop then asks the candidates for their books, beginning at the oldest. He searches each book until the lot is found. That candidate is then asked to step forward and his charge is given. Although the wife receives no formal charge, she also has a role to fill, which depends on the office. On rare occasions when only one man is nominated the lot is not used, but the story goes that John Sherk of Rainham requested the lot be used even though he was the only man. Sherk picked the book with the lot and accepted his call.

place for any self-glorification. At the time of the inquiry the only real qualification required is a willingness to accept the "call," and submission to the order of the church.[12]

An ordained Old Order Mennonite likens his ordination to King David's call from feeding his father's sheep to be king over Israel. King Saul's dishonourable end also demonstrates the Old Orders' principle when an ordained man violates the Word of God and his God-given powers. Just as God took the kingdom from Saul because of his sins, so the Old Order will also discharge their unfaithful clergy. The Old Order ministry are set apart, yet they are one of the number within the brotherhood. It is the office that sets them apart, not the person.

The theme of Gelassenheit, that is submission and yieldedness to God and the church, appears paradoxical to the qualifications of leadership. Nonetheless, the Old Order look unto Jesus as the perfect example of a submissive and obedient leader of the Christian church. An Old Order bishop commented that there is a very fine line between being firm and being stubborn when administrating a bishop's office. The role of leadership under the dynamics of Gelassenheit becomes very challenging for those called to the ministry. For this reason the ministry, like the apostle Paul, frequently request the prayers of the congregation. "Now I beseech you, brethren, for the Lord Jesus Christ's sake, and for the love of the Spirit, that ye strive together with me in your prayers to God for me" (Romans 15:30). The congregation's role in supporting their ministry in prayer cannot be overemphasized. They are to "Remember them which have the rule over you, who have spoken unto you the word of God: whose faith follow, considering the end of their conversation" (Heb. 13:7). We will conclude this topic with a testimony of an anonymous ordained man: "When Jesus called James and John to follow him he said 'I will *make* you fishers of men.'"

The Stand of the Old Order

The Old Order community emphasizes brotherhood as a body of professing Christians who stress unity, purity, humility, willingness to serve God seven days of the week, and of course non-resistance. Their evangelism parallels the later Anabaptist-Mennonite era—they are the "quiet in the land." For them a self-disciplined life is their light to the world. Their emphasis on humility limits any form of aggressive evangelism. Conversion and the new birth are tenets of their faith, but amendment of life must follow. Romans 6 is the closing text at a baptismal service.

True repentance by the Old Order is not measured in decibels of the convert, but rather by Zacchaeus' example of restitution, found in Luke 19:8. The Old Orders frown on a bold Christian testimony. Their emphasis lies more in such passages as: "Now our Lord Jesus Christ himself, and God, even our Father, which hath loved us, and hath given us everlasting consolation and good hope through grace, comfort your hearts, and stablish you in every good word and work" (2 Thess. 2:16-17). Their focus rests more on a "living hope." They also ponder over Jesus' words: "when ye shall have done all those things which are commanded you, say, we are unprofitable servants: we have done that which was our duty to do" (Luke 17:10).

The following event illustrates the Old Order position on over-confidence in one's faith. During the time of the New Mennonite movement in the 1870s, a threshing crew was doing justice to a classic Mennonite dinner when an adherent of the New movement boisterously declared his confidence in God and his own eternal abode in heaven. The traditional Mennonites frowned on such confidence, but they let the bold novice continue his boasting of the new faith. With a piece of meat on his spoon, he audaciously declared, "As sure as I will eat this piece of meat, I will get to heaven." But alas, the meat rolled off his spoon and fell to the floor close to where the family dog lay. The dog instantly consumed the important piece of meat.[13] The deafening silence that filled the room permitted each man to consider the values of his faith.

To the public, the Old Order may appear to be unyielding, but this is not their own perception. A brash young grandson, who later learned to appreciate the brotherhood, harped on his aged grandfather about the trivial issues and values held by the brotherhood. The aged man looked the youth in the face and said, "Look, we want a plain church and are striving to maintain those values. If these values mean nothing to you, you may go where your values are the norm, but don't dig up dirt here." Was the old man steadfast or just plain stubborn? Was he an arrogant bigot or was he sincerely concerned about the brotherhood? Historians continue to seek the answers to these questions in terms of their own social, cultural, economic or even ideological paradigms.[14]

I was challenged by the question, "How do you process change within the confines of Gelassenheit and Ordnung?" The words "How do you process change?" stand out to the Old Order. Admittedly the above question is honest and fair, but the dynamics of the Old Order brotherhood cannot be understood from a democratic perspective. Let us turn our attention to the story of the grandfather and his grandson. The grandson wanted to process change and the old man told him to learn to be content or leave. The Old Order brotherhood requires a voluntary commitment from its members and looks upon its members to present their ideas, not to push them. Remember the story where the young man was told to present his idea, but not to push it. The power in the Old Order brotherhood lies in peace and harmony, not in numbers or statesmanship because submission and obedience are the qualities for a brotherhood, not self-glorification and honour. A seasoned Old Order stated, "Could we not still say that it is hard to define in mere words the pulses that are the life of a Mennonite brotherhood—it is so inter-woven, it is so inter-locked."

The stand of the Old Order is a paradox. The Old Order request, no, they *expect* a total submission and obedience of members to the brotherhood. If the principles of the brotherhood are challenged, they become very unyielding. The aged man was unyielding to his grandson's gripes. The young man was to learn to appreciate the brotherhood and to be submissive and obedient, to practise Gelassenheit or to leave in peace. The Old Order stand is a voluntary commitment to be submissive and obedient to God and the brotherhood, but when "formidable egos" arise and one becomes lord over God's heritage, the delicate peace is destroyed.

Notes

[1] John L. Ruth, *The Earth is the Lord's* (Scottdale, PA: Herald Press, 2001), 131.

[2] Cornelius J. Dyck, *An Introduction to Mennonite History* (Scottdale, PA: Herald Press, 1981), 97.

[3] John L. Ruth, *Twas Seeding Time* (Scottdale, PA: Herald Press, 1976), 158.

[4] *Ibid.*, 165.

[5] Benjamin Eby, *Origin and Doctrine of the Mennonites* (Waterloo, ON: Markham-Waterloo Mennonite Conference, 1999).

[6] Abner Brubacher, Monthly Newsletter, Eagle Wings Discipleship Ministries, Aug. 2001.

[7] John H. Yoder, *The Legacy of Michael Sattler* (Scottdale, PA: Herald Press, 1973), 36.

[8] *Ibid.*

[9] Richard K. MacMaster, *Land, Piety, Peoplehood* (Scottdale, PA: Herald Press, 1985), 193.

[10] Horst, *Close Ups*, 118, 186.

[11] John L. Ruth, *Maintaining the Right Fellowship* (Scottdale, PA: Herald Press, 1984), 174.

[12] For lot, inquiry, and call see glossary.

[13] Milton, R. Good, *Folklore of Waterloo County* (Waterloo, ON: Waterloo Historical Society, 1981), 104.

[14] Ruth, *Maintaining*, 535.

A Scattered People

Chapter Nine

The Niagara Peninsula and Haldimand County Dissensions

The Old Order division left many congregations in a weakened condition. For reasons unknown today, Bishop Christian Gayman (Old Order) of Cayuga had fallen into disfavour with the main body as early as September 1884 and was put out of the fellowship. Gayman evidently went with Isaac Rittenhouse to the fall conference at the Moyer's meetinghouse.[1] (It was common at that time for lay persons to be present at the conference.) Bishops Amos Cressman and Elias Weber and others from Waterloo confronted Gayman about the disunity between him and Daniel Honsberger of Jordan. Honsberger had held with the Gayman group for awhile but by 1885 he returned to the main body. There had been some sharp words between Gayman and Cressman. Cressman had evidently criticized Gayman "as a witchcraft sinner without proof" and Gayman demanded reconciliation that Cressman was not ready for.[2]

The evidence suggests that the Haldimand County ministry was basically separate from the main body by the fall of 1885. On October 7, 1885, Bishop Gayman wrote to Minister Samuel Weber, "Last Friday we had a peaceable conference at Rainham. The home ministry were all present except Christopher Hoover (Deacon of Cayuga). The beloved brother Deacon Abraham Metz of Clarence, NY was present also and so was Abraham Kolb and Abraham Rittenhouse."[3] Gayman and his followers considered it a great injustice for Cressman and Weber to come into their district and act as they did. Perhaps Gayman did not appreciate that Honsberger had shifted his allegiance to Bishops Amos Cressman and Elias Weber, and the presence of the Waterloo bishops was threatening to Gayman. Gayman and his co-workers took council and decided to hold communion with the "peaceable" at "the Twenty" and believed that God's blessing was with them. Communion was also held at Rainham where "a goodly number took part," and he intended to hold communion the next Sunday at South Cayuga.[4] It is interesting to note that neither Bishop Abraham Martin nor any of the future Old Order ministry were present at "the Twenty" in 1885, and that Bishop Gayman felt free to write to Minister Samuel Weber in regard to his differences with the Waterloo bishops. A year later, in the September 11, 1886 Conference Report it was stated, "let Bishop Gayman stay where he placed himself."

The Gayman controversy dragged on. At the Berlin Conference of May 1887, Bishop Gayman had pleaded for patience and time for consideration. Nonetheless, a year later Gayman acknowledged at the conference that he had no desire to attend the regular conferences, but wished to hold a conference of his own.[5] (Evidence suggests that in Waterloo the Old Orders informally separated in the fall of 1887. Niagara district withdrew in the spring of 1888 and Bishop Christian Reesor of Markham tried in vain until 1891, three years later, to establish peace.) In Gayman's home district of Haldimand County it was only Deacon Christopher Hoover of the eight ordained men who stood by the Conference Mennonites, but in Lincoln and Welland only about half of the ordained men cast their lot with Gayman while the majority of the lay members remained loyal to the Conference.

The Old Orders in Welland County

The Mennonites in Welland County had by this time been reduced to a small congregation at Sherkston. Ministers Nelson Michael and Gilbert Bears, along with the majority of the congregation, held to the Conference Mennonites, while Deacon Jonas Zavitz had about six families who supported the Old Order movement. No resident minister was ordained for this small group. They had their preaching services filled by the neighbouring ministers from both Lincoln and Haldimand Counties, but this was not sufficient to assure that the congregation prospered.[6] The Old Orders included the (Sherkston) preaching appointment in Bertie Township until 1905, when it was discontinued even though Jonas Zavitz was still listed as a deacon for Welland County until his death in 1920. By 1931 the Conference Mennonites sold the meetinghouse at Sherkston and closed the chapter for the Mennonites in Welland County.

The Old Orders in New York

The New York settlement had early beginnings. Two Witmer brothers from Lancaster County settled in Niagara County, NY about 1811. David Habecker was an early minister and John Treichler and John Martin were the first deacons. The settlement spread south into Erie County and had two meetinghouses known as Goods and Clarence. This community always had connections with the Mennonites of Ontario since it was only about fifty kilometres from the border.

The Mennonite settlement at Clarence Center, NY also met challenging times. In about 1880 Bishop Jacob Krehbiel and a number of families left the Conference Mennonites and began to affiliate with the General Conference Mennonites. This movement weakened the fellowship at Clarence Center. Krehbiel also gathered the remaining few Mennonites from Black Creek and Stevensville in Welland County into his fold. Within a decade the Old Order division would again disrupt the community. Deacon Abraham Metz cast his lot with the Old Order Bishop Gayman while his co-worker Jacob Hahn remained with the Conference Mennonites. Such fragmentation had devastating effects on the church. After Jacob Krehbiel became inactive in the General Conference, his group declined and the members were absorbed by non-Mennonite churches.

Isaac Martin (1882-1964), an Old Order historian, remembered an elderly man by the name of Scherer, an Old Order from Clarence, who visited the Waterloo Old Orders about 1900. He evidently was one of the last remaining Old Order members at Clarence Center since the Old Orders discontinued New York from the title page of their Calendar of Appointments in 1906. The Conference Mennonites continued and experienced some real growth after 1920.[7]

The Old Orders in Lincoln County

The church at Vineland saw difficult years. The Hoch division of 1849 rent the community, and the Mennonite Brethren in Christ ("New"

Mennonites) movement during the mid-seventies caused further loss of members. Ten years later the Gayman controversy continued to weaken this once strong and growing community. The Old Order schism divided the ministry equally with Ministers Daniel Honsberger, Abraham Hunsberger and Deacon Philip Wismer who remained with the conference, while Ministers Abraham Rittenhouse, Joseph Wismer and Deacon Abram Culp cast their lot with the Gayman group (Old Order). The membership was not equally divided. Forty-one members were faithful to the Old Orders while seventy members remained with the conference at "the Twenty."[8] The forty-one members did not represent the congregation

After the 1889 division, the Old Orders at Vineland purchased land and built this meetinghouse north of the cemetery. In the forefront we see the stone wall that was built around the old cemetery for ninety silver dollars in 1833. Although not visible on this photograph, the Meyers Church ("The Twenty") stands east of the cemetery off to the right of this picture. When Minister Joseph Wismer died in 1927, the Old Order Mennonite congregation ceased to exist. In 1934 Abe Harder from Winnipeg bought the Old Order meetinghouse and moved it to Cherry Avenue and used it for a residence (W. M. Fretz). Courtesy of Larry W. Rittenhouse

but rather consisted of the ministry and their families, with several other older members. The Old Order meetinghouse was located northwest of the cemetery. The Old Order community never prospered. Abraham Rittenhouse directed his children towards Markham, and several of his daughters married brethren from Markham. By 1913, there were only a few remaining members at the Old Order Vineland congregation and Abraham Rittenhouse retired to his daughter's home in Markham where he died five years later. In 1921, Abram Culp passed away leaving only Joseph Wismer to serve the dying congregation. One may, however, never question Joseph Wismer's dedication. He was the minister, caretaker, and song leader for the Old Order church at Vineland. Wismer was known to have kept services by himself. He prayed and sang songs to his God. Albert Hauser and Michael Martin were the last members of the Old Order group. When Wismer died in 1927, Rev. S. F. Coffman of the Conference Mennonites assisted at the funeral service. The Old Order church at Vineland closed. Thus ended another Old Order appointment for worship. In 1934 the Old Order meetinghouse was sold to Abe Harder who had arrived from Winnipeg. He dismantled it and reconstructed it as a residence, so this Old Order community was reduced to memories.

The Old Orders in Haldimand County

The Rainham and South Cayuga congregations were the last foothold the Old Orders held in the old Niagara District. Bishop Gayman had been very influential and as a result the Old Orders were the larger fellowship in the area; however, by the end of World War I, Menno Hoover and Menno Sherk both decided to move to Waterloo. According to their views the Rainham community held no future for their families. When the last Old Order ordination was held in South Cayuga, there were two men suitable to be nominated. This ordination was during the David Martin division and the outspoken Menno Hoover evidently questioned the visiting Bishop Ezra Martin as to whether he had peace at home. Hoover was promptly disqualified and John E. Sherk was ordained minister in 1917. Sherk served the community until 1946 when he also moved to Elmira and laboured with the Markham-Waterloo Conference until his death. Waterloo Old Orders broke fellowship with the Markham and Haldimand County Old Order churches in 1929 or 1930, which ended all Old Order pulpit exchange between Waterloo and Markham and Rainham. After 1930 the Old Orders in Markham and Rainham were known as the Markham Conference until 1939 when the name was changed to the Markham-Waterloo Mennonite Conference.

Markham-Waterloo Mennonites used the South Cayuga meetinghouse until 1941. The Conference Mennonites continued to use this shared meetinghouse until 1965, when the reduced membership caused the congregation to amalgamate with the Rainham church. After John Sherk relocated to Waterloo, the Markham-Waterloo Mennonites held occasional services in the Rainham meetinghouse until 1955. During the time of these occasional services Mrs. Elias Helka (sister to Menno Hoover who moved to Waterloo) invited the ministry from Waterloo to her home for the noon meal. This more recent "Martha" was so encumbered with serving her much-appreciated guests that she elected to skip the morning service so her dinner may be prepared. Although her visitors were delighted with her intentions, they also appreciated the few "Marys" who were present at the service. Deacon Amsey Weber and Minister Ira Brubacher held the last worship service at Rainham on November 20, 1955. The former Old Order Rainham congregation by this time had only three remaining members.[9]

Scattered Families

The Mennonite Church had numerous small daughter Mennonite communities found in Middlesex, Elgin, Huron Bruce, and Perth Counties.[10] These scattered families were served by the ministers from Waterloo who were scheduled to hold preaching assignments every eight weeks. Worship service once in eight weeks was not adequate for their spiritual growth. These preaching assignments were at times adventurous, and at the worst wearisome and discouraging, for the ministers had to leave their homes for up to three days. Travelling these poor and often muddy roads in snow, heat and rain could be very trying. In general those people appreciated the services, but on several occasions the ministers returned home with questions on their minds.

On one occasion two ministers arrived at the Walkerton train station on Saturday expecting someone to meet them and take them to their desired destination. Night came and no ride arrived. Sunday came and went and still nobody appeared. Having had enough of the strange town, they boarded the first train that was homeward bound. On another occasion Minister Samuel Weber had completed his mission and was returning to the train station. Weber could not tolerate the driver's concept of time. His apprehension of missing the train compelled him to ask the driver for the reins and whip. Weber then drove to town according to his liking.

It is almost certain that the community straddling the Elgin-Middlesex boundary had no Old Order sympathizers because the Old

Account of building Meeting House.

				$	¢	$	¢
1882		Brought over from page	21.	237	00	164	41
Oct	3	Paid to J. & J. Large for Doors				6	38
"	"	" " G. S. Climie & Sons for pipe				5	50
"	4	" " Robert Carter for plastering & Chimney				28	00
"	5	" " W. J. Hamilton for lime				11	50
"	7	Received from Henry Bowman		5	00		
"	9	" from Moses Clemens, per D. Shuh		10	00		
"	"	Paid to Henry Strickler, for mason work				15	00
Nov.	6	Received from Henry Ludwig, per S. Hallman		5	00		
"	"	" " Levi Martin, on subscription		10	00		
"	8	Paid to Conrad Kraft, for liming 7¾ d. mason				6	75
"	"	" " Levi Martin for Boarding C. Kraft				2	00
"	10	" " David Shuh for Do. H. Strickler				9	00
"	"	Received from Christian Clemens		9	00		
Dec	29	Paid to Jacob Doersam for Lumber & lath				14	31
"	"	" " John Zurbrig for painting				2	75
1883 Jan.	12	" " John Orth, for drain from foundation				3	90
"	13	" for Drawing & Registering Deed				13	65
"	"	Received from J. Kolb per D. Shuh		22	80		
"	16	" J. Zurbrig for pieces of flooring			50		
"	19	" Samuel Ernst, (borrowed)		50	00		
"	"	Paid to J. Kurtz for Carpenter work (& 8 bolts)				41	47
"	"	Received from J. Kurtz on subscription		10	00		
"	27	Paid to P. Orth for 140 Tiles				1	00
"	"	" to Jacob Orth for Carpenterwork				22	50
Feb	22	Received from John Gole, on subscription		15	00		
March	8	Paid to D. Shuh. for bolts, nails, &c.				1	60
"	"	Paid over to D. Shuh, balance of Money on hand				24	28
		Total subscription		$374	30	$374	30

The above account shows the cost of building the Kurtzville meetinghouse.

Order-minded Abraham Brubacher, who had been ordained in 1877, had not been appreciated so he had moved to Ohio in 1883. The other ordained men of this community were of non-Mennonite background, and one can surmise that these men did not have the traditional feel of Gelassenheit. The appointments at Mosa and Middlesex Co. had been omitted from the Old Order calendar in 1890, as had Port Elgin.

The Wallace or Brotherston Settlement

The congregation in Wallace Township, Perth Co. went through some difficult times. It was included in the Calendar of Appointments in 1865. In 1869 Isaac Weber was ordained minister for this settlement, and Levi P. Martin was ordained deacon. In 1869 Montezuma Brothers donated land for a meetinghouse on the sixth line of Wallace (where the present Markham-Waterloo Brotherston meetinghouse stands). Brothers hired his brother-in-law, Jim Hargrove, to build the first church for community use. Brothers went with the "New Mennonite" (MBC) movement, and because he had donated the land he laid claim to the building. One Sunday morning, while the Mennonites were worshipping, he went up to the pulpit and, pounding his fist on it, declared that the Mennonites had no business in the meetinghouse.[11]

The Mennonites abandoned the church and worshipped in their homes until they built another meetinghouse in Kurtzville in 1882 on land donated by David Schuh. The new building was approximately twenty by thirty feet. The stone structure cost about three hundred and fifty dollars in addition to the free labour. Twenty-three families made contributions for the meetinghouse.[12] Of these, five families lived in Maryborough Township. It is surprising that these scattered settlements fared as well as they did when one considers the primitive roads and how far these people were removed from each other.

Deacon Levi P. Martin must have sensed that his Old Order inclinations were not being appreciated because he moved to Waterloo in 1884. At the time of the Old Order division, Bishop Abraham Martin happened upon an embarrassing situation. He, according to his calling, went to Wallace to administer communion. When he made his intentions known to the local ministry, Isaac Weber and Isaac Hallman, they informed him that they would prepare the necessary items for those in the congregation who desired to accept communion from Martin's hand, but they would not partake of communion from him. When the next day dawned and the congregation had been assembled, Bishop Martin arose to administer communion but nobody took part.

Later, at a convenient time, Bishop Elias Weber from Breslau served communion at the Kurtsville meetinghouse and the congregation took part, showing that they supported the Conference Mennonites. Nevertheless, the settlement did not prosper, and by 1902 the Mennonites in Wallace sold the meetinghouse to the Evangelical Association. The wife of Minister Isaac Hallman was the last Mennonite burial at the old Kurtzville cemetery. Time brings changes, and a century later these former Mennonite meetinghouses were again Mennonite places of worship. The Conservative Mennonites bought the Kurtzville location while the Brotherston property became a place of worship for the Markham-Waterloo Mennonites.[13]

There had also been a preaching assignment in Maryborough Township, Wellington County. It was probably at the Wyandot School and was included in the Calendar of Appointments from 1872 until 1890. The MBC fellowship had a church on the fourth line of Maryborough at one time, but it is highly unlikely that the Mennonites used that location.

Hay or Stanley Appointments

In 1829 the Huron Road was opened all the way to Goderich. The sudden passing away of Waterloo Minister, Henry Shuh, on January 8, 1837, while performing ministerial duties in Hay would indicate that the Mennonites had closely followed other settlers to Hay Township. A meetinghouse was built in 1846, about three miles south of Zurich. Daniel Lehman and Henry Newschwander were the early ministers and Abraham Vincent, Samuel Reesor, and Henry Baer severed as deacons throughout the early years. Another settlement was started in Stanley Township, which was adjoining Hay to the north. Henry Detweiler was ordained minister for Stanley in 1874 and Daniel Steckle became deacon in 1882. After Detweiler moved to Virginia in 1893, the Old Orders from Waterloo conducted a preaching appointment once every eight weeks until the end of 1954 for the last Old Order family living there. Over the years some of the youth from Stanley worked in the Waterloo area and married members of the Waterloo Old Orders.

By 1954, only Josiah Steckle remained at Stanley of the former Old Order Mennonite community. Josiah Steckle fellowshipped with the Markham-Waterloo Conference, and services were held in his home from March 1955 until November 1966. During the early years, services were held once every four weeks, but towards the end, services were held once every seven weeks. During the early sixties the Steckle family held several Markham-Waterloo Sunday evening youth singings so their children would become acquainted with the Waterloo youth group. In 1967 Josiah Steckle and his wife moved to Elmira and lived with their daughter until their deaths. This closed the Stanley chapter of the Old Order Mennonites.

The Mennonite Church in North Michigan

The desire for cheap land and the itch of frontier life lured the Mennonites into the hilly, sandy soils of North Michigan. In 1877 Elias B. Snyder from Waterloo bought twelve hundred acres for four dollars per acre. In 1879 he sold 240 acres to Minister Abraham Detweiler from Ontario who then settled in the Brutus district with some other families. This solid bush country lay about twenty-five kilometres south of the famous Mackinac Bridge at the Straits of Mackinac. The majority of the Mennonite settlers came from Waterloo, Ontario but there were also a few families from Indiana. In 1882 a railroad was constructed from Petoskey to Mackinac, which gave the settlers a market for their products. A meetinghouse was built just west of Brutus in about 1883. At this time Bishop Jacob Wisler ordained Jonathan Gehman as minister and Joel Snider as deacon. This congregation was affiliated with Ohio and Indiana, but it also maintained strong relations with Waterloo.

The 1886 division that occurred in Brutus may well have been influenced by the disturbance in Waterloo. Even though the Old Order Mennonite community was numerically larger than those who affiliated with John Funk of Indiana, Funk still asked Abraham Detweiler to desist from preaching. The Old Orders then worshipped in their homes until Bishop Christian Shawn of Indiana reinstated Abraham in 1896. According to historian Isaac Martin, both groups then shared the meetinghouse. In 1898, Bishop Abraham Martin of Waterloo presided over a baptismal service where three girls and one boy were baptized. By 1910, the Old Order community had about thirty-five families; however, when a number of families moved to Alberta, the community was weakened. The Conference Mennonites renewed activity to serve the community in 1919, and drew families from the Old Order community to the Conference Mennonites. This continued to weaken the Old Order community.

The North Michigan settlement was basically a logging community and its life reflected the logging industry; furthermore, the sandy soils were not very productive and the settlers found the long, hard winters discouraging. In early August 1925, Paul Brubacher and his father, Daniel, were making hay. The young man was having misgivings about his future in Michigan and when a dark cloud produced some snow squalls that early August day, he told his father that this was it, "I'm going to Pennsylvania." In a short time four young men boarded a train bound for the East—the community again lost some of her most valued resources.[14]

This Old Order community held numerous ordinations because so many moved away. There were five more deacons ordained after Joel Snider, but they all moved away. Those ordained who left were Joseph Detweiler, Jonas Brubacher, David Horst, Christian Leinbach, and Henry G. Martin. Owen Snider was ordained as minister in 1896, and when he became mentally ill, Daniel G. Brubacher was ordained minister in 1901, and advanced to the office of bishop in 1911. Henry Brenneman was ordained minister in 1906, and remained at Brutus until his death in 1943. By this time the Old Order community was basically extinct, while a small Conference Mennonite congregation remained. Bishop Daniel Brubacher responded to serve the Old Order community at Waterloo in 1939 when their bishop Jesse Bauman left them.[15]

Extinct Wellesley Settlement

An appointment for worship services held in a schoolhouse west of St. Clements began in 1860. A cemetery was started at the corner of Lobsinger Line and Hackbart Road in Wellesley Township. Ernest, Frey, Moser and Schmidt are some of the names found in this cemetery. Deacon Amos Cressman (1805-1881) is also buried there while his wife, who died three years later, is buried in Maryborough. The congregation failed and in 1885 the services were discontinued. John W. Martin (1877-1965), son of

Minister David B. Martin (founder of David Martin group) of Elmira, remembered going with his father to hold services at the Wellesley community.

In 1904 the unused portion of the cemetery was sold back to the adjacent farm and the cemetery was abandoned. The remnants of the cemetery can still be found at the southeast corner of the intersection. During the 1960s, when the Old Orders sought permits for their cemeteries adjacent to their new meetinghouses, the government officials confronted them about the abandoned Wellesley Mennonite cemetery. The Mennonites then re-assumed the care of the plot and presently pay one of their members to cut the grass amongst the fourteen graves.

Adventures in Florida

Early in the twentieth century, land agents from Florida spread colourful and enticing stories of virgin forest in northern Florida. These stories reached the Old Order Mennonite community in Waterloo. Daniel Horst became interested, and in the spring of 1917 he and his brother, Deacon David Horst from Brutus, Michigan, made an exploratory journey to Florida and came home highly impressed. Daniel's health did not lend itself favourably to the cold Canadian winters, and Florida's warm climate would agree with him. In November 1917, the Horsts boarded the train at St. Jacobs with several other families and met Daniel's brother David in Detroit. These were war years and the border-crossing was a challenge because several of the boys were of draft age.

Once in Florida, they settled south of Ponce de Leon where they engaged in produce farming and operated a lumber business. The lumber business ran into numerous difficulties. First the pine trees were too gummy to saw effectively so the equipment had to be modified. Secondly, during the war railcars were at a premium and often Horst could not obtain a railcar to move his sawed lumber to the inflated war-time market. After the war the prices dropped below profitable margins. Consequently, the sawmill enterprise was a failure. The produce enterprise fared better but the warm and different climate left many challenges to these people accustomed to seasonal changes. Neither was this settlement exempt from sickness. David Horst's wife did not fare well in Florida and so they returned to Ontario

The following is a coppy taken from the original list. taken by J. W. Brubacher,

1874 Jan	28	We give our money to the Russians without interest			
		Ludwig Koch	Paid	$20	00
		John S. Brubacher	Paid	20	00
		Michael B. Brubacher	Paid	5	00
		Samuel Hoffman	Paid	25	00
		Levi Bowman	"	30	00
		George B. Hoffman	"	6	00
		Samuel B. Hoffman	"	4	00
		John W. Brubacher	"	15	00
		David Betzner	"	10	00
		Daniel M. Brubacher	"	4	00
		Aaron Ziegler	"	5	00
		David Koch	"	20	00
		John M. Brubacher	"	10	00
				$174	00

The Old Order Mennonites supported the 1874 Russian Mennonite emigration to Manitoba. This a list of contributions designated for that cause.

in June of 1921. Daniel remained in Florida until the fall of 1921 when he also returned to Waterloo. The Florida adventure left the Horsts financially ruined but Daniel undauntedly pressed on and succeeded in raising his large family.

The Horsts had fellowshipped with the Old Orders before they moved to Florida but after they returned to Waterloo they soon began to fellowship with Conference Mennonites. This was the last attempt that any Old Order took to begin a new settlement until the Mount Forest settlement began in the 1960s. The pioneering spirit had ended.

The Russian Mennonites

Another branch of Mennonites would come into the Old Order community over the years. These Mennonites fled from Holland to Poland during the years of the Reformation's persecution. For over three centuries they prospered with only a nominal amount of persecution. The Mennonites refused to support the state church or the military by not paying their property taxes. Since the Mennonites already owned approximately three-hundred-thousand acres of land, the government in the mid-1800s put restraining measures on the community by not allowing the Mennonites to buy more land. The appeal by Catherine II of Russia to the Europeans to settle the Ukraine received the attention of thousands of Germans and the Mennonites took interest in this opportunity.

In 1886 four hundred families moved from Poland to Russia and founded a colony beside the Chortitza River in the Ukraine. About two decades later, from 1803-1806, another 365 families settled along the Molochnaya River.[16] These settlements were established at the same time as the Niagara Peninsula and Waterloo settlements in Ontario. Although the Ontario settlements began in the same era, the Russian colonies were much larger, which is also reflected by the numbers of these people who later migrated to Canada in the 1870s and the 1920s.

In 1861 the serfs in Russia were freed. Other political reforms began to threaten the Mennonites' religious freedom in Russia. The universal military service act of 1874 caused seventeen thousand Mennonites to migrate to Canada and the United States. The Russian Mennonites' religious freedom became jeopardized as the Russian people vented their anti-German feelings. Before the Russian Revolution destroyed the Mennonite communities in Russia, the highest courts in Russia were influenced by the "insidious propaganda talk of German oppression."[17] This heart-breaking story is beyond the scope of this book. We will only briefly touch on how these two migrations affected the Old Order community in Ontario.

Russian Mennonite delegations had been scouting North America two years before immigration began in 1874. Jacob Y. Shantz, a Mennonite entrepreneur, became agent for these often-penniless immigrants. During his efforts to help these people, Shantz may have travelled West as many as twenty-seven times.[18] Through Shantz's efforts a total of $33,974.00 was loaned by the Ontario Mennonites to assist the Russian Mennonites to establish their homes in Manitoba. The Ontario Mennonites also had posted bonds to the Canadian government for another $96,400.00. This was a significant amount of money at that time, but some of these settlers had left their homes unsold and needed assistance even to cross the Atlantic Ocean. The extreme difficulties those people encountered can be illustrated in the following story.

> John Dueck was the first child born in the Russian Mennonite community in Manitoba. During the winter of 1874, John was born in thirty-five below (Fahrenheit) weather. The cow and her calf were brought into the living quarters to help keep the kitchen warm.

During this winter there were numerous deaths. The conditions were so harsh that individuals who had lost their partners remarried shortly after they were widowed because to live alone was almost impossible. God blessed these people so that by 1888 their loans from the government had been paid. Two years later the direct loans to the Mennonites in Ontario were also paid and the books of the Ontario Committee were closed.[20]

In the 1870s, seven-thousand Mennonites settled in Manitoba. During the next forty-five years the settlement grew and spread over the Canadian West. By 1921 there were forty-five thousand Mennonites in the Canadian West and only 13,600 in Ontario.[21] These people were again preparing to help their brethren doomed in the catastrophe in Russia following the civil war and famine.

In 1920 the various Mennonite groups united and formed the Mennonite Central Committee to assist their Brethren in famine-stricken and war-torn Russia. 120,000 Mennonites were suffering from famine and the effects from the civil war. During July 1922, when the need was the greatest, MCC fed up to forty-three thousand people in Russia. (1) These people were desperately trying to emigrate to Canada but the animosity against the Mennonites, Hutterites, and Doukhobors in the Canadian West had led to the 1919 Order-in-Council that outlawed

(1) *Many of the horses had been stolen or destroyed; therefore, MCC delivered fifty tractor and plow units to Russia. Seventy years later Herb Enns would still remember those tractors and the spanking he received because he came home late. MCC's policy was to help all the people in the area where they were, not just the Mennonites. Nevertheless, children had priority over adults in the soup kitchens. Herb recalled the story of a family who sent their child to the MCC soup kitchen with the instructions to bring the soup home. The mother then added water to a child's portion of soup so there would enough soup for the whole family. Through divine providence the whole family was sustained by a child's portion of soup.*[19]

further immigration of non-resistant people. The political victory of William Lyon Mackenzie King in 1921 proved to be a blessing for the Mennonites. King, a native of Waterloo County, knew the Mennonites and was favourably inclined towards them. At the Mennonites' request King had the restrictive 1919 Order-in-Council rescinded in the winter of 1922.[22]

Very few people understood the extreme difficulties that had to be overcome in both Canada and Russia until the way was clear for the immigrants to arrive in Canada. Through the heroic efforts of B.B. Janz of Russia and David Toews of Canada, twenty-thousand Russian-Mennonites immigrated during the 1920s. This large migration of Mennonites also touched the Mennonites in Ontario. In 1924 the Ontario Mennonites took 1,340 immigrants into their homes and gave them assistance to re-establish themselves. There were many fond memories for those involved as well as many challenges as cultural differences arose and had to be bridged. These immigrants were to establish congregations in Waterloo, Leamington, and on the Niagara Peninsula. Even though some immigrants were placed in Old Order Mennonite homes, the cultural barriers kept the two groups separate from each other, aside from a few family relations.

Notes

[1] Conference Reports. Mennonite Conference, Sept. 12, 1884, 14, CGUC.

[2] Christian Gayman, Letter to Samuel Weber, Oct. 7, 1885, CGUC.

[3] *Ibid.*

[4] *Ibid.*

[5] L. J. Burkholder, *A Brief History of the Mennonites in Ontario* (Altona Manitoba: Friesen Printers, 1986), 198.

[6] J. C. Fretz, "The Early History of the Mennonites in Welland County, ON," *Mennonite Quarterly Review* (January, 1953): 73.

[7] ME, I, 618.

[8] Carson Moyer, *The Mountain Church at Campden* (Kitchener: Mennonite Historical Society, 1986), 3.

[9] ME, IV, 248.

[10] See Appendix A.

[11] Isaac Martin, "The Origin of the Mennonites," N.p, n.d., 11.

[12] Levi P. Martin, Deacon records 1873-1915. CGUC Mennonite Archives, 22.

[13] See chapter Twenty.

[14] Rachel Newswanger, *Undaunted Venture from Ontario to Michigan* (Kutztown, PA: Rod and Staff Publishers Inc., 2000), 3-4.

[15] Amos B. Hoover, *The Jonas Martin Era* (Denver, PA: Muddy Creek Library, 1982), 906-7.

[16] Cornelius J. Dyck, *An Introduction to Mennonite History* (Scottdale, PA: Herald Press, 1981), 166-170.

[17] Unruh, Heinrich, "Autobiography of our Father and Grandfather Heinrich Unruh, Teacher, Preacher and Elder of the Halbstaedter Mennonite Church (congregation) South Russia" (Author's collection, N.p., 1917), 29-30.

[18] Samuel J. Steiner, *Vicarious Pioneer: The Life of Jacob Y. Shantz* (Winnipeg, MB: Hyperion Press Limited, 1988), 155.

[19] Herb Enns, Interview with Author. Waterloo, ca. 1990.

[20] Steiner, *Vicarious Pioneer*, 147.

[21] Martin, Deacon records, 38.

[22] Frank H. Epp, *Mennonites in Canada* I. (Toronto: Macmillan Canada, 1974), 304.

[23] Frank H. Epp, *Mennonites in Canada* II. (Toronto: Macmillan Canada, 1982), 156.

The Markham (York) Settlement

Chapter Ten

Markham Before the Division

The Mennonite settlement in York County was always more scattered than the Waterloo community. The earliest settlers of the plain people in the York County area may well have been the Tunkers in Vaughan Township, who were present there in the 1790s. A bachelor, John Smith from Somerset County, Pennsylvania, came in 1799 on a scouting expedition, and by 1801 he had purchased two-hundred acres at lot 7, Concession 4, in Vaughan Township. What John's religious affiliation was is not clear but his brother Jacob Smith, who came in 1815 with his family, was of the Mennonite faith. Peter Musselman, who came in 1803, was the first minister for the Schmidt congregation in Vaughan Township, while Jacob Smith was deacon. In 1804 Minister Christian Troyer also arrived in Vaughan.

In 1824 Jacob Smith donated one acre of land for a meetinghouse and cemetery. The Schmidt meetinghouse was built the same year at a cost of $210.00. This building, constructed of white pine logs, has never seen any paint, and neither were there any songbooks in this meetinghouse because the people always brought their own. There was never a pulpit in the Schmidt meetinghouse; it only had a table constructed of two wide pine boards where the minister stood to preach. The meetinghouse was used until 1909, but the Old Order Mennonites discontinued its use in 1891. It was then closed until 1915 when it was used monthly until 1923. In October 1976 the Schmidt meetinghouse was moved to Black Creek Pioneer Village to be preserved and protected from vandalism. This building is the oldest existing Mennonite meetinghouse in Ontario and it was never altered. After the

1889 division Abraham Smith Sr., father of Bishop Abraham Smith, was the only remaining Old Order family in Vaughan Township and so he moved to Markham in 1891.[1]

In 1803 Henry Wideman and his family moved from Bucks County Pennsylvania and settled on Lot 24, Concession 8, Markham Township which was across the road from the present Widemans Mennonite Church. He was the congregation's first minister, but he was accidentally killed by a falling tree on June 24, 1810. Minister Martin Hoover and his brothers arrived in 1804. Four years later in 1808, Bishop Abraham Grove also moved to Markham and assumed the care of the new, expanding Mennonite community.

The Widemans meetinghouse was built in 1817. We should note that this meetinghouse at first had no pulpit, but had the traditional Lancaster County ministers' table. After the death of Abraham Grove on February 22, 1836, Ministers Martin Hoover and Daniel Kreiden moved back to the United States. Deacon Christian Wideman was alone in Markham Township with no minister. At this time Troyer was still a minister in Vaughan. He later affiliated with Daniel Hoch from Jordan. On March 13, 1836 Bishop Benjamin Eby performed four ordinations. Adam Wideman (age thirty-nine), Jacob Grove (age thirty-two), and John E Reesor (age thirty) were ordained as ministers and Daniel Hoover (age forty) as deacon.

The next year Jacob Grove was ordained bishop for the Markham district. During this time the church at Markham fell into a state of decline, to the point where some individuals were parents or even grandparents before they were baptized and became members of the church. This sad and disappointing state of the church made fertile grounds for the more charismatic Evangelicals and later for the New Mennonite movements. This sobering truth of the Markham district was also prevalent in other areas. In Markham, few of the first generation settlers left the Mennonite faith, but only about one-half of the second generation chose the Mennonite Church. By the time the fourth generation Mennonites began to select their place of worship only about three out of ten chose the church of their fathers.[2]

(1) *The annual conference was to be held at the Widemans Church in May of 1889. The conference was always held on the last Friday of the month, but in that year May had five Fridays and it so happened that the Conference or "Old" Mennonites assembled on the fourth Friday and held their conference while the Old Order came together on the last Friday to hold their conference. Finding the meetinghouse locked, they held their conference in the church's horse shed. One questions if it "just so happened" that both groups held their conferences at the same site on the traditional last Friday of the month. What is more significant is that this marks the formal break of the division. It is evident that the lines had long been drawn, but at that conference they were cut even more. Bishop Christian Reesor waited two more years before he cast his lot with the Old Orders.*

The Widemans meetinghouse was the central place of worship and it was there that the conferences were held. After the 1889 conferences at the Widemans church, the Old Orders chose Reesors as the place to hold their conferences.(1) The Old Orders shared the Widemans meetinghouse until 1928 when the Conference Mennonites rebuilt the church to be more suitable for the Sunday school.

The Altona congregation may have worshipped in a schoolhouse at the same location sometime before the meetinghouse was built in 1852, and the first service was held on January 19, 1853. (Mrs. Abraham Stouffer was buried there in 1835.) The Conference Mennonites used this meetinghouse until January 1919 when they discontinued having services there. The Markham-Waterloo group held services at Altona until September 15, 1974. Bishop Abraham Smith had Matthew 18 for his text and held council indicating that this might be the last regular service at Altona, and so it was.

The Reesors meetinghouse located at the corner of Markham Township was built in 1857. On November 18, 1836, a stove was bought for a *Schulhouse* (schoolhouse) on Lot 1, Concession 11, which is also the lot where the Reesors meetinghouse stands. How long services were held at this schoolhouse is not known. John E. Reesor, who was ordained in 1836, owned the land where the school and meetinghouse stood. By 1854 the place was listed in the Calendar of Appointments. At the time of the 1889 division the Old Orders claimed the Reesors meetinghouse while the Conference Mennonites took the meetinghouse at nearby Cedar Grove. The two groups never shared these meetinghouses. On October 23, 1994 Minister Gordon Bauman and Deacon Glen Horst held the last regular service at the Reesors Church. Gordon Bauman had Isaiah 55 for his text. The membership at that time had declined to six members.

The Almira meetinghouse is located on Lot 32 Concession 5, Markham Township. There had been scheduled appointments in the area since 1852. On January 12, 1860 a meeting was held by the "Mennonist" (Mennonite) Church for the purpose of building a meetinghouse. A thirty by forty foot brick building was built and in 1875 horse sheds were added. The first service held in the new Almira meetinghouse was on September 30, 1860. After the 1889 division both the Conference Mennonites and the Old Orders used Almira. The Conference Mennonites discontinued Almira in 1956. Jacob H. Wideman and Aaron D. Grove conducted the last service. The text was Matthew 24:14. The Markham-Waterloo Mennonites held their closing service on December 27, 1970. Bishop Abraham Smith had the opening and Christian Frey had Matthew 2 for his text. The fifty-four people present sang numbers 94, 93, 344, and 150 from the Church Hymnal and so closed another chapter of Old Order Mennonite history.

In the Wake of the Division

Bishop Christian Ressor tried to hold a neutral position after the division of 1889. No doubt he knew that his small congregations would suffer if they were torn asunder by the division. Reesor's fellow ministers and the majority of the people had sided with the Conference Mennonites. However, by 1891 Christian Reesor's preaching was no longer accepted by the Conference Mennonites and neither had there been any affiliation with the Waterloo Old Order Mennonites since 1889. (1894 was the first year that the Old Orders included Markham in their Calendar of Appointments.) In 1891 Bishop Reesor united with the Old Orders and on November 30, 1891 he, with the help of two lay members, ordained Christian Burkholder as minister and Tilman Reesor and John B. Reesor as deacons. John Reesor and his wife had only been baptized earlier in 1891. He served faithfully as an Old Order deacon for over fifty years. Christian Reesor also ordained Christian Gayman Jr. as minister on July 16, 1893 and on August 5, 1906 Levi Grove was called to be a minister; he had only been baptized ten months before.

As the Old Order Mennonite brotherhood entered the new century, the church was confronted with new problems: the automobile and the telephone. During the first decade if a couple purchased an automobile they were denied communion. This became an even more thorny issue as the years passed. In 1915 Bishop Christian Reesor died and the contentious car and telephone issues within the community delayed the bishop ordination for six more years! Bishop Freeman Rittenhouse of Cayuga assumed the bishop work in Markham during those years. The Mennonite church at Markham was not prepared to witness effectively during World War I. Under the pressure of the 1918 conscription, many people who had previously been unconcerned were baptized. The young men in danger of being drafted into the army were baptized in the spring while older ones, including some grandparents, were baptized later. It was evident that the war roused many people from their spiritual slumber, but tradition is not easily broken. Some young girls whose boyfriends had been baptized during the war waited until after marriage to accept baptism and commit themselves unto God. After the war, the communities in Haldimand County and Markham began to drift away from the Old Order community at Waterloo.

Challenging Years

At the spring conference in 1921 the decision was made to hold a bishop ordination for the Markham district. Minister Levi Grove caused some disunity because he already had a telephone in his home. After some visitation a confession was made and he went through the lot when Christian Gayman was ordained bishop on May 5, 1921. Bishop Freeman Rittenhouse from Cayuga and Bishop Ezra Martin from Waterloo presided over this ordination. Bishop Gayman was a strong leader and well respected. The church at Markham was at peace during his administration, but when he died suddenly in January 1927, the church at Markham entered a different era.

Old Order Bishop Ezra Martin, from Waterloo, ordained Levi Grove as bishop on June 12, 1927. Minister Thomas Reesor was also in the lot. Levi Grove and his brother had at one time attended Baptist Church meetings against their parents' wishes. Although Levi returned to the church of his fathers to seek his life companion, he did not leave all of the Baptist teachings behind him. The subtle shift in emphasis of doctrine put Levi out of step with the fellowship and caused ill feelings and disunity within the church.

On September 25, 1927 Bishop Levi Grove ordained Abraham Smith as a minister. Of the five candidates, only Abraham Smith did not possess a car at that time. Bishop Grove had stated that none of the candidates would have to put away his car if he was chosen by lot as minister, but since it was Abraham Smith who was chosen, Markham could still fellowship with Waterloo because, as yet, none of the Markham ministry had possessed cars.

In 1928 Abraham Smith attended the Old Order conference in Waterloo in peace. This is an interesting note because Smith always preached in English. At this point he was the only ordained man in Markham without a car, as Bishop Grove had by this time also purchased an automobile. Perhaps Grove lost touch with the Old Orders' Gelassenheit because of his Baptist inclinations. The strained relations with the Old Order community at Waterloo and Markham are revealed by the following happenings. There is a story that, during the late twenties, Bishop Ezra Martin from Waterloo had gone to Markham on the train to preach at the Markham community, but nobody came to the station to meet him. Ezra commented later that you cannot quarrel alone. In either 1929 or 1930 Bishop Levi Grove met Bishop Ezra Martin at the train station in his car. This offended Martin and the Waterloo Old Order relations with Markham were severed. With their affiliation with Waterloo severed, Markham printed their first separate Calendar of Appointments in 1932. This year is counted as the official date when the Old Order Mennonites from Waterloo separated from the Old Order community at Markham, even though the division had occurred about two years previous.

The Old Order Mennonite community in Pennsylvania had experienced a division in 1926 over the car issue. The evidence suggests that in the late twenties Markham had been more interested in affiliating with the Weaverland Conference of Pennsylvania than with the Old Orders from Waterloo, who drove only horses and buggies. Bishop Ezra was well aware that a former marital stipulation was endangered. When the former Bishop Paul Martin had married the widowed daughter of the late Bishop Christian Reesor, the agreement had been that the church relations with Markham would not be severed during this relation; however, Bishop Ezra had this woman for his second wife when the relations with Markham terminated.

The Groffdale Conference was the horse-and-buggy Old Order group at the 1926 division in Pennsylvania and consequently, the Old Orders from Waterloo maintained fellowship with the Groffdale Conference. There were a few of the older members in Markham who continued to commune with the Old Orders at Waterloo. Abraham Bearinger from Waterloo held the funeral service for Mrs. Albert Reesor in Markham on July 12, 1944, in the German language. Four years later, in 1948, the last of the Old Order members passed away and closed another chapter in Old Order history.

The Transition of the Car and Telephone within the Old Order Circles

The bubble burst again in the American Midwest. The Old Order division had first climaxed in the Midwest and so did the telephone issue. In 1907 a spilt occurred within the Old Order community in Ohio and Indiana. The horse-and-buggy faction were known as the "Martins," or Old Orders, and those who accepted the telephone and cars were called the "Wislers." In 1926 this automobile split developed in Pennsylvania. Those driving cars were known as the Weaverland Conference, or "black bumpers," and those driving horses and buggies were called "Wengers" after their founder Bishop Joseph Wenger, or Groffdale Conference, and have continued to freely fellowship with the Old Orders from Waterloo.

The Weaverland Conference were concerned with retaining their separation from the world. They were mindful of the admonition,"Stellet euch nicht dieser Welt gleich" (Be not conformed to this world, Romans 12:2) as they sought to establish their Ordnung. Thomas Reesor from Markham was present at the Weaverland Conference when a discussion about Ordnung took place, and he suggested the black-bumper idea, which carried. (Reesor's stepmother was from Pennsylvania and one could assume he took the opportunity to visit family relations in Pennsylvania at the time of the Weaverland Conference.) To be a visitor at the conference would have been tolerable, but to take part in conference discussion was out of the ordinary. In short, Reesor associated with both the Weaverland Conference in Pennsylvania and the Old Orders in Waterloo. Such behaviour was out of order, but evidently neither side challenged Reesor.

The Weaverland Conference finally agreed that members have only black, chromeless touring cars. (The late model cars at that time had solid tops and glass windows as we know cars today.) The story goes that

Bishop Levi Grove of Markham had to change automobiles in order to conform to this regulation when Markham sought to affiliate with the Weaverland Conference in about 1930. By 1935 the touring cars were no longer manufactured and the Weaverland Conference then decided to accept solid-top cars but only out-of-style models. This move frustrated the local car dealers who had invested considerable money in the obsolete touring cars which now had little resale value. Only the Weaverland Conference has retained, to any degree, the concept of a chromeless black car for the laity. In Ontario the Markham-Waterloo Conference ministry possess black-bumper cars so they can maintain a peaceable pulpit exchange with the Weaverland Conference. It is only the "black car" that has remained a universal Ordnung for all the churches that affiliate with the Weaverland Conference. In Ontario the black-car Ordnung did not become firmly established until after 1939. Dark colours were encouraged but not all cars were black during the thirties when members went to Markham for communion. (Levi Martin had a dark blue car before he was married.)

The transition from horse and buggy transportation to the use of the automobile was a prolonged, contentious process for the Old Orders of Markham and Rainham. Members obtained cars as early as 1918, without church censor, and by the late 1920s it must have been evident that the Old Orders from Waterloo were not in harmony with those in Markham and Rainham. Nevertheless, the acceptance of the automobile in Markham was not without strife. There were also those who did not respect their bishop, and there was no communion for several years. Help was requested from Pennsylvania and Bishop Joseph Hostetter obliged and came to Markham, and peace was restored and communion was again held. The passing away of Bishop Levi Grove on April 2, 1936, left Markham without a bishop. On June 7, 1936, Bishops Moses Horning and Joseph Hostetter ordained Abraham Smith as bishop. During the thirties there were families from Waterloo who went to Markham to have communion. Bishop Levi Grove had not been as receptive towards these nonconforming Old Orders from Waterloo as Abraham Smith would be; nonetheless, Grove and Deacon Joe Barkey were willing to come to Waterloo on October 27, 1935, and serve communion at the home of Mrs. Nathaniel Martin.[3] As the Great Depression began to release its grip on the economy, more and more people from the Old Order community began to purchase cars and the number of those who fellowshipped with Markham increased.

Notes

1 Clarence Smith, Letter to Author, 1995. Eldon D. Weber, *A Historical History of Waterloo Township by Ezra E. Eby* (Kitchener: self published, 1984), 81-82.

2 Epp, *Mennonites in Canada* I., 234.

3 Elisabeth Martin, Diary, Oct. 27, 1935, Author's collection.

Challenging Decades

Chapter Eleven

A Vision to Hold

Peter Shirk, the Bridgeport miller, was quite confident in the Old Order Mennonite church after the division. In his letters to Jacob Mensch of Eastern Pennsylvania, he repeatedly wrote very positive comments: "In the upper churches there is peace and unity, both in the church and among the ministry, as far as I know, and they all hold fast to the old foundation as our forefathers held to it, and the blessing seems to abide with them. Quite a number of young people joined the church this fall."[1] His opinion of the lower churches reveals that Peter's relations with the "Conference Mennonites" was deeply marred. He resented the fact that some of his children chose to associate with those churches. He wrote on March 19, 1893, "They come to our children to entice them to their church where they have more freedom, and need not put away what the church demands to which their parents belong." Peter also fretted about the Conference churches' singing school.[2]

Peter's personal views on the Conference Mennonites are fruits of the shattered relations that developed as the division tore across family ties. One should never suggest that Peter was alone in his biased thoughts. He was just one of the few who wrote his feelings, which are now on record. Peter obviously never dreamed the day would come when his beloved church would also sanction singing schools. By the 1930s, singing schools were accepted by the conservative Old Orders. In retrospect it is also difficult, from an Old Order perspective, to reconcile Peter Shirk, the progressive businessman, with Peter Shirk, the conservative churchman. He and many of his contemporaries in the Old Order Church at that time were of the opinion that temperance in the use of alcohol and tobacco meant moderation, not total abstinence.[3] It would take the Old Orders over half a century to make the transition from moderation to total abstinence.

One could question whether Peter comprehended the controversy the telephone in his mill would cause the Old Order community in later years. The apparent agreement between him and his brother-in-law, Bishop Abraham Martin, about having a "business" telephone in his mill led to the inconsistent telephone usage which would haunt the community for decades. About 1930, John Sauder's buggy shop in St Jacobs would sport a telephone. A decade later Noah Reist's butcher shop and Emanuel Reist's welding shop had telephones. Furthermore, the Old Order community today would find Peter Shirk's involvement as a Waterloo Township clerk from 1892-1912, and his membership on the Berlin High School Board from 1878-1904, unacceptable.[4]

Peter Shirk had a brother in the church who took a different view of the telephone. In 1923, Moses Martin made the following stipulations when his son-in-law took over his farm: "That he will not acquire the use of the telephone service, or an automobile, or a lawn mower on to the said lands and premises during the lifetime of the said party and his wife."[5] To Peter Shirk the Old Order community had been stable, but the bishop who led the church during the first decade of the twentieth century had many more concerns.

The Brubacher and the "ditch" controversies (to be discussed later) were heavy burdens for Bishop Paul Martin. In a letter dated June 29, 1908, Paul confided to his friend, Bishop Jonas Martin, of Pennsylvania: "Es ist bedauerlich wie die alte Mennonite Gemeinde verteilt wird zu dieser zeit. Blosz um Menschen Meinung und zeitligen Sachen wo ein mahl alles vergehen tut. Der Mench kan zu geistly werden, Aber er kan auch zu lasz werden. Der Heiland sagt der Weg ist schmal für die kinder Gottes." (It is deplorable how the old Mennonite church is divided at this time merely for human reasoning and temporal things, which someday all will perish. It is possible to be steeped in law, but it is possible to be too lax. The Saviour says the way is narrow for the children of God.) He closed his letter by lamenting that: "Es ist eine sehr bedenklig zeit zu diese zeit" (These are perilous times).[6]

Evidently, Bishop Paul Martin and Bishop Jonas Martin of Pennsylvania exchanged many letters and shared similar challenges.

In 1909, Minister Tobias B. Martin also expressed his concerns to Frank Hurst of Lancaster County. In his letter he quoted a verse from hymn number 108 in the Old Order hymnbook, *Lieder Sammlung*:

Alle Christen hören gerne	Every Christian heareth gladly
Von dem Reich der herrlichkeit,	Of the kingdom of glory
Denn sie meinen schon von Ferne,	For they think already, from afar
Daz es ihnen sei bereit;	That it is prepared for them.
Uber wenn sie hören sagen,	But when they hear it spoken of,
Daz man Christi Kreuz muz tragen,	That man must bear the cross of Christ
Wenn man will sein Jünger sein,	If we want to be foll'wers.
O! so stimmen wenig ein.	Oh! So few agree to it. (1)

(1) *The poet emphasizes a characteristic of Anabaptist theology. To the Old Order, the cross of Christ is something undesirable to the flesh which a believer voluntarily accepts. To do so is to be an obedient doer of God's commandments, not just a hearer. Although this ethic is universally expressed by all sincere Christians, there are few churches in which such complete dedication is expected from all members. The Old Order voluntarily accepts afflictions and troubles for the sake of Christ and the unity in the brotherhood. To many Christians the cross of Christ is a voluntary acceptance of bodily affliction in one's life that one cannot avoid. Christ accepted the cross at Calvary because He loved the human race, not because He had no other choice. The Anabaptists accepted the cross of Christ because they loved Him. This voluntary acceptance of the cross of Christ distinguishes the faithful Christian from a nominal believer.*

Tobias further lamented that people of sound mind are unconcerned about spiritual welfare. They carry on in life as though there is no God to fear and there are no two ways towards eternity.[7]

The bicycle, considered a new invention at that time, also caused contention within the Old Order community. Bishop Paul Martin put Levi Bauman out of the church because he obtained a bicycle to go to work. Later David Frey used his bicycle to travel to work at the tile-yard and was obliged to put it away. The bicycle was an issue during the David Martin division, and in all probability is the reason that group will not tolerate bicycles even today. By the 1930s, bicycles were tolerated by the majority of the Old Orders. Theron Schlabach has noted that "Old Order people have been very discriminating. They have accepted technology if it has fit, or even helped, their ideals of family, small community, and close-knit congregation. They have rejected what they have perceived as hindrances to those ideals."[8] When, at the close of the twentieth century, preacher Ervin Shantz collapsed on his bicycle from heart failure, the people's attention was turned to his sudden death and not to the fact that he was riding a bicycle. Furthermore, by the close of the twentieth century one could see young girls riding bicycles, which in former years would not have been considered fitting.

Electricity was another technology that tried the patience of many within the Old Order community. Bishop Ezra Martin was of the opinion that electricity is used for lights and water pumps and thus is necessary to farming.[9] Therefore, in the 1920s when August Sauder bought a house with electricity in the village of St. Jacobs, it was suggested that electricity could be convenient for the elderly couple. In about 1935, a progressive farmer by Lexington had electricity installed at his farm. However, not all of the Old Orders held that view, and for decades these irregularities existed. It was through patience that those who had hydro, those who did not, and those who had diesel generators accepted each other as one fellowship. This was a time of transition and challenge as the Old Orders faced a rapidly moving society and modern technology.

There was another technology some liberal Old Orders dabbled with—the camera. During the pre-war years some youth had portraits of themselves, but not all were so-minded. A grandfather commented that his wife once took care of his portraits—they found their way into the stove. Urias Martin, a preacher, never posed for a picture and was offended if photographed. A photographer once pressured him for a picture with his coat and hat. Annoyed at the persistent photographer, he put his coat on a hanger, placed it on a hook, and put his hat on top and said, "Now take a picture of my coat and hat." Old Orders deem photographs as images, and thus a form of pride. The moderate Markham-Waterloo Mennonites possess cameras, but moving cameras are not acceptable.

One may suggest that the Old Order Mennonites were, at the turn of the century, experiencing transitional pressures the Conference Mennonites had faced several decades before. When the first locomotive arrived with its eight cars at the Elmira station on the evening of October 12, 1891, did it not spell progress and a new era? The railroad had cut through the core of the Old Order Mennonite community and likely influenced those people. Before transportation and communications were convenient, the infrastructure dictated a life of simplicity and a general separation from the urban community. During the nineteenth century the Old Orders' ethics of simplicity and separation from the world had been neglected,

The following three photographs are pictures of Old Order Mennonites. The first photograph was taken in 1863 which was before the 1889 division. Photographs two and three are of Old Orders from Waterloo that were taken during the first two decades of the twentieth century. During the early 1900s it was common for the young girls to take off their capes, which they wore at church, and to go to the "time" in the shown attire. I have included these photographs with some apprehension because I believe we need to respect those who lived before our memory, yet lest we become smug like Peter Shirk (see page 153) it was deemed necessary to include them. These photographs underscore the fact that the Old Order community struggled for several decades with how to express itself according to rudiments of its faith in a rapidly changing society. Since there remains an Old Order church today, there were surely those at that time who understood the traditional faith of their forefathers, but there were others who failed to appreciate the theme of Gelassenheit. At this time I request any reader who may recognize the individuals in these photographs to respect their wishes that they may remain anonymous. Maybe Ministers Daniel Brubacher of Conestogo and David B. Martin of Peel had reasons to be dissatisfied with the Old Order community during their time. Their reactions to the issues they faced may be debated, and the fact that the Conestogo congregation did not hold communion for seven years during Bishop Paul Martin's time reveals that this was a difficult era for the Old Order Mennonites of Ontario.[10] Let us respect those who lived the faith before us and learn from the past so that we may "Be watchful, and strengthen the things which remain, that are ready to die: for I have not found thy works perfect beforGod."(Revelation. 3: 2)

This is the wedding picture of Abraham F. and Christina Rittenhouse of Vineland, Ontario. Abraham had taken for his wife a woman of the Baptist church and was married by a Baptist minister. The marriage certificate was witnessed by John Rittenhouse, Abraham's father, and Samuel H. Moyer. Such marriages outside of the Mennonite church were all too common during that era. Abraham evidently remained faithful to the Mennonite church until his death in 1918, and was ordained minister in 1871. At the 1889 division he associated with the Old Order movement and his brother John was ordained minister in his place at the Vineland church. Courtesy of Larry W. Rittenhouse

but they were now at a threshold, at a time of transition, during which the Old Order community evolved to *voluntarily* cling to their ethics of simplicity and separation from the world. This transition bridged several decades and two world wars.

The Brubacher Church

The decade from 1907-1917 was one of several disturbances. Bishop Abraham Martin had passed away in 1902, and Paul Martin had been ordained bishop in the same year. In 1907 Minister Abraham Brubacher returned home to Ontario to reside with his daughter, Mrs. Menno Brubacher. Abraham Brubacher had been ordained minister for the Mosa congregation in Elgin County, Ontario, but when his congregation did not appreciate his conservative views, he moved to Ohio in 1883, and joined with the Wisler movement.[10] His returning home to his daughter soon erupted into a messy domestic dispute that would shatter family ties and spill over into the brotherhood, resulting in much confusion.

While living at Menno Brubachers', Abraham and his wife noticed that Menno was unduly familiar with the hired girl, who was also a member of the church. They tried to admonish Menno to see his folly, but he evidently saw no need to break off the relationship with Miss Metzger and she took an offence towards Abraham. Abraham Brubacher moved to the home of another one of his daughters, but these marred relations eventually leaked to the public. The rumours provoked Miss Metzger's father, a non-communing member, so that he sued Abraham Brubacher for libel. Due to the court proceedings which followed, Minister Abraham Brubacher and Minister Daniel M. Brubacher, Menno's father, were put in the ban. Menno and Miss Metzger were also excommunicated for their alleged behaviour, a matter both denied. Nevertheless, in her last days Mrs. Menno Brubacher acknowledged the error of Menno and Miss Metzger. Minister Abraham Brubacher was the only one of these four who was reconciled with the Old Order church.

Minister Daniel Brubacher sided completely with his son and refused to accept the counsel of others. Daniel and his son Menno stood alone. Menno's wife became emotionally ill; and although she partially recovered, she remained an invalid for the rest of her life. Since she was seldom able to attend church services, Daniel Brubacher began to hold services at the home of Menno Brubacher. By 1911 Daniel invited his children to attend these services which were held only once every six weeks until 1917.[11] Although many stories travelled about the community concerning the Brubacher affair, a man who was raised in Menno's home as a foster child saw nothing; indeed he had no evil thing to say. Were there more misunderstandings obscuring the reality of the problem? Did Miss Metzger's charming (witchcraft) abilities reflect negatively in the community? There was a story of an individual whose buggy wheel stopped going around when he drove past her place. A contemporary's concern was that this deviation from Gelassenheit may be taken as a warning to future generations.

The Brubachers joined with the David Martin group in 1917, and Daniel Brubacher was ordained bishop and Menno was ordained as minister. In 1920 the David Martin group built the meetinghouse in Woolwich. Daniel Brubacher had expected the new meetinghouse to be built on his farm because the Wallenstein meetinghouse had been built on David Martin's farm. The

Martins felt this was too much out of the way and accepted a one-acre lot donated by Tilman Martin at 1877 King Street North. The Brubachers participated in building this meetinghouse, but after they had preached there several times, they permanently separated from the David Martin group. They had about twenty members in the beginning, but the outlook for the youth was bleak—they were all cousins. The group had relative peace for ten years but then discord began to break the group apart. In disgust some forsook the Mennonite faith, but most joined the Old Order Mennonites. By 1940 Menno Brubacher, his wife, three daughters, and Miss Metzger were detached from all others. After Menno's death in 1953, the women stood alone until a minister from the Conference Mennonites convinced them to become part of their fellowship.

The Turbulent Decade—Woolwich Municipal Drain No. 1

There was another scandal that rocked the Mennonite community during the same era that the Brubacher problem surfaced. This dispute also began in innocence. Several Mennonite farmers had contacted the township engineer about a drainage problem on Lot 46, and part of Lots 47 and 84 GCT, Woolwich Township. On September 7, 1908, the township engineer, C. D. Bowman, sent a letter to Moses C. Martin requesting he sign the petition which Bowman had drawn up. On September 15, 1908, the Woolwich council considered the petition under the Municipal Drainage Act of Ontario.[12] The council ordered Mr. Bowman to prepare a report for the work proposed. In retrospect, one must question whether the five Mennonite petitioners understood the Municipal Drainage Act's proceedings and that these proceedings would almost divide the church.

It was common for the Mennonites to petition the local council for improvements. In the midst of the drainage issue, two other petitions were also forwarded to the Woolwich Township council. In 1909, four Mennonites submitted a petition for a road between lots 85 and 86. This proposal failed because the railroad objected to having three crossings within one mile of track. In 1910, the Woolwich Township council received another petition to have a bridge built on lot 10 across the Conestogo River. The public voted down this proposal.[13] (Half a century later, in 1962, the Mennonites built a bridge at the same site.) In the above two petitions there were objections and the petitions failed, but not so with the Ontario Municipal Drainage Act. Once a report was filed under the drainage act, proceedings could not be stopped without court orders. The Municipal Drainage Act does not allow a few vocal protesters to stop a project. The Act holds a property owner at the headwaters of a watershed liable for his run-off downstream.

One could surmise that a storm was already brewing in the spring of 1909, or even some time before, because the story is that communion was not held at Conestogo for seven years during this era. In any event, David Sauder, one of the petitioners, sent the following note to the clerk on May 22, 1909: "I hereby 'wishdraw' my name from the petition for Municipal Drain in Township of Woolwich."[14] Although the note was read to the council, the council moved on the same day to order the clerk to prepare a by-law authorizing the work. David Sauder understood that peace within the brotherhood meant more than a drain, but his objection was not enough evidence for the council to stop proceeding. On June 6, 1909, the council passed by-law No 564:

> A by-law to provide for drainage work in the Township of Woolwich, in the County of Waterloo, and for borrowing on the credit of the Municipality the sum of $3063.03, the proportion to be contributed by said Municipality for completing same.
>
> The whole length of the ditch is 15,567 feet. The upper end, 1530 feet, is to be an eight-inch tile drain and the balance an open ditch.
>
> About 350 acres in the water shed is a very level tract of swampland and consequently will be greatly benefited by the construction of this ditch. The balance of the land in the watershed, which includes about thirty-one hundred acres, is rolling land. The water discharges on the level area above described and flooding the same. These lands I have assessed for relief from injuring liability.[15]

Sixty-five owners were assessed by this by-law, and it would be those assessed for injuring liability who protested. On July 3, 1909, a Court of Revision was held at Conestogo Township Hall for by-law 564. "The court heard the appeals of Isaac Martin and others and confirmed the assessments as made by the engineer. Eli M. Martin's acreage be decreased by seventy-five acres. Henry Horst's acreage be increased by eighty-five acres. Council passed a resolution making those parties who are assessed for benefit liable for the maintenance of the said ditch provided no further appeals be entered. Signed by J. J. Wilkinson."[16] It is questionable whether this Court of Revision caused the trouble, or whether it was what the last phrase in the above quotation suggests.

This may not have been the last of the appeals, because at this time there was a strange silence in the township records concerning Municipal Ditch Number 1. The only reference from 1910, shows that the township paid her solicitor forty-seven dollars for Ditch Number 1. The *Elmira Signet* did not record the township minutes or any reference to the disputed ditch during the time in question. Court records are not available, and a fire destroyed the Municipal Drain referee's records. The question remains why the tender was not accepted until February 14, 1911. "Moved that we accept the tender of C. Peterson of St. Jacobs for making of Municipal Ditch No. 1, for the sum of $3028.00 provided he signs an agreement satisfactory to this council. Carried."[17] Folklore abounds in conflicting stories. Tales still linger that there were court proceedings concerning the "ditch," and Mennonites are not to go to court. (Was this litigation or was it the standard court of revision?) Local folklore has it that a judge condemned the Mennonites for refusing to pay their assessments for the Municipal Drain and said that they should be ashamed of their behaviour.

The root of the turmoil appears to have been a short drain that crossed diagonally across Mr. Lackner's field, beginning at Three Bridges Road and continuing until it met the Listowel Road. Although this ditch was not part of Municipal Ditch Number 1, it lay in its watershed and the farms above the ditch in question had to pay "injuring liability," but they had no outlet for tile drainage for their farms. Not all that transpired is clear, but the facts are that Mr. Lackner did not want a ditch across his field and the Mennonite community took Lackner to court and dug a ditch on his farm.[18] Furthermore, fifty years later a Mennonite farmer who bought the Lackner farm raised some eyebrows in the community when he installed a large tile and closed this open ditch. A contemporary commented that the church had supported the aggression against Mr. Lackner and now, when it was in their hands, the ditch must go.

The township records reveal that the ditch across Mr. Lackner's farm is not a registered Municipal Drain. Therefore, the next owner could close the ditch on his own, providing he gave those farms above him an outlet for their tile drains, which was done. Why was there such an uproar about a ditch less than half a kilometre long? Since the property in question lay within the watershed of the above Municipal Drain, legal action against a non-complier would have been normal procedure. Nevertheless, court action was not the Mennonite way. As a result, they forced Lackner to yield and dug the ditch, much to his offence. Why was a large tile not installed at that time? According to the evidence found, the offence resulted from the non-resistant Mennonites doing what they wanted against Mr. Lackner's wishes. The offended Lackner later stated he would never sell his farm to a Mennonite, but after his death this happened.

A contemporary felt that some of the Mennonites were aggressive in having the ditch made, while others who were not benefited by the ditch, and yet were taxed for it, were strongly opposed.[19] Isaac Martin notes, "Some of the church leaders thought members should stay out of it, while others said you cannot get away from it. Some people struck by the drainage business who were not Mennonites, felt the Mennonites were taking advantage of them. (It seems the Mennonites started the whole thing.) There was confusion all around."[20] The township records clearly state that it was the Mennonites who had "asked" for the drain and "ask" was what the Mennonites thought they had done. In 1909, they asked for a road and in 1910, they asked for a bridge on GCT Lot 10 at the Conestogo River, but these were voted down. They did not fight over their rejected proposals, but the Municipal Drain was different. The Drainage Act is designed to give fair treatment to all and a person may go to court and challenge the fairness of the engineer's report, but the Act does not allow one to ignore one's liabilities. The highlands owners (the injuring liability) were responsible for the flooding of the lowlands. Some of the Mennonites understood this, but others apparently did not.

Notes

[1] Peter Shirk, Letter, 1895. From "The Family History of Peter Shirk,"Bridgeport, ON: n.p. n.d.

[2] Peter Shirk, Letter, 1893. From "The Family History of Peter Shirk," Bridgeport, ON: n.p. n.d.

[3] *Ibid.*, 9.

[4] *Ibid.*, 7.

[5] Urias Martin. Letters and legal documents dated before 1940, Alma, ON.

[6] Amos B. Hoover, *The Jonas Martin Era* (Denver, PA: Muddy Creek Library, 1982), 380.

[7] *Ibid.*, 390.

[8] Theron F. Schlabach, *Peace, Faith, Nation* (Scottdale, PA: Herald Press, 1988), 208.

[9] Private Conversation.

[10] Private, anonymous letter.

[11] L. J. Burkholder, *A Brief History of the Mennonites in Ontario* (Altona, MB: Friesen Printers, 1986), 209, 281.

[12] Elizabeth Rudy, "History of the Brubacher Church." (Author's collection, N.p., 1958), 2.

[13] Woolwich Township Archives. Municipal Drain Number 1 File.

[14] Woolwich Township Minute book, 1900-1914.

[15] Woolwich Township Archives. Municipal Drain Number 1 File.

[16] *Ibid.*.

[17] *Ibid.*

[18] *Ibid.*

[19] Private Conversation.

[20] Isaac Martin, "Origin of the Mennonites." N.p. n.d., 14.

[21] Rudy, "History," 1.

The Ultra-Conservative Old Order Churches

Chapter Twelve

Beginnings of the David Martin Group

The confusion that arose out of the "ditch" mêlée left some individuals deeply concerned. Elizabeth Rudy remarks, "Apparently Minister Daniel Brubacher and Minister David B. Martin and several others were hard against the way things were going. They saw that the government had the right to force all those within the watershed to pay."[1] We do not know what knowledge these men had of the Drainage Act, but common sense led them to believe the government was right and all the unrest was wrong. In 1909, Deacon John Nahrgang from the Peel congregation was aging and an ordination to replace him was deemed proper. Amos F. Martin, Elias Weber, Aaron Bauman and Christian B. Frey were nominated for deacon. Two of the nominees were apparently considered involved in the "ditch" dispute, because people came to them for advice in regards to the "ditch." (It had been agreed that no person involved with the "ditch" be nominated.) Minister David B. Martin of Peel felt there was no peace and on the day of the ordination, after the people were come together, the ordination was cancelled.

The disunity was so apparent that communion services were disrupted in the fall of 1909. In a brotherhood of believers this is a very grave situation. At this time Bishop Paul Martin wrote to his co-worker, Bishop Jonas Martin from Lancaster County: "Der geistlig hochmuth und der machnichs geist ist die ursach von allen unruh; wo dei geistlig armuth recht gefield wird, da ist friede und liebe." (Spiritual pride and the "doesn't matter spirit" are the reason for all unrest; where Gelassenheit is felt there is peace and love.)[2] Bishop Paul further laments the disunity within the brotherhood to Jonas and one can gather that the telephone Old Order division in Indiana and Ohio also cast a dark cloud over the brotherhood in Waterloo.

As the legal wrangling concerning the ditch dispersed, the air cleared and communion was held in October 1910, but Minister Daniel M. Brubacher and some of his family did not take part.[3] One could gather that Daniel was at this time a member of the main body, but was excommunicated soon afterwards, because in 1911 he was holding services at the home of Menno Brubacher.

Catharine, the wife of Minister David B. Martin who died August 11, 1914, was so dissatisfied with the church that she did not accept communion again in her lifetime. On the evening of her funeral the boys asked their father about their mother's state as a non-communing member. The old minister replied that the Word of God is pure and clean, but we have made it so dirty that it is not fit to drink.[4] (1) These words must have pierced her son's, David W. Martin's, heart. He had been ordained deacon for the Peel congregation in June 1913. Deacon David W. Martin was a very conservative and exacting man. He was the son of Minister David B. Martin. David W. Martin served in all three offices: deacon, minister and bishop and is commonly referred to as "Bishop Dave" and it is from him the group received their name.

Deacon David W. Martin and his bishop, Ezra Martin, had a personality clash which may be traced to former generations. The two Martin immigrants, David and Peter, were first cousins, but there were

(1) *Ezekiel 34:18-19 NIV was the passage David B. Martin quoted: "Is it not enough for you to feed on the good pasture? Must you also trample the rest of your pasture with your feet? Is it not enough for you to drink clear water? Must you also muddy the rest with your feet? Must my flock feed on what you have trampled and drink what you have muddied with your feet?"*

David B. on one occasion conducted a funeral for the Brubacher group. He used Ez. 34 as his text and said that the Old Orders are the Shepherds who have dirtied the clear water. It was evident that David Martin had lost confidence in the Old Order Church, perhaps over the "ditch" issue.

apparently conflicted relations, which were passed on for generations. The immigrant David Martin family was more conservative and exact in nature than were the easy-going Peter Martin descendants. There was also a subtle rivalry between the descendants of these two families.[5] A leading Mennonite genealogist has noted that during the 1800s these families rarely inter-married.

Let us digress a little to comment on the Martin genealogy. David Martin, who settled along the Grand River at Lexington, was a first cousin to the more popular Peter Martin, who settled on Weber Street a little south of the Woolwich-Waterloo Township border. Peter's descendants became nicknamed *die grozfüszige* (big footed) Martins, while David Martin's descendants were honoured with the nickname of *die gscheide* (smart) Martins. The author came to realize that he shared the same dilemma as the old time storyteller, Mathias Martin. He is a descendant from both immigrant Martin families and is therefore *halb gscheid* (half smart).

The following illustration reveals the communication problems that existed between Deacon David W. Martin and his bishop, Ezra Martin. The use of the bicycle was an issue at that time. Bishop Ezra Martin felt he could tolerate members who were carpenters having bicycles, because in his opinion it was a very convenient means of transportation for the carpenters. For the exacting Deacon David W. Martin, such inconsistencies could not be tolerated. To fulfil his responsibilities Deacon David W. Martin went to visit an erroneous brother who allowed his sons to have bicycles, even though they were not carpenters. Deacon David W. Martin did not possess the most tactful personality; in this case he failed to accomplish his mission.

When Deacon David W. Martin was leaving, the erroneous father told his son to get on his bicycle and pass the deacon with his horse and buggy to open the gate so he would not have to climb out of his buggy to open the gate. The annoyed deacon went to his bishop and said he would not visit anybody in regards to bicycles unless he could excommunicate such an erroneous member. Bishop Ezra expressed surprise that Deacon David Martin was so bold, being ordained only a very short time.[6] The exacting deacon could not deal with his members as his conservative conscience directed him; furthermore, the people soon learned they could duck behind the more lenient bishop. The above incident reveals the differences in interpretations of the ban.[7] David wanted the *personal* authority, which in time became David Martin custom, so he could excommunicate a person on issues pertaining to the Ordnung. The more traditional view would be that the power to excommunicate is the Word for all gross sins and for those who go against the order of the church. The church is given power by the Word to maintain discipline within her confines. The rite of excommunication is too holy and sacred to be placed into the hands of fickle human beings, for it is the power of God to keep the church pure and in order. Men who are ordained to the office of bishop or deacon are by virtue of the office called by God to excommunicate the sinner that the church may be kept pure. In the David Martin group, excommunication is more disciplinary, as opposed to the love with which the Old Orders execute the ban. The different attitude the David Martins hold toward the ban results in fewer restored fellowships after the ban has been applied.

The ruined relations between the Peel ministry and the rest of the conference were so complete that Minister David B. Martin and Deacon David W. Martin stepped out of the conference in the Spring of 1917, on the question of the use of the ban. After several weeks the two Davids held services in the Peel meetinghouse on an "off" Sunday. They were denied further use of the meetinghouse and therefore began to hold services in both David Martin's and Daniel Brubacher's homes. (The Martins had invited the Brubachers to join the fellowship.)

The first years were turbulent, and at times discouraging for the new group. In May 1918, Daniel Brubacher was ordained bishop and then the group held its first communion services. Forty-eight members from about eighteen families participated. In September of the same year, Enoch Horst was ordained preacher for the Wellesley district. The following month Menno Brubacher was ordained minister for the Woolwich district with Tilman Martin and David W. Martin sharing the lot. During the summer of 1919 the Wellesley Meetinghouse was built on the old David B. Martin farm near Wallenstein. (This meetinghouse was rebuilt in 2000 and they installed flush toilets which the Old Orders have refused to do to this day.) The next summer a meetinghouse was built in Woolwich on land donated by Tilman Martin northwest of St.

In July 2000 the David Martin group tore down the first meetinghouse they built east of Wallenstein on Line 86. The old meetinghouse, which had stood between the fence and the present meetinghouse, was much smaller and had its sidewall facing the road. The meetinghouse pictured here is the second Mennonite meetinghouse in Ontario to have the convenience of the flush toilet. The Old Order group has continued to resist this modern convenience.

Jacobs. This selection of the location of the Woolwich Meetinghouse resulted in a rift. The Brubachers half-heartedly supported building the house. In the end they withdrew from the David Martin group on the question of shunning in the fall of 1920.

Bishop David W. Martin was known for his exacting ways and the strict application of the ban. Onlookers have questioned his position, but they have also admitted that he kept order in his church. There was unity in Ordnung and in helping each other in financial need. The David Martin group has received the derogatory nickname "New Borns." The David Martins feel they received this nickname because of their founder's emphasis on the new birth and a regenerated life.[8]

Bishop Dave, as David W. Martin was known, was a man who was both despised and well respected. We'll include two stories about him; the first by an outsider and the second by a man who worked with him.

Story one: David and his hired man were planting potatoes with the single furrow plough. Every third furrow they would plant the potatoes. On one occasion David told his hired hand to plant potatoes in the second furrow drawn, but the hired man objected and said that this is only the second furrow. David told him "Des es de Roy" (This is the row). When the sprouting potatoes revealed the truth, the imprudent hired man brought it to David's attention. The hired hand was again told, "Des es de Roy."[9]

Story two: We continued to work together even though my father was put in the ban. One evening after a day's threshing at David's place, my father was sick from the threshing dust. He was sensitive to threshing dust and knew it, but that day he helped too much in the barn. When we were about to go home David saw his neighbour was sick with fever. David stopped us and said my father is not ready to go. David went in and got a quilt and tucked it around the shivering man, a man he had excommunicated from his church.[10]

The Bann and Separation

The two David Martins had challenged the Old Orders by a letter on the question of the observance of the ban. David Martin had written his view concerning the observance of the ban and presented it to his co-workers, challenging them to prove his position was wrong according to the Word. The rest of the ministry never accepted the challenge—no doubt the thought came to preacher Urias Martin, as he would later express himself: "The word of God is sharper than any two-edged sword, but we may never strike with it." Since David Martin was never challenged, he took the opinion that he must be right and the others wrong.

Separation from other fellowships was very rigid, to the point where the David Martins would not attend funeral services, weddings, or churches of other denominations. The following incident reveals their position. Mrs. Tilman Martin's funeral was held on February 15, 1931 in the home of her husband, who had been excommunicated previously and therefore was out of church fellowship. Tilman, now a member of the Old Order, wanted his wife to be buried beside him and therefore the burial would have to be at the Conestogo Old Order meetinghouse. Martin Frey, a David Martin preacher, was invited to conduct the normal service at the home, but was told by his bishop to stay away. Urias Martin had been asked to be present if the intended plan collapsed, and when Frey did not come Urias was asked to conduct the service. When Urias stood behind the table, three of Tilman's daughters and their husbands arose and went to another room. Urias conducted the service with six empty chairs belonging to immediate family members. These six people ate separately while the main service was held at the Conestogo meetinghouse. To voluntarily separate oneself from family members for the sake of conscience takes courage and, as in the above case, can be extremely difficult. Actions like those above set precedents for the group, which remained strong in the David Martin group. Each fellowship within the Old Order circles has some form of separation from those outside the fellowship. To exclude certain family members from being pallbearers because they are divorcees has at times not been understood, but lifestyles of others not acceptable by the fellowship are generally excluded from any form of worship. However, they still may be welcome to worship as a visitor. Most Old Order groups feel that to separate oneself from those outside the fellowship is different from shunning a person in the ban.

The ban will not be effective when there are no strong brotherhood bonds. The purpose of the ban is to remove or break a sinner from sinful life or thoughts. A person can live comfortably in sin, but when put in the ban, this comfort is removed. The sin becomes open before God and man. It is sin that bars one from the presence of God and also separates the sinner from a church that desires to be pure. The church must cast the sinner and his sin aside if she desires to be pure. It is the sinner's role, by God's grace, to put away the sin. The purpose of the ban is to convince or convict the sinner of his sin. If the ban is to be effective the sinner must (1) feel the *love* of the brotherhood, (2) sense the church's willingness to forgive as Christ forgives and (3) understand that it was the sin not himself, as a person, that the church condemned. Therefore, by cleansing himself from his sin, he can again be accepted into the fold. Beyond the confines of Gelassenheit and brotherhood, the principle of excommunication and shunning is seldom understood because the drawing effect of the love of the brotherhood is not understood. Some people view it as a means to whip a member back into line, not an act of love where the congregation weeps on the behalf of the one who sinned.

The David Martin People

Menno Shirk married one of old David B. Martin's daughters and Menno Hoover took one of Martin's granddaughters for his wife. They both decided to move from Rainham to Waterloo. They desired more fellowship for themselves and their young families, and Menno Hoover and his wife were accepted into the David Martin fellowship in November 1918. In August 1920, Menno Sherk was accepted into the fellowship while his wife waited until 1921 to join the group.

The Sherks and the Hoovers had difficult adjustments to make. In Rainham they associated with the Conference Mennonites and became familiar with the pre-millennial doctrine which dominated the Conference theology at that time. Neither were they accustomed to the David Martin group's rigid administration. The David Martin records indicate that membership was a very personal matter. Frequently, the husband and wife were dealt with separately. If the wife did not shun her expelled husband then she would also be put out because she stood by her husband. Although one may not agree with this approach, it must be remembered that it is the David Martin interpretation of shunning which is similar to that of the Old Order Amish. (The Amish interpretation of the ban reflects their emphasis on the Dortrecht Confession, while the Mennonites hold a more mild interpretation, as did the Swiss Brethren.) The David Martin interpretation of the ban is their voluntary commitment to being submissive and obedient to their brotherhood.

This young church was not without troubles. On May 4, 1924, Bishop Enoch Horst and Minister Amos Bearinger were excommunicated on the interpretation of the ban. Amos returned to the Old Orders while Enoch moved with his family to Mornington Township where they lived and worshipped alone. David Martin was appointed bishop by church council on August 17, 1925. The group was struggling to maintain its numbers eight years after its beginning. There had been sixty-five members who joined the fellowship during the first years, but by 1925 thirty-nine had withdrawn (Brubacher group included) or were excommunicated, and nine had died. During these years thirty-eight were baptized and received into the fellowship, which brought the total membership to fifty-five. On October 12, 1930, Deacon Franklin Housser, originally from Cayuga, joined the fellowship and remained a member until his death on February 18, 1933.

The present-day rigid isolation of the David Martin group developed over the years. During the thirties both Menno Hoover and Menno Sherk visited their former friends and relatives in Rainham. It took them two days to drive to Rainham in a horse and buggy. In the fall of 1946, preacher Paul Shank from Virginia was accepted into the fellowship along with six members. This was unique because Shank's members were totally English and had the telephone, while the David Martin group at that time held German worship services and had no telephone. There were too many differences, so the two groups parted ways.

In October 1951, Robert Lahman was baptized in Virginia and later moved to Waterloo and married Mary Martin. Until about 1970 the David Martins had many English sermons from the English-speaking Robert Lahman. They then feared that they might become completely English and overreacted. There were no more English services for Lahman. Over the years he became an outcast, although some of his family remained within the group. In 1952 the David Martin group accepted and baptized another outsider, Esther Schlueter of Lutheran background. Her home life left much to be desired, so as a teenager she left her family and made her home with the David Martin people. She married Jacob Martin, a grandson of David B. Martin.

The membership grew slowly, so that by 1942 there were fifty-six married members and thirty-three youth, of whom sixteen were baptized. The group was also blessed with ninety-two children. In 1945 the centre Wellesley meetinghouse was built at 4401 Ament Line. By 1952 the David Martin group consisted of forty-four married couples, one widow, and 183 youth and children. Bishop Enoch Horst and then Bishop David W. Martin married a total of fifty-two couples in a space of about thirty-five years, but disunity was brewing.

In October 1952, Menno Hoover and Isaac Bauman were put in the ban. In January 1954, three more families were excommunicated. Two years later, on March 11, Minister Elam Martin was expelled for the second time over the interpretation of the ban. On December 23, 1956, David Martin expelled his son-in-law, Deacon Samuel Horst. On the Sunday following the above excommunications, Bishop David W. Martin stated in the Wallenstein meetinghouse that from this time forward there would be no more religious discussions with outside people: "We have lost too many people," he told the congregation that day.[11] Up to that time David W. Martin had been a little more receptive to other people, but they then chose to completely isolate themselves from other religious denominations.

During the thirties yet another wave of revivalism swept through the community when the Plymouth Brethren's revival meetings caused confusion among the Old Orders. This movement had accepted dispensationalism and placed a very strong emphasis on the new birth and the doctrine of eternal security. The positive and aggressive air of this movement clashed with the Old Order humility ethos. As a result, the David Martins minimized the idea that Jesus washed away our sins and stressed that it is only by the grace of God that we face His judgement.[12] The above view, and David Martin's autocratic position on the bishop's office and the ban, created confusion. A major rift in the David Martin group occurred in 1957. Minister Elam Martin organized a new group under the name of the "Orthodox Mennonites," then commonly known as the Elam Martin church.

The David Martin group continued to spread west into Wellesley Township beyond Crosshill. In 1987 the David Martins built a meetinghouse at 5161 William Hastings Line a little west of Crosshill. Towards the end of the twentieth century the David Martins were faced with the challenge of obtaining enough farms for their people. In March 1999 they began purchasing farms in the Maxwell-Badjeros area, and by December 2000 the settlement consisted of thirteen families. A year later they controlled about ten thousand acres in the area.[13] A meetinghouse was built at 633492 Sideroad 60 and Minister Edwin Martin and Deacon Noah Frey serve this new community. Since the David Martins have always attended the public schools they have no parochial schools.

The David Martins were ultra-conservative during the early years, but their outlook towards economics changed over time. By 1979, they, as a group, unanimously accepted the telephone. This left Bell Canada scrambling to satisfy all of its new customers living on side roads. Also surprising is their acceptance and use of electronic technology in their numerous shops. The use of the computer, fax machines and other on-line services has kept their shops abreast of industry as a whole. By the end of the twentieth century the David Martin community consisted of about 350 households. The community had 145 shops which average about five thousand square feet. These shops are large enough to warrant a separate shop telephone line, even though the shops are built in close proximity to the residences. Close to thirty per cent have smaller shops that are served by residential telephone lines. None of these shops use electricity from the public utilities. Diesel-electric generator units power all these shops with some of the larger shops sporting eight hundred horsepower units. Moreover, none of these shops own or operate trucks or any licensed motor vehicles. They rely on truckers who specialize in hauling for the David Martins, and other rapid delivery services, for their transportation needs.

In the early 1980s the David Martin group used only public transportation, such as buses, trains and taxis, if they wanted to travel beyond the range of horse-drawn vehicles. This would also change so that by 1990 they did not hesitate to ask their neighbours, or other people who make it a business, to drive people to the doctor, hospital, or shopping in the city. In this regard they are more comparable to the Old Orders who also hire private individuals to provide transportation for them. With the Maxwell settlement came the hiring of chartered buses for social purposes. Hiring a chartered bus for taking men to demolition jobs or barn raisings had been common for some years.

The David Martin agricultural community also began to adopt modern sealed silos and silo-unloaders. Farm tractors, however, are not allowed. They only use stationary belt-drive diesel engines for their threshing, silo filling and chopping needs. By the late 1960s they began to make deals with their neighbours to cut their grass and bale their hay. The neighbour with the tractor and baler generally has his hay piled into his barn by the David Martin people if he custom-bales their hay. By the year 2001 they also began to dabble with large bales which are handled by forklifts. When it comes to harvesting grains and corn silage they have resisted modern machinery. The binder and thrashing machines are still used for harvesting and the corn binder and cutting box to fill their silos.

The David Martin homes have a unique pattern. The living quarters are very plain, but tidy, with distinctive colours of blue, green and purple everywhere. They have no electric lights in their living quarters, but do in the laundry. Freezers, refrigerators and propane stoves are typical household appliances.

The David Martin people are very reserved and will not communicate with others about their personal and church life, but in business they are open. Nevertheless, they have an excellent business reputation. With them a deal is a deal, and very rarely will they cancel a deal. There are very few bad accounts within the group and they effectively help one another. No other Mennonite group is so uniform in dress, colour and structure of buildings; even their flowerbeds are similar. A local store once sold two bolts of tablecloth in one day to the David Martin women. As the news of this pretty tablecloth spread through the community, the telephone orders came in by those who had not even so much as seen it, but true to David Martin ethics those orders were firm.

A close observation of the David Martin people suggests that after the division in 1957 the more conservative element followed Elam Martin. Before the division the David Martin people had led quite simple lives on their farms. Ten years later the old hayloader was on its way out, while the Elam Martin people continue to use the hayloader until the present. The acceptance of the telephone in 1979, along with computers and other electronic equipment, suggests that the earlier simplistic lifestyles were giving way to a far more business-oriented community of the twenty-first century. In 2002 a local machinery dealer was elated because he had found a new market for skid-steer loaders. He had just sold his first skid-steer to a David Martin farmer.

A Personal Experience

The Mennonite community was drawn together in 1984 in a very different way. An arsonist was wreaking havoc in the Mennonite community around the Conestogo area. A total of seven large barns went up in flames within the space of one year, although two fires were not the work of the arsonist. The whole community shared the burden and anxiety, not just the Mennonites, as the police sought to arrest the arsonist. As a result, the David Martin group also came and helped on several occasions to reconstruct some of these barns.

The following year the David Martin people lost one of their barns due to a lightening strike. The author and his neighbour decided to return the much-appreciated favour and went to help the David Martins build their barn. People from outside the immediate community seldom, if ever, arrive at such David Martin sites; therefore, knowing the dynamics of the group, we were not chilled by the cool reception we received. There was no direct communication for some time as we continued to labour with the David

Martins. After they had sorted out who the outsiders were, they cautiously received us and then invited us to come along for dinner. Because I had driven, I was asked to do some errands and deliveries in the afternoon. Although they were very reserved until they understood our mission, the author felt they appreciated the fact that we were willing to share of our time during their loss. There was nothing amiss in their order during the noon meal, but the coordination and the systematic manner by which they conducted their labours caught my attention.

The Orthodox Mennonites[14]

Beginning in 1953 there was considerable unrest within the David Martin group which resulted in numerous excommunications. Minister Elam Martin was put in the ban in March 1954, but was later reinstated. Two years later he was again put in the ban because of his interpretation of Matthew chapter 18. The excommunicated Minister Elam Martin was cautious. He contacted John Dan Wenger, a radical Old Order bishop from Virginia, but there were no further interactions because Wenger demanded re-baptism of all the David Martin people. Elam Martin also had a lengthy discussion with preacher Ervin Shantz about Matthew chapter 18. Shantz agreed with Martin's views.[15] Martin also once attended an Old Order service, but the rest of those expelled from the David Martin fellowship encouraged him to hold services on his own. On New Years Day, 1957, Elam Martin and his small following met in the home of Anson Hoover for the first time.

Evidently there had been contacts with Peter Nolt of Lancaster County, an Old Order renegade minister, because on February 24, 1957, Peter Nolt preached for Elam's group. The Nolts were in fellowship with Elam's group until the fall of 1959 when it became evident that the Nolts were not prepared for Elam's ultra-plainness, and they separated. Several Mexican-Mennonite families also worshiped with Elam's group in 1957. The Mexican-Mennonite families are frequently on the move with some coming and others leaving. In 2003 there are Mexican Mennonites fellowshipping with this group.

During the winter of 1958, Elam's group and Deacon Samuel Horst's group, united as one fellowship and held their first communion on April 6, 1958, with about forty communing members besides the children.

(Horst had been excommunicated on December 23, 1956.) The Samuel Horst group had kept to themselves for eight months, envisioning reconciliation with the David Martin church, but when it became evident that it was not possible, they joined with Elam's group. Then in 1967, Minister Noah Brubacher, with a small following, united with the Elam Martin Mennonites. (2)

(2) *Noah Brubacher had left the Old Orders during the late 1950s with three other families and associated with John Dan Wenger of Virginia. He later fellowshipped with the "35ers," a nicknamed group in Pennsylvania. Noah Brubacher had been ordained by John Dan Wenger and served these three families in Waterloo. This group was concerned about the drift and laxness of the Old Order Mennonites during the 1950s. Furthermore they were convinced that Christ's return was imminent and had little concern about their children's social life. As years went by they realized their children needed fellowship and they associated themselves with the Elam Martin group.*

A meetinghouse was built in 1962 on the Lawson Line and Moser-Young Road corner in Wellesley Township. The dedication service was held on June 24, 1962, with Romans 12 taken as the text. The question of the group's name arose with the new meetinghouse. Since the Old Order were registered as the Old Order Mennonites, the Elam Martin group agreed upon calling themselves the Orthodox Mennonites. On the night of Friday, May 14, 1971, the meetinghouse burned down. It had been vandalized the previous week and was repaired and ready for service. A new building was speedily erected so that six weeks later, on June 20, the second meetinghouse was dedicated. Mark 12 was the text chosen for that occasion.

For a number of years there was peace, but in the winter of 1974 there was major unrest. The beard seemed to be the issue, but the matter of bed-courtship had also been a disputed issue, even though the youth had abandoned this practice. (3) The fact that Elam began to accept the David Martin group's interpretation of the ban ultimately resulted in a division between Anson Hoover and Elam Martin in March 1974. The Elam Martin group had forty-five members and sixty-two children while the Hoover faction had sixty members and 107 children. Beginning in 1979 the Elam Martin group began to relocate in Howick Township (Gorrie).

In the Waterloo Old Order district the telephone and the use of farm tractors were issues gathering steam during the 1980s. The conservative wing of the Old Orders became very uncomfortable with these new innovations and when it became clear that the use of the telephone and tractors in barns would be allowed, several families moved to the Gorrie area and later others moved into the Kinloss area and sought fellowship with the Orthodox Mennonites. This transplanting of the ultra-conservatives from the Old Order to the Orthodox continued, so that by the year 2001 thirty-seven families had made the transition. The result of this transition is that their genetic pool has greatly enlarged and there have been no first-cousin marriages since the 1960s, which are common in the other ultra-conservative groups. The genetic pool has shifted, for thirty per cent of the members have one-hundred per cent Old Order background while only nine per cent of the original members are one-hundred per cent David Martin heredity. As a result of this move the Orthodox Mennonites are more of an Old Order splinter group than a part of a David Martin division.[17]

The Orthodox Mennonite Church has three meetinghouses: North Howick, built in 1986 and located at 44189 Glenannon Rd. Huron County; Wroxeter, built in 1995 and located at 42680 Orange Hill Rd. Huron County; and Kinloss, built in 2000 and located on Hayes Lake Ave. Kinloss Township, Bruce County. The church also fellowships with two small groups in Snyder Co., Pennsylvania and Trigg Co., Kentucky.

(3) *The Mennonites have often been associated with the shady practice of bundling. The Elam Martin group recognized the practice as evil and worked to eradicate the problem. One should never justify the practice of bundling, but neither have we a right to pass judgment on our forbears. (This practice was common throughout society; it was not just the Mennonites.) Vera and Olive Schweitzer remark that "When a young man came a courting in pioneer days, a cabin full of family members did not afford much privacy, so a young couple would simply be put to bed fully clothed. The time permitted for courting would depend on the patience of the family."[16] Furthermore, the old houses became quite chilly during a cold winter night when the lonely cook-stove's attempts to heat the house failed. It became very tempting for a girl to invite her friend to the warmth of the bed. In the 1920s it was still common for a boy to see his girlfriend only once in four weeks. The boys in those days were shyer and more reserved in the presence of a girl's family. No doubt bundling was a questionable practice in pioneer days, but the present frequent dating practices makes bundling an unacceptable practice as premarital sex is believed to be sin.*

In 2001 there were approximately 120 families within the Orthodox circles in Ontario. They have six parochial schools with a total attendance of 180 students in Ontario. The American groups each have a school with approximately twenty students each.[18]

Simplicity, frugality, and brotherhood describe the Orthodox Mennonite community. They have largely resisted shifting the centre of faith from obedience to Christ to the experience of salvation. When one walks into their community it is like a rural community of the early twentieth century. One will find no electricity, telephone or any modern electronic devices. Their farms are worked exclusively by horses and manual labour and when they go to the bush to cut wood for their kitchen wood stove and heating purposes, they are content to use the crosscut saw, wedges and sledge. Stationary diesel engines are used for threshing grain, silo filling, and running the shops. They do not run electric generators, but use line shafts and belts and pulleys to run their shops, and neither do they use air compressors or hydraulics, but rely on mechanical devices to operate their shop equipment. However, they are not devoid of ingenuity. The need to load skids of merchandise onto highway trucks led to the invention of horse-drawn forklifts. Furthermore, the Orthodox Mennonites still avoid hiring private transportation except for emergencies. Their worship services follow the traditional Old Order Mennonite pattern. However, they will preach in English for an English audience and routinely hold English services once every four weeks.[19]

These people desire to live quiet and simple lives. They certainly do not consider themselves deprived of any good thing. Even though they do not have such luxuries as flush toilets in their homes, they do have water piped into the house and a comfortable place to live. An explorer in Antarctica whose ship had not been able to pick him up in the fall captured these thoughts in 1912, "The luxuries of civilization only fulfil the wants they require." He had been holed up in an ice hut for the long Antarctic winter and had not been able to shower or bathe for over half a year. The Old Order Mennonites all understand that contentment does not come from the accumulation of earthly things, but as the departed Minister Urias Martin used to say, "Die unzufriddaheit fühdra macht nett satt" (feeding discontentment will never satisfy). The words of the apostle Paul, "that godliness with contentment is great gain" (1 Timothy 6:6), are frequently spoken during their worship services.

The Hoover Group

Anson Hoover was alone with his following after the split in March 1974. A need for ministerial help prompted two ordinations. Anson's brother Tilman was ordained deacon by lot on October 15, 1974, and on April 29, 1975, Amos Sherk was ordained minister for the Hoover fellowship. The Hoover group was short-lived. In 1976, Anson Hoover was excommunicated for reasons not clear to those outside the group. It was suggested that the excommunication was the result of there being too many changes and there being members who supported the traditional practice of bundling, which Hoover did not. Evidence suggests that Hoover was not used fairly—the point in question was confirmed in a letter eighteen years later and the Orthodox Mennonites loosed Hoover from the ban. By then Anson Hoover had abandoned the Orthodox Mennonites and associated with the Conservative Mennonites.

After Hoover was banned, Amos Sherk was advanced as bishop by church council on October 3, 1976. The two factions of the Orthodox Mennonite Church then worshipped separately in peace. The Elam Martin group had some unrest and did not hold communion in 1979. In May 1984 Minister Edward Martin returned to his former Old Order community and was excommunicated by the Orthodox. (He was later released from the ban by the Orthodox Mennonites but not accepted as a member.) In 1986 the Hoover group experienced disunity, and they excommunicated their bishop, Amos Sherk. The deacon released Sherk from the ban and this triggered disintegration, which would in the end annihilate the Hoover group. It came about suddenly and there was no clear reason why this turmoil occurred, but the end result was that about seventy members switched their membership back to the David Martin church during the following year.[20] Deacon Tilman Hoover then elected to join the David Martin church and was in 1987 accepted as deacon by the David Martin group.

Those of the Hoover group who united with the David Martins were required to set aside all practices and customs where they had differed from the David Martin church. They were to return to the David Martin fellowship "empty" of their previous Ordnung. The Elam Martin and Hoover groups were strong supporters of the Canada Pension Plan exemption, but when the above group returned to the David Martin fellowship, they were required to cancel their exemption because the David Martin group never took interest in obtaining Canada Pension Exemption.[21] The Hoovers and Elam Martin fellowships had their own parochial schools, but the David Martin children always attended the public schools. As a result, the former Orthodox Schools, Red Hill and Beachville Parochial, were then operated by the Old Orders. There were some definite changes for these estranged Hoovers, but the news drifted across the community that those who returned felt they had lost thirty years of their lives by leaving the David Martins.

The remainder of the Hoover group, except for a few families, united with the Elam Martin (Orthodox) church. On April 26, 1987, the reunited Orthodox Mennonite Church held communion services. Twenty-nine married couples and twenty youths participated in this solemn joyous occasion. These former Hoover members also relocated in Howick Township.

Hoover's co-worker, Amos Sherk, questioned Charlotte Martin's opinion that Hoover was excommunicated because he "preached the gospel too freely, that is, preaching about salvation by faith alone rather than works."[22] Even Hoover himself disagreed with Charlotte; he thought it was the bundling question that led to his excommunitcation. One may ask if Charlotte's perception is the common misunderstanding of Old Order values. Is this not the subtle variation between Pietism and Anabaptism?

It is the author's belief that faith and works generate more tension within the Protestant churches than within the plain groups, where faith and works are considered mutual partners. Tension results when faith and works are separated, because how do works blend with salvation by faith alone? "Even so faith, if it hath not works, is dead, being alone" (James 2:17). In the plain churches the two virtues are intermingled with a strong emphasis on being "good stewards of the manifold grace of God" (1 Peter 4:10). Their concept of a faithful stewardship to God and the church—Gelassenheit—motivates the work ethic; furthermore, faith is the foundation of their simplistic way of life. They have more confidence in the brotherhood's Ordnung than in theology and higher education, which they reject as human reasoning and a hindrance to their faith. Gelassenheit and Ordnung, the key pulses that drive the Old Order community, are both saturated with faith and works. It is not works that destroy the Old Order community; destruction comes when personal values are placed above those of the group and power politics come into play.

The "New" Elam Martin Group

A few families remained in the Waterloo area from the scattered Hoover group. These laid claim to the otherwise abandoned meetinghouse on Moser-Young Road. On January 17,1993, the group chose Elam Martin, son-in-law of Bishop Elam Martin of the Orthodox group, as their minister. Elam Martin performed four marriages in this closely related group and ordained his son Alvin as a minister. Three of these marriages were first cousins. In the year 2001 they had six married couples, two widows and three homes with unmarried siblings. In the spring of 2002 Elam excommunicated his son Alvin on differences in interpretation of how church order should be held. Then in November of 2002, Elam died and the group was left without an official leader.

The "original" Elam Martin group owned the Beechvale Parochial School. When the original group dispersed they rented the school property to the Old Order Mennonites for ten dollars a year, with the understanding that the property be maintained in its former condition. The "New" Elam Martin group send their children to the Beechvale School for a tuition fee. The "New" Elam Martin group and the Orthodox Mennonites are open to discussion concerning their faith in God and welcome a visitor at their worship services. However, they will not attend a service outside of their group. This custom is also shared by David Martin and Orthodox Mennonites and may well be the only custom that all three ultra-conservatives share.

Notes

[1] Elizabeth Rudy, "History of the Brubacher Church" (Author's collection, N.p, 1958), 1.

[2] Amos B. Hoover, *The Jonas Martin Era* (Denver, PA: Muddy Creek Library, 1982), 384.

[3] Rudy, "History," 1.

[4] Private Conversation.

[5] Private Conversation.

[6] Private Conversation.

[7] See Glossary regarding "ban."

[8] Private Conversation.

[9] Private Conversation.

[10] Private Conversation.

[11] Private Conversation.

[12] Anson Hoover, Conversation with Author, 1998.

[13] Private Conversation.

[14] Based on the Orthodox Mennonite Church records by Amos Sherk at Conrad Grebel University College, and on the Anson Hoover church records of 1917-1918, Author's collection.

[15] Ervin Shantz, Conversation with Author.

[16] Vera and Olive Schweitzer, *Canadian-German Folklore* 5 (1975), 31.

[17] Sherk, Amos. Letter to Author, 2000.

[18] *Orthodox Mennonite Church Directory*. Third Edition, 2001. 43067 Howich-Turnberry Rd. ON. N0G 2X0.

[19] Amos Sherk, Letter to Author, 2000.

[20] Private Conversation.

[21] Private Conversation.

[22] Charlotte Martin, "My Relatives, Ultra-Conservative Mennonites," *Ontario Mennonite History.* XVI (1998): 6.

Liberty Threatened

Chapter Thirteen

The Old Order Community and Theology before World War I

Nestled on their quiet farms, the Old Order Mennonites were only partially sheltered from the rapidly changing times across the countryside. In 1898 there was no small stir when the first car rolled into Berlin from Toronto with a top speed of fourteen miles per hour, but to the Old Order such an invention surely would have been something out of this world. Even though the telephone arrived at St. Jacobs in 1887, it would not affect them for another forty years. However, the arrival of hydro in St Jacobs in 1917 would stir the Old Order community within twenty years. When the milldam at St Jacobs washed out in 1905, we can be sure that it caught the attention of the Old Order people, as did the train wreck in 1902 about one mile south of the present-day stockyards. The erection of the German Emperor's monument at Berlin's Victoria Park in 1897 would have been shrugged off as *Hochmut* (Pride). The Children of Zion's 1890 prediction about the world's end, or the evil conditions of the world, disturbed the Markham community to the point that some of the older members discouraged the young people from marrying because they thought the end of the world was at hand. The Old Orders' immediate reactions to the above events are unknown, but they certainly did not escape the effects of the pulses that drove their community.

Theological matters also affected the Old Order community. A generation would pass away before the effects of Darbyism and its beliefs of dispensationalism and premillenialism, as advocated by Cyrus I. Scofield at the 1893 Chicago Exposition, would trouble the Old Order people. (1) This theological system made inroads into the Conference Mennonite Church during the 1920s and even more so during the 1930s. So strong was the movement that the Mennonite Conference of Ontario in 1940 took the "liberty to request Goshen Mennonite College and the Mennonite Publishing House not to neglect the pre-millennial view of prophecy."[1]

(1) *John N. Darby (1800-1882) was the founder of the dispensational system of eschatology. One of the basic tenets of the teaching is that God deals differently with mankind during the various eras (dispensations) of time. Time is divided into seven different dispensations: innocence—before the fall of man, conscience—from the fall to Noah, human government—from Noah to Abraham, promise—from Abraham to Moses, law—from Moses to Christ, grace—the church age, and the kingdom—the millennium. This scheme is based on an overly literal interpretation of the Old Testament teaching that Jesus' message was that of an earthly Jewish kingdom, which the Jews did not accept. Since the kingdom was rejected by Israel, its establishment was postponed and the church age instituted as an expedient. Another consequence of this line of thought is that the Sermon on the Mount and the ethical teachings of Jesus are kingdom truths and don't apply directly to the church age, but are applicable during the millennium reign.*

Dispensationalists believe that the present era closes with the pre-tribulation rapture of the saints to Christ. With the church gone, Satan will sorely oppress Israel and the nations of the world for seven years. Christ will then return with the church and set the stage for a reign of peace for a thousand years—the Millennium. After the millennium age Satan will again attempt to revolt against God but will be destroyed and cast into the lake of fire while the saints will find their eternal home with Christ.

The weakness of this inspiration is that it fails to see that God's ways with the human family have always been the same—that is salvation has always been by grace through faith in God's promises. Those of the Old Testament times accepted God's promises by faith while those of the New Testament era by faith accept the immaculate sacrifice of Christ. It is only by the grace of God that the Jew or Gentile can be saved.

A notable Mennonite evangelist, John Coffman, was impressed by Dwight L. Moody and Scofield's interpretation of the book of Revelation and wrote in his diary in 1893, "a better line of thought than I ever had of that book."[2] At an early date, Darby's new doctrines filtered into the Conference Mennonite community. The "quickening" Conference Mennonites of this era also developed their own form of theology, in which they began to emphasize redemption and conversion calling it "the plan of salvation" and referred to matters such as non-resistance and nonconformity in a rather negative-sounding tone as "restrictions." These thoughts were further extended in Daniel Kauffman's writings that "tended to freeze the separation (of non-resistance and nonconformity) into 'Old' Mennonite theology."[3] To the unlearned Old Order, "theology" meant little, and they wondered why there was a "plan of salvation." They believed the Lord required that they "do justly, and to love mercy, and to walk humbly with their God" (Micah 6:8).

James Juhnke has noted that at the close of the nineteenth century

> all Mennonites in 'North' America and the Old Order groups in particular faced a special problem in adapting their religious understandings and rituals to the transition from persecution to toleration. . . . But in the transition, what assurance was there that the powerful forces of *American individualism* would not overwhelm and destroy a central Anabaptist-Mennonite commitment—commitment to the church as a community of believers responsible to each other and to God?[4]

Through organization and education the Conference Mennonites sought to shore up their defences and under the leadership of John Funk and Daniel Kauffman, as editors of their church publications, a great degree of stability was established.[5] One of the greatest ironies in Old Order history is that the principle of regulating dress and association with the world was borrowed from the American culture itself.[6]

Plain and simple attire has long been a Mennonite tradition, but distinctive dress codes and regulations have not. Although the Conference Mennonites began this trend about 1890 and continued it for half a century, the Old Order stressed simplicity and humility. Moderate use of alcohol and tobacco were Old Order customs long after the Conference Mennonites decreed such things vices. When the war broke out and the problems arose over military exemptions, the Old Order Mennonites looked to the Conference Mennonites for guidance since they lacked the organization and will to challenge the government. The evidence suggests that the Old Order community in Ontario struggled long with the transition from being a suffering, persecuted people to being a tolerated community, or even a prosperous community who strove to maintain their faith and practice.

The Local Community and the War

Waterloo County was German from its beginnings. The German-speaking Mennonites were the foundation of the community. After the Napoleonic war had left Europe in shambles, thousands of Germans migrated to America. Many of these were attracted to the German-speaking community along the Grand River valley where a strong German culture developed. The Governor General of Canada addressed the citizens of Berlin on May 9, 1914:

> It is of great interest to me that many of the citizens of Berlin are of German descent. I well know the admirable qualities—the thoroughness, the tenacity, and the loyalty—of the great Teutonic Race, to which I am so closely related, and am sure that these inherited qualities will go far in the making of good Canadians and loyal citizens of the British Empire.[7]

The Germans were proud of being German and well respected until August 4, 1914, when Britain declared war on Germany.

Three weeks later jingoism made its first attack when some unknown persons threw the bust of the German Emperor into the lake in Victoria Park, Berlin. This deed caused a general indignation throughout the city, but wartime passions also hounded others. Dr. H. A. Sperling, a German pastor of St Peter's Lutheran church, was slandered and accused of sending money via the United States to Germany. For reasons unknown he was never convicted or vindicated, yet he served as pastor at the church until 1940. Rev. C. R. Tappert, an American German who was pastor of St. Matthew's Lutheran congregation, failed to reckon the tenor of the times. In a public letter he stated, "I am not ashamed to confess that I love the land of my fathers—Germany. Yes I love her!"[8] The passions of the English people flared, and one night a gang of soldiers routed Tappert out of his bed, assaulted him, and made him march through the streets of Berlin. This brought about his resignation from St. Matthew's church and his return to the United States. Two soldiers were convicted of assault but were only given suspended sentences.

Tensions were high. People receiving any German publications were suspected, but we must also remember that only a few years before, eighty per cent of the students at the Berlin Public Schools participated in German classes. In March 1915, all German instruction was discontinued in the Berlin schools; furthermore, the "Made in Berlin" labels only furthered the wartime turmoil. On May 19, 1916 only eighty-one out of 3,057 votes were in favour of keeping the city name of Berlin. There was little public interest when a vote was taken and Kitchener (named after a British army general) was chosen as a name to replace the former proud name of Berlin.

On August 13, 1917, an unusually contentious law was passed—the Military Service Act, or the conscription law. This law almost divided the nation since the French were completely against it. The December 17, 1917, election was contested on the conscription issue and the Waterloo North riding witnessed one of the must controversial elections in history. W. D. Euler, the Liberal candidate, was against conscription because in his mind it opposed the principles of democracy. He was pitted against W. G. Weichel, the Union candidate, who was the Conservative Member of Parliament. As the heated campaign continued, disunity increased. Former friends began to disagree as the debate became more intense. Euler, the ex-mayor of Kitchener, accused Weichel of not representing the will of his people. Both candidates rallied the populace at well-attended meetings where they were booed and cheered, but on November 14 when Prime Minister Borden arose to speak to a crowd of six thousand people, he was disgraced. When Dr. Honsberger rose to address the people he was confronted with shouts and jeers and told to sit down. The people shouted, "We'll listen to Euler." Mayor Gross tried to calm the agitated audience, but failed. When Prime Minister Borden stood to speak, the people shouted, "Sit down Borden" and "We want Laurier." This uproar caught the attention of the Canadian press. Kitchener was accused of acting in true German fashion, which meant being disloyal to Canada. Public pressure forced the council to apologize to Borden for the mêlée, but when the votes were counted on December 17, Euler won by the largest majority in Waterloo North's history.[9] Where did the Mennonites stand during such a tumult? The Mennonites had been disenfranchised and to vote would have effectively eliminated their military exemption.

Unprepared for War

Except for the War of 1812-14, when about twenty Mennonites were pressed into service as teamsters, the Mennonites in Ontario had enjoyed religious liberty during the nineteenth century. In November 1813 the battle by the Thames River was lost for the British and they told the Mennonites, "To make their Escape from the enemy as well as they could."[10] It is evident from the list of claims that the men unhitched their horses from their wagons and fled, leaving the wagons and equipment as enemy spoil. The Mennonites claimed losses to the government for 1250£, or the equivalent of over ten percent of what they paid for Waterloo Township. We should remember that in 1759, the Mennonites offered such services to General Braddock; however, by 1914 the Mennonites also took a stand against non-combatant service.[11] This position was by and large granted to them but not without difficulties.

World War I was a very challenging time for the Old Order Mennonites. The confusion and disunity of the "ditch" incident (see chapter eleven) remained in everyone's memories, and these recollections were rubbed sore by the David Martin division in the spring of 1917. Popular opinion said the division focused on the ban, which is valid, but there were other issues that also reflected on the Old Order community. Why did the Old Order nickname the David Martin people "New Borns"? Were old David B. Martin and Daniel Brubacher out of order to suggest that the church should have compensated Mr. Lachner for his portion of the "ditch"? Several generations later it is fair to suggest that most Old Orders would agree with Martin and Brubacher that leaving Mr. Lachner offended was an error, yet that is how the issue ended.

Table One
Old Order Baptismal Records

Year	**Boys**	**Girls**
1911	12	11
1912	12	15
1913	20	17
1914	16	16
1915	21	16
1916	18	22
1917	20	12
1918	**84**	**27**
1919	3	11
1920	6	9
1921	13	25

To state that the Old Order community was indifferent is too strong, because many in the Old Order brotherhood were sincere in their faith. However, one cannot deny that the Old Order community had difficulties finding its place as a separate people during the first half of the twentieth century.

These issues became apparent in several ways. During the patriotic fervour of the War, several Old Order Mennonite couples took a pleasure trip to the Elora Gorge. This incident may well have been forgotten had they not taken portraits of themselves, which was against their minister's convictions. Moreover, in light of the military-service issues, such frivolous behaviour in public reflected a misunderstanding by the Old Order people of the urgency of the times. The group included a young man in his mid-twenties whose conscience had not yet led him to be a member of the church. Evidently he had many friends who were also apathetic to their personal faith in God. In the exceptionally large baptismal class of 1918 (see table 1) we find that about half of the converts were twenty years old and older, and over one-quarter of these were twenty-two years old and older. This "clean up" class occurred when the war was in its fourth year and after the conscription law was placing the Mennonites under a lot of pressure. It aroused the attention of the military officials in the local London barracks who sent out an officer to investigate the sincerity and integrity of the matter.

On the afternoon of Sunday, June 11, 1918, an investigating officer from the London district was present at the Elmira meetinghouse. He and Minister Urias Martin sat inside the men's door and watched the eighty-four boys file in the young boys' door and sit down at their appropriate places. The young men were called outside and lined up along the north wall of the meetinghouse. The officer then asked to see the boy's exemption or membership cards. After he had inspected about half a dozen cards, the officer was satisfied that there were no draft-dodgers present. He and Urias Martin went along with Noah Bearinger to his planning mill for further discussion. The problem lay in the interpretation of the Wartime Elections Act of August 13, 1917, which limited military exemption to those who were part of the Mennonite community on the sixth day of July 1917. The unusually large baptismal class of 1918 prompted the officials to make sure there were no boys from other denominations (prior to July 1917) amongst the Mennonite boys.

The baptismal records show there was little concern about the war until 1918. Table One indicates that the number of applicants was constant for the years previous to the war. (The 1914 applicants would have been received before war was declared.) The next three years had only a few persons more until matters became earnest in the spring of 1918, when farm exemptions were cancelled. The years after the war show the expected decline in numbers for several years.

The Mennonites and the Law During the War

The Mennonites had enjoyed complete military exemption in Canada, except for the event of 1813. After 1849, they were no longer compelled to pay militia fees or render service to the armed forces, provided their men could present certificates to the authorities proving that they were members of the Mennonite, Tunker, or Quaker churches. For over half a century the Mennonites of Ontario suffered no harassment or bother of any kind for their non-resistant faith. When the War Measures Act of 1914 was passed, it gave broad powers to the Government. There was a complete change in Canadian attitude towards the non-British immigrant population, which came to include the German-speaking Mennonites as the war continued. Except for a letter in 1915 to the Governor General stating the tenets of the Mennonite faith, the Mennonites of Ontario remained in the shadows.[12]

After the passing of the Military Service Act in August 1917, the Mennonites delivered another appeal to the Canadian government in October 1917. They again stated their gratitude for past exemptions and privileges and said:

> Since the passing of the 'War-times Elections Act,' we humbly seek to know the position of the government for all of our members relative to this Act, so that we may conduct ourselves accordingly; realizing that in matters of war we cannot conscientiously give our voice, and in respect to government we are to be submissive to its laws, excepting only the higher laws of the Gospel in all righteousness.[13]

In the spring of 1918 the German advances greatly alarmed the Allies. Germany had conducted V. I. Lenin, a Russian exile safely back to the politically unstable Russia from Switzerland. Lenin rose as leader of the Communist party and won the resulting bloody civil war. Early in 1918 the civil war forced Russia to sue for peace. Peace on the eastern front allowed Germany to concentrate all its might on Western Europe. Germany's advances shocked the Allies and the call for more conscripts

Forty-two Excepted for Leaves of Absence

The confusion over how to interpret the law became an annoyance to the officials and a concern to the Mennonites. In the Canadian West, after a test case, the Mennonites were "excepted" from military service, provided the young men could present written proof that they had been raised Mennonite and were part of the Mennonite community before July 2, 1917. They received a blanket exemption through the August 13, 1873 Order-in-Council's "Schedule of Exceptions." The Russian Mennonites had negotiated with the Canadian government before they immigrated to Manitoba that they were an exception as pertaining to military service.[15]

In Ontario the Mennonites were obliged to seek their military exemptions via other means, such as religious exemption or as farmers. When the farm exemptions were cancelled in the spring of 1918, the Ontario Mennonites were in a grave position because the tribunals seldom allowed religious exemptions. The most restrictive order-in-council was passed on October 25, 1918. It was then clear that the Ontario Mennonites were not covered by the 1873 "Schedule of Exceptions"' and neither were they eligible for exemptions under the act. It was only through manipulation of the local politicians that the Ontario Mennonites were granted exemptions by the way of leave of absence without pay.[16]

Even though the Ontario Mennonites had been in Canada almost a century before the Russian Mennonites arrived, the Ontario Mennonites had far more difficulty seeking exemption from military service than their brethren in the West; however, the Mennonites in the West encountered far more public animosity after the war than did their Eastern Brethren.

became urgent. The first call for conscripts in October 1917 revealed that ninety-five per cent of the eligible Canadians had claimed exemption. It became evident that those interested in the war effort had already volunteered, but with the adverse situation in Europe, the local tribunals were under heavy pressure to give the government the benefit of the doubt when they processed these exemptions.[14]

The situation became very serious for the non-resistant people. Early in November 1917 Bishop S. F. Coffman from Vineland received a letter from E. L. Newcombe, the deputy minister of Justice. The letter stated: "Under paragraph 7 of the Schedule of Exceptions to the above Act, Mennonites are excluded from the operation of the Act and have no duty to perform thereunder. . . . the matter has been thoroughly discussed by the Military Service Council and the opinion now is that if Mennonites should be prosecuted for non-compliance with the Act the answer to the prosecution would be that they are Mennonites and on proof of the fact, undoubtedly prosecution would be dismissed."[17] A letter of thanks to the Canadian government was carefully drafted by the Mennonites in November 1917, but was not sent. In the same month S.F. Coffman received a letter from J. L. Byler of Markham stating that he had asked a local tribunal official "what they would do with any Mennonite that they deemed was not necessary for the production of food." The official replied that they would likely be called for such duties as Army Transport work.[18]

Being conscripted for non-combatant service was real for the Ontario Mennonites, but not all officials interpreted the law the same. The London Ontario tribunals continued to hold that the Mennonites of Ontario were "excepted" from the Military Service Act while other tribunals viewed the Mennonites as needing to seek exemptions, which then forced the Mennonites to seek exemption through the tribunals. For this reason the Mennonites of Waterloo were by and large unscathed during the war, while in other areas of Ontario approximately 130 men were imprisoned.[19] The confusion over how the law should be interpreted haunted both the government officials and the Mennonites for the duration of the war.

S. F. Coffman, the primary spokesman for the Mennonites in Ontario, laboured persistently to keep the Mennonite men from military service, but he would learn that what he said in his home pulpit could reach official ears. Sir Percy Sherwood of Ottawa, the Chief Commissioner of the Dominion Police, wanted the following statements from a Sunday morning sermon clarified, "What good are the soldiers, they produce nothing, they earn nothing, they don't earn the clothes they wear, they do nothing but destroy. If any of you are producing food to help win the war, don't do it. If you are producing food to feed the needy, alright go on."[20] The bishop testified that he was only encouraging his people to remain steadfast in the non-resistant faith and had no intentions to slander the government or the soldiers. He was personally excused. Adhering to the non-resistant faith is never popular, but such bold statements must be spoken with care and may come at a cost.

On April 19, 1918, the Manpower Bill cancelled all exemptions for those in class one (ages nineteen to thirty-four) and stipulated immediate call-up for the unmarried men from nineteen to twenty-three. This had a serious impact on the Canadian farmers and others in need of workers. The tribunals were bypassed because "time does not permit of examination by exemption tribunals of the value of civil life."[21] This turn of events troubled the non-resistant people. Those cherished exemption laws could be changed.

Local members of Parliament, J. A. Calder, F. S. Scott, W. D. Euler and E. L. Newcombe, were supportive of the Mennonite and Tunker's non-resistant beliefs. They persuaded the military authorities that the Mennonites "would be of little use to them under any circumstance holding the belief which they did and that it was better to leave them at their present occupations, if it could be done."[22] Although this sentiment was not flattering to the Mennonites, Mr. Scott captured the predominant opinion of the MP's view: "It is however bringing about the object which you desire and my own judgment is that the less said about it the better."[23] Exemption was the key issue, and whether it was gained at the cost of reputation was of little importance.

In May 1918, the government requested that a list of the names of the bishops, and others with signing authority, be sent to Ottawa. Each Mennonite who was eligible for military service was given a certificate of membership by his bishop that was to be used in claiming exemption via "leave of absence" without pay. Under this gentleman's agreement the Mennonites were allowed to apply for exemption from service, but the officials in Ontario understood when the Mennonites reported to the military headquarters that "they were granted exemption which was understood to be 'from combatant service' and were given a 'leave of absence without pay for the duration of the war.'"[24] This final arrangement was the work of several local parliamentarians and military authorities and reveals the flexibility of the authorities. By law the Mennonites in Ontario at this time had no legal exemption.

The uncertainty of the Mennonite exemption remained. On July 5, 1918, C. Lesslie Wilson, Ontario Registrar, informed L. J. Burkholder that the Mennonites were not "excepted" from the Military Service Act and that all persons needed to register. The letter continued to challenge Burkholder on the lines of his faith, citing even historical events when the Mennonites were active in non-combatant service. The last paragraph of this letter stated:

> In view of what has been passed between us, I venture to again call your attention to the advisability of the members of your community holding a conference with a view to seeing whether you cannot see your way to make a compromise on the subject of non-combatant service with Hospital Corps or other non-combatant units. With the example of your brethren during the Napoleonic Wars and during the American Civil War, it seems to me that you should find some better use for your young men than having them sent to prison.[25]

It is interesting to note that Mr. Wilson was evidently not aware that the Mennonites had been pressed into military transport in 1813, and that in 1756 they had helped the British in army transport. Neither would he have understood why Bishop Funk, who died in 1766, was concerned that the Mennonites were losing their sense of Gelassenheit.

D. W. Heise, a Tunker leader from Markham, stated in the spring of 1918, "The lines are still being drawn tighter, but we believe our God is ABLE."[26] The church laboured hard to help her men remain steadfast in the faith. They printed a list of questions that were typically asked at the tribunals. These tribunal hearings were intimidating to any farm boy who had no experience in such legal matters. The men were admonished to use simple words they understood in order to avoid misunderstandings that would arise from the careless use of words. The following questions were selected from the above list, and give the reader an idea of what an applicant could expect:

> 1. What process of reasoning led you to the views you hold?
> 2. What sacrifice have you ever made for your conscience?
> 3. What attempts did you make to improve things around you before the war broke out?
> 4. Your country is in danger. What do you propose to do for it now?
> 5. Why is it wrong to prevent evil from happening to someone else—to protect women and children from inhumanity?
> 6. You have been telling us about Christ's conscience. What does your conscience say?
> 7. If war is evil, why did not Christ condemn it? Did he not

even say, "He that hath no sword, let him buy one," "Render unto Caesar the things that are Caesar's," "If my kingdom were of this world then would my servants fight," and "I came not to send peace, but a sword"?

8. Would not Christ help the wounded and sick? Do you think He would show discrimination in His acts of mercy? Would it not be pleasurable to Him if you helped the wounded and sick also?

9. How can doing the same thing, such as ambulance or relief work, be right under civilian control and wrong under army control?

10. Do you pay taxes indirectly if not directly? Do they not help the war? What is the moral difference between helping to pay for the war and fighting in it?

At the beginning of the war, the Mennonites knew what they believed in regard to their role in war, but they waited far too long to get a good understanding of their legal rights within the law. The Mennonites waited until almost three years after the war began before they contacted a law firm, McCullough and Button of Stouffville, Ontario, to inquire about their legal status.[27] It was not the Mennonite way to use the services of lawyers, but they were learning that the government was not about to grant them special liberties if they were not ready to persist in asking for them.

The legal wrangling that occupied Coffman and other leaders in the Mennonite church during the last year of the war was very new to the Peace Churches. Within the Old Order community, it would be the most recently ordained ministers, Minister Thomas Reesor of Markham, Minister Urias Martin and Noah Bearinger of Waterloo, a lay member, who accepted this formidable challenge.

Even though the Old Order community anticipates that all their men will remain true to their traditional faith, experience has revealed that some will leave the church. In order to claim the non-resistant faith one must learn submission to God and the church, and to forsake acts or even thoughts of revenge. The love of God within the heart of man enables man to love his enemy as himself. The spirit of Jesus on the cross is not of human flesh, yet it is the core of the non-resistant faith.

The non-resistant faith has never been popular. The thought of being vulnerable lambs amongst vicious wolves does not appeal to men. Neither are people inclined to humbly accept loss and destruction and accept the words: "Dearly beloved, avenge not yourselves, but rather give place unto wrath: for it is written, Vengeance is mine; I will repay, saith the Lord" (Romans 12:19). Jesus said, "I lay down my life for the sheep" (John 10:15). That yieldedness, Gelassenheit, is exemplified in this passage. There is a significant difference between laying down one's life and giving up one's life in a battle. Christ laid down his life without a struggle even though unlimited power was at his disposal. Love is the only defense a non-resistant believer has, and of unbearable situations Jesus said, "But when they persecute you in this city, flee ye into another . . . " (Matthew 10:23). The challenge to voluntarily lay down all earthly things, including one's life, is continuous. Unless the principles of Gelassenheit radiate from the heart, it becomes very difficult to live a non-resistant life.

Conscientous Objectors' Experiences During the War

The Waterloo Old Order community was virtually unscathed by the war. Six men (Jeremiah S. Bauman, Norman S. Bearinger, Leander Clemmer, Henry Freeman, Peter M. Martin, and John M. Martin) were called to report to the London army camp. These six men, who were called up, were baptized on May 19, 1918, before the large class of that summer. Norman Bearinger evidently did not understand the consequences of deserting the army when he left the London army camp. When he arrived home the Old Order community wasted no time in telegraphing the London officials and promptly put him on the next train bound for London. The London officials overlooked this deviance as the folly of a novice farm lad. Since this episode occurred over three years after the war began, one could suggest that the Old Order community was still quite naïve about war and their exemption from military service. Jeremiah Bauman did some fatigue duties around the army kitchen, like peeling potatoes, without donning the uniform.

During this time Urias Martin, a recently ordained minister, was scheduled to go to the London army camp as a spiritual adviser for some of these boys. The night was long and sleepless as the young minister considered his mission. He chose to go out in the quiet of the night and

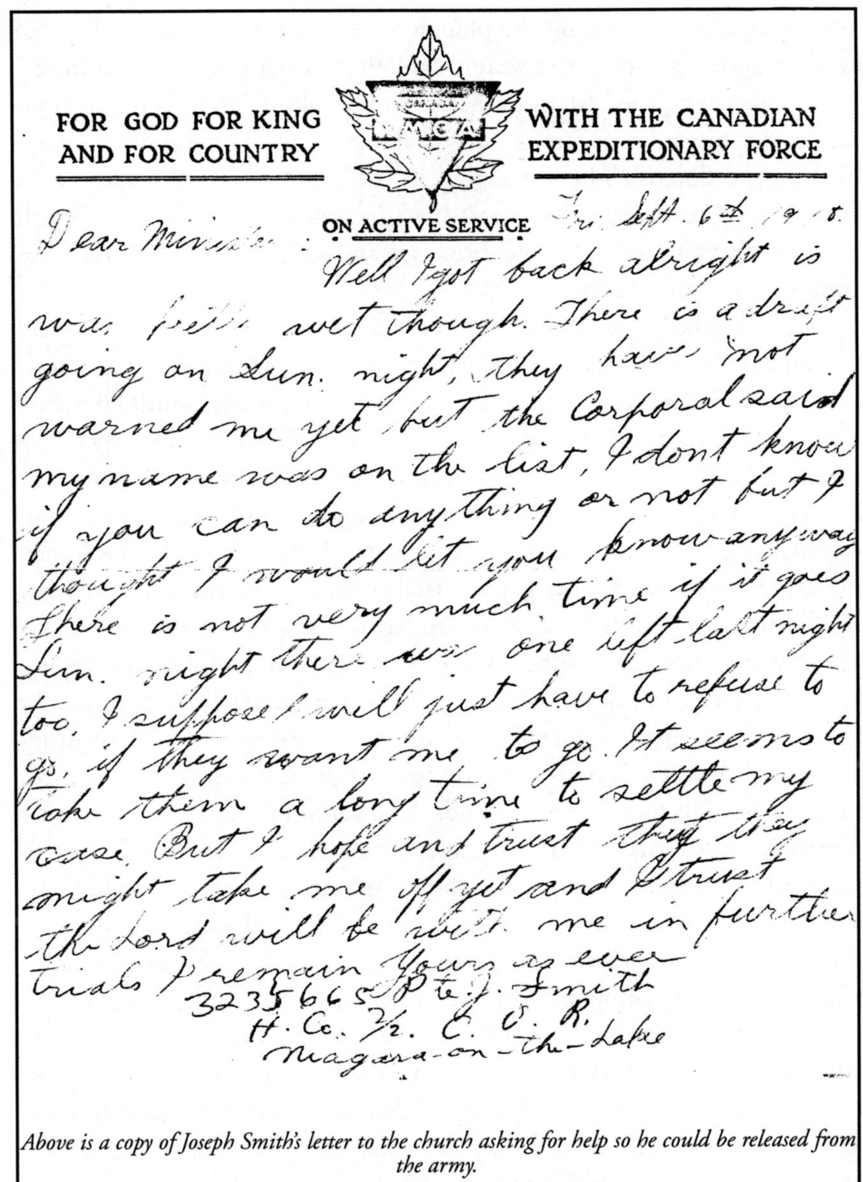

FOR GOD FOR KING AND FOR COUNTRY

Y.M.C.A.

WITH THE CANADIAN EXPEDITIONARY FORCE

ON ACTIVE SERVICE

Fri. Sept. 6th 1918.

Dear Minister:

Well I got back alright is was pretty wet though. There is a draft going on Sun. night, they have not warned me yet but the Corporal said my name was on the list, I dont know if you can do anything or not but I thought I would let you know anyway There is not very much time if it goes Sun. night there was one left last night too. I suppose I will just have to refuse to go, if they want me to go. It seems to take them a long time to settle my case. But I hope and trust they they might take me off yet and I trust the Lord will be with me in further trials I remain Yours as ever

3235665 Pte J. Smith
H. Co. 1/2. C. O. R.
Niagara-on-the-Lake

Above is a copy of Joseph Smith's letter to the church asking for help so he could be released from the army.

to shock grain. In later years Martin would recall that he discovered that shocking was harder on the body than a sleepless night.

When Freeman and Clemmer received their notice to report to London, Freeman was very concerned. While ploughing on a hot and muggy day, Freeman sat on the plough to let the horses rest. He then fell into a trance and heard the words, "not to be careful about the future." The burden was lifted from his heart. In the fall of 1918 Minister Urias Martin accompanied Freeman and Clemmer to the London army camp. Because the Spanish Flu was raging in the camp, they were allowed to return home with orders to report back in a month. Before that month was past the war was over and Freeman and Clemmer never served the army camp at London.

In the Markham district matters were different. Some men were conscripted into the army while others were court-martialed and jailed. Most Old Order men were soon released, but Joseph Smith, the first man called, had a long and difficult experience. When he was called, the church told him "don't make any trouble and we'll soon have you out." But alas, neither Smith nor the church understood that once a man voluntarily puts on the uniform, in the eyes of the officials he has joined the army. Smith made this grave mistake unaware of the consequences. He followed the orders until it came to bayonet practice where the dictates of his conscience made him decline. He was now guilty of disobeying military orders. He never spoke of all the challenges that he faced. In order to force Smith's compliance, the army transferred him to other camps. In spite of this Smith never implied that he was physically abused. In time he developed some friends and some of the officers became sympathetic towards him and gave him menial assignments. Smith marched in some military parades, but when he was at home on leave he faced another awkward problem. To attend an Old Order Mennonite church service in uniform was taboo; however, he was also forbidden by military orders to remove his uniform when on leave. Smith was in training camps for over half a year, until the end of the war, and discharged as any other soldier. Even though the church was not able to gain Smith's release from the army, one could still suggest that the contact the church made with the military officials on Smith's behalf was profitable to him as the following incident would indicate.

The men who had true convictions against war, but had no association with an historic peace church known by the government, faced the greatest challenges. E. J. Swalm of the Tunker Church witnessed a sad and sobering incident. While Swalm was under military arrest and waiting his court-martial, a young man, John Reid, took a firm stand against bearing arms. His beliefs as a conscientious objector were not upheld or understood by his pastor whose church did not adhere to the doctrine of non-resistance. His own pastor was ashamed of Reid's position and told the military authorities that "they should give no recognition to his profession of pacifism and even advised them to treat him roughly, calling him a coward."[28] Reid was even denied court-martial and sent overseas. He refused to accept his gear and march, but lay on the ground. They literally carried him to the patrol wagon and took him away. Swalm "remembered how sad it seemed, as he shoved a couple of dry bread crusts under his belt, in case they might try to starve him."[29]

One reason some 130 men were detained as conscientious objectors was that the Tunkers had recently changed their name to Brethren in Christ and were not recognized by the government as a religious denomination that adhered to the non-resistant faith. It was June 25, 1918, before the Canadian government accepted the Brethren in Christ's non-resistant position, even though the group was referred to in the 1793 statute. The Jehovah's Witnesses and Plymouth Brethren were also given a two-year hard labour sentence, and served time in the Kingston Prison until six months after the war.[30] Some of these men, like Reid, were tortured. David Wells, a Pentecostal, died three weeks after he was detained.[31] The members of the Peace Churches faced challenging times, and those who stood alone were often given even less consideration.

Ernie Swalm, a conscientious objector, was drafted into the army. Ernie was a twenty-one year old single man living on his father's farm near Collingwood, Ontario. He was a member of the Brethren in Christ church, which was not at that time acknowledged by the government as a non-resistant church. He was to report for duty in Hamilton, on May 7, 1918, without fail. Since Ernie was the first man of his church to be called up for service, his future was very uncertain and he did not know if he ever would return home again. On that day Ernie was found in Hamilton where he informed an officer of his CO convictions. The officer coolly replied that it was not his responsibility to deal with his request but said, "I'll give you this tip. Don't try anything like that, my boy, for we've had two or three that tried that here. Until we got through with them, they were mighty glad to carry on and be a soldier. I'd advise you to profit by their mistakes."[32]

The next captain who interviewed Ernie first tried to flatter him and then tried to scare him, saying that Ernie better take service or they would put him in chains and take him overseas to the front lines to stop bullets to save better men coming up behind. Ernie was then ordered to put on his uniform but he refused. After some more threats and verbal abuse he was placed under arrest by Sergeant Hartley and taken to the Guard Room where, to his surprise, he met seven or eight other COs who had taken the identical stand that Ernie had taken. At this time the boys took courage and thanked God. The next day they were forcefully stripped of their civilian clothes and had a fatigue uniform put on them. They were remanded for a district court-martial and were given light duty around the camp, such as cleaning up the yard. During the time before their court-martial Ernie and his friends faced many threats and scoffings. The soldiers even pretended to have it arranged to shoot them, but when the Sergeant heard about that, there was an end to such recklessness.

Ernie and his friends were charged not as conscientious objectors, but as defaulters for disobeying a lawful command given by a superior officer because they refused to put on the uniform. To this charge the COs had to plead guilty. (Even though Swalm's and Smith's charge were identical the officials made a difference since Swalm had never voluntarily identified himself with the army.) Three days later the sentences of eighteen COs were read in front of the whole battalion. They were made an example of to intimidate the rest of the soldiers from taking a similar course. The COs were then ushered away and taken to the St. Catharine's prison to be held there until the provincial sheriff could take them to the federal prison at Kingston.

Life in prison was drab indeed. The prison menu was simple. One pint of oatmeal porridge sprinkled with a dessertspoonful of sugar but no milk, three slices of unbuttered bread, and a cup to get water at the spigot. This was the menu three times a day except for a pint of beef stew at noon once a week. Again they were fortunate that S. F. Coffman, the Mennonite bishop at Vineland, was a personal friend of Mr. Bush, the governor of the jail. Since the COs had the rating as "Trusties," Mr Bush gave them special privileges. By June 25, 1918, the Tunker situation was clarified and the government again recognized the Tunkers, or Brethren in Christ, as a non-resistant church. Their men received an indefinite leave of absence without pay and were allowed to go home. There were limits to the liberty the Canadian government allowed, but it also was evident that the men who were part of the traditional Peace Churches received better treatment and more respect than their counterparts who stood alone on their personal convictions.

The Non-Resistant Relief Organization (NRRO).

The general public resented the Mennonite exemption from military service. Public pressure prompted the Peace Churches to form an organization by which monetary relief could be sent to those who were suffering due to the war. The first meeting was held at the Wideman Mennonite church in Markham on November 19, 1917. This action was taken over three years, starting when the war began and continuing after conscription became a reality. On January 16, 1918, members from the Amish, Tunker (Brethren in Christ), Conference Mennonites, Mennonite Brethren in Christ, and Old Order Mennonites were present at the home of C. N. Good in Kitchener. At this meeting they adopted the name "Non-Resistant Relief Organization," developed a mandate, and agreed to send a committee to present the proposal to the government at Ottawa. The officials in Ottawa declined to accept any money for relief purposes because they were not authorized to do such work, but commended the idea and suggested the funds be directed towards some existing relief organization.

The NRRO distributed approximately seventy-five thousand dollars to various relief organizations in 1919. In 1921 the Mennonites of Ontario assisted the famine-stricken Russian Mennonites through NRRO. The NRRO continued to be the arm for international relief for the Ontario Mennonites until it was absorbed by the Mennonite Central Committee of Canada (MCC Canada) in 1963.

The Old Order community in Ontario suffered from dissension during World War I. In the Rainham and Markham districts members were beginning to purchase cars, much to the displeasure of the Waterloo district. Since it was the Old Order faction that condoned cars and promoted the relief fund, the conservative element did not readily support the relief fund. Another sensitive issue at that time was Bishop Ezra Martin's purchase of Victory Bonds which caused some members to refrain from communion.[33] Even though the Old Order minister Urias Martin and lay member Noah Bearinger attended most NRRO meetings during 1918, the Old Orders from Waterloo never held a collection for the NRRO until after the war had ended. The opportunity to appease public animosity by voluntarily sending assistance to those who suffered from war had been squandered due to internal strife. In our story we will discover that in later years the Old Orders supported the NRRO.

Notes

[1] Frank H. Epp, *Mennonites in Canada* II (Toronto: Macmillan Canada, 1982), 558.

[2] James C. Juhnke, *Vision, Doctrine, War* (Scottdale, PA: Herald Press, 1989), 22.

[3] Theron F. Schlabach, *Peace, Faith, Nation* (Scottdale, PA: Herald Press, 1988), 318.

[4] Juhnke, *Vision*, 71.

[5] *Ibid.*, 127.

[6] *Ibid.*, 119.

[7] W. H. Heick, *The Lutherans of Waterloo County During World War I* (Kitchener: Waterloo Historical Society, 1962), 23.

[8] *Ibid.*, 25.

[9] Gerhard Enns, *Waterloo North and Conscription 1917* (Kitchener, ON: Waterloo Historical Society, 1963), 60-68.

[10] D. N. Panabaker, *Statement of Losses, Block 2 Residents , War of 1812* (Kitchener, ON: Waterloo Historical Society, 1928), 8.

[11] MacMaster, Horst, and Ulle, *Conscience in Crisis* (Scottdale, PA: Herald Press, 1979), 99.

[12] L. J. Burkholder, *A Brief History of the Mennonites in Ontario* (Altona MB: Friesen Printers, 1986), 262. For a complete study of the Mennonites during World War I see pgs. 365-386 in *Mennonites in Canada,* I by Frank Epp and pgs. 163-197 in *Limits on Liberty* by William Janzen.

[13] Burkholder, *A Brief History*, 264.

[14] William Janzen, *Limits on Liberty* (Toronto: University of Toronto Press, 1990), 174.

[15] *Ibid.*, 193-195.

[16] Epp, *Mennonites*, I, 378.

[17] Janzen, *Limits on Liberty*, 186.

[18] *Ibid.*, 188.

[19] *Ibid.*, 184.

[20] Epp, *Mennonites in Canada* I, 377.

[21] Janzen, *Limits on Liberty,* 179.

[22] Letter from F. S. Scott to S. F. Coffman, June 15, 1918, CGUC.

[23] *Ibid.*

[24] Burkholder, *A Brief History*, 268.

[25] Lesslie C. Wilson. Letter dated July 5, 1918, CGUC.

[26] D. W. Heise. Letter dated July 29, 1918, CGUC.

[27] Janzen, *Limits on Liberty*, 342.

[28] E. J. Swalm, *Non-resistance Under Test* (Nappanee, IN: E.V. Publishing House, 1938), 36.

[29] *Ibid.*

[30] E. J. Swalm, Conversation with Author.

[31] Janzen, *Limits on Liberty*, 431.

[32] Swalm, *Non-resistance*, 32.

[33] Letter from Noah Bearinger to Thomas Reesor, December 5, 1918, CGUC.

The Continuing Challenge

Chapter Fourteen

The Conference Mennonites

The 1889 division left only about thirty families with the Conference Mennonite Church in Woolwich Township. The building of the Floradale Church in 1896, the St. Jacobs Church in 1915, and then the founding of the Elmira Church in 1924 are evidence that there was some movement of the Old Orders to the Conference Mennonites during the first decades after the division. The Conference church had natural growth, but why didn't the Old Orders build a meetinghouse in the years between Peel in 1901 and Fourth Peel or Olivet in 1956? Table Two reveals that from 1920 to 1930 the membership in the Old Order Church only increased by 170 members, yet from 1920 to 1929, inclusive, the baptismal records show that 172 boys and 197 girls were accepted into the church. Thus two-hundred potential members had drifted away from the Old Order Church. Of the eighty-four boys baptized in 1918, only one-third remained Old Order until death, while another third selected the Conference Mennonite Church as their place of worship, and the remaining third eventually went with the Markham division in 1939. This chapter will detail the events leading up to the Markham division of 1939. The Old Orders generally acknowledge that there will be some movement by their members because it is a voluntary commitment. They also feel that the Ordnung is more important to them than numbers.[1] For these reasons, the Old Orders are not greatly troubled by divisions: they

Table Two—Old Order Statistics

Year	Martins	Conestogo	Elmira	NWoolwich	Peel	Totals
1906	160	60	60	60	30	370
1911	170	110	160	90	50	580
1920	210	118	160	114	100	702
1930	212	129	180	179	172	872
1936	208	123	203	227	189	950
1940	140	109	136	177	168	730
1940	67%	89%	67%	78%	89%	77%

Bottom row are the per cent of the members in 1936 that stood by the Old Order in 1940. Data for year 1906. [2]

are more concerned with having a brotherhood of committed believers than with having a large membership.

The percentage row on Table Two does not necessarily reflect the full picture since it ignores the natural growth of the Old Order Church. From 1936 to 1939, inclusive, there were 177 youth baptized and accepted into the brotherhood. The Markham division drew considerable members from the Old Order Church, but it is fair to suggest that there was also movement to other groups. Both Elmira and Martins congregations lost about one-third of their members in the division while Conestogo and Peel only lost eleven per cent. Since Urias Martin was minister of Martin's congregation and Bishop Jesse Bauman was the congregational leader of Elmira, one could suggest some leadership related influences, but other factors also influenced the picture. An Old Order historian feels that the Conestogo and Peel congregations were more conservative for several decades after the 1889 division.[3]

The Elmira congregation, historically known as the West Woolwich congregation has a complete set of membership records dating from 1918 to 1940 due to the diligent work of the late Isaac G. Martin. In these congregational records Isaac never included the youth, but rather listed the number of families. (See Table Three.) From 1930 on he also included the older single women and men. In 1939, Old Order bishop Daniel Brubacher served communion to 116 members, or fifty-two households and twelve widows and single sisters, at Elmira. Jesse Bauman held

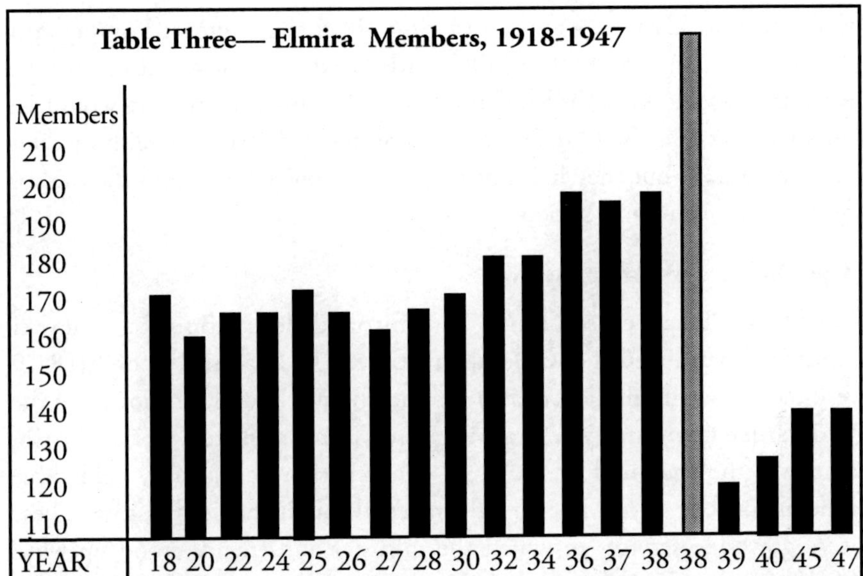

communion for sixty-five members while forty-nine individuals remained undecided and took no communion. From the total of 230 adherents in 1939, 116 were decidedly Old Order and twenty of the undecided forty-nine also joined the Old Orders by 1940.

These records reveal the gravitation of the renegade adherents towards the Markham division in 1939. Beginning in 1932, I. G. Martin listed thirteen non-communing adherents, but by 1937 this number had increased to twenty-five. The 1938 bar in Table Three indicates the number of adherents in the Elmira congregation just before the division. From a low of 164 members in 1927, after the mid-twenties decline, there was steady growth for the next decade which peaked with 230 adherents in 1938.

Several observations can be made from these statistics. From 1920 to the division, neither the Martins nor Conestogo congregations experienced any real growth. Elmira had nominal growth but it is evident that the people were moving north and west into the Peel and North Woolwich districts. In Table Three one can see the trend of movement away from the church to the point that the Elmira congregation experienced negative growth. This coincides with the formation of the Conference Mennonite congregation at Elmira in 1924. One could suggest that the Old Orders' way of resisting all changes created a stagnant environment. In the 1980s an Old Order leader implied that during the early thirties the Old Order Church was due for a revival. It would be unfair to say that the Old Order Mennonites had lost their faith or their spiritual vision, but they had not yet learned how to maintain their ethos in a rapidly changing society.

The Old Orders After the War

World War I had caused much hardship and destruction, but another scourge also afflicted the world at this time. The Spanish Flu of 1918-19 resulted in twenty million deaths around the world and did not leave the Old Order community unscathed. The young minister, Urias Martin, who was the shepherd of the large congregation at Martins, held three funerals in four days while this flu raged through the community. These were graveside services in which the minister and friends stood up-wind of the family of the deceased. Public events were cancelled or forbidden by law. The people were so fearful that when the banker in St. Jacobs succumbed to the dreaded illness, the undertaker had to drag the body down the stairs because no one volunteered to assist him. Minister Urias Martin commented years later that the congregation was easy to lead during the war and flu, but this situation would not last.

In 1907 the telephone had rent the Old Order community in the American Mid-West. The telephone issue burned low during the war years, but by the mid-twenties the telephone became problematic. To maintain order, the Old Order community excommunicated all those who accepted the telephone. About 1925 the deacon from the Martins congregation approached Aaron Weber and informed him that if he did not put his telephone away by Saturday he would be put in the ban. Years later Weber, who joined the St. Jacobs Mennonite Church, commented that that day it was his turn to be stubborn.[4] In any event Weber was the last individual that the Old Orders formally expelled from the church because he accepted the telephone; however, Weber was not a lone example, as there were many who switched membership after the war because they desired to have the telephone. After Weber's excommunication, the Old Order church took the position that those who installed a telephone had put themselves out of the church and no longer formally excommunicated them.

One Sunday morning, about 1925, at least six families from the Old Orders were accepted as members at the St. Jacobs Mennonite Church. (1) The loss of so many members from his congregation, including his own brother, was a great burden to Minister Urias Martin. In later

(1) *I was not able to determine the exact number of families received into the St. Jacobs Mennonite church on that occasion. The Meeting Calendars indicate that the Conference Mennonite membership was stable or in a state of decline from 1921 (1845 members) to 1925 (1761 members). By 1926 the Conference membership had risen to 1826 members. In 1926 the St. Jacobs congregation had 158 members and the Elmira church fifty-six. Two years later, in 1929, the St. Jacobs membership had increased to 213 and Elmira had 141 members. During the thirties these congregations experienced nominal growth. The evidence suggests that during the twenties considerable gravitation occurred from the Old Order Mennonites to the Conference Mennonites, but after Markham was separated from the Waterloo Old Orders this gravitation was directed more towards Markham. In any event the telephone and car issues caused numerous members of the Old Order community to gravitate to other Mennonite churches during the third decade of the twentieth century.*

years he shared with his son that it was hard to see so many of his age leave and not to go with them. Fifteen years later, Martin would get a telephone except that his father-in-law, one of the most conservative members of his congregation, deterred him (if his conscience didn't), because it had been stipulated that there was to be no telephone on Martin's property as long as the old people lived.[5]

The Old Order community lay quietly in the great pastures of Waterloo County with the breezes of change gently drifting over them. They were committed to being a separate people who were strong in their faith in God. However, they were weak in expression and perhaps somewhat stagnant in their vision. Was their traditional meetinghouse schedule of having services once in four weeks sufficient for spiritual health? Diaries reveal that some people only attended services once in four weeks. Fellowship over a Sunday noon meal was traditional and Mr. Lachner, a non-Mennonite farmer, sarcastically commented that the new portion of Listowel Road west of Floradale Road would only be used by the Mennonites to go visiting on Sundays. It was also common to remain at home all day, especially during the time when the horses were worked hard in the fields. Rest for their horses was part of their culture, and it was not considered prudent to travel long distances during the cold of winter. As a result, it was common for the family to finish their daily chores and then to spend the day at home. In some families it was customary to spend the Sunday in work clothes, while in other homes the family always changed into their Sunday clothes. Another practice was to have Sunday-at-home clothes that were worn when the family did not attend church. Memories linger of observing father sitting in the living room rocker smoking a cigar with his German Bible across his knees.[6]

The Great Depression of the thirties created many hardships. The people in the cities suffered more because they could not grow their own food. Herbert Enns, a Russian Mennonite, remembered those years because he had to postpone his marriage since he would not have been able to support a wife. Another Mennonite lad recalled walking along the railroad tracks searching for coals that fell between the tender and locomotive. Years later a woman questioned why widows were not given money so that children could stay at home and families not be broken up. The answer was that there was no money. An aged Mennonite farmer with means also understood that there was no money available. He would have been willing to sell a four-thousand-dollar mortgage for two thousand dollars in order to receive cash so he could live.[7]

The Great Depression was challenging, and at times discouraging, for the people of that era. A day labourer asked a farmer if he could go into his bush and cut another foot off the stumps with his sweep-saw. He needed wood to heat his house but he had no money and no work. Half a century later a successful businessman reflected that "to work hard all year and then to have nothing left was not nice." He had lost his farm during the early thirties. Even though there were hardships, the people adjusted. Those who lived during those years have commented that people were as content in those years as they were later.

Strained Agricultural Changes

During the twenties hydro power arrived in many villages, but the rural lines were built later. Although hydro power would create some confusion and disunity within the Old Order community, the more progressive members readily accepted Bishop Ezra Martin's opinion—"water pumping and lights, that's part of farming." By the mid-thirties the farming economy had picked up and a few progressive Old Order farmers were installing hydro. Nevertheless, the conservative element's disapproval of hydroelectric power would continue to strain the unity of the Old Order community for years. By the 1970s diesel generators for electric power were acceptable by the even more conservative David Martin group, while the Orthodox Mennonites continued to avoid them. In order to maintain the balance of peace, the Old Order community's custom was that no ordained men used electric power. During the 1980s a newly ordained Old Order minister created quite a stir when he installed a diesel electric generator to operate his farm. Small electric generators were preferred by the conservative element as opposed to hydroelectric power. By the close of the twentieth century it became acceptable for the Old Order ministry to use hydroelectric power.

The farm tractor was another product of prosperity that would alter the Old Order community. Steam tractors used to power threshing machines had been accepted as necessary pieces of equipment, and when the gasoline engine replaced steam power the community also embraced this new invention. The use of tractors for the fieldwork, in the opinion of some, challenged their simple lifestyle; therefore, the use of steel wheels versus the rubber tire was another issue that would strain peace within the Old Orders of Ontario. The farm tractor has revolutionized the farming industry and the Old Order communities have been struggling to preserve their simplistic lifestyles and yet remain competitive within the industry as a whole.

[1] The most liberal wing of the Old Order Mennonites began in the Markham area. The Old Orders from Waterloo who affiliated with Markham became known as the Markham Mennonites in the Waterloo district. In this book the Markham Mennonites from Waterloo will be referred to as Markham.

[2] Frank H. Epp, *Mennonites in Canada* I. (Toronto: Macmillan of Canada, 1974), 269. For the year 1911, see Winfield J. Fretz, *The Waterloo Mennonites: A Community in Paradox.* (Waterloo, Ontario: Wilfrid Laurier University Press, 1989), 116. For years 1920-40 see Isaac Martin records.

[3] Private Conversation.

[4] Private Conversation.

[5] Urias Martin. Letters and Legal Documents, ca. 1920. Aaron Martin's collection, Alma, Ontario.

[6] Private Conversation.

[7] Private Conversation.

A Revival Close to Home

Chapter Fifteen

Conquering the World for Christendom

In 1828 and 1832 several reforms were passed by the British parliament that transferred the power of the Anglican nobility to the middle classes. These far-reaching changes increased the influence of other churches and fed revivalistic zeal in England. In America, revivalism reached its zenith at the Cane Ridge Camp Meeting in 1801: "An estimated thirty thousand people —or ten per cent of Kentucky's population—attended the revival."[1] The harsh pioneer life had desensitized the people and when they were brought under the influence of the gospel the meetings were often charged with emotions and hysteria of individuals shouting and rolling on the ground. Religious renewal was manifesting itself throughout the Western World.

Western Christianity with the "innate superiority of the Anglo-Saxon race" was, by the end of the nineteenth century, set to conquer the traditional religions which predominated in both Asia and Africa.[2] Cultural and commercial imperialism accompanied the evangelical-minded Britons as their missionaries set out to conquer many parts of the world for Christianity. The famous English explorer David Livingstone declared in 1857, "I go back to Africa to try to make an open path for commerce and Christianity." Was he an agent of English commerce or a missionary of the church?[3] Or was it similar to the climate of American expansion which culminated in the Spanish-American War of 1898? At the close of the nineteenth century the "superior" Anglo-Saxon race was participating "in a movement which fully expected to conquer the world for Christendom and to do it quickly."[4] It was an era of many missions to "that Dark Continent" and Asia, a time when to Christianize meant to teach European and White North American ways to those "foolish and pagan heathens" in far away lands.

There were several pulses driving the Western World. Individuals like Karl Marx were becoming bold enough to question the "Holy Writ," while others deemed it essential to compare the Bible with the findings of modern science. The American Civil War also left a vacuum that was filled by a "social gospel" (1) while others resisted these modern advances with a cry to hold to the fundamental Biblical truths. "They (the fundamentalists) sensed that the culture in which they were located was clearly turning away from its religious past and from the shared assumptions that they and other Americans had long sustained."[6]

(1) *The social gospel movement was active from the American Civil War to World War I. This movement held the same Calvinistic overtones that fundamentalism did. It was liberal and highly optimistic in its views, believing that since the evils of slavery were now history, God would open the way for redemption and sanctification to the whole American social system. The optimism of this movement faded away with the carnage of World War.*[5]

Fundamentalism Versus Old Order Mennonitism

Fundamentalism built on many aspects of the American religious past. Revivalism, Pietism, Methodism and the Wesleyan holiness movement were all drawn together as these Christians arose to defend Christianity from the "higher criticism" of the Bible. Fundamentalism was a defence of the faith with a strong emphasis on a personal conversion experience. Fundamentalists also emphasized the absolute accuracy of the Scriptures that highlighted the doctrines of creation and the virgin birth of Christ. Communism, atheism, and the beginnings of modern psychiatry were all part of the free-thinking dogma of the nineteenth century. Although Fundamentalism opposed modern science and Darwin's and Marx's free thinking, the movement was not totally anti-modern for it adopted the teachings of dispensational premillennialism. It was also often aggressive, highly self-assertive and individualistic. Fundamentalism was yet another movement that clashed with the Anabaptist-Mennonite theology of humility, Gelassenheit, and brotherhood.

Perhaps the Old Order Mennonite ethos of brotherhood was at odds with the individualism of the new Protestant movements. They emphasized Jesus' work on the cross, meaning grace, but did not stress a life of obedience to a brotherhood. They also emphasized the resurrecting power of Christ rather than the Anabaptist doctrine of first dying with Christ at the cross and then being lifted by the Spirit of Christ unto newness of life. Discipleship, or living a life submissive and obedient to God and the Brotherhood, was understood differently by the

> (2) *The shift of emphasis from discipleship and the cross to grace alone has troubled the Mennonite people for centuries. Over the years Pietism, then Wesleyan holiness, was followed by Fundamentalism. Dispensationalism also emphasised the grace of God and passed over the ethical teachings of Christ since they pertain to the "kingdom" or the millennium era.*

Fundamentalists. (2) In Frank H. Epp's words, for the Mennonites life was "an exercise of faith that manifested itself in obedience to the teaching and life of Jesus." It was much more a "gradual guidance into all truth by the Holy Spirit—a system of logic for the absolute trustworthiness of the Bible."[7] Frank H. Epp also notes that:

> Because of their more pronounced cultural conservatism, and an even greater appetite for quietistic ruralism, the Amish and Old Order Mennonites noticed and integrated outside influences more slowly that did the Conference Mennonites. Emphasizing a practical Christianity and discipleship, they were disinterested in the scholarly debate or doctrinal correctness, which characterized the Fundamentalists.[8]

Nevertheless conservatism and ruralism would not shield the Old Order Mennonites from the evangelical fervour that was moving closer and closer to their communities.

In 1879 Charles Russell began publishing the *Watchtower* and organized the group known today as Jehovah's Witnesses. By 1900 the Pentecostal movement had spawned many charismatic revivals in both

America and Europe. This was an era when revivalism swept across the North American continent. Before the American Revolution only about six per cent of the adult population were church people. By 1870 that figure had risen to eighteen per cent and by 1956, sixty-one per cent of Americans were church people.[9] Another medium of revivalism appeared in 1909—the Scofield Bible. Its popularity was expressed by the approximately three million copies that were sold during its first fifty years in print. The Scofield Bible also challenged the Old Order Mennonite community. It was not the translation of the Scofield Bible that troubled the Old Orders, but the footnotes the author placed in the text and the doctrine that was advocated in those notes.

An Overview of Dispensationalism

Dispensationalism is a theological and historical system teaching that God established different ages ("dispensations") in salvation history and that human beings are called to respond differently to God, depending upon the dispensation in which they live. While dispensationalists maintained that they were reading the Bible "literally," in fact the Bible was read according to the rules of interpretation appropriate to the "dispensation" at the time of the reading.

The dispensationalist programme taught by C. I. Scofield and contained in his Bible translation and notes (published in 1909) maintained that God had divided all of history into seven dispensations. Scofield maintained that the first five dispensations had already passed; the sixth and the seventh referred to the present and the coming ages, respectively. The sixth dispensation was the "age of grace," extending from the cross until the beginning of the thousand-year (millennial) Kingdom. The seventh dispensation was the millennial kingdom itself, the thousand-year reign of Christ and the saints when righteousness and peace would prevail. One pressing question was when the millennial reign would begin – a question whose answer was thought to lie in the Scriptures themselves, properly understood and interpreted. Dispensationalists therefore undertook to interpret the "signs of the times" as well as biblical prophecy in order to discover where they stood in the divine calendar of End-times events. Many dispensationalists were "premillennialists," believing that they were living at the turn of the sixth and seventh dispensations, just before the second coming of Christ.

The emphasis on the nearness of the End Times encouraged revivalist preaching. Society was considered doomed, and it was imperative to save as many souls as possible before the impending last judgment. Furthermore, the ethical teachings of Christ in the Sermon on the Mount were said not to apply literally in the present (sixth) dispensation. Christ's difficult ethical teachings pertained to the "future kingdom of the millennium" rather than to the present age. The focus fell on "personal salvation" (by God's grace) rather than on discipleship.

The Baptist churches were greatly influenced by Scofield's work, as were the Plymouth Brethren and some Mennonite churches. (3) Dispensationalism was never a part of Old Order Mennonite thought. It is difficult to discern whether the Old Orders understood the depths of dispensationalism, but one thing is certain: during the 1960s the renegade Old Order, Menno Sauder, was still busy distributing anti-dispensationalist literature within the Old Order community. It is evident that some of the more radical statements made by the dispensationalists had caught his attention.

(3) Some early Anabaptists believed they were living in the End Times. Melchior Hoffman believed that Christ would return in his lifetime, and was instrumental in encouraging the militant apocalypticism of Münster. That tragedy marred the reputation of the Anabaptists, and apocalypticism was explicitly rejected by Menno Simons and the surviving Anabaptist groups. Ontario Mennonites were introduced to premillennialism (the teaching that the thousand-year reign of Christ would begin soon) by the preaching of S. F. Coffman and C. F. Derstine during the first half of the twentieth century. The Old Order Mennonites, however, have continued to reject premillennialism.

Old Order Eschatology

The Old Orders were farmers and not theologians. They were literalists who accepted the Word in its simplicity. The Old Order preacher, Abraham Bearinger, (ordained in 1935) occasionally quoted Revelation 10:5-6: "And the angel which I saw stand upon the sea and upon the earth lifted up his hand to heaven, and sware by him that liveth for ever and ever . . . that there should be time no longer." Bearinger's quotation underscored the simplicity of Old Order eschatology—the end of time is certain and final. Old Orders also quote Matthew 24:36-39: "But of that day and hour knoweth no man, no, not the angels of heaven, but my Father only . . . But as in the days that were before the flood they were eating and drinking, marrying and given in marriage, until the day that Noah entered into the ark, and knew not until the flood came, and took them all away; so shall also the coming of the Son of man be." The word that "the day and hour knoweth no man" was convincing to the Old Order.

The aged minister, Ervin Shantz, (ordained in 1947) was asked the question, "What is your view about the millennial reign?" The old man paused for a moment then began, "Vas Mich besht bahst" (that which is the most reasonable to me). He was hesitant, and no doubt agreed with his co-worker that he can wade through the Bible, but when he comes to the Book of Revelation he must swim. Shantz continued to answer the question clearly indicating he stood in the traditional Mennonite view, being amillennial. Eschatology is too controversial for the Old Order, and Revelation is seldom chosen as a text. An Old Order father once told his son, "You must first study the gospels, because salvation is not found in the Book of Revelation." Daniel Kauffman truly mirrored Old Order thought when he wrote: "We get most out of our investigations if we do not assume to know too much, but meekly take our place as humble learners and diligent students, in faith receiving what God sees fit to reveal."[12]

The Old Order Community is Troubled by Revivalism

Revival meetings were a common occurrence in the first decades of the twentieth century, but they only affected the Old Orders when their members began to attend these meetings outside of the church. In the fall of 1927 Israel Martin was saved at some evangelistic meetings at the Elmira Conference Mennonite Church. He soon became very active in witnessing for the Lord and for years operated the Golden Rule Book Store in Kitchener. About 1929 Mr. John Martinson, a Baptist who lived just south of Wallenstein, had a spiritual concern for the children in the Wallenstein area and started a Sunday school in the old Zion Methodist Church (formerly used by the

Black community of the area). During the summer a preaching service followed the Sunday school. Various churches took part in these services including Baptists and Pentecostals.

Two years later, in August 1931, Mr. Harter, a Pentecostal evangelist, held a series of meetings:

> John Martin (an Old Order youth) was gloriously converted to God. The sudden, violent death of his brother in a level train crossing had been God's way of arousing conviction and concern in this careless and indifferent young man. His conversion produced a great change in him so that he soon became a bright witness for his Lord. Through his testimony his brother Noah and a friend, Henry Bauman, were saved along with his fiancée, Miss Melissa Brubacher, a few months later. All this caused a great stir in the Old Order Mennonite Church, and these strange new teachings were condemned by the ministers, and others viewed these developments with grave concern and alarm.[13]

At the same time the four Hoffman brothers were also converted and began to testify concerning their faith amongst the Old Order youth at their singings. Sidney Hoffman, who had been a respected Old Order youth, very aggressively confronted Ervin Shantz and indicated that his evangelism would in time overwhelm the Old Order Church.[14] Although Sidney's optimism failed to materialize, the pessimistic Old Order who thought the *Hawkesviller* (the Hawkesville Brethren fellowship) would fail were also wrong. Some strong comments slipped by zealous lips on both sides. One of the early brethren said, "Even if I killed my mother-in-law, I'd be saved."[15] Such a radical statement was sure to enter the gossip mill. A lively discussion centred upon what was the original language of the Bible. A naive Old Order woman said, "Why, German, because it is written 'Adam wuh bist du' (Adam where art thou)." Being devoid of theological knowledge, the simplistic Old Order woman reasoned that since her Bible was German, German was the original language of the Bible. It was an era of theological awareness for the ex-Old Orders and the Old Order community as a whole.

There were other impulses driving this movement. A Russian Mennonite immigrant who worked for an Old Order, Israel Hoffman, was also instrumental in promoting the new teaching. When Anna Martin, the hired maid, became involved in this new teaching, her mother and brother arrived one day and took her home. The strange doctrine was reason enough to cut short the promised time of employment. Although Martinson's revival meetings did not necessarily attract large crowds, the Old Order converts of those meetings generated quite a stir within the Old Order community when they spoke zealously of their beliefs at the young people's "time" (later the events were called singings).[16] The "time" became a stumbling block to some of the "wild ones" who were steeped in the new movement and marred the Old Order testimony of that day. There were also Old Order youth who out of curiosity attended Martinson's meetings but remained faithful to the Old Order church.

Beginnings of the Hawkesville Bible Chapel

John Martinson's meetings in the old log church bore fruit. In October 1931, these zealous Christians organized and opened a Sunday school in the home of Nathan Martin in Hawkesville. The group relied on visiting speakers. Henry Janzen, a Russian Mennonite Brethren bishop and Frank Guthrie, of the Plymouth Brethren, were instrumental in organizing the congregation. The Mennonite Brethren were the most enthusiastic premillennialists within the Mennonite circles, but it became evident that this fledgling group also desired Calvin's teaching of eternal security.

Sunday, September 9, 1934 was a milestone to the young assembly. John Martin and a brother had gone to old Bishop Ezra Martin and told him that they were leaving the Old Order fellowship.[17] They had generated turmoil within the Old Order community for about three years. That day marked the beginnings of the Hawkesville Plymouth Brethren. This movement was distinguished by weekly observance of the Lord's Supper, and by the idea that the ministry should be based on the gifts that God has given rather than on the church's ordination. Later in the afternoon Henry Janzen baptized fifteen converts by immersion in the Conestogo River by the Wallenstein railroad bridge. This event attracted a large crowd estimated to have been about a thousand curious onlookers who were there to witness a new and almost unheard of thing. Among these spectators stood an Old Order youth, Henry Weiler. Some of the Hawkesville Brethren later objected to the doctrine of eternal security and left the fellowship. These still cherished Mennonitism and sought fellowship at the Conference Mennonite churches at St. Jacobs or Elmira.

This new assembly was not ready to abandon all of its Mennonite past. At a meeting held on September 13, 1934, they agreed to observe the rite of feet-washing once a year and recommended that former Mennonite women still wear their distinctive head coverings. They also believed that Christians should abstain from combatant service. It was at this meeting that the assembly's direction was turned towards Hawkesville Plymouth Brethren affiliation. By 1939 the assembly had outgrown its building and a new Gospel Hall was erected. Even though the congregation's theology differed little from the Methodist or Baptist faiths, the assembly had to endure scorn and derision from other denominations, and this may well have been an overreaction to the aggressive evangelism of the group. The Hawkesville Plymouth Brethren assembly was another movement in which the Old Order ethos of living one's faith was misinterpreted as earning one's salvation.

It would be dishonest to suggest that the Old Order community was not guilty of cold ethical formalism and such formalism is a disgrace to the blood of Christ, but the Old Order focus on Gelassenheit and simplicity has never blended well with charismatic evangelism and Calvinistic eternal security. The Old Order have never emphasised the fact that they are saved. Such a statement is too audacious for them. Their emphasis on dying with Christ on the cross of Christ develops an unassuming manner that focuses more on peace, that is, peace with God and man.

1 John 3:20-21 captures the Old Order view of being saved: "For if our heart condemn us, God is greater than our heart and knoweth all things. Beloved if our heart condemn us not, then have we confidence toward God." In short, if they have peace with God then they have confidence in God. The importance of living in peace with man is supported in Romans 12:18 "If it be possible, as much as lieth in you, live peaceably with all men." The Old Order emphasis is not "I'm saved" but "I have peace with God and man." The emphasis on being "saved"

was foreign to them, as was the doctrine of eternal security. To the Old Order a *Frema Geisht* (strange doctrine) had entered their midst and it is evident that they may not have been charitable to those who carried this Frema Geisht.[18] Nevertheless, the confusion was not over after approximately fifteen families had separated themselves from the Old Order and established the Hawkesville Chapel. The Frema Geisht was still with them and would be instrumental in producing another schism.

The beginnings of the Hawkesville Bible Chapel left a mark on the Old Order community. They had been accused of not being saved, and those who left the community and joined the more evangelical and charismatic fellowships were called the "saved" Old Orders. The Old Order's unconcerned attitude towards moderate use of alcohol and the use of tobacco was offensive to the revivalistic individuals, as were questionable courtship practices. There was reason enough for the Old Order to examine themselves without even addressing the theological differences in regard to eternal security and eschatology.

Misunderstandings and Faulty Interpretations

The openness of the Hawkesville Brethren to declare their salvation caused an overreaction in the Old Order community, and it took them about two generations to achieve a balance again of teaching a "living hope." To declare, "I'm saved" was far too bold for the Old Order, but they definitely believed in having a living hope in Christ their Saviour.[19] The Old Orders' concept of "saved" takes on another dimension: "Now being made free from sin, and become *servants to God*, ye have your fruit unto holiness, and the everlasting life" (Romans 6:22). Salvation through the blood of Christ is not the point in question. This is understood by all Christians. However the emphasis of Old Order Mennonitism is not "I am saved," but I am an "unprofitable servant" of Christ (Luke 17:10). Adam Clarke, a devoted Methodist, puts the Old Order thought into words: "For though we are not saved for our good works, yet we are saved that we may perform good works, to the glory of God and the benefit of man . . . obedience to the will of God is the very element in which a holy or regenerated soul lives."[20] The Old Orders overreacted to the Hawkesville Brethren's "I am saved" position because it clashed with Old Order humility. Meanwhile, the Old Orders' stress on "works" clashed with the Brethren's viewpoint of "I am saved."

There were numerous spiritual debates at this time and neither faction appreciated the other's view. For the Hawkesville Plymouth Brethren it was paramount that one *knew* he was saved. For an Old Order it was far more important to him that he *understood* that he had been converted. When the prodigal son returned to his father, the son had repented and said "I am no longer worthy to be called your son" (Luke 15:21). The Old Order thought parallels those of the prodigal son, "make me as one of thy hired servants." Being *servants* of God, it is more expedient for the Old Order to humbly labour for Christ than to boast about what Christ has done for them. However, for John Martin, one of the Hawkesville Brethren, to witness for Christ was imperative. There was a lot of room for argument. The following incidents will illustrate the tension between the two groups.

John Martin and a friend drove up to an Old Order Mennonite's home. The Mennonite's response from the porch was "If you want to know if I am saved I can tell you from here." John was not deterred by such a cool reception. At another time an Old Order blurted out to him, "Dieah reiszet euch in da Himmel" (You tear your way into heaven).[21] Noah Martin, a founding member of the Hawkesville Brethren, commented years later that he was surprised that anyone followed them when he considered their overbearing aggression in the beginning.

John Martin appreciated Minister Urias Martin who believed that one could know that he was saved. We can also be sure that Urias knew the words of Paul, "If in this life only we have hope in Christ, we are of all men most miserable" (1 Cor 15:19). One day John approached Urias and challenged him if he was saved. Urias very adeptly avoided John's controversial questions and thereby deprived John of being able to say to others that Urias told him he was "saved."[22] Nevertheless, Urias on another occasion had voluntarily confessed to Emanuel Brubacher that he thought he was saved.

Urias had worked a year in Alberta as a young man amongst the Conference Mennonites. While working there he attended a revival meeting where he experienced a deep spiritual renewal. Some twenty years later Urias commented on this experience to a group of young boys in his home. One of the boys, Emanuel Brubacher, made reference concerning this to another Old Order in the community. The idea that an Old Order minister had been "saved" at a worldly revival meeting caught the attention of several people. Emanuel was obliged to take several witnesses with him and go to Urias and confirm the statement. Urias acknowledged that Emanuel's story was true and the issue died.[23] It is certain that Urias believed in a hope in Christ, but the argumentative approach of John Martin and his aggressive interpretation of Calvin's eternal security doctrine prevented spiritual reasoning with the more passive Old Order interpretation of a hope in Christ. Out of this spiritual confusion arose the Old Order opinion that the Hawkesville Brethren believed that they could be Christians without bearing the cross of Christ. It is certain that the Brethren would also have agreed with the above quote from Adam Clark, "we are saved that we may perform good works, to the glory of God and the benefit of man."

The feelings were strong and it was not advisable to discuss issues relating to the Frema Geisht. Over the years Amsey Weber (1912-) observed that the Hawkesville movement was instrumental in arousing the Old Order community to review its ways, and may be considered a stepping-stone towards spiritual renewal for the Old Orders of Ontario. During the thirties the Old Orders were accused of not preaching salvation but building their salvation on works or their Ordnung. Some considered the Old Orders as a "mission field," and funerals a time to preach salvation to the "unsaved" Old Order relatives of the deceased. These accusations may have held some truth as the group was seeking its identity as being a separate people, but in general it was a misunderstanding of what Ordnung really meant to the Old Orders.

Notes

[1] John Driver, *Radical Faith: An Alternative History of the Christian Church* (Kitchener, Ontario: Pandora Press, 1999), 270.

[2] James C. Juhnke, *Vision, Doctrine, War* (Scottdale, PA: Herald Press, 1989), 143.

[3] Theron F. Schlabach, *Gospel Versus Gospel* (Scottdale, PA: Herald Press, 1980), 22.

[4] Juhnke, *Vision*, 158.

[5] ME, V, 834.

[6] *Ibid.*, 319.

[7] Frank H. Epp, *Mennonites in Canada* II (Toronto: Macmillan Canada, 1982), 56-57.

[8] *Ibid.*, 82.

[9] Loraine Boettner, *The Millennium* (Philadelphia, PA: The Presbyterian and Reformed Publishing Company, 1957), 42.

[10] ME, I, 557.

[11] George B. Fletcher, "The Millennium. What it is NOT and What it IS" (Pamphlet, Berachah Baptist Church, Hampton, VA, no date), 16.

[12] Daniel Kauffman, *Doctrines of the Bible* (Scottdale, PA: Herald Press, 1928), 578.

[13] David M. Martin, *Wallenstein Bible Chapel* (Wallenstein, Ontario: Wallenstein Bible Chapel, 1968. Author's collection), 6.

[14] Private Conversation.

[15] Ken Bechtel, *Three Score Years* (Elmira, ON: Bauman Printing, 1984), 35.

[16] See Glossary regarding "time."

[17] John Martin. Conversation with Author, 1980.

[18] See Glossary regarding Frema Geisht.

[19] Private Conversation.

[20] Adam Clarke, *Clarke's Commentary* VI (New York: Abingdon Press, no date), 439.

[21] Private Conversation.

[22] John Martin. Telephone Conversation with Author, 2000.

[23] Emanuel Brubacher. Conversation with Author, 1990.

The Markham-Waterloo Conference

Chapter Sixteen

The Frema Geisht, or Strange Doctrine

As early as 1922 Emmanuel Martin and Simeon Martin, the carpenter, were influenced by an evangelist, Alex Stewart, and for a time were involved in a small assembly that soon was disbanded.[1] Although Simeon Martin was never a member of the Hawkesville Bible Chapel, he entertained a more progressive spiritual outlook. When Jesse Bauman (1892-1967) was ordained minister for the Elmira congregation on July 4, 1923, he considered himself very unprepared for his calling. That fall Jesse and his wife Rebecca visited Simeon Martin who would remember clearly that, "Jesse did not leave as he came, and he began in an unusual way to preach the gospel."[2] Jesse soon showed ability in his calling and he preached as a learned man. His shift away from Gelassenheit towards evangelism caught the attention of some in the congregation who complained to the elderly bishop, Ezra Martin, about this Frema Geisht. Bishop Martin tried to calm these members by saying that Jesse preached the same thing but only used different words. However, concerns continued to abound.

Thomas Reesor, Bishop Ezra Martin's brother-in-law, wrote the following to John Huber of Pennsylvania on April 11, 1934: "There is quite a bit of apprehension in Waterloo about the young Bishop Jess Bauman. He appears too friendly with a revival movement in the district, a new sect called Plymouth Brethren. Not a few of the young people of Ezra L. (Old Orders) group are taken up with the movement. I am very much concerned with Jesse's stand as it will be a great disappointment if he should swing in that direction. By all accounts he is pretty firm in his convictions."[3] Aden Brubacher had heard of these rumours but dismissed them as such. One Sunday on the way home from services, Aden told his wife, "I have heard stories that Jesse preaches a strange doctrine, and today we *heard* it." Brubacher did not follow Jesse in the 1939 division, but waited several years before he joined the Markham Church.[4]

In time Jesse's beliefs were interpreted as a Frema Geisht, which was akin to the teachings of the Hawkesville Plymouth Brethren movement. This teaching did not vanish when the Brethren separated and began their own assembly in 1934. The effective proselytizing by the Hawkesville Brethren continued the commotion within the Old Order fellowship. Jesse's faith was comparable to that of the Plymouth Brethren and he enjoyed their frequent visits to his farm. Those of the Old Order community wished that the Brethren would leave Jesse alone, and his wife apparently shared similar concerns. One day when Simeon Martin desired to introduce a visiting evangelist to Jesse, he was not at home. Jesse usually enjoyed such visits, but when Martin suggested to Jesse's wife that they await his return, she blurted, "I'd rather you just go." As a minister's wife she already had borne the brunt of far too much criticism of Jesse's new ways.[5]

In retrospect one could suggest that Jesse Bauman did not have the feel of Gelassenheit—the concept of a yieldedness to the brotherhood which is the heart of Old Order Mennonitism. For example, in later years he was ready to use the church for a missionary's slide presentation when the Conference Mennonite Church of mid-century was not.[6] The issue was neither right nor wrong but he failed, as a minister, to comprehend the values of the brotherhood. May one suggest that Jesse had embraced pietistic individualism or even some Wesleyan holiness and lost the focus of the traditional Mennonite heritage? Jesse also had private reservations concerning the last article of the Dortrecht confession because it seemed too amillennial, and he was reluctant to preach against externals such as hood ornaments on cars and "when others did, his *zeugnis* (testimony) that followed began 'Ja and Amen to the Word of God' rather than referring to the sermon."[7] His daughter shed light on the situation when she stated that Jesse was inclined to go with the Hawkesville Brethren but his wife refused.[8] Jesse's Hawkesville Brethren inclinations were read by the Old Order as a Frema Geisht and this resulted in a schism led by Jesse Bauman.

The Year 1939

In September 1939 the world entered World War II. The Great Depression had created political instability in the world, especially in Germany. Hitler had rebuilt Germany after World War I and developed a powerful army. In Europe one country after another collapsed before Hitler's powerful army. Although these events had no immediate effect on the Old Order community, in the end the war did.

At this time the Old Order brotherhood was struggling to accept their new bishop, Jesse Bauman, ordained bishop in 1933, with his Brethren ideals, but old Bishop Ezra Martin had been able to still Jesse's critics. During the winter of 1939 a certain rather simple individual placed Jesse in a bind. He convinced Jesse to publish him and a certain widow in the marriage banns. The widow had not consented to her publication in the bans and raised an objection. Now the members were sure that Jesse was not fit to be bishop, but we must remember that the secretive nature of the Old Order tradition concerning those to be published in the bans required the bishop to keep such requests confidential. Jesse was in a very awkward position. This episode only revealed that the bishop was losing the confidence of the people, and his tendency to choose texts out of order did not strengthen the congregation's respect for him. (1)

(1) *On March 22, 1936, Jesse used Eph. 4 as his text for council meeting when the norm would have been Matt. 18. On Jan 1, 1938, Jesse selected Gal. 3:23-29 as a New Year's text when traditionally Luke 2:29-52 would have been expected. Occasionally a minister will select a text outside the expected window for a special service such as a council meeting, but it is interesting to note that Jesse's deviations were always away from the norm towards a more pietistic preference.*[9]

The aged bishop's moderating effect came to an end. Bishop Ezra Martin had been frail for some time, so the Spring Conference in 1938 was held in his home, but his passing away on March 22, 1939 closed an era.[10] On April 14, 1939 the Spring Conference was held at the Conestogo meetinghouse. Isaac Martin noted in his diary, "No agreement formed to hold communion." Toleration and forbearance were exchanged for mistrust and disunity as the delicate bond of peace was shattered. On April 27, 1939 the ministerial body were again assembled but peace eluded them. On Sunday, May 7, not all the testimonials affirmed Jesse's message. (After the message is delivered and the speaker is seated, the remaining ordained men testify or comment on the message. If the testimonials are not in agreement with the speaker, it is considered very serious.) The tension was increasing. On Ascension Day, May 18, Jesse Bauman and Urias Martin held the normal Old Order service at the Conestogo meetinghouse and no testimonials were given by the other ministry present. These strained weeks were to come to an end; on Tuesday June 6, 1939, a conference was held at the home of Elias Weber. Isaac Martin noted in his diary, "The heads of the church are now divided." The Old Order community remembers that day as a parting of ways. Jesse Bauman left and joined the Markham group.

With the division now final, the leaders agreed that the new Markham group could share the Martin's and Elmira meetinghouses on the Sundays the Old Orders worshipped elsewhere. This mutual agreement stipulated that the Markham group could not introduce changes to the meetinghouses against the wishes of the Old Order church, for example, adding a lobby to the meetinghouse for the men or installing pews with a full backrest. The Old Orders, however, did permit the Markham group to change the hymnbook shelves to accommodate the Markham group's English hymnbooks.

Although this painful division separated many families, it was not as bitter as the 1889 division had been. The 1889 division centred on Gelassenheit, an intangible doctrine, while the 1939 split focused on the car and telephone, which are tangible things. I have never heard that either party excommunicated the other group. They disagreed and separated but continued a workable relation in their social lives. Bishop Amsey Martin of the Markham group once asked the Old Order minister Edward Martin to preach at his son's wedding which was held by the Markham group. This sharing of the pulpit created ripples that ended such endeavours.[11] There was no further preaching in the Markham group's meetinghouses by Old Order preachers.

The Old Order people continued to worship as before and by June 25 they began to hold their instruction meetings for the youth. A class of thirteen boys and twelve girls had made application for baptism. The church evidently moved promptly to have the vacant bishop's office filled. By July 21, 1939 Bishop Daniel Brubacher had moved to Waterloo from Brutus, Michigan. The Old Order community in Brutus was almost extinct and so Daniel agreed to accept temporary responsibility in Waterloo. In a few years he moved to Pennsylvania, at which time Addison Gingrich was ordained bishop. On August 6, Daniel Brubacher baptized the class of twenty-five converts at the Martins meetinghouse. In September 1939 the Old Order ordained Daniel Martin as minister to replace the vacancy left by the departure of Urias Martin. The Old Order brotherhood had now filled all the offices left vacant by the division, and continued to hold services according to their former practices.

Beginnings of the Markham-Waterloo Conference

Even before the formal separation from the Old Order brotherhood on June 6, 1939, about twenty-five families from Waterloo were communing members at Markham. These families had parked their cars outside the fence and attended the Old Order Mennonite church services. Those who separated themselves from the Old Orders were now faced with the challenge of structuring a new Mennonite church. On Saturday, June 10, 1939, Jesse Bauman and Urias Martin were at a conference in the home of Bishop Abraham Smith at Markham. There they established fellowship with the Markham Conference and marked the beginnings of the Markham-Waterloo Conference. On June 11, Urias Martin and Jesse Bauman attended the services at Altona in Markham and no doubt took part in the service.

With the affiliation with Markham established, the new group was ready to hold services at Waterloo. The following Sunday, on June 18, 1939, Bishop Abraham Smith and Minister Thomas Reesor held services at the Elmira meetinghouse and Deacon Joseph Barkey read the text. This meetinghouse was familiar to Thomas Reesor. He and John Bowman had held services at the Old Order Elmira Harvest meeting on September 8, 1938, only ten months previous.[12] At that time Reesor had been misinformed that the majority of the people favoured the use of cars, but when he reached the pulpit he soon realized that the majority were disappointed in this move. Reesor had made a radical move to step behind the pulpit. Within the Old Order fellowships the pulpit is only shared by conference members of like affiliation. Perhaps Reesor would not have taken part in this service had it not been for Bishop Jesse Bauman's permission. Such actions alienated the people from Jesse.

The Old Orders of Waterloo had ceased to affiliate with Markham in 1930 because of the automobile issue. When the Markham-Waterloo Conference was formed in 1939, the conference continued numbering the calendar using 1931 as its beginning. (The 2001 calendar is the seventieth edition of the Markham-Waterloo Calendar of Appointments.)

The Markham group held its first instruction services on July 23, 1939 at Elmira. There were sixteen boys and four girls in the class for instruction prior to baptism. Bishop Moses Horst and Minister Israel Snyder from Ohio were present. During the first year, visiting ministry were very common, especially those from Markham. Bishop Jesse Bauman baptized this class at Elmira on September 10, 1939, with Deacon Joseph Barkey assisting him. The traditional Harvest Meeting (Thanksgiving Day) for the Old Orders is the first Thursday in September. The newly established Markham group elected to hold their Thanksgiving service on the national holiday, which falls on the second Monday of October. Consequently the Markham group held their first Thanksgiving Day on October 9, 1939 at the Elmira meetinghouse.

Evidently, Aden Brubacher's feeling that Jesse Bauman embraced a Frema Geisht was more than an intuition. On Friday, November 17, 1939, Isaac Martin wrote in his diary,

> A general Conference was held at West Woolwich (Elmira) in the presence of the following bishops, ministers and deacons; Jesse Bauman; Urias Martin; Bishop Abraham Smith, Minister Thomas Reesor, both of Markham; Bishop Moses G. Horst, Minister Abraham Good, of Ohio; Bishop Joseph Hostetter, of Pennsylvania; Minister Paul Hoover; and Deacon Joseph Bechtel, of Indiana. Jesse Bauman was not in harmony with the Conference Resolution.

At the conference Jesse promoted Sunday school and evening meetings. When Jesse refused to comply with the Conference's position of rejecting Sunday school and evening meetings, he was given until Sunday morning to change his position, which he did not. On Sunday, November 19, Isaac recorded in his diary, "Jesse Bauman was not permitted to take part in service." That meant Jesse had been set back as a bishop and no longer permitted to speak in the Markham-Waterloo Conference.

This action caused further confusion in the fellowship. Martin Frey and Selina Martin had been published the third time on November 19, 1939 and the wedding was planned for the following Tuesday. Jesse Bauman approached Martin Frey and asked him with which group he intended to associate. When Frey replied that he would fellowship with Urias, it was mutually understood that Jesse would not take part at the wedding. There was no small stir among those involved, who wondered what to do with no bishop to marry the couple. Bishop Smith from Markham could not legally officiate at the marriage because he was never present when the bans were published. The late Bishop Ezra Martin had obtained the necessary marriage papers for Urias Martin but had never given them to Urias. Urias was not prepared to take the opportunity to ask Ezra Junior for the papers but the bride's father was. The story goes that Ezra Jr. requested that Urias and his wife come for a dinner and a visit. That Monday night Urias and his wife visited Ezra Martin's and he then gave Urias the most coveted papers of that day. The commotion, turmoil and anxiety of that Monday all passed away when Urias officiated at the wedding of Martin Frey and Selina Martin. This is one of the known instances where the division created some very anxious and uncertain circumstances.

The Assimilation of Jesse Bauman's Followers

A meeting was held at Jesse Bauman's home on November 22, 1939 and Jesse and his followers agreed to make arrangements to hold meetings at the Elmira Conference Mennonite church. On December 3, 1939 Jesse held his first evening service at the Elmira church. Further services were held at St. Jacobs and Bloomingdale. By the spring of 1940 most of Jesse's followers were leaning towards the Conference Mennonite Church, and on July 7, 1940 Jesse and most of his sympathizers were received into the Elmira congregation.

The merger was not without suspicion on the part of the Conference Mennonites. Some people feared the supposed eternal security view that

Jesse was deemed to hold. Glenn Brubacher notes, "Jesse felt that when someone had tasted the heavenly Gift, he would never turn against Christ. The idea in his mind was very much unlike Calvin's view of eternal security, which the Brethren group held—theologically that is."[13] One can assume that Jesse's group had drawn from the Brethren's teachings. Jesse's followers wanted to be baptized even though they were all baptized in the Old Order church. This idea of rebaptism was not acceptable to the Conference Mennonite district overseer, Bishop S. F. Coffman from Vineland.[14] Neither was the Elmira congregation (Conference Mennonites) in agreement with Jesse's group that the Old Orders were still in heathen darkness.[15] Jesse brought with him about fifty members and over thirty unbaptized children.

Jesse Bauman's life is mirrored by other zealous and emotional Mennonite preachers. Daniel Hoch, Daniel Brenneman, and Solomon Eby all found themselves outside of the Conference Mennonite fellowship, even though they endeavoured to preach the Word as the Spirit led them. Although Jesse was pressured by some of his followers to establish a new church, he, unlike Hoch and Eby, declined and with the majority of his followers sought to unite with some existing church. By the sixties the Conference Mennonite church's eschatology shifted towards the former traditional amillennial view, as noted in the *Mennonite Encyclopedia:* "Relatively few Mennonite scholars espouse dispensationalism. . . ."[16] This shift alarmed the remnant of Jesse's group and in the late 1960s eighteen members left with their children and united with the Hawkesville Brethren in their newly-constructed chapel at Wallenstein.[17] Although Glenn Brubacher, in his essay "the Frema Geisht," minimized Jesse's eternal security leanings, Darby's premillennialism remained in the Elmira Mennonite church for years, and this thinking had been familiar to Jesse's people.

Conclusion

The flurry of revivalism during the first decades of the twentieth century did not leave the Old Order church unscathed. There were those who had a feel for Gelassenheit and were true to the faith of their fathers; however, they were not prepared for these new and more radical views. Some had become static and lax in attending worship services, and were also in need of a renewal and a closer walk with God.[18] The Hawkesville

Plymouth Brethren movement, and then the schism of 1939, drove the Old Order community to study the Word and achieve greater understanding of their beliefs. The uncertainty of World War II helped to strengthen the Old Order community's religion.

The teaching of eternal security affected a few of the Old Order leaders to the extent that they could barely teach and support the traditional Old Order principle of believing in a living hope. It would take a number of decades for the Old Order church to regain its former stability. The upheavals of the 1930s fostered the establishment of the family altar. There was a gradual shift towards more wholesome reading, more religious singing, and more edifying conversations.[19] The accusations made by some disgruntled former Old Orders, that they never heard God's way of salvation preached in the Old Order church, is unfair and untrue. Such individuals failed to develop the feeling of Gelassenheit and Ordnung and did not appreciate the church of their fathers. Unappreciated doctrines are of little spiritual value.

The turmoil of 1939 was a three-way affair. There were the traditional Old Orders who resisted change and remained as the Old Order. Those of Old Order orientation who desired access to the car and telephone followed Urias Martin, united with Markham, and became informally known as the Markham group. Jesse Bauman's people embraced more modern forms of worship, including revival meetings and Sunday school. These people in time scattered amongst the Conference Mennonites, Hawkesville Brethren and Pentecostals.[20] Married couples that were not in agreement about these differences found the Markham group a good compromise. If one party desired further liberty and the other saw no need for change, the more middle-of-the-road way became convenient. Family ties significantly influenced the decisions of many, and thus the division did not follow the lines that had formerly divided the Old Order community. There were many reasons why people chose the Markham church. It took the Markham church a number of years to establish formal Ordnung.

For the first two years the Markham group only used the Martins and Elmira meetinghouses. Once every five weeks the Old Orders used both meetinghouses and therefore the Markham group had no meetinghouse to worship in. On these Sundays they began to hold services at homes in the North Woolwich area. They made an agreement with the

Old Orders to use the North Woolwich meetinghouse so on May 11, 1941, they held their first service there.[21] After this North Woolwich was included in the cycle. Martin's and Elmira meetinghouses are jointly owned between the Old Order and Markham groups, but the Old Orders retained sole ownership of the North Woolwich meetinghouse even though the Markham group share the building expenses.

Since Bishop Amsey Martin resided in the North Woolwich district, George Brubacher was ordained for the Elmira congregation in 1942. At times George's sermons mirrored those of Jesse. There was a stir when George's wife uttered an audible prayer during the service in 1946. This expression may well have been quite normal within Pentecostal circles, but within an Old Order community it was considered the manifestation of a strange spirit. The appropriate confessions were made and peace was restored, but traces of Jesse's teachings also lingered. During the sixties some of the Markham group carried the Scofield Bible in church. These members largely became the target of the Wallenstein Chapel's effective proselytizing campaign during the late sixties and were won over to the chapel.

Many members appreciated Minister George Brubacher. However, the occasional hint of the Brethren's teaching escaped his lips, which would frustrate some members, like the father whose sons had left the fellowship to worship at the Chapel. George faithfully served the Markham church until he suddenly passed away while preaching at the Montrose church on April 16, 1978. Silence filled the well-filled meetinghouse as he was carried outside and Minister Noah Martin arose to proceed with the service.

The building of the Montrose and Goshen meetinghouses were also occasions when underlying values surfaced. In 1950 the Markham group built their first meetinghouse about two kilometres north of West Montrose. This meetinghouse deviated from the traditional Old Order seating arrangement in that it resembled the Conference Mennonite churches (cathedral style) with the pulpit at the gable-end of the building. When the Goshen church was built five years later it was constructed in the customary Old Order amphitheatre style with the pulpit along the side of the building. The Markham meetinghouses have since always been constructed in the amphitheatre style. All Markham meetinghouses have lobbies for both the men and women, while the Old Orders have lobbies only for the women.

The different seating arrangement at Montrose has been a point of contention, and the reason why it was built differently is not clear. Several opinions have surfaced —one being the availability of some used pews which were purchased. These pews were installed in the cathedral style. The second reason is more enlightening and supports the third. It has been said that Isaac Martin believed that eventually the casket would be brought into the meetinghouse for the funeral service and supported the cathedral-seating arrangement. (The Old Orders bury their dead and then go to the meetinghouse for worship, comfort and encouragement.) The third view suggested that after the Markham group had separated from the Old Order, at least some of them desired to be different from the Old Orders. Five years later, when Goshen was built, the pendulum had swung the other way and the more vocal part desired to be more like the Old Orders. They were, in the opinion of some, to be Old Orders with cars and telephones. Time has revealed that, in the beginning, the Markham Mennonites esteemed the Conference Mennonites above the Old Orders, but as the years passed by this estimation reversed, and the Markham group are now far more associated with the Old Orders than with the Conference Mennonites.

Notes

1 David M. Martin, *Wallenstein Bible Chapel* (Wallenstein, Ontario: Wallenstein Bible Chapel, 1968), 6.

2 Ken Bechtel, *Three Score Years*, (Elmira, Ontario: Bauman Printing, 1984), 33.

3 L. Freeman Private collection.

4 Private Conversation.

5 Bechtel, *Three Score Years*, 33.

6 *Ibid.*, 46.

7 *Ibid.*, 35.

8 *Ibid.*, 35.

9 Isaac Martin. Diary, 1936-40, CGUC.

10 *Ibid.*

11 Private Conversation.

12 Isaac Martin. Diary, 1936-40, CGUC.

13 Glenn Brubacher, "The Frema Geisht." (Unpublished college essay, n.d. Author's collection), 15.

14 *Ibid.*, 18

15 Bechtel, *Three Score Years*, 35.

16 ME, V, 241.

17 Bechtel, *Three Score Years*, 36.

18 Isaac R. Horst, "Mennogespräch." *Mennonite Historical Society of Ontario* 6 , 2 (1988): 12.

19 *Ibid.*

20 Bechtel, *Three Score Years*, 36.

21 Angus Bauman. Diary, May 11, 1941, Leonard Freeman collection, Elmira.

Old Orders During World War II

Chapter Seventeen

Prelude to War

The Great Depression had crippled the world's economies, leaving millions of people without work. Furthermore, the Treaty of Versailles had unduly restricted the German economy, thus when Hitler promised the Germans prosperity they voted him into power in 1933. Hitler rebuilt the German armed forces and thereby violated the Treaty of Versailles. By March 1938 Austria had fallen to German aggression. By March 1939 the Germans occupied Czechoslovakia and were secretly preparing to invade Poland. Most of Europe was still war-weary from World War I and was not eager to challenge the growing German power; however, everybody feared the impending war.

On September 1, 1939, the German army smashed into Poland and within weeks Poland fell. France and England declared war on Germany with Canada following suit. By June 22, 1940, Western Europe had collapsed and England stood alone facing the German might. England's position was very critical and Canadians became concerned when German submarines were spotted in the Gulf of the St. Lawrence and Japanese warships were sighted off the Pacific coast. Canada committed herself to the war and the Peace Churches were again faced with conscription and military service.

The Challenges of the Peace Churches in the West

World War I had ended with no real exemption from military service for the Peace Churches. A very restrictive order-in-council of October 25, 1918, had stated that "[the Mennonites] were not eligible for the 'exemptions' under the act."[1] Fortunately for the Mennonites, these amendments were not carried out before the war ended. Almost two decades later, in 1936, the Russian Mennonites in Western Canada inquired if the October 1918 order-in-council was permanently binding. They were assured that it was not, since it had been passed under the authority of the War Measures Act.[2] The Mennonites' exemption lay in the statute of 1868, which stated that the provision is subject to "such conditions . . . as the Governor-in-Council may from time to time prescribe." This clause was reason for some serious apprehension among Mennonites in the West who had immigrated in the 1920s. For the Old Orders in Ontario there is no evidence to suggest that they were concerned, or even aware, that such legislation existed since their freedom had not been seriously challenged.

By the winter of 1939 the international situation showed an apparent trend towards war, which could affect the non-resistant Mennonites in Canada. In the spring of 1939, the members of the Peace Churches (all Mennonite groups, Amish and Brethren in Christ) felt joint action would be important. Joint committee meetings were arranged where statements were prepared and examined, and an essential mutual agreement was established. It should be noted that all these actions were taken before war was declared; however, in the Canadian West the *Russlaender* (those who arrived in the 1920s) and the *Kanadier* (those who came in the 1870s) could not agree. The Kanadier had left Russia in the 1870s because they feared losing their non-resistant status in Russia. The Russlaender had remained in Russia and accepted alternative service in lieu of military training.

A meeting on May 15, 1939, revealed the sharp division in the Mennonite brotherhood in the West on the question of alternative service during war. The Kanadier rejected any kind of compulsory alternative service in lieu of military draft, while the Russlaender had found such an arrangement satisfactory in Russia during World War I and were willing to render a broader range of services, including medical and ambulance work at the front. The descendants of the Swiss Mennonites were willing to perform some form of alternative service if it were entirely separate from the military.[3] The issue was tabled but the war clouds drew closer.

The Mennonites in Western Canada definitely experienced more difficulties during World War II than did their eastern brethren. In June

1940 two Mennonite churches in Alberta were destroyed by fire.[4] In Manitoba, in the town of Gretna, the magistrate imposed a two-hundred dollar fine and a year of hard labour on six young men refusing to go into the military. The Mennonites in Saskatchewan also had their problems. In December 1941 seventy Mennonites out of 126 who had applied for alternative service, were denied military exemptions and ordered to take military training.[5]

The story of Sam Martin's prison experience also reveals that the authorities in the West were not prepared to grant the Mennonites exemptions without some difficulties. Sam Martin of Duchess, Alberta, had his CO status denied. Martin refused to don his military uniform and received three twenty-eight day jail sentences for his continual refusal to put on his uniform. When he refused a fourth time he was then sentenced to ninety days in a military prison. Martin again refused to don his uniform which led to his fifth sentence of eighteen months of hard labour in the Lethbridge jail. During his confinement Sam was forced to live on bread and water in a cell without heat or clothes (he was stripped except for his underwear) for forty-nine days. He received three blankets to sleep but they were taken away every morning. His army uniform was always with him in his cell but he chose not to put it on. After a doctor warned the army officials that Martin's health was endangered he was transferred to the provincial jail where he received better treatment. After spending over a year and a half in prison, Sam Martin was finally released several months after the war had ended.[6]

Table Four
Number of Conscientious Objectors During World War II

Province	Number
Manitoba	3021
Ontario	2636
Saskatchewan	2304
British Columbia	1665
Alberta	1184
Nova Scotia	29
Quebec	28
P.E.I.	3
New Brunswick	2
Total	10872

The book *Sam Martin Went to Prison* was bought by the Markham church and given to their youth during the 1990 Gulf War. It reveals the grim reality that the difficulties the COs in the West encountered were caused by the local official's interpretation of the law. The Canadian law had made the provision for exemption from military service, but not all the officials had the same interpretation of this law. In this story of the Old Order Mennonites in Ontario, time does not permit elaboration on the military problems of the West. However, it is important to bring to the reader's attention the fact that three quarters of all the Canadian conscientious objectors lived in the Canadian West.[7]

Formation of Alternative Service (AS)

By May 10, 1940, Western Europe had collapsed in catastrophic defeat. With the United States and Russia remaining neutral, only Britain and her dominions stood in Hitler's path to world domination. Under these grave conditions Canada reacted and passed the National Resources Mobilizations Act (NRMA) on June 21, 1940.

As the wartime preparations gained momentum, the Peace Churches realized more and more the gravity of the impending wartime problems. The Peace Churches gathered together under the initiative of E. J. Swalm, (chairman of the CHPC) and on July 22, 1940, the Conference of Historic Peace Churches (CHPC) of Ontario was born. The East was now united and prepared to negotiate with the officials as one voice; however, the West remained divided. The first requirement of the NRMA was that all citizens between ages sixteen and sixty register in August 1940. In Saskatchewan some Mennonites refused to register because they reasoned that registration would identify them with the war. Fourteen people were jailed for not registering, and when they were released they still refused to comply. They were jailed again. In Ontario the Mennonites registered according to law and also registered with the CHPC. The military authorities later recognized this formal registration with the CHPC and as a result the members of the CHPC received their postponement (1) from military service without personal interviews, which were so problematic in the West. (2)

(1) *During the Second World War the Canadian lawmakers avoided the use of exemption when addressing the role of the conscientious objectors (COs). The COs were not exempt from military service, their military service was indefinitely postponed in lieu of alternative service.*

The CHPC drafted a detailed alternative service proposal and delivered it by letter to the officials in Ottawa on October 16, 1940.

(2) *The following happenings are interviews with the officials in the West.*
A young Mennonite...came before the Board and one of the questions was: "Did you go to school?" Answer: "Yes" Question: "Did you ever have a scrap in school?" Answer: "Yes"—"Well, you are not a conscientious objector, your application is not accepted, get out!!!"
Another boy came before the Board. "Are you a Mennonite and a Conscientious Objector?" Answer: "Yes." "Why is it that you are asking for a postponement?" Answer: "Besides being a Mennonite and a Conscientious Objector, I am a farmer and I am the only one working on the farm." Answer: "I do not care a hoot about your farm, we want you, your application is not accepted, get out!!!"[8]

By the fall of 1940, the Russlaender were also ready for joint action with the CHPC and on November 12, 1940, a delegation of eight members, four from the East and four from the West, met with deputy ministers of the National War Services. The deputy ministers resisted the idea of alternative service under civilian control, which the CHPC desired, and the delegation resisted the deputy's view of non-combatant service under military control. The Mennonites' objective of service in the agricultural and forestry industries held little value to military officials whose army was in dire need of men. On November 22 the delegation met again with the deputy ministers. This meeting did not go well.

B. B. Janz of Alberta had personally presented a new proposal where an ambulance and/or medical programme would be acceptable if it was under the supervision of the Red Cross. He did not completely reject alternative service under military control. This is what the military had wanted to hear.[9] E. J. Swalm had received this message the evening before from Bishop J. B. Martin of Waterloo. For the CHPC this was a desperate attempt to thwart Janz's plan for alternative service under military supervision. The deputies tried to exploit the Mennonite division, but the Mennonites were determined to remain united. A stalemate was inevitable after Deputy L. R. LaFleche and Jacob H. Janzen clashed. LaFleche had challenged the delegates: "What will you do if we shoot you?" This was too much for Janzen, who had experienced the Russian civil war, and had survived several desperate episodes in the Soviet Union. "Listen General" he replied, "I want to tell you something. You can't scare us like that. I've looked down too many rifle barrels in my time to be scared in that way. This thing is in our blood for four hundred years and you can't take it away from us like you'd crack a piece of kindling over your knee. I was before a firing squad twice. We believe in this."[10]

The delegation decided to spend the night in prayer. Since they were sceptical of LeFleche, they proposed to meet with Hon. James G. Gardiner, Minister of National Defence. Gardiner had learned to know the Brethren in Christ, respected them, and was surprisingly sympathetic towards the CHPC's cause. He gave his ear to the delegates as they explained their position and assured them: "There's a hundred and one things you fellows could do without fighting and we'll see that you get them."[11] On the day before Christmas 1940, an amendment was passed paving the way for Alternative Service under civilian control.

The Kanadier stood aloof until February of 1941, when their delegates to Ottawa were informed that, "it is impossible at this time to dismiss you from all service because of the agitation amongst the people."[12] Despite the disappointment, the Kanadier leaders accepted the verdict and cooperated with the government's Alternative Service (AS) programme, along with the "Russlaender" and CHPC. For the duration of the war a commendable level of cooperation continued between the Mennonites and government officials. Even though the Jehovah's Witnesses were granted alternative service like the Peace Churches, they chose not to cooperate. Over ninety per cent of all prosecutions of postponed COs during the war were Jehovah's Witnesses.[13]

Alternative Service Work Camps (AS)

The announcement for the first call-up for the AS was on May 29, 1941. The Minister of Mines and Resources reopened some of the Depression-era work camps that provided work in national Parks and highway construction. On July 1, 1941, the first groups were sent to the camps in Montreal River, Ontario, Riding Mountain National Park, Manitoba and Lac La Ronge, Saskatchewan. These men were required to serve four months, which was mandatory for military training; however, by November the situation changed and the men were informed that "each and every one of them is subject . . . to alternative service work for the duration of the war."[14] During the war the Minister of Mines and Resources opened a total of eight camps.

The camp at Montreal River in Ontario was the first camp organized. The COs began to arrive in July 1941. During the first summer, up to

165 men were working at the Montreal River Camp. In July, 1942 the camp was closed and those who were not farmers were transferred to the British Columbia Forestry Service. The Montreal River Camp was reopened during the winter of 1943, but was then closed in preference of the Selective Service (SS) programme. All told, 478 men served at Montreal River Camp. Of these, fifty-five were Old Orders.[15]

The Japanese raid on Pearl Harbour in Dec., 1941, had damaged the United States' navy and left the Pacific coast open to Japanese attack. The B.C. government did not have sufficient manpower to protect its vital forests from the feared Japanese incendiary bombs. The Federal Minister of Mines and Resources arranged a contract with the B.C. Forest Service to have AS workers transferred and serve as forestry workers. During 1942, an average of 740 AS workers were stationed in British Columbia of whom about two hundred were from Ontario. On June 1, 1942, a number of non-farm Old Order Mennonites left Kitchener for Green Timber Forest Service Camp in British Columbia to serve as forest rangers. These men were told they must serve there for the duration of the war. The B.C. Forest Service had nineteen CO camps open in 1943. Fourteen of these were on Vancouver Island. The Old Order Mennonites of Ontario for the most part only have memories of Montreal River Camp, although there were a few who were stationed on Vancouver Island. The numerous camps in the West were primarily stationed with Mennonites of Russian or Dutch descent.

The acute manpower shortage that developed as the war progressed resulted in the reduction of the men in the Forest Service to 450 men by December 1943.[16] By March 1944 the Japanese threat along the B.C. coast was over and the federal government cancelled the contract by B.C. Forest Service.

The threat of enemy sabotage was the primary reason the COs were sent to the B.C. Forest Service, but less than eight percent of the man hours were devoted to the seasonal fire-fighting task. During the two years the AS workers were in B.C., they fought a total of 234 fires, but none were started by enemy action. Reforestation accounted for forty-three per cent of their time—AS workers planted over seventeen-million trees. Approximately three-hundred miles of roads were improved or constructed under the request of National Defence authorities.[17] These improvements resulted in permanent assets for the B.C. Forest Service. The balance of the time was spent in cordwood production and other miscellaneous projects. Assisting the B.C. Forest Service was one of the greater contributions made by the AS workers.[18]

Selective Service and Red Cross Contributions

Selective Service (SS) was phase two of the Alterative Service programme. SS allowed the men to work productively for a limited wage.

The Canadian total war effort resulted in an acute manpower shortage by the end of 1942. In January 1943, a delegation from the CHPC met with the federal deputy minister of labour, Arthur MacNamara. He asked the delegation their opinion on having AS (Alternative Service) workers employed in private industry. The CHPC favoured the possibility of their men making a far greater contribution to their country, but they feared the disparity of earnings would generate unrest among their people. The CHPC favoured group employment so it would be easier to provide religious guidance, and they desired that the work would be clearly for the public, that is for their country. In April 1943, an order-in-council paved the way for a far more complex plan for the COs of Canada. After considerable dialogue between the government officials and the CHPC, a scheme was arranged where the AS workers would serve in Agriculture, Experimental Farms, Feed Mills, Food Processing, Meat Packing, Cheese-making, Creameries and Dairies, Canning Factories, Teaching, Hospital Service, and Medical and Dental Services.[19] The implementing of this major task was the responsibility of the Department of Labour.

Service contracts were the avenue by which the Department of Labour directed AS workers to a place of employment it deemed a priority. If a CO applied for a service contract, he became a Selective Service (SS) worker. For a farmer to qualify for an SS worker (hired man), he had to have enough livestock or work to warrant a labourer according to the Department of Labour's standards. (E. J. McLoughry, the Waterloo County agricultural representative, had significant input in these farm-related regulations for the Old Order Mennonites.) The Mennonite Church took great pains in trying to be fair to all its members. The poor members who had almost lost their farms during the Depression were in no position to expand their farming operations to qualify to keep their own sons at home. There were hurt feelings when these sons had to work away from home or even outside the community. The SS workers were given the opportunity to accept such a contract in lieu of spending their time at the AS camps. Aside from the Jehovah's Witnesses, almost all COs chose to accept a service contract after that option became available in the spring of 1943.

In Waterloo County the Mennonites were privileged to have E. J. McLoughry serve on the board of administration. If a Mennonite farmer qualified to have a labourer, and an AS worker wanted to work, for his uncle for example, McLoughry would recommend this to the board. The Mennonites received many such favours from the quiet work of McLoughry.

These service contracts were at times short-lived and involved seasonal work in canning factories. A number of Mennonites from Waterloo were given contracts to work at a Simcoe canning factory while several other boys were called to work in a Chatham canning factory from September 12, to October 6, 1944. The industrial contracts stipulated that a worker labour for five eight-hour days in a week. This left the men with a lot of spare time, which some put to good use. It was evidently accepted for Selective Service workers in industry to find gainful employment during their off hours, which some did at the Simcoe canning factory where they worked extra hours for which they received full pay.

It was mentioned above that the CHPC was concerned about equality in the wages earned by its men. Equality was gained by a system of wage deductions payable to the Canadian Red Cross. The government froze the wages of the SS workers at twenty-five dollars per month. The employer agreed to forward the balance of the SS worker's wages to the Canadian Red Cross, which meant that about half of a SS worker's wages was forwarded to the Red Cross. In the West, where the Mennonites were hired for higher-paying jobs, the Minister of Labour approved a scale of payments for the Red Cross with a maximum of fifty dollars per month.[20] By the summer of 1944, twenty-five dollars per month proved to be insufficient for a man with dependants, and amendments were made, but not without the Canadian Legion protesting this "conchies pay boost."[21] These Red Cross payments were not discontinued until the spring of 1946, which was a full year after the war in Europe had ceased.[22]

The Red Cross contributions were a welcomed gift to the Red Cross at a time of great need. Approximately $2,250,000 was paid to the Red Cross by the COs across Canada during the war. The sacrifice the COs made cannot be reckoned in monetary values alone, but one must realize that it was about half of their pay. It was like a tax that was deducted from their pay cheque; they only received what was left and at times this caused financial difficulties. Young men who were farming and qualified for Selective Service were also required to make Red Cross payments of twenty dollars per month. Although the COs felt the burden of their meagre service, one cannot compare this sacrifice to that of families who lost sons in battle.

A young Mennonite was distressed because his Red Cross payment was due and he had no money to pay. He was grateful to God, who moved an anonymous brother to mail him the twenty dollars.[23] Even though it was a burden at the time, a contemporary stated that he didn't feel the Red Cross payments deprived them, because after the war the economy boomed and they all had a fair chance in life.

It was not just the Red Cross payment that troubled the Mennonites. The uncertainty of the times and the ridicule directed towards them by the general public had a sobering effect on the youth. However, the disrupted social life of those requested to work beyond the Mennonite community was another matter. One Old Order Mennonite, while home on leave, told his father that he was exposed to the radio. Without contacting the CHPC or the government officials, his father went and took his son home. Such a break of a service contract was equivalent to deserting the army. This action created a conflict for the CHPC that was very difficult to resolve.

It was a challenge for the youth to be removed from their familiar confines and to enter a different culture. Mistreatment was not a problem because an abusive boss could be reported and the SS worker transferred. However, one SS worker discovered he had a tough boss. When his boss went to town he was asked to move some straw to the other side of the mow. The next time the boss went to town he was told to move it back where it had been. As a CO it was not fruitful to complain, but even the most zealous workaholic will be tempted to balk when he is asked to work without a purpose.[24]

The Demobilization of Alternative Service Men

On May 7, 1945, the hostilities in Europe ceased. It became obvious that the demobilizing of the AS men was more of a political manoeuvre than an economic question. There was a substantial cost for the government to keep the Alterative Service programme in operation, but the Canadian Legion and others were making it clear that the "conchies" should not be discharged until the regular service men were at home and had found employment. A. MacNamara, Deputy Minister of Labour, wrote, " . . . Conscientious Objectors have gotten off very, very lightly . . . Ninety per cent of the public will resent the relieving of the Conscientious Objectors of further contributions until our boys who are serving are relieved from further service and returned to their homes."[25]

MacNamara addressed a very vital point—the Conscientious Objectors had gotten off very, very lightly. The Canadian government had been generous enough to foot the bill for the Canadian Alternative Service programme and it even paid a token fee of fifty cents per day to those who refused to participate in the Selective Service programme. Very few Mennonites, if any, refused Selective Service. Such generosity was not found in Russia during World War I, nor south of the border during World War II. During World War I the Russian Mennonite community contributed over fifteen hundred thousand dollars in 1917 alone to support their men in Civilian services.[26]

American Mennonites were confronted with conscription as early as 1940, even though they did not enter the war until after the Japanese attacked Pearl harbour in December 1941. After much dialogue with the officials they organized Civilian Service Camps, but President Roosevelt expressed opposition to the state's paying the COs wages.[27] As a result, the Peace Churches of the United States picked up a tab of $3,032,286.75 for the privilege of having Civilian Public Service camps for their men in lieu of joining the armed forces.[28] It cost the American Mennonites an estimated thirty-five dollars per month to have a man in a Civilian Service Camp, while the Canadian COs earned twenty-five dollars per month. In the case of the Old Orders of Ontario the men were in their home community most of the time. The Military Problems Committee had its share of frustrations in keeping the system running smoothly, but by and large the Peace Churches of Ontario were thought to "have gotten off very, very lightly."

The number of COs (all denominations) who participated in the Red Cross payments across Canada was 10,851.[29] Of this total 7,543 were Mennonites, of whom about eighty per cent were farmers. It has been estimated that another forty-five-hundred Mennonites volunteered to enlist in the armed forces.[30] Some of these may have been alienated from their home churches long before the war, but there were those who denied the traditional non-resistant teaching and enlisted against the wishes of the church. One Sunday morning the St. Jacobs Mennonite church excommunicated four of their young men because they had enlisted in the army. Two boys of Old Order heritage also enlisted, but there are no records or stories that any enlisted from the David Martin or the Markham groups. Those who had enlisted found it difficult to be reconciled to their congregation of origin after the war because they had denied the traditional non-resistant faith.

The community as a whole exerted a lot of pressure for the young men to enlist. The anti-German propaganda was very effective, as Fred Snyder would discover. In 1941 Snyder believed it was his patriotic duty to serve, but when he saw the destruction of the German cities, he realized that war was appalling on both sides. After the war he commented that when a person enlists, "You park your brains at the door and you change overnight . . . In the military you don't think, you just follow instructions."[31] Nevertheless, we must respect those who fought in the war. Sleeping in muddy slit trenches, being shell-shocked, and seeing your buddy fall was real for those at the front. The horrible memories the soldiers brought home with them had to be buried with time, and the careless comments of the plain people at times deeply offended those men. A farmer commented that if the war had continued a few more years, he could have paid for his farm. Such thoughts were selfish, inconsiderate, totally inexcusable, and would surely offend a veteran.

One of the reasons that the Mennonites had "gotten off very, very lightly" during the war was the knowledge that Prime Minister W. L. Mackenzie King had of the Mennonites. King, a native of Waterloo County, had gone to school with Mennonite children and had learned to respect and appreciate the Mennonites. Respect has to be earned, and when the Peace Churches approached Major-General L. R. LaFleche in 1940, they were strangers to him. As a Frenchman from Quebec, he probably had heard little about the non-resistant faith. Therefore, he gave little consideration to the Peace Churches' request for some form of Alternative Service. Hon. James G. Gardiner's favourable connections with the Brethren in Christ and the understanding and cooperative position of E. J. McLoughry all contributed to the fact that the Peace Churches were treated fairly during World War II.

Honourable Humphrey Mitchell, Minister of Labour, who was in charge of the Alternative Service programme, made the following statement concerning the "conchies": "Conscientious Objectors have willingly undertaken heavy and difficult work during the war. Their services have been available at several periods when critical situations developed due to labour shortage." He also felt that "The average conscientious objector in Canada is entirely sincere in his desire to do everything short of actual combat duties to be of service to his country in time of war."[32] The officials understood that the conchies' fifty cents a day wage was not much of an incentive and stated that: "The work performed under the circumstances was surprisingly satisfactory."[33]

In all likelihood, the key to the success of the Alternative Service programme lay in the cooperation of the Peace Churches' leadership with the government officials responsible. The persistent efforts of E. J. Swalm, chairman of the Historic Peace Churches, caused him to visit the officials in Ottawa eighteen times during the war.[34] In spite of such doggedness, J. F. MacKinnon, Chief Alternative Service Officer, pays special tribute to the cooperativeness of the Mennonites:

> The Mennonites cooperated in every way from the beginning of Alternative Service. There was very close cooperation between the Mennonite bishops and the Alternative Service officials. Perhaps it can be said that this group contributed more than any other group to Alternative Service... the bishops were always willing to discuss mutual problems and to go as far as possible to cooperate within the limits of their conscience.[35]

The Peace Churches appreciated the cordial and friendly relationship between them and the Canadian Government. On September 25, 1945, E. J. Swalm, J. B. Martin and Elven Shantz delivered the following letter, in person, to the Right Honourable W. L. Mackenzie King:

Honourable Sir:

We, the undersigned, duly authorized representatives of the Conference of Historic Peace Churches, do hereby present a brief statement of our appreciation and gratitude to you and your Government for the kindly consideration you have shown to our participating groups, namely: Mennonites, Brethren in Christ (Tunkers), and Quakers, during the years of war from which we are presently emerging.

We have, as you are well aware, a traditional and Scriptural background which causes us to hold very strong convictions against taking part in war. The opportunity of service to our country as provided in Alternative Service was, with few exceptions, very acceptable to us and greatly appreciated.

We believe that your administration in preserving inviolate the right of conscience and the religious liberty of minority groups, exercised a Christian virtue which is the basis of all true democratic government.

We believe this will result in the blessing of the Eternal God resting on yourself and the people of Canada whom you have so efficiently led for an unprecedented length of time.

We hope and pray that our people may ever be mindful of this great kindness and that the Parliament of Canada may continue to extend such liberties in the future.

Respectfully submitted by,
E. J. Swalm, Chairman of Historic Peace Churches
J. B. Martin, Chairman of Military Problems Committee
Elven Shantz, Secretary of Military Problems Committee

Prime Minister King cordially accepted this letter and thanked the Peace Churches for their cooperation.[36]

The Canadian government was remarkably accommodating towards the Mennonites during both of the World Wars. Towards the end of World War I, when law removed the Mennonites' provisions for exemption from military service, the local Members of Parliament were still able to work out an informal arrangement that allowed the young men to receive "leaves of absence" from the army. During World War II the church leaders feared that public pressure would erode their exemption from military service and laboured hard to have the alternative service programme established. Both of these arrangements were a compromise in which the Mennonites received their cherished military exemptions at a time when they were legally conscripted into the army.

The freedom of religion is not necessarily guaranteed by civil law. Laws can change, as the Kanadier in the West discovered when the 1873 Order-in-Council, which granted "entire exemption from any Military service," was effectively cancelled by a new Order-in-Council of December 24, 1940, which paved the way for Alternative Service in Canada.[37] Exemption from military service in a time of war will only be possible if the Conscientious Objectors' testimony demonstrates peacefulness and non-resistance during a time of peace. The Plain and/or Peace Churches must command the respect of their neighbours and the officials during a time of peace if toleration is to be expected during times of war. It is evident that the government's concession only came about once sympathetic politicians laboured on behalf of the Peace Churches. The Old Order Mennonites' exemption from Canada Pension Plan (CPP) was no exception.

Nevertheless, the Old Order Mennonites have a greater calling than to retain the respect of their neighbours. Freedom of religion, like salvation, cannot be earned. It is a gift from God. Christians are not to be surprised if the world hates them: "If the world hate you, ye know that it hated me before it hated you" (John 15:19). Furthermore, "Woe unto you, when all men speak well of you" (Luke 6:26)! Christians must fear God more than man and this includes to . . . "live peaceably with all men" (Romans 12:18). During times of persecution, God, for reasons unknown to His people, withdraws this gift and His children suffer for His name's sake. The theme of Gelassenheit was born during a time of persecution and if the Old Order live according to the peaceful laws of Christ their neighbours may learn to respect them as the Swiss respected their Anabaptist neighbours.

Relief Work After the War

The war left large parts of Europe in ruins and the people had little means to sustain themselves. In order to help stabilize these war-torn countries the United States, through the Marshall Plan, helped re-organize

Europe and sent about thirteen billion dollars in food, machinery, and other products to Europe so these countries could rebuild their roads and restructure their economies. A massive amount of relief entered Europe, and the Mennonites took part in helping those in need.

Millions of people were displaced during the war and these endured extreme hardships. An example of this is found in *Up from the Rubble* by Peter J. and Elfrieda Dyck, where 614 persons fled from the Ukraine beginning October 7, 1943. This group endeavoured to stay ahead of the retreating German Army, and was on its disastrous journey for twenty-two months. By the time they arrived in West Germany there were only thirty-three persons remaining in the group.[38] Many more Mennonite refugees surfaced in Germany after the war. MCC chartered a ship, the *Volendam,* and transported 2303 refugees to Argentina in 1947. This was the first of several chartered voyages of refugees that MCC sponsored.

When MCC called for old horse-drawn equipment to be shipped to South America to help these refugees in getting started, the Old Order community of Ontario also responded. For several years after the war, thousands of relief bundles (clothes and canned food) were shipped to Europe. Old Order deacon Angus Bauman makes frequent reference in his diary to preparing and sending bundles to the needy in Europe. In November 1945, a number of families in the Old Order community butchered and canned a cow that was sent to Europe. The following year reference is made to preparing about four thousand cans of beef for relief. By 1948 the Old Order community was supporting a meat-canning for relief enterprise at Seranus Martin's cider mill in Floradale. In 1951 there was an apple butter campaign for relief, and the Old Orders donated about four-hundred bags of apples for this project. The next year two tons of apple butter were canned at the St. Jacob's cider mill as an Old Order donation.[39] Although the Old Orders do not write about their relief projects, I felt it necessary to reveal the shift in support of the NRRO or MCC as opposed to the World War I era. The Waterloo Old Order Mennonites were not united in relief support in World War I, but by World War II the group as a whole was supportive of relief work. One may suggest that the Old Order community had found its sense of identity and became more willing to cooperate with the Mennonite community as a whole in such relief projects.

Notes

[1] William Janzen, *Limits on Liberty* (Toronto: University of Toronto Press, 1990), 195.

[2] *Ibid*, 198.

[3] T. D. Regehr, *Mennonites in Canada 1939-1970: A People Transformed* (Toronto: University of Toronto Press, 1996), 39.

[4] Janzen, *Limits*, 206.

[5] Janzen, *Limits*, 215. It should be noted that during World War II conscription was only for national defence. That meant all men were required to take military training, but those who declined to volunteer for service overseas were on call for national defence.

[6] William Janzen and Frances Greaser, *Sam Martin Went to Prison: A Story of Conscientious Objection in Canada and Military Service* (Winnipeg, Manitoba: Kindred Press, 1990).

[7] Conscientious Objectors include Amish, Doukhobors, Hutterites, and Mennonites.

[8] Janzen, *Limits*, 221.

[9] Regehr, *Mennonites*, 48.

[10] *Ibid.*, 48.

[11] Janzen, *Limits*, 208.

[12] *Ibid.*, 210.

[13] J.A. Toews, *Alternative Service in Canada during World War II* (Winnipeg, MB: Christian Press Ltd., 1959), 51.

[14] Regehr, *Mennonites*, 52.

[15] Angus Bauman, Diary, May 11, 1941, Leonard Freeman collection, Elmira.

[16] Toews, *Alternative Service*, 87.

[17] *Ibid.*, 88.

[18] Camp life has been well described by Noah Bearinger's account of personal experience. His article, "No Spears of Iron" appeared in the June and July 1986 edition of the *Family Life,* an Amish publication.

[19] Janzen, *Limits*, 226.

[20] Toews, *Alternative Service*, 93.

[21] *Ibid.*, 91.

[22] *Ibid.*, 72.

[23] Private Conversation.

[24] Private Conversation.

[25] Toews, *Alternative Service*, 71.

[26] Guy F. Hershberger, *War, Peace & Nonresistance* (Scottdale, PA: Herald Press, 1981), 95.

[27] Melvin Gingerich, *Service for Peace* (Scottdale, PA: Herald Press, 1949), 57.

[28] Hershberger, *War*, 125.

[29] Toews, *Alternative Service*, 95.

30 Regehr, *Mennonites.*

31 *Ibid.*, 38.

32 Toews, *Alternative Service*, 110.

33 *Ibid.*, 111.

34 E. J. Swalm, Conversation with Author, 1985.

35 Toews, *Alternative Service*, 111.

36 E. J. Swalm, Conversation with Author, 1985.

37 Regehr, *Mennonites*, 49.

38 Peter & Elfrieda Dyck, *Up From The Rubble* (Scottdale, PA: Herald Press, 1991), 89.

39 Angus Bauman, Diary, 1933-1954, Leonard Freeman collection, Elmira.

Old Order Mennonite Life

Chapter Eighteen

In this chapter the term Old Order Mennonite includes all Old Order Mennonite groups, while Old Order reflects only the largest group or the main body from which the other groups originated.

Their Order of Worship

The order of worship within the Old Order Mennonite circles has been remarkably constant. The service begins when one of the leaders announces a German hymn. (The Old Order Mennonites hold their services in German, except the Markham group which uses English exclusively.) After the congregational singing has ended, a deacon rises to read the text chosen by the minister who is to have the main sermon (frequently referred to as the minister who "has the text"). During the early 1800s the Waterloo County deacons remained seated to read the text but this custom has long since changed.

The minister who speaks first has the "opening message." This speaker frequently comments on the song that was sung and delivers further admonition as the Spirit leads him. The ministers do not formally prepare their sermon with notes, but spend time in reading, meditation, and prayer. When they rise to speak, they frequently comment that they covet the prayers of the congregation while they commit themselves to the guidance of the Spirit to bring a message to the congregation. The concept behind Mennonite leadership is servitude—they are servants called by God to lead the flock. The office or position of the ordained men is highly respected by the congregation and those who reveal a truly humble attitude are admired, while aggression and over-confidence are not accepted. At the close of the "opening," the minister asks the congregation to kneel and join him in silent prayer and to be mindful of the minister who is to have the "text."

The minister who has the "text" is normally a visiting minister from another congregation. The length of the sermon is about one hour. When the minister takes his seat, any minister or bishop who did not speak now speaks and the deacons give testimony. To give testimony means to acknowledge that they are in agreement with what was said, or they can make further brief comments regarding the messages brought by both speakers. (1) When the testimonies are ended, the speaker who had the "text" rises and asks the congregation to kneel with him in prayer. This prayer is always audible and ends with the recitation of the Lord's Prayer. At this time the song leader announces a closing song for the congregation. The main speaker then rises and says the benediction and any further announcements are made. The congregation is then dismissed.

(1) *There is some flexibility within the Old Order Mennonite circles. It is customary to the Old Orders to have at least two testimonies, therefore, ministers have at times testified to each other's messages, and aged men from the congregation have been asked to give testimony.*
One Markham congregation stands for the last prayer so the interpreters can sign to the deaf-mute members in a inconspicuous manner.

Men and women are seated separately. The women always sit to the right of the minister in the meetinghouse while the men sit to the left. The schoolchildren and youth also have their appropriate places, with boys sitting in front of and to the left of the minister and the girls in front of and to the right. The seating arrangement also reflects the custom that the woman sits to the left of her husband on the buggy, and at formal events such as weddings. This reflects the distinctive role between men and women which will be discussed later.

Meeting Calendar Data and Its Purpose

Why did the nineteenth-century Mennonites choose only to use their meetinghouses once in four weeks, or at most every other week? Is the custom traceable to the era of persecution, when no set schedule would have been possible? Or does it reflect the difficult pioneer days? We may never ascertain the reasons why services were held irregularly. The Mennonite culture has always promoted social interaction. Visiting the brethren on Sunday is beneficial for all, but the Mennonites' spirituality was challenged by the once-in-four-weeks' services.

For seventy-four years (1858-1932) the Mennonite community of Woolwich had a four-week cycle for its meetinghouses. This meant the Martins location was used on the first week, West Woolwich (Elmira) on the second week, and North Woolwich and Conestogo continued this cycle on the third and fourth weeks with Martins beginning the cycle again on the fifth week. Because of this cycle, and since they used heavier and slower horses for transportation along poorly maintained roads, it was common during those long years for people to attend church services only once or twice a month. This cycle gave the Mennonites ample opportunity to attend church services in other local denominations and there is evidence that this occurred. At the turn of the century there were Old Order children who had memories of attending the Lutheran Sunday School in Elmira. In 1932 when the Old Orders began to hold services at two meetinghouses on each Sunday, the opportunity to attend services increased. During these decades unarranged visitation was common on Sundays. If church services were in another district, people would simply drop in on an acquaintance on Sunday morning, stay for dinner, and visit in the afternoon.

After services began to be held at more meetinghouses on one given Sunday, visiting practices developed along other lines and people began to attend services other than those of their home congregation and then visited people in that congregation. The terms "home church" and "having company" developed out of this practice. When one's meetinghouse is listed in the calendar one has "home" church and expects to "have company" from anyone in the larger community whose congregation is not listed in the calendar of appointments. For the Mennonites this movement of the people throughout the larger community is considered to be beneficial for the brotherhood. The interaction between members is encouraged throughout the whole community. The community remains a fellowship of many congregations and does not become congregational. It is interesting to note that only the Ontario Old Order Mennonites have retained this form of informally visiting members throughout the community as a whole.

The second positive effect of only having "home" church about half of the time is that the ministers also are free to move around and serve at other congregations throughout the community. It is customary that the "home" minister, the one ordained for that congregation, has the opening part of the service, while the visiting minister has the main sermon or the "text." Consequently, the Mennonites have a variety of speakers that preach at their services on Sunday mornings. Since the Mennonites rely on an untrained, self-supporting ministry, the sharing of each one's personal talent in presenting the Word gives the people a varied presentation of and emphasis on the Word. (The Old Order Mennonite ministers in the United States rotate among the congregations and thereby give the laity a variety of speakers.)

The traditional visiting custom is to just drop in without a formal invitation. This is no problem on the part of the hostess. When they have "home" church the women are prepared for company, as they expect to have visitors. In the Old Order Mennonite circles the women prepare excellent meals and the visiting women help the hostess prepare the dinner and clean up after the meal. The men and boys rarely help in the kitchen in the presence of company, but they always help to eat. Small errands like fetching a few extra chairs are common, but the fact remains that Old Order Mennonite men are in general novice cooks.

The Old Order Mennonite congregations in Ontario regularly worship and then visit with other congregations within the community as a whole. The meeting calendars show which meetinghouses are open and thus encourage visiting.

Singing as Part of Life

All Old Order Mennonite groups encourage singing. Youth gather in homes on Sunday evenings to socialize and sing. At weddings the guests draw together to sing. Even the youth on bus trips are known to pass time in singing hymns. The David Martin group will stop singing if the driver joins in and sings with them. They will not worship with others in any way. (The David Martin people are great singers. They have been known to sing at a barn-raising when rain stopped the work.) For the occasions listed above, four-part acappella singing in English is the norm but German songs may also be included.

Congregational singing amongst the Old Order Mennonites is in unison. (The Old Order sing one song at the beginning of their services and one at the closing, while the Markham sing two English songs, both at the beginning and ending of their service.) Their German hymnal *Lieder-Sammlung* and the Markham group English hymnal *Mennonite Hymns* do not have music written in them. The concept of a brotherhood, that is oneness, influences the Old Order Mennonites' singing ideals. Choirs are not acceptable within their circles because they tend to elevate one member above another in estimation of their ability to sing. Likewise choristers remain seated in the audience and are simply called *Forsinga* (song leaders). These men are asked to lead in the singing, but they are not conspicuous to others unless they slip up and pick a tune that will not fit to the metre in which the song is written. Such an embarrassment was described by one song-leader as, "an excellent way to humility." Another song-leader commented and said, "there is no better way to make a fool of one's self." A song-leader's job is a challenge some experts would decline, because without pitch-pipe or musical notes, a tune must be picked from memory or personal notes while the minister reads a verse or two of the song he announced. The first number of words are solo until the congregation recognizes the tune and joins in.

It is surprisingly rare but a Forsinga may stumble on occasion. In the Elmira meetinghouse some time ago the minister announced the first song and read the first verse. The unfortunate song leader began singing a tune that did not match the hymn. The singing stopped short and deafening silence followed. Then another courageous singer made an attempt to sing the song, but his tune also clashed and silence ruled again. A third try ended in like embarrassment. At this time the minister suggested that they could sing the next song, which created no further problems for the humbled Forsinga. It was the song-leader's duty to announce the closing song and he announced that troublesome number that had held the song-leaders at bay and without a ripple led the congregation through that song as the closing hymn.

The singing schools of the 1800s brought with them too much change and the Old Order rejected the innovation, but by the 1930s the Old Order were holding their own Singing Schools and taught a limited amount of theory and used the hymnbooks of their preference with shaped notes.

The *Philharmonia* was the hymnbook used by the Old Order for social singing until the second decade of the twentieth century when the *Church and Sunday School Hymnal* was introduced at the youth singings and was used until in the late 1970s the *Christian Hymnal* was introduced into the Old Order circles and it became the main hymnal for social singing. The German hymnal *Glaubens – Lieder* also found its way into the Old Order community in the 1970s.

By the late 1990s the Old Orders recognized that the old *Philharmonia,* printed in 1875, was still very much a part of their heritage since the tunes they sing in their Sunday services are found in this hymnbook. Furthermore, the desire to preserve and promote these older hymns with an emphasis on discipleship convinced the Old Orders that it was time to print the hymnal again. The style in which the music was written was changed to the conventional manner, but it still includes the metre number of the song and its relation to the German hymnal *Lieder-Sammlung* tune index. The Old Order in Ontario published the new edition of the *Philharmonia* in 1999. In 2002 Vineyard Publications, an Old Order enterprise, published a hymnal, *Musical Meditations.* The songs of this small hymnal are written and composed almost exclusively by Josiah Weber, a member of the Old Order Mennonites.

The Markham group has used numerous hymnals for their social singings. *Crowning Day* and *Life Song Number Two* were used, along with the *Church and Sunday School Hymnal* for several decades after the group began in 1939. By the 1960s *Radio Favorites* and *Favorite Songs and Hymns* had replaced *Crowning Day* and *Life Song Number Two*. When the *Radio Favorites* and *Favorite Songs and Hymns* went out of print, youth sought new songbooks like the *New Songs of Inspiration* series and other modern songbooks. By about 1990, a number of members expressed interest in compiling a new hymnbook that would include some of their old favourites found in those old out-of-print books. The new *Inspiring Favorites* hymnbook, published in 1992, was the fruit of their labours. The Markham group has been much more open to modern songs than are the other Old Order groups. Since the 1950s the song leaders of the Markham group have exercised their liberty more and more to choose tunes of their liking in the congregational singing as opposed to the traditional tunes of the *Philharmonia.* Over the years some of the older members have commented on the *Frema* (unfamiliar) tunes used during worship services. The use of tunes more popular with the youth encouraged four-part acappella singing within the Markham group. Some members have sung four-part music from memory in church since the 1960s.

After the division of 1939 the Markham group developed the order of singing one German song and one English song for both the beginning and ending of their services. As the German preaching was slowly discontinued, the singing of German also ended during the last quarter of the twentieth century so that by 1997, the Markham group sang two English songs at the beginning of its worship services and also two English songs at the conclusion of the assembly. At that time the German hymnbooks were removed from the meetinghouses they did not share with their Old Order friends.

The singing school is a tool that generates interest in singing. It is primarily a youth social event held in the community schoolhouses or farm shops during the fall or winter. Because the Old Order Mennonites value home life very highly, they consider it improper for married couples to spend much time at evening social events. During the fifties the Markham district held evening singing school in the Reesor's Meetinghouse. They had also purchased hymnbooks with notes before the church divided in 1964. (2)

Several members with music skills are generally asked to teach these singing schools. Some basic rudiments of music are taught as well as new songs. It is acceptable for the teacher to use a pitch pipe or a tuning fork during these lessons, but there is no accompaniment by any musical instrument. Four-part music is taught and in general the singing is faster than during worship services, though still slow compared to the singing of other churches. In short, one could say that the singing schools are refresher courses or a continuation of the music taught in their parochial schools. The Orthodox Mennonites had several sessions of singing school while they were in Waterloo County, but after moving to the Gorrie area they have until now discontinued singing schools.

(2) *In the Waterloo district the meetinghouses are never used for such functions because there is no lighting installed and it is not deemed appropriate to use the house of God for such social activities. How the Old Order view their meetinghouse is a paradox. They are quick to suggest that the meetinghouse is only a structure, not a church or a sacred spot. It is the congregation or the people that constitutes the church. Yet few things are more contentious than building or renovating a meetinghouse.*

Community German schools were also part of Old Order life. These were held on Saturday afternoons and some older members were present. The teacher was often an individual with a good command of the German language and of his own volition, or through the encouragement of other brethren, arranged to hold a German school. However, few Saturday German schools are held since the introduction of teaching German letters, phonics, and some basic grammar in their schools. The purpose of teaching German at school was to support the use of the German language for the groups who treasure the traditional mother tongue and continue to worship in that language.

The Variance of Customs within the Old Order Groups

The Waterloo Old Order Mennonites' custom of how the ministry enters the meetinghouse does not follow the order of either the Franconia or Lancaster Conferences before the divisions. In Pennsylvania the ministry gathers together in the anteroom and then they walk into the auditorium together once the congregation has started to sing, while in Waterloo the ministry enters the meetinghouse with the aged brethren, then go to their place behind the pulpit, and at the appointed time announce the first song.

The Old Orders of the United States have soundly rejected the pulpit after the Lichtys Meetinghouse-pulpit-dispute in 1889. They have retained the traditional singers' table and the preachers' table. In Ontario, however, the long Franconia-style pulpit had been part of the Mennonite heritage from their beginnings and the Old Order Mennonites maintained that tradition after the division in 1889. There were exceptions to having pulpits in Ontario. In 1817 the Widemans meetinghouse was built and in 1824 the Schmidt meetinghouse was built; neither had a pulpit. The Schmidt meetinghouse never had a pulpit, but Widemans eventually did.

The Lancaster Old Orders have a table in the centre of the auditorium where a group of song leaders sit while the Franconia custom was that the song leader sit amongst the congregation. The Ontario Mennonites retained the old Franconia tradition.

The Ontario Mennonites borrowed another Franconia custom. The Old Orders of the United States follow the Lancaster order that the deacon reads the text after the first prayer. The Franconia tradition was for the deacon to read the text after the first song before the "opening message" and this is still the Waterloo Old Order custom. The Markham group had followed the Franconia order, but in the late 1970s they adopted the Lancaster Old Order Mennonite order and the text is read after the first prayer.

The Waterloo Old Orders do not follow the Pennsylvanian custom of the congregation rising for the benediction at the close of the service, but rather remain seated for the benediction. The Waterloo Old Order Mennonites' practice of having church services on New Year's morning is a custom foreign to both Lancaster and Franconia, but why did the Waterloo Mennonites abandon preparatory services on Saturdays before communion when both conferences in Pennsylvania held them? (The Orthodox Mennonites reintroduced preparatory services during the 1990s.)

The Home and Family

The home and family are the foundation of every nation—"The hand that rocks the cradle rules the nation." The Mennonite emphasis on home and family is equal to the emphasis on the church insomuch that a minister commented that at times he finds it hard to decide which of the two should take the pre-eminence. Historian John Ruth stated that in the past the Mennonites did not always clearly distinguish where the home started and the church stopped. The marriage vows are sacred to them—"What therefore God hath joined together, let not man put asunder" (Mark 10:9). Separation is rarely exercised, but remarriage is never acceptable while the other partner is living. To the Old Order Mennonite marriage is no experiment; it is always for life.

The family altar and prayers are not spoken lightly. Few Old Order fathers pray an audible prayer, yet they endeavour to fulfill their role to the best of their abilities. The ministers often admonish the flock of the importance of bringing up their children in the fear of the Lord.

The roles of men and women are clearly defined. They know what their roles are and what their culture expects of them. Married partners freely help each other, although it is well understood what each of the roles are. The woman's role is housekeeping: "To be discreet, chaste, keepers at home, good, obedient to their own husbands, that the word of God be not blasphemed" (Titus 2:5). However, biblical exhortation does not stop there: "Likewise, ye husbands, dwell with them according to knowledge, giving honour unto the wife, as unto the weaker vessel, and as being heirs together of the grace of life; that your prayers be not hindered" (1 Peter 3:7). The Old Order Mennonites emphasize, "being *heirs together* of the grace of life." This equality in Christ and the biblical teaching of headship, as interpreted by the Old Order Mennonites, may well appear paradoxical to those outside their circles. The distinction of roles brings us to the teaching of the headship of Christ, man and woman.

Perhaps the most conspicuous garment worn by the Mennonites is their headgear—this being the woman's prayer veiling and the man's black hat. According to their interpretation of 1 Cor. 11:3 "the head of every man is Christ; and the head of the woman is the man; and the head of Christ is God." They understand that a man uncovers his head to pray while a woman covers her head to pray. They also draw from this chapter that a woman is to be subject to the man, or the man is the head of the woman, even though, they are "heirs together" in Christ. " . . . Wives be in subjection to your own husbands . . . whose adorning let it not be that outward adorning of plaiting the hair, and of wearing of gold, or of putting on of apparel; but let it be the hidden man of the heart . . . even the ornament of a meek and quiet spirit" (1 Peter 3:1-4). A strong emphasis is placed on 1 Cor. 14:34, "Let your women keep silence in the churches: for it is not permitted unto them to speak; but they are commanded to be under obedience, as also saith the law." Old Order Mennonite women are never ordained, but the wives of ordained men receive a special place in the church and are, in reality, partners with their husbands' calling. At times of church council, women are given equal privileges with the men. In essence women are equal to men but not in function. Within the Old Order Mennonite circles, the role of leadership, according to their interpretation of the word, belongs to men—"the head of every man is Christ."

Amongst the Old Order Mennonites it is not considered appropriate for married women to enter the work force. A woman's role within the Old Order Mennonites is to keep house and bear children, which is indeed a high calling from God. Proverbs 31:10-31 may be considered a model for Old Order Mennonite women: "the heart of her husband doth safely trust in her." Furthermore, "she will do him good and not evil all the days of her life." Also note verse 30, "a woman that feareth the Lord, she shall be praised."

Although modern women may assume that Old Order Mennonite women are very limited by tradition, the opposite reflects Old Order women's feelings. Freedom of mind and soul is found in serving the Lord in His appointed way. I, as a man, have disqualified myself from presenting an Old Order Mennonite woman's view concerning the prayer veiling and the order of headship. I, therefore, asked a woman (who wishes to remain nameless) to define this paradox of servitude and freedom from her perspective.

> For the Mennonite woman, the wearing of the prayer veiling or head covering is not burdensome. Rather, it is a scriptural symbol of recognition that she accepts the order of headship—God, man, and woman (1 Cor. 11:3). She also recognizes that God is a God of order, not a respecter of persons (Romans 2:11). The prayer veiling becomes so much a part of a woman's life that she feels "incomplete" when her head is uncovered. "For this cause ought the woman to have power on her head because of the angels" (1 Cor. 11:10). I do not feel a woman will earn her salvation by wearing a prayer veiling because it is written, "For by grace are ye saved through faith . . . not of works, lest any man should boast (Ephesians 2:8-9). Yet at the same time I feel a sense of spiritual peace through obedience by wearing a covering. It serves as a reminder that a bold, forward spirit is not befitting to a woman with a prayer veiling. [Note the theme of Gelassenheit expressed here.]
>
> To an outsider, Mennonite women appear restricted when they honour the sequence of headship, but in reality they are free. A Mennonite woman desires that her husband is the head of the home yet together they are partners in the work of Christ. When the order of headship is regarded, there is harmony in the home for each one is working in God's order and there is no strife in seeking or coveting the other's position. I've never felt restricted—it is just relaxing to live in the order of God. Obedience to God's order is an expression of an inner liberation.
>
> A woman that feareth the Lord.

Simplicity—Occupation and Lifestyle

The simplicity theme predominates both the lifestyles and occupations of the Old Order Mennonites. Places of employment for their youth are invariably sought amongst their own people. The Old Order generally prefer agricultural work above other occupations because the youth are more sheltered from outside influences. Numerous Mennonite shops and other small businesses become second choice for males. The girls are expected to work as domestics so that they may learn the art of housekeeping. Older single girls may find occupation in rural stores or other small businesses. Occasionally they take ownership of a small business like a store or bakery. The Markham girls tend to venture into the work force at a younger age, and at times the Markham boys seek employment outside the Mennonite community. Their driving licence gives them opportunities in other industries beyond the Mennonite community. One at times questions if these changes support the Mennonite ethic of simplicity and humility.

In order for farming to be economically viable, the cash flow must increase as farmland values rise. This unavoidable equation has challenged the Old Order Mennonite community, because as production rises so does the need for automation. Manual labour has its limits when trying to remain competitive, but the Old Order have adapted and entered the economies in which they can compete. The long-standing tradition of helping each other during harvest and other occasions along with the sharing of equipment has helped the Old Order community remain financially viable even though they avoid large modern equipment.

As newer options, such as air-conditioned cabs, became available on large farm tractors, the focus on simplicity led the community to shun these luxurious units. Endeavouring to maintain their quiet and simple lifestyles, during the 1980s the Old Orders chose to reject the large, over-one-hundred-horsepower tractors and the convenient and luxurious cabs. The acceptance of pull-type combines and the unrestricted use of farm loaders inside barns were contentious issues that were resolved during the last quarter of the century. More modern milking equipment was accepted in the nineties, as milk quality issues demanded these changes. These compromises have allowed the Old Order community to remain competitive in the farming industry and continued to strengthen the community, since more of their youth are required on the farms because the large units are not accepted.

The David Martin group has adopted a far more progressive lifestyle in business and economics. They readily accept government grants while the Old Orders shun them. They hold the opinion that all inventions can be used if they are profitable for material gain, but inventions should not be used for pleasure.[1] This is quite different from the traditional Old Order view where most new inventions are rejected, or at the least viewed with caution, until the cause and effects of the invention have been proven over time. In the David Martin church if an invention is considered beneficial and practical for the community and does not conflict with their culture, it is then allowed by the group. Even though the above ideals are confirmed by the evidence of their business operations, the official views of David Martins cannot be obtained because they decline to discuss such matters.

The Old Orders and the Orthodox have incorporated more of the traditional theme of simplicity into their vocations. Although there are various shops within the community, modern computerized machines are generally not found there. Computers are taboo, as is most electronic equipment. There is a definite concern about electronic equipment; nevertheless, the telephone, a bone of contention for years, was acknowledged as a business tool in 1989 and allowed by the Old Orders. That decision was too drastic for some Old Orders who then chose to move to the Gorrie area and fellowshipped with the Orthodox group who have no telephones.

The use of hired transportation has become more and more common as the Old Order community spread across numerous townships. In the thirties it was common for an Old Order to decline a car ride offered by a neighbour. Eden Martin offered Urias Martin a short ride home from the Clemmer farm, but Urias deemed it proper to walk instead. Over the decades this attitude changed and during the last quarter of the century, semi-retired individuals with cars or vans have sought employment driving their Old Order neighbours and relatives to go shopping, to the hospitals and doctors, and even on trips to Mennonite communities in the United States. In order to minimize the use of private drivers to commute to the Mount Forest district, the idea of chartering buses was entertained. In March 1988 the Old Orders arranged a chartered bus on a designated route from

Waterloo to Mount Forest on Monday morning with a return trip in the evening. A reverse route from Mount Forest to the Waterloo Stockyards is also scheduled for Thursday morning with a return trip in the evening. Chartered buses have become a common means of transportation for the Old Orders when there are special services such as ordinations or funerals. There are frequent Mount Forest runs that include a Sunday worship service. The hiring of private drivers became more common after the Mount Forest settlement began.

The hiring of transportation has also become part of the David Martin group over the last two decades. During the late 1990s the use of chartered buses has become commonplace; furthermore, the David Martins hire numerous small truckers to haul their freight. They are becoming more and more dependent on outside forms of transportation for their shopping and personal life.

The Markham group is the most liberal of all the Old Order groups. Their farming operations blend well with their outside neighbours. When an individual displays his wealth or spends too freely, the neighbourhood gossip train may carry the story that "he had had a lot of money." Modern conveniences are part of their lives, but those who exercise simplicity are well respected. Their community is challenged to feel the rudiments of Gelassenheit when they tend to accept the conveniences of the world.

The Old Order Mennonite community has long been identified by their well-kept farms. Large bank barns were the norm in the past as well as large and cosy houses to accommodate their families. Over the years it has been a challenge for those with means not to deviate from the simplicity theme and build "rich" houses. The warnings of Jeremiah the prophet resound across the Old Order communities: "Woe unto him…That saith, I will build me a wide house and large chambers, and cutteth him out windows; and it is ceiled with cedar, and painted with vermilion" (Jeremiah 22:13-14). Opinions vary in what is considered "rich," but the traditional Old Order Mennonite value of equality is at stake when Old Order Mennonite families with means can be identified by their "rich" homes. One who has financial means should never live in a way that is identifiable as rich. The Old Order Mennonites are taught to bear riches as though they had none. They are to be of those, "that use this world, as not abusing it: for the fashion of this world passeth away" (1 Corinthians 7:31).

With riches comes power, not unity, with power comes the abuse of power, not equality, and with abuse of power comes disunity not peace. For these reasons it is paramount that within a brotherhood of believers those who are so blessed with money do not display their wealth. Simplicity by virtue of choice is one of the chief cornerstones of Old Order Mennonite beliefs, whether it be their attire, houses, farms, or the way they live.

The Old Order Youth

"The sleep of a labouring man is sweet . . . " (Ecclesiastes 5:12). The Old Order Mennonite children have the work ethic deeply ingrained into their character. They are taught that when they eat the fruit of the labours of their hands, "happy shall they be, and it shall be well with them" (Psalms 128:2). Continuing education rubs hard with their simplistic lifestyles; therefore, education beyond elementary school is seldom sought but rather discouraged. Individuals may pursue further education by means of correspondence or night-school courses, but this is not the norm. Their culture demands that children learn to work and even enjoy working. Barn raisings and other such social events at times drive the competitive spirit, which helps to motivate strong work ethics. The womenfolk are present at these events to prepare the meal. The girls also get the opportunity to work amongst the older women and are taught positive work ethics. During these events youth have the opportunity to appreciate that working to help others can be one of the greatest satisfactions in life. The Old Order Mennonite work ethic is to work to the best of their abilities, to learn to provide for themselves and to be willing to help others—be it in the church or otherwise.

Social life and free time is also part of the Old Order Mennonite community, albeit not adequate according to general society's values. Saturdays for the most part are work days; Sundays and religious holidays are the times when the youth and adults relax and socialize. The Sunday evening singings are the traditional youth activities for the Old Orders. During the instruction services (for baptism) the Old Order youth are encouraged to retire early. Baseball games on their farms substitute for singing during those weeks. Creative youth at times contrive additional activities, which may not always be accepted by the church. Youthful frivolousness is discouraged so the lasting regrets of youthful folly will not follow them in later years. The Old Order Mennonites teach, "When I was a child, I spake as a child, I understood as a child, I thought as a child: but when I became a man, I put away childish things" (1 Corinthians 13:11).

Courtship is considered a very serious undertaking by the church and casual dating is considered worldly. Some families discourage dating before age eighteen and long courtships are frowned upon. The ideal model is for the youth to first make their commitment to God and the church before they begin dating. Dating outside of their fellowship is taboo as is premarital sex. The Old Order Mennonite churches' model is for youth to have a pure courtship. Only the David Martin group has retained the old custom of bundling and accepted moderate use of alcohol and tobacco. Their culture has adopted an interesting twist. It is common to see a David Martin smoke, but only cigars or a pipe; never cigarettes.

Mid-week social activities have always been part of the Markham youth. The earliest events were skating on private ponds and baseball games held at the farm. By the fifties these events had evolved into the use of public diamonds for baseball and a private arena for indoor skating and hockey. The highly competitive game of hockey is at odds with the traditional Mennonite ethos of simplicity and submission. The use of the public arenas for hockey has been a contentious issue in the Markham group since 1966 when the private arena at Martins Tile closed. During the Gulf War the Markham church ruled out the use of public arenas for members and organized a private outdoor rink for their youth activities. The Markham youth activities are far more sophisticated than those of all other Old Order groups. Aside from normal midweek socials they have three annual events: the June picnic, where baseball, volleyball and races are held; the Thanksgiving afternoon Bruce Trail hike where a two-hour part of the trail is walked and is followed by a wiener roast and picnic supper at some park (in the morning the youth normally attend church services); and the Christmas programme, which resembles the old-time school Christmas programmes.

Old Order Mennonite Holidays

Religious holidays play a significant role in the Old Order Mennonite community. They begin the New Year by conducting a New Year's worship service where Luke 2:21-40 is the traditional text. (The Orthodox use Ephesians chapter six.) Family gatherings dominate their social life during this season. The American Mennonites do not hold worship services on New Year's day and there is no evidence that the custom was borrowed from the Franconia conference but the fact that the Lancaster German hymnal has nine News Year's songs is interesting as they do not have services on that day. What transpired over the years is beyond the scope of this work, but we do know that the two New Year's hymns Benjamin Eby included in the *Gemeinschaftliche Lieder-Sammlung* in 1836 are currently being used by the Ontario Old Order Mennonites.

Good Friday, a traditional Christian holiday, is also held by the Old Order Mennonites. Unlike many of the Christian churches the Old Order Mennonites do not hold communion services on Good Friday. Any one of the crucifixion chapters are chosen as the text. The Old Orders also include the preparatory theme on Good Friday along with the crucifixion texts. There may be some guests entertained, but the afternoon is generally spent quietly at home or visiting aged members.

In the past, Easter Monday was classed a holiday, but at present very few people regard it as such. It was more of a social day when the older people went visiting and the youth sought fellowship with one another, or when they were working away from home it was a day in which they were free to go home and be with their parents and do as they pleased. The Monday after the Day of Pentecost was another such holiday. The importance of these holidays has faded away during the past fifty years. Levi P. Martin bought a saddle and wrote a letter on Easter Monday 1866. In 1900 his son, Isaac, went to town in the forenoon and was at home in the afternoon. Clearly, the observation of the Easter holiday had begun to decline in the nineteenth century.

Having commemorated the birth, death and resurrection of Christ, the Old Order Mennonites also deem it expedient to observe His ascension. Ascension worship services are held on the sixth Thursday after Easter. Various Scriptures relating to Christ's ascension are taken, but Acts 1 is the most popular. If the weather has been challenging, some fieldwork is done in the afternoon; however, in general, Ascension Day is a social holiday for all. (3) Older people go visiting while the youth spend time together and at times go fishing. They would covet Isaac Martin's luck in 1901 when he went fishing in the evening and caught twenty-two fish.

(3) *On Ascension Day 1866 Levi P. Martin wrote in his diary, "I was in the meeting at Martins in the forenoon and at home in the afternoon, there were some boys here." In 1907 Isaac Martin found himself on the plains of Iowa with the Stauffer Mennonites. Since he arrived on Good Friday, his diary reveals little of the work patterns for Good Friday. On Ascension Day, however, he was working all day with no mention made of worship services. In 1906 Isaac Martin worked all day Good Friday while working in North Michigan. These diary entries reveal that some outreach settlements did more work on holidays then the Old Order community today normally would. At the beginning of the twentieth century the Old Orders held Good Friday services at Martin's and on Ascension Day the Conestogo meetinghouse was used. Because of this routine the youth in the Peel district barely realized that Ascension Day was a religious holiday since they never had services at their meetinghouse. The youth at Peel always went fishing.*

Pentecost always falls on a Sunday so it never becomes a special holiday, but the day held some significance since it was historically called "Whit" Sunday. Recognition is given during the services to Acts 2 and the outpouring of the Holy Spirit.

Erntefest (Thanksgiving or Harvest meeting) is another holiday when worship services are held in the forenoon, and the afternoon activities resemble those of Ascension Day, with the older people visiting the aged and infirm and youth enjoying their day amongst themselves. Until 1940, Harvest meeting was generally held around the middle of September, but after the division it was normally on the Thursday preceding the first Friday in September. The Old Order also incorporate the preparatory theme into their Harvest meeting services.

Sacred or Important Events

Important events are times that an individual remembers for the rest of his or her life. Birthdays are remembered, but gifts and birthday parties are not part of the Old Order Mennonite culture. It is not deemed proper to focus the attention on individuals because they are brethren. One may surmise that the account of Herod's birthday party and the beheading of John the Baptist also affected the Mennonites' attitude towards birthday celebrations (Matthew 14 and Mark 6). The first day of school and the last day of school are two milestones for Old Order Mennonite children. Elementary education is deemed important, but learning how to work and appreciate health and strength in labour are considered equally essential. Joining the youth group at age fifteen is another highlight for Old Order Mennonite children (for the David Martins it is sixteen). For the girls this event means putting their hair in a bun and beginning to wear the devotional head-covering for church services. There is a variation among the groups at what age girls wear the covering all the time. The David Martin and Orthodox girls put up their hair as soon as they leave school.

The following events have a more sacred air. By the time the youth are in their mid to late teens they are deemed to be growing out of childhood and becoming responsible for their spiritual lives. Recognizing their need of a Saviour and submitting themselves to the Word of God and the church is classed as the most important decision a person can make. In the spring the Old Order Mennonite churches give an invitation to those who desire to join the church. Individuals so inclined are taught the eighteen articles of the Dortrecht Confession on six consecutive Sunday afternoons at the appointed meetinghouses. On each Sunday three articles are taught, and after the instruction of each article the minister asks the applicants if they believe in that article and if so to answer "yes." On the day of baptism the whole congregation witnesses the baptism and the vows that are made. The converts are then received into the fellowship and are considered communing members.

The Old Order Mennonites practice closed communion where only members in good standing are welcome to partake of the sacred emblems. For this reason *Umfrage* (council meeting) is always held before communion service. Matthew chapter eighteen is the text at Umfrage. Humility, personal peace with God, peace amongst the brethren, and forgiveness are the key points stressed. After the schoolchildren and members of other congregations are dismissed, the ministry retires to the lobby and the participating members, in groups of up to a dozen people, go into the lobby and one by one:

1. Express their peace with God and fellowman.
2. Express a willingness to accept reproof from other members. Their American brethren also include a willingness to have Matthew 18 applied to them.
3. Express agreement to how and what the ministers preach and encourage them to continue preaching the Word without fear of man—that is to warn the sinner, encourage the despondent, and to rebuke and exhort with all longsuffering and patience.
4. Express appreciation of how the ministry is trying to lead the church and to support the Ordnung—the order of the church.
5. Express a desire to be a partaker of Holy Communion if it can be held in peace.
6. Express concerns about the church and her administration.

The aged men go out first to the lobby, then younger married men, then the aged women, followed by younger married women. The youth who are members are present and not excluded from the council chamber, but seldom venture to give counsel. A novice should learn in silence or express his concern in private to the ministry and other aged members. Old Order Mennonites' administration is not a democracy. Old Order Mennonites seldom, if ever, vote on issues pertaining to church order. The ministry take the counsel from the Umfrage to their conference where the opinion and values of the people are considered and applied. The Umfrage has a very important function within the Old Order Mennonite church.

After the conference has been held, communion services are held, as marked in the Calendar of Appointments.[3] The bishop walks down the aisles and first gives the bread (the bread is cut in three-centimetre-square bars from which the bishop breaks off little cubes to give to the members). The wine is passed by the bishop in a common cup to the members of the congregation. The service is brought to a close and the youth and children who were present during the administration of the emblems are dismissed. The members who partook of the emblems remain seated and participate in feet-washing, according to John 13:1-17. Upon the conclusion of feet-washing the bishop presents the conference report to the congregation. There are slight variations among the Old Order groups when the conference report is given: for example the Orthodox give their conference report at their preparatory service. (Not all groups have a printed conference report.) See appendix "B" for copies of conference reports.

Order of an Old Order Conference

" . . . the servant of the Lord must not strive; but be gentle to all men," (2 Timothy 2:24).

An ordained man of the Markham group wrote the following order of their conference. There may be minor variances between the different Old Order churches such as the place and time where the conference is held and the order in which the conference is conducted, but as a whole there remains a similarity.

> The Markham Waterloo Conference is held twice a year at the North Woolwich meetinghouse. The bishops sit behind the pulpit, and the ministers, followed by the deacons, sit according to seniority in the men's section of benches closest to the pulpit. The service begins at 9:00 with a hymn, followed by a short opening message by one of the bishops, based on either Ephesians 4:1-16 or 1 Peter 5:1-9, which is concluded with a silent prayer. After the Conference Report of General Recommendations is read, each one present gives a brief personal testimony that might include an expression of peace with God, a desire to be partaker of Holy Communion and a willingness to continue labouring in his particular office in the church. Included in these testimonies are the reports from the council meetings by either the bishops, if they were present, or the home minister. In this way the counsel and concerns of the whole church are made known.
>
> At this point the meeting becomes open for discussion. Issues needing a decision, brought forth by the bishops, are generally dealt with first, such as requests for church membership by formerly baptized individuals, planning an ordination to fill an empty office, etc. The concerns and suggestions from the council meeting reports are focused on next. Finally, if time permits, personal concerns may also be raised.

After an issue has been discussed, each brother is asked to give his counsel, beginning with the senior bishop and ending with the most recently ordained deacon. If a member has no comments he is considered to be in agreement. Voting is not their practice; decisions are made by consensus. The importance of unity among the ministry is indicated by the fact that if only one member is opposed to the issue being discussed, no change will be made.

In order to avoid stalemates, it is not uncommon to hear statements such as, "I don't agree with this, but I won't oppose it." This allows a person to stay true to his own convictions without holding the whole conference body at an impasse. When all issues here have either been discussed or postponed for the next conference, the meeting is concluded by an audible prayer, another song, and the benediction.
The meetings are seldom over before 2:30 and sometimes last until 3:00 p.m. A short lunch break is taken at the Spring Conference, but in the fall a 2:45 p.m. dinner is served at the home of one of the church members, with close neighbours helping to serve. The remainder of the afternoon is spent in fellowship.

Occasionally, unscheduled ministers' meetings are held throughout the year to deal with concerns that need immediate attention.

Gelassenheit is the foremost theme at an Old Order conference. Yielding to the conference body is very important. The desire of a conference member is highlighted by an old bishop: " . . . remain true and in humility, which is what the Lord demands of all his servants."

Preparatory and Erntefest Services

Now an historical tangent. In 1879 Joseph Wismer from Jordon (Vineland) wrote to Samuel Weber and asked him, "On what ground or reason is the Harvest Meeting (Erntefest) held on a Thursday in September?" The answer to that question is found in the old Meeting Calendars.

We know that the American Old Orders hold preparatory services on Saturday afternoon before they hold communion. The Ontario Old Order

Mennonites have often wondered why this custom did not follow the Mennonites to Ontario. In the 1837 Calendar of Appointments, the earliest known edition, not even Christmas and Ascension Day are listed; however, it lists Saturday, September 16 as *Fast-tag* (Fast Day) at Martins, Benj Ebys (First Mennonite), and Union (Hageys). Council meetings were held the following Sundays and then the Semi-Annual Conference was held at Benj Ebys on Monday, October 9. The Annual Conference was held at Meyers, in Clinton Township, Lincoln County, on Friday, October 13. Communion services were held October 22 to November 26. Aside from holding a "Fast Day" before council meeting, the order of events did not change within the Old Order circles for over one-hundred and sixty years. We should note that during the early years it was common to hold communion on Easter Sunday, and on occasion on Saturdays or Ascension Day.

The 1848 calendar shows spring council meetings were followed by the Semi-annual Conference held on March 31. Communion services were held on April 16-May 29, with the Annual Conference held at Benj Ebys, Berlin on May 26. In the fall council meetings were held from August 20-September 10. *Busz und Bet-tag* (repentance and prayer day) services were held on Saturday, September 2. The Semi-Annual Conference was held at Benj Ebys on Saturday, September 16, 1848. During the eleven years from 1837 to 1848, the Mennonites changed their "fast day" to "repentance and prayer day."

In 1852, we find a change and the answer to Joseph Wismer's question. Busz und Bet-tag as a Saturday service was discontinued, but a new appointment, Erntefest, was listed for Thursday, August 26, 1852. From here on Erntefest was always listed on a Thursday. Evidently the people did not attend these services too well because the Conference passed the following resolution in 1861: "That harvest services should be more general, and observed by all members."

In 1858 a notice appeared inside the cover of the calendar: "An allen Plätzen, wie in diesem Calendar angemerkt ist, wo das heilige Abendmahl gehalten werden soll, wird auch jedesmal Samstag vorher um 2 Uhr Nachmittags, eine Vorbereitungs-Versammlung gehalten." (At every place where this calendar is marked to have Holy Communion, on the previous Saturday at 2:00 pm there shall be preparatory service.) It was customary to hold communion on Saturday or Sunday after the Annual Conference, and that year the conference was held as usual on the last Friday in May at Meyers (Vineland). The communion service was booked for the next day and did not give time for the planned preparatory service. (The reason for this communion service's falling next to the conference was so that the ministry from the other districts could hold communion together as one body.) In the fall of 1858, Erntefest was listed on Thursday, September 16, and appears to be an event separate from the former preparatory services. This suggests that it was a new venture.

The 1859 calendar is missing, but the 1860 calendar does not have the above notice inside the cover and Erntefest appears to be evolving into a harvest meeting; however, the 1861 calendar has a very interesting twist in it. On Saturday, April 13, an appointment is listed for the 2:00 p.m. service to be held at Ebys and Hageys. On Sunday the 14th communion was held at Ebys and Hageys. This pattern was consistent so that the lower parts of the Waterloo district, Markham, Cayuga, Meyers and Clarence, N.Y. all held preparatory services that year, but Martins, Conestogo, West Woolwich (Elmira), and Schmitt of Vaughan Township did not. North Woolwich was listed as Hemblings since 1858, but there were no communion services held at Hemblings in 1861. In subsequent years there were no more Saturday *Vorberitungs-Versammlung* (preparatory services) listed in the meeting calendars and Erntefest was always held on Thursday.

Why the Canadian Old Order Mennonites do not hold preparatory services and their American brothers do has often been a question amongst the Old Order Mennonites of Waterloo. One can only surmise, but perhaps the Woolwich churches' reaction towards preparatory service in 1861 was a counter-response to the infiltration of Wesleyan holiness into the Mennonite brotherhood by the Methodists of that day. Did the

(4) *Elias Ebys diary (1872-1878) records that there were preparatory services held at Ebys (First Mennonite) meetinghouse during those years. One of the most outstanding entries is recorded for April 11, 1873 when Elias was at Ebys on Good Friday. On Saturday he was also at Ebys for preparatory services, and then he was at Ebys on Easter Sunday for communion. It is evident that preparatory services were held at Ebys, even though it was not listed in the meeting calendar. When these services were discontinued is unknown, but the Old Order Mennonites did not hold preparatory services after the 1889 division.*[3]

Woolwichers sense that Protestant influence even though they were more in the backwoods? But why did they spurn preparatory services that their conservative brethren in Lancaster County held? The truth is unknown. One can only surmise that the conservative-minded brethren from Lancaster County, who arrived after the War of 1812-14 and settled in Woolwich Township, were never in true harmony with the earlier settlers from either Franconia or Lancaster districts.

Another view of Erntefest is that Good Friday was substituted for the spring preparatory services. In time council meetings were always over before Good Friday and communion, then began the first Sunday after Easter; therefore Good Friday always fell between council meetings and communion. In the fall Erntefest is held after the council meetings are past and precedes the conference that is held on Fridays after Erntefest. Communion then follows the conference. Thus the spring preparatory services were incorporated into the Good Friday services, and the fall preparatory services integrated with Erntefest. This opinion holds true with the Old Orders who incorporate the theme of preparatory services in both Good Friday and Erntefest services.(4)

Marriage—That Sacred Bond for Life

Marriage is God-instituted and is the ultimate bond between a man and a woman. It is for the welfare of the human race, and when both parties honour their marriage vows God's blessing flows upon the union. For this reason dating is considered a serious undertaking and discouraged for those under eighteen years of age. Dating outside the fellowship is not accepted and is considered unscriptural and in violation of the twelfth article of the confession of faith. Furthermore, dating before baptism can be likened to placing the cart before the horse.(5)

Weddings are very special social events held during the week and usually in the bride's home. The service and the actual ceremony are about two hours long. Many admonitions are given with regard to the responsibilities of married life and state that divorce was not part of God's original order. All Old Order Mennonite groups forbid the wearing of jewellery, and therefore there is no exchanging of wedding rings.

"Lo, children are an heritage of the Lord: and the fruit of the womb is his reward" (Psalms 127:3). This passage reflects the Old Orders'

(5) Pioneer life was very demanding and communication was difficult. As a result, there were unique marriages. Bishop Abraham Grove arrived at Markham in 1808. The next year a young man, John Reesor, came to Grove's home on horseback. Grove asked him what his purpose was and Ressor suggested that he could help split wood. Grove was not satisfied with Ressor's answer and asked him again what he wanted. Reesor then found the courage to ask Grove whether he could have his daughter Annie for his wife. Grove implied that she was too young. Ressor then asked Grove if she could cook "mush." Abraham's affirmative answer satisfied Reesor whereupon Grove said that he must ask his daughter. Annie accepted Reesor so Abraham married them and Annie rode away on horseback with her husband to begin keeping house at the age of fifteen.[4]

Among the Old Orders today no bishop would marry even his daughter before she was a member of the church. Although it is not certain, it is highly unlikely that Annie would have been baptized at her age. During the nineteenth century it was all too common that married couples, even those with children, had not been baptized. This problem ended in the Waterloo district at the time of the 1889 division, but in Markham it lingered on until after World War I.

position on having a family. The modern buzzword "contraceptive" is seldom spoken. Their belief is clearly stated in Hebrews 13:4 "Marriage is honourable in all, and the bed undefiled: but whoremongers and adulterers God will judge." The model Old Order Mennonite marriage is a home with a mother and children supported by a loving, caring father.

Amongst the Old Order Mennonites the home carries yet another important function: it is the centre of social life. In it guests are entertained, youth hold their social gatherings, weddings are held, and children come together to play. The children's whole world revolves around their mother and home. Going out to eat is seldom done and considered a deviation from the established ways. As a separate people, they do not freely socialize with those outside their fellowship. If one wants to understand the Old Order Mennonites, the word "pleasure" has to be substituted with "simplicity" in their thoughts. As pleasure dominates the lives of most people, in like manner humility reflects upon the Old Order Mennonites' life. Their values concerning relations to the state, church order, courtship, marriage, and the home set them apart as a peculiar people.

At the End of Life

"And it came to pass, that the beggar died, and was carried by the angels into Abraham's bosom: the rich man also died, and was buried. And in hell he lift up his eyes, being in torments, and seeth Abraham afar off, and Lazarus in his bosom"(Luke 16:22-23). The Old Order Mennonites equally emphasize heaven and hell. To them there is no question that "It is a fearful thing to fall into the hands of the living God" (Hebrews 10:31).

The traumatic death of twenty-seven-year-old Elam Kraemer drew a large crowd of young people to the Conestogo Meetinghouse in January 1969. He had died instantly when a jack slipped and he was crushed under a car. The meetinghouse was filled to its limits, which meant the young boys were seated double on the last two benches. The first row was perched on the vertical edge of the lazyback, while the second row sat between the feet of those perched on high. On this solemn occasion, Minister Noah Martin was led to speak from the book of Ecclesiastes. The first verse of the last chapter was a clear warning to any indifferent youth that they must "remember now their Creator." Noah did not preach about Elam; he spoke to the living who sat before him on that cold winter day. This funeral service, heart-rending as it was, was typical of any Mennonite funeral message. The message was directed to "the living" for they "know that they shall die: but the dead know not any thing" (Ecclesiastes 9:5). The Mennonite ministers always remember the bereft and give words of condolence and encouragement, but they still hold to the conference resolution that was held on Friday September 6, 1867 at Berlin, "Resolved that preachers at funerals should be careful neither to praise and glorify anyone, nor to condemn anyone, as this is beyond our right."[5]

John Weaver, a founder of the Old Order community in Indiana, expounded the Old Order vision when he informed his cousin Samuel Weber about the death of his wife in 1879. " She is departed from us, and as you may well imagine there is a large place vacant; however, we try to comfort ourselves as well as we can with these thoughts—what God has done is well done."[6] An Old Order widower of many years stated, "Death is something we do not question." Neither do the Old Order Mennonites disregard the reality of the last Judgment. The words of Jesus "depart from me, all ye workers of iniquity" (Luke 13:27) are believed to be as true as, "in my Father's house are many mansions (John 14:2)." The Old Order Mennonites seldom share their deep confidence and hope in God with those outside the fellowship. The defence for such restricted behaviour at a time of death is that the more confident Protestant values rankle with the Old Order Mennonites' unassuming and quiet way of mourning. With the reality of the Judgment in mind, the Old Order Mennonites approach death and mourning with reverence and Godly fear.

The Old Order Mennonites' openness at a time of death is also at variance with the way the Protestant Churches speak of death. Since the ethos of Gelassenheit failed to cross the English Channel, few English hymns support that theme. When relating to death, the English poets are somewhat inclined to gloss over the realities of death. Some popular hymns like *Asleep in Jesus, Abide with me, Silently they pass away,* and *Some sweet day* make a definite allusion to death, but when the German author writes, "Bedenke Mensch das Ende, Bedenke deinen Tod." (Think man about your end, Think about your death), he comes right out to the point. Neither did the following poet hesitate to pen his thoughts, "Komm Sterblicher! Betrachte mich . . . Denk auf die letzten Stunden . . . O Mench gedenk ans Ende!" (Come mortal man look on me . . . think on your last hour . . . O human think upon the end.) Their hymns are not silent concerning their hope in God—"Mein ganze Hoffnung steht allein in Jesu Tod und Leiden." (All my hope stands alone in Jesus' death and suffering.) The Markham hymnbook contains some hymns about death and dying, but these are not usually sung at funerals.

The Old Order manner of burying their dead is also straightforward and to the general public may seem crude or unsympathetic. After the public viewing in the churchyard, the casket is carried to the cemetery for burial with the family following. In the presence of the family, the body is lowered into the grave and a hymn is sung. The most common has the following words, "Nun laszt uns den Leib begraben, und die feste Hoffnung haben": (Now let us bury the body and have a steadfast hope). In a very straightforward, open manner the Old Order Mennonites lay their dead to rest, but not without hope in Christ.

This hope in Christ is real to the Old Order Mennonite people. In the event of a sudden tragedy their hope becomes a very present help in a time of trouble; nevertheless, they do not question God's ways at such times but rather state that tragedies are God's way of drawing his people to him. Sudden tragic deaths in the community draw large crowds to the funeral, and then the brotherhood has a responsibility to support the bereft family; indeed tragedies are ways that God speaks to his people.

The Old Order Mennonites acknowledge that all believers in Christ receive inner strength from God at a time of bereavement. It is the author's conviction that all Christians share the same benefits in Christ. The Old Order Mennonite faith and culture shifts the emphasis on certain values. It is this shift of emphasis that the author desires to portray, rather than suggesting that the Old Order Mennonite life is the only way.

It is a very sad occasion when death is self-inflicted. These rare occurrences draw in another dynamic for the Old Order Mennonite communities. Those outside their fellowship are not part of the brotherhood—that family of believers. In the case of suicides, the Old Orders do not bury the body in the row with the others, but along the fence off to a side from the rest. It becomes very challenging to separate

The customs vary a little between the Old Order Mennonite groups in how they bury their dead. In general, several neighbours are appointed to dig the grave by hand. Frost in the winter and soggy soil during the spring have challenged the grave-diggers. These occasions are considered a time of fellowship and a way of getting acquainted with each other. The Old Orders always close the grave immediately after the body has been lowered. The Markham group waits until the family has returned to the meetinghouse for the funeral service before they begin to close the grave, but the Old Orders will, in the presence of the family, gently begin to close the grave while the graveside hymn is sung. The young men of the home congregation who are not closely related generally close the grave. The shovels are normally put away before these men, who are dressed in their suits, enter the meetinghouse to attend the remaining part of the service. In this picture the David Martins evidently forgot to put away the shovels.

immediate family ties from the family of believers. Nevertheless, when one passes away outside the fellowship, that challenge remains. The Old Orders do not sing at such occasions, but will hold a funeral service. The David Martin group will not bury such a person or any other non-member in their own cemetery, but will lay them to rest in a public cemetery; neither will they hold a funeral service on such an occasion. Several from their number have been buried in the Hawkesville cemetery as a private internment with only a few men present to close the grave.

The Old Order Mennonite community is not part of the Provincial Perpetual Cemetery plan. They continue to maintain their cemeteries at their own expense. They have assumed the responsibility of the old abandoned Mennonite cemetery just east of Crosshill in order to satisfy the government that they are sincere in maintaining their cemeteries. No plots are sold; cemetery care is part of the general maintenance of the church property. The Old Order Mennonites rely on the community to manually dig the grave. Such working together builds and strengthens the community. Only on rare occasions have family members outside the fellowship hired a machine to dig a grave.

Notes

1 Abraham Martin, Article, no title, n.d., n.p. Author's collection.

2 Elias Eby, Diary, CGUC.

3 For the order of service see Benjamin Eby, *Origin and Doctrine of the Mennonites* (Markham-Waterloo Mennonite Conference, 1999).

4 Clarence Smith. Conversation with Author, 2000.

5 Conference Reports, Sept. 6, 1867, CGUC, 8.

6 Samuel Weber, Letter, February 2, 1879, Author's collection.

The Privilege—Religious Freedom

Chapter Nineteen

Canada Pension Plan Exemption

The Mennonite community as a whole went through changes after World War II. It brought its numerous relief organizations together under Mennonite Central Committee Canada (MCC Canada) in 1963. This inter-Mennonite organization united the Canadian Mennonites in many activities they wished to do together. The Mennonites' focus on peace-witness also changed from supporting the traditional non-resistant faith and assisting conscientious objectors at times of war to actively promoting peacemaking through government lobbying and assisting victims of war without concern for political loyalties.[1] MCC Canada became the primary official government contact body for the Mennonites of Canada.

The Canadian government introduced the compulsory Canada Pension Plan (CPP) in 1966. This social welfare programme was promoted as a universal plan for all Canadians. However, it was more than a welfare plan; it was a pension plan into which the government required everybody to pay. It supported the aged and those who lost income in the event of disability. A number called the social insurance number (SIN) was also legislated at the same time. The Old Order Mennonite community viewed CPP as an insurance scheme and firmly believed that it violated their faith. They believed that it was the brotherhood's responsibly to take care of one another. Old age pension and children's allowances, as well as other government grants, such as agricultural subsidy payments, have always been strongly advised against by the church. When CPP became law the Old Order Mennonites felt that they were "now being coerced into accepting a form of life insurance."[2] The Old Order Mennonites were of the same mind as their forbears a hundred years before. In the September 9, 1864, conference it was resolved: "Since it is a general rule that most professing Christians rely on institutions (insurance companies) . . . to cover damages by fire . . . Therefore we see the need that we, as members of one body, of which Christ is the head, to return to the system of the apostles, help and assist each other among ourselves when we suffer damage by fires."[3] The Old Order Mennonites understand that within a brotherhood they take care of each other. Government insurance schemes are not acceptable.

The Old Orders (both Amish and Mennonite), the David Martin group excepted, made their first appeal in April 1966 to Joseph W. Willard, deputy minister of National Health and Welfare via their spokesman, an MCC representative, Elven Shantz. (Levi Frey from the David Martin group had stated to Shantz that they were not interested in seeking exemption from CPP.[4]) Although these government officials appeared to be sympathetic to the Old Order Mennonites' dilemma, their response according to the law was negative and the request for exemption was denied.[5] Nonetheless, the Old Orders persisted, and on October 16, 1966, they presented another brief to Mr. Benson, Minister of National Revenue, and others, but Prime Minster Lester Pearson was absent due to a visiting dignitary. Again the Old Orders felt they received sympathetic consideration. Mr. Benson had promised "his personal support in favour of the Old Order and Amish brethren in the revision."[6] However, "the government was not willing to take the brethren into special consideration on this matter and in November 1966, Prime Minister Lester Pearson replied, 'It is not considered advisable to introduce amending legislation to exempt from the Plan . . . (CPP).'"[7] The government's unbending position disappointed the Old Orders. They then approached a Kitchener law firm for legal advice on whether CPP infringed on the freedom of religion. J. E. Lang studied the question and concluded: "To say that a group could avoid such a law on the grounds that it prevented them from freely practising their religion would put the Government of Canada in the inequitable position of being unable to effect any legislation for fear of offending some groups."[8] This avenue failed to bring the desired results, but, by April 1967, the Kitchener Chamber of Commerce had become involved. The Old Order then proposed to the government that they would pay the CPP premiums if the monies were allocated to a charity of the Old Orders' choice. Not all of the Old Orders were comfortable with this compromise and the government also had difficulty with the proposal, and declined.

In the spring of 1967 the Old Orders paid their income tax only and sent along a form letter addressed "To Whom It May Concern":

> I am a member of the Old Order Mennonite Church. We believe that the needs and losses of the brotherhood should be taken care of first by the individual, then the family, then the Church, as we are taught by the Holy Scriptures. Our forefathers have established the system in the church long before the Dominion of Canada was formed, and we cannot conscientiously participate in a compulsory social insurance system.
>
> While it is our desire to extend love and mercy to every man in need regardless of religion or creed, we are very conscientious as stewards over the material things the Lord has entrusted to us. I am therefore not including the Pension deduction payment with my income tax return.[9]

The Department of Revenue responded and informed the Mennonites of their legal obligation to pay. Again the Mennonites were firm and begged the government to review the situation. Nonetheless, by the summer of 1967, the government began seizing milk and cream cheques from the Old Orders to collect payment for their overdue CPP payments. This action caught the media's attention. Furthermore, the Kitchener Chamber of Commerce became more deeply involved. In a study they found that because the Old Orders declined old age pension and children's allowances they were saving the Canadian taxpayers approximately four hundred thousand dollars per annum.

The Kitchener Chamber of Commerce presented a brief to the Minister of Revenue on October 16, 1967. Some of the points were: the Mennonites were sincere; they had never been a social problem; and to exempt them would effect a savings rather than an expense to the Treasury. The brief concluded: "The Kitchener Chamber of Commerce has committed itself to support of the Old Order plea for exemption from both contributions to and benefits arising out of the Canada Pension Plan."[10]

The Mennonites also presented a brief at that time. In their lengthy brief they acknowledged that governments are ordained by God for maintaining order in a country, and that they pray on behalf of the government. They continued: "We believe that the church is the body of Christ seeking to do the will of God, and as such demands a higher allegiance than does that of the state." Their concern was: "We see the social security as a direct threat to our religion. To be forced to accept such programmes is to be compelled to substitute a government welfare programme for a church-centred programme."[11] Edgar Benson, Minister of Revenue, at this time indicated that he was not happy with the seizures of milk cheques, and pledged personal support in amending the Act. This commitment failed to materalize; a year later the Old Orders had not received word as to when a conference would be held. The 1968 election gave Canada a new government and consequently the Old Order in January 1969, met with the new Minister of Revenue, Jean-Pierre Cote, who was also opposed to changing the law.

The Hutterites from the Canadian West also began to seek exemption from CPP. The government now had to respond to both the Old Orders in Ontario and the Hutterites on the prairies along with two members of Parliament, Mark Smerchanski from Manitoba and Max Saltsman from Ontario. In the Kitchener area the public also felt that the government should be more accommodating. As a result, the matter was brought before the Cabinet early in 1970, but it decided against granting exemption.[12]

In April 1970 the Hutterites again requested reconsideration for exemption, but the government sent a letter to them and denied that request. The Old Orders and the Hutterites continued to seek some means of being excluded from CPP. Their reprieve came with the sympathies of the new Minister of Revenue, Herb Gray. On December 7, 1971, Gray listened intently to the Old Orders submissions and suggested that it might be possible to bring the matter before the Cabinet for reconsideration without first consulting the provinces.[13] The former officials held that the provinces must first be consulted before reconsideration could be made and had refused for that reason. The Old Orders were deeply impressed with

Gray's position and through Gray's favourable influence the government announced two weeks later that it would amend the CPP Act to accommodate both the Old Orders in Ontario and the Hutterites in the West. Although the government made this commitment in December 1971, the amending bill was not brought into the House of Commons until June 1973. Bill C-22, as this bill was called, met some strong opposition, but there were also those in Parliament who supported Bill C-22. After over a year of debates and committee revisions it was finally passed in the House of Commons on November 7, 1974.

The persistence of the Old Orders and Hutterites had succeeded. Their conviction that CPP encroached on the church's responsibilities to take care of their own members drove them on in requesting their desired exemption. It was a learning experience for the Old Orders since not all groups shared the same level of conviction. The Markham group never had full support of all the members because many members worked in the general workforce and had the deductions taken off their paycheques. Conversely the Orthodox Mennonites became frustrated with the Old Orders' willingness to compromise and had to be encouraged to cooperate with the others.[14] Meanwhile, the David Martin group had elected to accept CPP from the beginning. Noah Martin always felt that the government began to consider the Old Order cause more seriously after certain government officials clearly understood that the Mennonites declined accepting old age pension and children allowances, and did not cash their subsidy cheques. During the parliamentary debates Mr. Stanley Knowles, MP Winnipeg North Centre, said:

> When a person says he does not want to pay a certain tax or a premium because it is a matter of religious conscience, I want to be sure of that. The question to put to our witnesses who are here today, has already been put: "Do you mean this? Have you demonstrated it by not accepting old age security even though you pay a tax for it? Do you mean this by not accepting family allowance even though you pay tax for it, and do you mean it by not having taken widow's or disability or pension benefits under the Canada Pension Plan?"
>
> You have already said that you have demonstrated the sincerity and the honesty of your religious conviction by letting

> it cost you money. I think we have to accept that as an honest religious position and therefore even those of us who do not like to breach the universality of this Canada Pension Plan should go along with this bill. As a matter of fact that is why I voted for it.[15]

Mr. Knowles' remarks verify his awareness that the Mennonites' refusal to accept certain government benefits demonstrated a sincere religious conviction.

The Mennonites also learned that many government officials also professed to be Christian, and saw that it was needful to recognize another man's beliefs. At one time a government official rebuked a Mennonite by stating that he also was a Christian. The Old Orders' interpretation of the Word and their definition of religious freedom did not always harmonize with those of Parliament. When asked to define religious freedom, Prime Minister Trudeau replied:

> Religious freedom exists, I take it, when people are free in their conscience and they can exercise their beliefs freely within the country, belong to a church of their choice, and so on. But, in some cases, if morals which flow from their metaphysics—if I can put it that way—are not morals accepted by the community in which they live, it is unfair to say that preventing those moral precepts from applying is an attack on religious freedom . . . And in this particular case, the morals of this small minority are in direct conflict with the scheme of social welfare which the governments of today have adopted in order to serve the communities better. And therefore, while they may continue practicing . . . believing the same kinds of faith, but in this particular case there is no practical way not to be bound by the ethic or the morals of the policies...(sic) when the government adopts laws which are good for the majority, I don't think that freedom of religion permits people from opting out (of CPP).[16]

Mr Trudeau's interpretation of religious freedom was definitely quite narrow in the Old Orders' minds; indeed, the Mennonites' exemption from military service during the wars would not have been possible if the above view had been applied during the wars. Furthermore, neither would the Old Order's exemption from jury duty and their parochial schools have been possible. This successful exemption from CPP indicates the considerable flexibility of Canadian politics at that time, but the many refusals also clearly indicated the reluctance of the government to accommodate such minority groups as the Old Orders.

The dialogue between the Old Orders and the government did not end with the passing of Bill C-22. The Social Insurance Number (SIN) also made the Old Orders uneasy. They had no desire to be linked to CPP by a number that was designed to organize both personal income tax, CPP, and other social plans. After some more discourse, both parties agreed on those averse to using the SIN could use an alterative number beginning with "zero" which would distinguish the Old Order and was valid only for income tax proposes.

After all these years of lobbying the government for exemption from CPP, the Old Orders sent a letter of acknowledgement to the government on December 6, 1977. They again stated that in their opinion it is the church's responsibility to take care of its needy:

> More significant than the economic aspects of the pension plan for us are the spiritual and moral values that are derived from meeting each other's needs.
>
> We continue to find looking after the needs of our dependent elderly, sick incapacitated and orphaned a greater joy than a burden. Our members are encouraged not to become dependent upon or add to the burden of government by accepting family allowance, Old Age Pension, and Canada Pension cheques, Hospital Insurance Plan assistance or Children Aid services. To our knowledge all our members continue to trust in God and look to their fellow believers for help in times of need.

The Old Orders reaffirmed their "complete satisfaction with the existing exemption provisions." Their closing sentence was: "We, therefore, pray that the Commission will be led to recommend continuance of the provision to exempt from participation in the Canada Pension Plan all those who have religious convictions against the same." The letter was dated Dec. 6, 1977 and signed by Edward M. Bauman, Old Order Mennonite bishop: Amsey Martin, Markham Waterloo Mennonite bishop;

Joseph N. Jantzi, Old Order Amish bishop; Arthur Gerber, Beachy Amish bishop; and Amos M. Sherk, Orthodox Mennonite bishop.

The Old Order—Oath and Jury Duty

The swearing of the oath of allegiance was for centuries a troublesome issue for the Mennonites and the Quakers in England. About 1695 the Quakers achieved the concession that permitted them to solemnly affirm: "I do sincerely promise and solemnly declare before God and the World that I will be true and faithful to King William and Queen Mary."[17] This affirmation was a reaction of the Church of England to make sure England remained a Protestant country because a Catholic's allegiance would be to the pope. It is noteworthy that an affirmation was accepted at such an early date.

Our next point of interest is the first successful Mennonite petition of 1809 in Upper Canada. This Act granted the Mennonites and Tunkers the same privilege as the Quakers to make "affirmation or declaration" instead of taking the oath where such was required. Furthermore, it "also disqualified the Mennonites and Tunkers from giving evidence in criminal cases, from serving on juries, or from holding any office or place in government."[18] To be disqualified from serving on juries was of no concern to the Mennonites who ultimately drew away from the courts. Nevertheless, John Erb's stint as a Justice of the Peace during the 1812-14 war reveals that the above stipulations were not always rigidly enforced. In reality there was no political body in the Waterloo settlement before 1820, and the Mennonites felt they were forced to deal with civil affairs.

The conference of 1864 resolved that it was not in accordance with the non-resistant faith to be active in canvassing and voting for public offices and, furthermore, the 1883 conference denied a Mennonite his membership if he was elected as a township councillor. These discussions at the conference reveal that the Mennonites were far more active in politics than the 1809 Act stipulated. Samuel Weber's son, Moses, recorded in his diary that his father went to Berlin as juryman in March of both 1863 and '64. This indicates that the Mennonites were involved in matters they later avoided and then declined.

Voting was not new to the Mennonites. They had been very active in Pennsylvania before the Revolutionary War. The war had set them apart from politics, but evidently they again took interest in the political affairs, even though the church advised against it. Though some Mennonites dabbled in politics, the conservative element drew away from such activity. At the turn of the twentieth century some Old Order Mennonites voted and those who voted were expected to vote Liberal.[19]

In 1974 the Canadian laws changed and the Mennonites were randomly called up for jury duty like all other Canadian citizens. To serve on jury duty was against the dictates of the Old Order Mennonites' conscience, and neither were the judges interested in the non-resistant Old Order who refused to swear the oath but would only affirm. As a result the Old Orders, with the assistance of MCC Canada, convinced the reluctant Sheriff Schmitt that a form letter be used and sent to the Sheriff's office of the local court, and the Old Orders were thereby excused from jury selection.

The Old Order Schools

Illiteracy limits an individual both spiritually and economically. For that reason the early settlers in Ontario, including the Mennonites, organized schools that were held primarily during the winter months. Attendance was erratic and there were few textbooks. Teachers with limited abilities were hired during those years. Nevertheless, people learned to read, even though there was some very rough spelling and grammar. Formal education in pioneer days was only for the upper class. However, this changed in 1842 when the Ontario government assumed the responsibility of educating the general public. The Common School Act divided the province into school sections, and in time a standard curriculum for the schools and regular attendance until a child was fourteen years old became law. High Schools, or grammar schools as they were called, opened in Galt (Cambridge) in 1853 and Berlin (Kitchener) in 1855. For over a century the people of Ontario received their education in these lowly country schools, but with the passing of Bill 54 in 1964, things were about to change.

Bill 54 abolished fifteen-hundred small schools across the province and created the large central township schools, where the children had to be transported to and from school. The intent was that large capital costs, such as gymnasiums, could be used by more children, and teachers in such schools would have more time for tutoring than those in the eighth-grade setting.

Many people resisted this change, but the plain people were the most sceptical of all. In April 1964, Old Order Minister Ervin Shantz wrote to William Davis, Minister of Education, and inquired if it were possible to keep the small schools open, and whether fourteen-year-olds were required by law to attend high school until age sixteen. (At this time the Old Orders were not sure of their legal status.) On June 15, 1964 Davis indicated that the small schools could remain if the local board of trustees agreed. In regard to the fourteen-year-old question Davis wrote: "In accordance with the provisions of clause C of subsection 2 of section 6 of The Schools Administration Act, apparently a child will still be excused from attendance at school if he has attained the age of fourteen years and his parent or guardian requires his services on the farm operated by the parent or guardian."[20]

The year 1965 was a frustrating time for all involved in school matters in Woolwich Township. The township school board was accountable to the general public, while the Old Orders were seeking concessions to maintain the small country schools. Even though three of the five-member school board in Woolwich Township were of Old Order parentage, the board voted in favour of consolidation of the small schools. Furthermore, there were some among the Old Order who were quite sceptical of the idea of holding their own schools. Meanwhile, Leonard Brubacher of the Markham group saw the transportation of schoolchildren as a business opportunity and formed a school bus company. The township school board sought to accommodate the Old Orders by opening the Three Bridges Schools as an Old Order public school. This compromise did not satisfy the Old Orders whose reasons for withdrawing were:

1. They were uncomfortable with the modern teaching of evolution.
2. They did not appreciate the emphasis on space travel.
3. They opposed physical training and the required clothes.
4. They rejected the use of TV as a teaching aid.
5. They feared the exposure of their children to the profanities and pornography of the larger society in the large consolidated schools.
6. The Old Orders deemed the long bus rides to and from school unprofitable to their children.

7. They did not appreciate the idea that some of the grade seven and eight students would be transported to separate Junior High Schools.

Since the curriculum was under the control of the County board of Education, only points 3, 5, and 7 were addressed by the Three Bridges "Mennonite" School.

By the spring of 1965, it became clear that the township board rejected the Old Orders' plea. At the Elmira meetinghouse on June 1, 1965, the Old Orders concluded that starting their own private schools was their next option. By September plans were in place to build or open the schools. In September 1966 the following parochial schools opened in Waterloo and Wellington County:

- Amish Parochial School #1 (New one-room school building) OO Amish
- Balsam Grove Parochial School (Renovated chicken house) OO Mennonite
- Beechvale Parochial School (Renovated farm house) Orthodox Mennonite
- Cedar Grove Christian Day School (Former school) Beachy Amish
- Martins Parochial School (Portable classroom) OO Mennonite
- Red Hill Parochial School (Renovated farm house) Orthodox Mennonite
- South Woolwich Parochial School (Portable Classroom) OO Mennonite
- Winterbourne Parochial School (Renovated farm house) OO Mennonite
- Winfield Parochial School, Wellington Co. (Renovated farm house) OO Mennonite

This parochial school endeavour had to overcome numerous hurdles. Although parochial schools were legal in Ontario, the government educators strongly discouraged the venture. Mr. Bornhold, the area educational supervisor, told the young novice teacher Amos Sherk, "You should have at least Grade twelve." Sherk replied, "I'm working on it, it takes time."

Sherk touched on the two vital points that directed the Parochial Schools towards success—perseverance and time. Another asset to the endeavour was the hiring of Mr. James Bauman, a certified teacher, to supervise the parochial schools. All those with whom he worked felt Bauman's commitment: "I will endeavour to help these teachers, board members, and families attempt to go in the educational direction they wish to go, providing that direction can be pursued without compromising academic progress and success."[21] Mr. Bauman's presence helped ease the public educators' concerns as the Parochial School endeavour launched on a very uncertain path. Bauman's closing comment at the first teachers' summer school (a crash course) was true: "Let's face it. It's going to be rough." There were many skeptics in the Old Order community during those first years, but time and perseverance prevailed. Skepticism slowly gave way to confidence and the community fully supported the parochial schools.

These schools are church-supported but are administered by a local three-man board from each school community. This local board is responsible for hiring the teacher and maintenance of the property. However, a separate committee consisting of teachers with ten years of teaching experience and several men from the community administer the curriculum. Also, experienced teachers are teamed with those of little or no experience to help them when going gets "rough." A group of retired teachers annually administer standardised tests to the students to help maintain academic uniformity over all the schools. Finally, there is a five-man board that handles the legal affairs and endeavours to peacefully solve human misunderstandings.

The Parochial Schools are continually challenged. Although the law changed in 1968 so that students were required to attend school until age sixteen, the Old Orders continued to keep their children out of school at age fourteen, as before, in full knowledge of the Minister of Education and his subordinates. The Canadian government's introduction of the metric system brought with it the need for metric-formatted-arithmetic textbooks that were compatible with the eighth-grade class setting. No satisfactory metric books were available for the eight-grade classroom, therefore, the Old Orders worked from 1980 to 1990 to make their own arithmetic textbooks. The need for grades seven and eight history textbooks became apparent in the late 1980s. The community did not appreciate the patriotic influence of the standard history books. A group of individuals accepted the challenge to produce two history textbooks that included a brief course of Mennonite history. In 1996 *A Goodly Heritage* was printed and the following year *Pleasant Places* was found in the classrooms. In 1995 the community also assumed the responsibility of including special children in their schools.

The struggle to administer the parochial schools continues. To fulfil the academic requirements within the ethos of the Old Order brotherhood remains an on-going effort that many in the community do not comprehend. The very heart of these schools rests upon the dedication of those who build and maintain this private education system. A teacher was asked what a child should know before he or she goes to school. She replied: they should know how to take care of themselves, be able to follow instructions, and be taught to finish a job—perseverance. Academics are important, but without an understanding of the above three virtues one's life is extremely difficult. The tension between high academic standards and the ethos of Gelassenheit and humility make it difficult for the parochial school to maintain a balance.

For the Old Order people education incorporates a broad sense of values. As implied above, academic standards are important to them. Nevertheless, because their children are taught the Pennsylvania Dutch German dialect as their mother tongue, it is difficult to maintain a good command of the English language. The values of Gelassenheit and equality discourage the elevation of outstanding or gifted students above their classmates. Although it varies how parents and teachers handle such circumstances, the model role is based on humility and gifted students are directed towards those values.

Teaching children how to get along with others is another important role of the Old Order schools. A parent stated that we should teach our children that it is better to patiently accept a false accusation than to be rightly accused for a wrong we have done. These values are the core of Gelassenheit and the Old Order faith and pose a continual challenge to the Old Order community. Nonetheless, if the community understands these values and endeavours to live them, the schools become an avenue to support the faith.

Though religion is the basic focus of Old Order Mennonitism, child evangelism is not. High morals are stressed and supported in every way.

Biblical values and Bible stories are part of the Old Order schools, but the teaching of doctrine is not. The Old Orders believe that the sacredness of the Scriptures is lost if there is only talk and no action. For this reason religious studies in the Old Order schools are limited to morning devotions (citation of the Lord's Prayer), a noon prayer or giving of thanks for the food, and a closing prayer or song. Classroom study of Bible characters and spiritual hymns are the extent of the religious studies in the Parochial schools. Academics in sincerity, morals in entirety, and community as a brotherhood are the principles that drive the Old Order schools.

Notes

1 T. D. Regehr, *Mennonites in Canada 1939-1970: A People Transformed* (Toronto: University of Toronto Press, 1996), 394.

2 William Janzen, *Limits on Liberty* (Toronto: University of Toronto Press, 1990), 257.

3 Conference Reports. Sept. 9, 1864, 7, CGUC.

4 Letter, MCC files. MCC office, Kent Avenue, Kitchener.

5 *Ibid.*

6 *Ibid.*

7 *Ibid.*

8 Janzen, *Limits*, 251.

9 Form letter, Feb. 23, 1967. Author's collection.

10 Janzen, *Limits*, 255.

11 "The Old Order Mennonite and Amish Basis of Objections to Government Sponsored Social Security Programmes." Manuscript donated to author's collection by Edward M. Bauman, Joseph N. Yantzi, and Noah B. Martin. N.P., Oct. 16, 1967, 1.

12 Janzen, *Limits*, 260.

13 *Ibid.*, 264.

14 Noah Martin, Conversation with Author, 1985.

15 Minutes of Proceedings, Thursday, October 18, 1973, Author's collection.

16 Janzen, *Limits*, 262.

17 Frank H. Epp, *Mennonites in Canada* I (Toronto: Macmillan of Canada, 1974), 98.

18 *Ibid.*, 103.

19 Private Letter, Author's collection.

20 Ervin Shantz, Records. Letter from William Davis to Keith Butler, June 15, 1964, Author's collection.

21 James Bauman, Article. Floradale: n.p, n.d., 5.

Twentieth-Century Settlements

Chapter Twenty

Barwick Settlement

During the mid 1960s several families from Markham and Waterloo districts moved to the Rainy River area in Northern Ontario and other families from Indiana joined them. They formed the Pine View congregation and on August 25, 1968, Marion Hoover was ordained minister for the community. On May 5, 1971, Walter Martin was ordained deacon. The congregation consisted of various cultures, and by 1974 the Pine View church left the Markham fellowship in favour of the Conservative Mennonites.

Hoover was blessed with a very strong voice and could captivate the attention of an audience. Hoover occasionally visited the Waterloo community from 1968-74, and I well remember how Hoover, in no uncertain terms, informed the North Woolwich congregation of those “ungodly neckties.” (Only the Ontario Old Order Mennonites wear neckties; the American Old Orders do not.) This was during the time when convictions against the use of tobacco and the wearing of neckties were strengthening. Hoover’s forthright administration would occasionally create problems for him over the years, but one always knew where he stood.

Beachburg Settlement

In 1979 several families of the Markham group sought to establish a new community. Scouting trips were taken to Manitoba and the Ottawa River Valley in Renfrew County. Their ultimate choice was the Beachburg area in the Ottawa Valley. Three families moved to Beachburg in June 1980. By September 1980 the Riverside Parochial School was opened for the children of these families. More families took interest in this daughter settlement so that by 1983 there were ten Markham households in Beachburg. On November 28, 1984, Merlyn Martin was ordained minister and Oscar Martin ordained deacon. On December 7, 1994, Kenneth Martin was also ordained minister for the Beachburg congregation.

From the very beginning the Waterloo ministry has scheduled a minister and deacon to serve the Beachburg community every three weeks. This schedule has continued until the present and has provided a good variety of ministry in rotation. Since 1994 Beachburg has church services every Sunday rather than the former schedule of once every three weeks.

In the summer of 1983, the Mennonites assumed responsibility for an old union cemetery on Zion Line. At the same time they purchased an adjacent lot. They moved a set of portable buildings onto it and started using the location for their meetinghouse the following spring. Services had been held in an old farm house on Grants Settlement Road which also housed the school. In 1999 the Riverside Parochial School was moved to a new building located on Pappin Road. This location is also used for the youth's midweek baseball games and skating.

The Beachburg community experienced some sensitive growing pains as people moved to the community and others left for various reasons. Nonetheless there remained a dedicated core of members that, along with support from the mother community, stabilized the settlement during the shifting of members. In 2002 the Beachburg community consisted of seventeen households, made up of sixteen families and one single person.

Brotherston Settlement

After World War II the Markham community was torn between those who wanted more activity, such as Sunday school and prayer meetings, and those who were comfortable with the traditional Gelassenheit theme. In 1950 it was agreed to place songbooks with notes in the meetinghouses. This compromise failed to restore peace. When Cecil Reesor was ordained minister in 1952, he did not completely support his bishop, Abraham Smith, and withdrew from the conference in 1959. Two years later in 1961, Alvin Baker was ordained minister, and he did not support Bishop Smith either.

One day at council meeting, Baker declined to go out into the council room with the other ministry; however, after the other ministry was in the council room, he arose and asked for a public council. This radical move ended that council meeting. For about half of the three years that Baker served the conference, no communion was held at Markham. In the fall of 1964 Bishop Smith told the congregation that he would stand with Waterloo and serve communion to those who agreed with him. About thirty members stood with Smith while the remainder of the congregation formed the Steeles Avenue Mennonite Church.

There was little future for the few remaining members at Markham because of the urban development. In 1972 Bishop Abraham Smith and his family followed some of his members who had moved before into the Howick-Wallace Township area. Beginning in 1972, there were church services held in the homes, and in 1973 these appointments were listed as Mayne. The small congregation had rented a vacant church on the fourth concession of Wallace Township at the Howick Township line. The congregation deemed it appropriate to ordain a deacon to assist Bishop Abraham Smith in serving the community. On December 3, 1973, an examination service was held at the Mayne Church for the ordination of a deacon. (The Mayne Church was later moved to the Milton Agricultural Museum.) On this day one of the trustees from the vacant Brotherston United Missionary Church on the sixth approached Minister Noah Martin and asked him if they would be interested in purchasing the Brotherston church. Noah referred the man to Bishop Smith and in due time the property was purchased for five thousand dollars. After being absent for a century the congregation returned to the original site of the first Mennonite Meetinghouse in Wallace.[1]

On August 27, 1974, John Drudge was ordained minister to assist the aging Bishop Smith. The small congregation experienced difficulties in blending the Markham and Waterloo cultures. Bishop Abraham Smith died in 1980 and the stabilizing effect of the old bishop was soon missed. In the fall of 1981 Deacon Ibra Martin withdrew from the conference and joined fellowship with the Countryside Mennonite Church. In the spring of 1984 John Drudge was silenced by the conference. His interpretation of Gelassenheit, charismatic administration, and the preaching of the second work of grace had caused the people to lose confidence in him. Drudge withdrew with a following of 127 members and formed the Crystal View Mennonite Church in Floradale. There were several other families who left the Markham group at that time who then sought fellowship with the Conference Mennonites.

The Brotherston congregation was challenged by the continual tension that hung over the community during Drudge's administration. After Drudge's departure, the Waterloo community served the Brotherston congregation for several years. On December 14, 1988, Edgar Bauman was ordained minister for Brotherston, and on November 29, 1990, Elmer Bearinger was ordained deacon. The congregation again had its own ministry and with the former tensions set aside, it prospered. By 1993 the old church was too small and the congregation decided to tear down the old church and build a new meetinghouse. The congregation had sought to relocate across the road but the township rejected the plan. However in 2001 additional land was purchased on the west side and the much-needed parking lot was enlarged. By the spring of 2002 the membership had again outgrown the meetinghouse and the congregation was divided into two separate congregations. These congregations share the meetinghouse on alternate Sundays.

Chesley Settlement

During the early 1990s there was considerable interest in starting daughter settlements for the Old Order community. Farms were purchased in the Teeswater area in 1991, in Chesley in 1992, and in Kinloss in 1993. The first family moved into the Chesley area in 1993. The community was in harmony with the parent community and experienced steady growth. A meetinghouse was built in 1998 and by 2001 two ministers and a deacon had been ordained. The Lilac Grove School was opened in 1995, and by 2002 there were twenty-six households in the area and several other properties had been purchased.

Kinloss Settlement

From its beginning the Kinloss settlement had very conservative leanings. A number of farms were purchased in 1993 north of Lucknow in the Kinlough–Holyrood area, and the first settlers arrived the following year. There was rapid growth, so much so that by the late 1990s about thirty farms had been purchased, even though not all were occupied at that time. The settlement agreed to forbid the installation of hydro and telephone in their homes and farmed exclusively with horses. These in-house regulations created tension, not only with the main body, but also internally. The unrest stifled growth for a few years. Some of the group were still not content and leaned towards forming their own church. After a few years of contention these separated from the Old Order group and joined fellowship with the Orthodox Mennonites in Huron County north of Gorrie. The remainder of the Kinloss settlement continued to commune with the main body of Old Orders, but they have their own set of understood guidelines which the community follows. Having settled their differences the community again prospered so that by 2002 the two groups combined owned about sixty properties in the area. The two groups continue to work together during the week and cooperate with their parochial schools.

Mount Forest Settlement

In the later 1950s, George Martin was introduced to the Mount Forest area by his boss, the owner of Martin's Apple Juice. George was impressed with the soil and recognized the area's potential to be a Mennonite settlement. Meanwhile, Isaac Horst visited Wallace and Howick Townships and felt the people were averse to the Mennonites. By the mid 1960s Isaac Horst and George Martin agreed to settle in the Mount Forest area. In November 1967, George's son-in-law, Amsey Bearinger, moved to a 150-acre farm. Isaac Horst moved to his farm in May of 1968, and Urias Weber and Edwin Martin moved in the fall of 1968. The following year another seven families joined the settlement. The community continued to grow, so that by 1972 there were seventeen families in the area and another six farms purchased.

The Mount Forest Mennonite community faced an air of pessimism during the early years. According to Old Order traditions, all out-reach settlements had failed—Wallace, North Michigan, and Port Elgin to name a few. During the first years those who had ventured outside the norms were asked who they thought they were. Did they think they could accomplish what others could not? As the community grew, the opposition waned. During the early years approximately five farms were bought every year by the Mennonite community, but as the negative attitudes dispersed the Mount Forest community prospered, so that by 1980 there were almost seventy farms bought by the Old Orders. Twenty years later the community had doubled in size, and close to one hundred and sixty families lived in the Mount Forest district.

The parent community served those in Mount Forest during the first years. In 1969 the community bought and remodelled an old Anglican church. For the first two years the services alternated in the homes of Horst and Bearinger and the Farewell church on a seven-week cycle. Beginning in 1971 services were held once every four weeks. In 1972 a meetinghouse was built and Melvin Sauder ordained as deacon, and the following year Elam Weber was ordained minister. In the year 2001 the community had four meetinghouses and eight two-room schools.

One of the pioneers indicated that it was a dramatic cultural change to move to a complete English neighbourhood. "We were well-received by most of the natives, although some were understandably apprehensive." With direct interaction this soon disappeared and in time confidence was won. It is evident that the venture was a success. The reasons may well have been the timing of the whole issue. The thrust behind the movement was *land*. Two centuries before it was land that drew the Mennonites into Waterloo County. As it was two hundred years ago so it was again when the Mount Forest settlement began. There was a rapid influx of new settlers and therefore a community could be formed.

Other Small Settlements

Several small settlements were founded during the 1990s. A few families moved into the Teeswater area in 1994. For several years it appeared as though the settlement could prosper, but by 2002 some of those families left the Old Order group and the remaining families were considering moving away.

In the mid 1990s three farms were purchased east of Dunnville about twelve miles from Lake Erie. Daniel Brubacher and his sons farmed there until 2001 when they sold their farms and moved to Kinloss and joined the Old Order community there.

In 1999 Ivan Gingrich took interest in the Lindsay area. He purchased three farms and moved in 1999 to Lindsay. Several other farms have been purchased recently so that five properties were owned by the Old Order Mennonites by 2002. The future of this settlement at this time remains unknown.

Notes

[1] For the early history see chapter nine regarding the Wallace or Brotherston settlement.

Epilogue

Chapter Twenty-One

The Old Order Mennonite community and the Anabaptist ethos of Gelassenheit are synonymous. Gelassenheit, as viewed by the Old Orders, is in part paradoxical. There is a strong emphasis on "submissiveness" to God and man: "Submit yourselves therefore to God. Resist the devil, and he will flee from you" (James 4:7), yet the "steadfastness" of the apostles and the martyrs is admired and they are considered perfect examples to follow. "A double minded man is unstable in all his ways" (James 1:8).

During the World Wars the Old Orders, along with the Peace Churches, patiently persisted as they sought exemption from military service. In the Canada Pension exemption issue, the Old Orders again displayed a remarkable level of "patient persistence" as they sought exemption from the public Social Insurance Plan. Throughout these times the Old Order demonstrated steadfastness in their beliefs by not fully submitting to the government, but at the same time expressing submission to the authorities within the dictates of their interpretation of the Bible. In other more resent issues the same values have been displayed.

Their conspicuous uniformity in dress and their personal aversion to public attraction are demonstrations of "courageous meekness." This is especially manifested by the women's head covering or veil. In total submission to their faith in God the sisters accept the headship of man while they receive a blessing from God. This acceptance of the headship of man does not mean the women are slaves to the men, but parallels the man's submission to the headship of Christ. It is a matter of *order* not of *power* because under the theme of Gelassenheit, power dissipates under the umbrella of submissiveness and yieldedness. This may appear a mystery to those outside the Old Order Mennonite circles, but for those within the confines of Gelassenheit the husband and wife are partners together with Christ under the manifold grace of God. "As every man hath received the gift, even so minister the same one to another, as good stewards of the manifold grace of God" (1 Peter 4:10).

Christian stewardship is another characteristic of the Old Order Mennonites. They consider themselves unworthy servants: "So likewise ye, when ye shall have done all those things which are commanded you, say, We are unprofitable servants: we have done that which was our duty to do" (Luke 17:10). Yet they are taught to labour to the best of their ability: "Servants, obey in all things your masters according to the flesh; not with eyeservice, as menpleasers; but in singleness of heart, fearing God: And whatsoever ye do, do it heartily, as to the Lord, and not unto men" (Col. 3:22-23). Hand in hand with stewardship goes thrift and success, yet Gelassenheit denotes suffering and persecution. The Old Order Mennonites have been challenged to combine these contrasting values. The fruits of thrift and wealth draw them toward the things of the world, while the theme of Gelassenheit directs them towards a simple and humble lifestyle. There is a never-ending challenge to harmonize these virtues in the community of believers in God.

It is difficult to separate the culture from the beliefs of the Old Order Mennonites because the two are so interwoven in Gelassenheit. The Old Orders appear to decree that there shall be no change, and it is this decree that enables them to control change as they move through transitions of change. Furthermore, Gelassenheit empowers the Old Order community to resist change.

Within the Old Order brotherhood all members are considered equal and, in theory, each person is to esteem his brother or sister in Christ better than himself: "Let nothing be done through strife or vainglory; but in lowliness of mind let each esteem other better than themselves" (Philippians 2:3). Without that spirit of yieldedness to the brotherhood, that complete resignation to God's will, that self-abandonment and a total commitment to being a disciple of Christ one cannot maintain a fellowship based on voluntary devotion. A demonstration of democracy within the brotherhood is in opposition to the principle of self-abandonment where one meekly places his ideas before the congregation and then quietly allows the brotherhood to determine his fate. However, the Old Order Mennonites are as human as all other people, and there are times when the peaceful ethos of Gelassenheit is over-stepped and personal views are pushed upon the brotherhood. If such individuals then quickly step back into line, the ripples smooth over and the issue is forgotten. However, if individuals use democratic tactics to force change on the community, the bond of peace is weakened and confidence in the brotherhood is undermined. Without confidence in the brotherhood there is no unity or peace, and where unity and peace fail there is no brotherhood and fragmentation results.

In an Old Order Mennonite fellowship the liberties in Christ take on an added dimension. In 1 Corinthians 8:13 we read " . . . if meat make my brother to offend, I will eat no flesh while the world standeth, lest I make my brother to offend." Such willingness and yieldiness is also taught in Romans 14:17-19: "For the kingdom of God is not meat and drink; but righteousness, and peace, and joy in the Holy Ghost. For he that in these things serveth Christ is acceptable to God, and approved of men. Let us therefore follow after the things which make for peace, and things wherewith one may edify another." Though the Old Order Mennonites believe in the liberties in Christ, they are taught it is wrong to do things that offend others even though they have no conscience against the matter. The importance of forbearing one another in love is one of the basic tenets of their faith. (1) Though the Old Order Mennonites believe in a Christian brotherhood, their relation with God is personal.

Faith in God must be personal while being in harmony with the brotherhood. For lack of ability to give a proper testimony, individuals have at times expressed that they believe as the church does. However,

(1) *The following incident demonstrates this virtue. An Old Order Mennonite who was financially secure was approached by a brother in the church and asked why he continued to use his old well-worn harness. He received the following answer: "Yes, I could afford in new harness but what if I then tempt a brother who cannot afford a new harness, to buy one." A bishop once stated that those with means should conduct their lives in a way that their wealth is not displayed.*

they are taught that they should "...be ready always to give an answer to every man that asketh you a reason of the hope that is in you with meekness and fear" (1 Peter 3:15).

This study shows that the virtues that envelop Gelassenheit had little in common with the charismatic revivalism of the 1800s. However, it is also evident that early Anabaptism was not at odds with revivalism. One could suggest that the Old Orders over-reacted towards revivalism during the 1800s as promoted by the Methodists and later the Fundamentalists. As a result of this over-reaction against the charismatic air of those times, the Old Order Mennonites have declined to become involved in any form of aggressive evangelism. Are the Old Order Mennonites truly averse to evangelism or is their emphasis on cross-bearing and discipleship simply not as appealing to those outside as traditional revivalism?

The Old Order Mennonite brotherhood supplies the spiritual, social, and economic needs of its people. Nonetheless, such voluminous benefits include a price—a voluntary commitment to minimize personal values and to be obedient and submissive to the brotherhood. Many people covet the social and economic stability of the Old Order Mennonite community, but are not willing to pay the price. Moreover there are also times when those within the fellowship are not willing to pay the price and yet reap the benefits for a time. The community is patient with such because it takes maturity for a person to grasp Gelassenheit. However, those who continually resist the order of the community and fail to voluntarily submit themselves to the brotherhood become "fence crowders" and cause the community to drift from the principles the group strives to maintain. The numerous divisions within the Old Order Mennonite communities are the result of the brotherhood developing varied values. Since the foundation of the brotherhood is a voluntary commitment, one cannot coerce individuals to comply with church order, and yet it is evident that order strengthens the fellowship. A community with a strong sense of Gelassenheit finds it easier to maintain order and peace within the brotherhood.

The cherished Old Order Mennonite teaching of non-resistance is also directly related to the theme of Gelassenheit. Without Gelassenheit the non-resistant belief ultimately changes to pacifism. Pacifism encourages peace activity, but a pacifist is seldom prepared to suffer the spoiling of his personal goods and to accept the ridicule that a non-resistant individual must during a time of war. World War II Mennonite statistics indicate that as the theme of Gelassenheit weakened, so did the commitment to the non-resistant faith. From forty to sixty per cent of the men in the main Mennonite churches chose alternative service during World War II while the rest voluntarily enlisted in combatant or non-combatant services. In the Old Order groups from ninety-three to one hundred per cent chose alternative service, while the conservative groups (like the Amish Mennonites) had seventy-six per cent in alternative service.[1] Although these are American Mennonite statistics, one can presume that Canadian numbers would be similar. Although Old Order groups remained true to their non-resistant faith during World War II, how their eighteen-to twenty-three-year-olds would respond today remains unknown, but if the theme of Gelassenheit is understood they would likely react as their forefathers did. It remains certain that the non-resistant faith is never popular, and during the time of war it will collapse if not fortified by the theme of Gelassenheit.

During prosperous times it becomes exceedingly difficult for people to "feel" the peaceful theme of Gelassenheit. Nevertheless, if the Old Order Mennonites lose this vision then it may well be with them as J. Winfield Fretz wrote concerning the Waterloo Mennonites: "If it [the Mennonite church] no longer conceives of itself as a fellowship of believers, as a voluntarily disciplined body of followers of Christ, it will have lost its reason for existence."[2] It is very challenging during prosperous times to grasp that salvation is more than a verbal confession. To the Old Order Mennonites salvation means discipleship in the fear of God. They have confidence in Christ and believe in the mercies and love of God. "It is of the Lord's mercies that we are not consumed, because his compassions fail not." (Lamentations 3:22). The prophet also felt Gelassenheit when he wrote, " . . . what doth the Lord require of thee, but to do justly, to love mercy, and to walk humbly with thy God?" (Micah 6:8).

The allures of society sometimes draw young people away from the church of their fathers. They find it easier to express their faith in the more evangelical way. The Protestant emphasis on rising with Christ from the tomb is more appealing than the Anabaptist view of dying with Jesus at the cross and the strong thrust of discipleship. It takes Gelassenheit—

that peaceful surrender of self—to allow one to make the voluntary commitment to submissively and obediently serve God through the context of the brotherhood.

Gelassenheit and a strong commitment to God are upheld by many Christians outside the Old Order Mennonite communities. The difference is that the Old Orders endeavour to practise these principles as a brotherhood, while most other Christians generally do so as individuals. It is their strong emphasis on biblical values of Gelassenheit, Discipleship and Brotherhood that separates the Old Order Mennonites from their Protestant neighbours. Salvation is a gift from God and is only attained through the blood of Jesus Christ our Lord.

The pen and paper are willing instruments in portraying how the Old Order Mennonites feel their religion through the ethos of Gelassenheit. The portrayal of Gelassenheit in this book is idealized.At times the human element mars that perfect theme of yieldedness and peace and individuals lose focus of their place within the confines of the brotherhood. Nevertheless the goal of having peace with God and man within the confines of Gelassenheit is available to every Christian.

Notes

[1] J. A. Toews, *Alternative Service in Canada during World War II* (Winnipeg: Christian Press Ltd., 1959).

[2] J. Winfield Fretz, *The Waterloo Mennonites: A Community in Paradox* (Waterloo: Wilfrid Laurier University Press, 1989).

Appendix A

Appointments for Worship

Appendix A is the unpublished work of the late Isaac G. Martin. I have taken the liberty of adding additional information from my research.

An outline of the 1837 Calendar of Appointments.

Henrich Eby, Berlin, Upper Canada, printed this calendar. The appointments are given throughout the year as follows:

Benjamin Ebys	every 4 weeks	First Mennonite in Kitchener
David Ebys	4 "	Corner of Erb St.& Hallman Rd
Geigers	8 "	South of Baden
George Bechtels	4 "	His residence in Blenheim Township
Hallmans	4 "	North Dumfries
Cressmans	4 "	Breslau
Latschars	8 "	West of Manheim
Martins	4 "	North-west of Waterloo
Samuel Bechtels	8 "	Little west of Hespeler
Schneiders	4 "	Bloomingdale
Stauffers	8 "	A residence in Blenheim Township
Union	2 "	North of Preston [Hageys]
Wanners	8 "	North of Hespeler

Stauffers, Hallmans, Latschars always had one of the following minister's names included beside the appointment which indicated who was to preach there on that Sunday. The names were Benjamin Eby, Johann Weber, Jacob Hallman, Heinrich Weber, Martin Bear, Joseph Bauman. George Bechtel evidently was also a minister at that time and meetings were held at his residence. There is no indication that there was a calendar printed from 1837-1848, and it is uncertain whether this was because of the 1837 Revolution.

This is a list of all the appointments recorded from 1837-1901.

Aldboro: Aldboro Township, Elgin County. This appointment was first included in the calendar of 1874 and was discontinued in 1890. The meetings were held in a school several miles east of Clachen. The place at present is known as Bothwell. The settlement had settlers from both Waterloo and Vineland districts.

Almira: Markam Township, York County. This appointment first appeared as "Elmira" in 1861, but it was changed to "Almira" in 1867.

Almira: On Jan. 12, 1860, a meeting was held by members of the Mennonists Church for the purpose of nominating trustees for the building of a meetinghouse. In March of 1860, a parcel of land was purchased from Adam Wideman for twenty-five dollars and a thirty by forty foot brick building was erected. The first service was held on Sept. 30, 1860. Minister Adam Wideman who had served the church for about twenty-five years died on Jan. 28, 1861. The story goes that he was only present one Sunday at the new meetinghouse. On June 16, 1861, nominations were held for a minister, but the ordination was postponed on account of difficulty between Caspar Wideman and Prefect Jacob Burkholder. July 14, 1861, Jacob Wideman was ordained minister by Bishop Jacob Grove. (Abraham Wideman was excused from the lot by his own request.) In 1875 horse sheds were built. The following information is from the diary of the late Jacob B. Grove—Ontario Conference final meeting before the church was relocated was held on Aug. 14, 1955, by Brother Elmer Burkholder. On Feb. 5, 1956, the Markham-Waterloo Conference held its first services. Song number thirty-nine in *Lieder Sammlung* and number 188 in the Church Hymnal were sung. Bishop Abram Smith had the opening. Deacon Henry Gingrich, Waterloo, read Heb. 12 and the message was delivered by Fred Nighswander. Cecil Reesor, Carl Reesor and Joseph Barkey gave testimonies. In the afternoon a joint service was held by the two Mennonite groups which was also attended by many Brethren in Christ. The meetinghouse was filled. The Conference Mennonites had their opening services on Mar. 18, 1956 with fifty-three people present. On Sept. 23, 1956 the Conference Mennonites closed the Almira congregation. There were only thirty-four members at that time. Jacob H. Wideman and Aaron D. Grove conducted this last service—text was Matt. 24:14. On Dec. 27, 1970 the last meeting was held by the Markham Waterloo Conference at the Almira Meetinghouse. Songs numbers 94, 93, 344, 150 from the Church Hymnal were sung. Bishop Abraham Smith had opening remarks—had served there for forty-three years. Christian Frey from Waterloo had Matt. 2 for his text. There were fifty-four present that day.

Altona: Pickering Township, Ontario County. This meetinghouse was included in 1852 and was used until 19—. The first reference to Altona is the burial of Mrs. Abraham Stouffer in 1835, on Lot 30, Con. 9, Pickering Twp. On Feb. 9, 1850, the Mennonist Society held a meeting at Stouffville in regards to building a meetinghouse. Samuel Hoover, Abraham Stouffer, and Martin Nighswander were the trustees and a meetinghouse was built by 1852. A schoolhouse was at this location before this date.

Baumann: Waterloo Township, Waterloo County, was a residence Northeast of Breslau. It was included in 1849 and 1850 every four weeks. It was probably held at a school near Elias Bauman. "Isaac Y. Shantz" was apparently in the same neighbourhood. It was included from 1851 to 1857.

Bechtel, George: Blenheim Twp., Oxford County, was a residence included from 1837-1848.

Bechtel, Samuel: Waterloo Township, Waterloo County, was a union meetinghouse and school near Hespeler. [I. G. Martin indicated that it stood near the Wanner church.] The Tunkers and Mennonites both used it. It was included from 1837-1862; however, after 1849 it was listed only as Bechtel. The building was removed about 1870, and a large boulder was set into a cement block to mark the place.

Berg: Clinton Township, Lincoln County, first appeared in the 1848 calendar but probably was used earlier. This place was upon the mountain ridge near "Vineland." It was discontinued in the Old Order Mennonite Church Calendars in 1898.

Bertie: Bertie Township, Welland County. This congregation was located in the southeastern part of the county and was included from 1873-1909.

The "Old" Mennonites then called it "Sherkston."

Biehn: Wilmot Township, Waterloo County. This place of worship was included in 1867, and a meetinghouse was erected on the John Biehn farm southwest of Haysville in 1870. The congregation has been known as the Nith Valley Mennonite Church since 1976. Other sources indicate that the Blenheim congregation joined the Biehn congregation to form the Nith Valley Mennonite Church.

Blandford: Blandford Township, Oxford County. It was included in 1849 when "George Bechtel" was discontinued. A log meetinghouse was built and used until about 1908. At this time the Blandford meetings were discontinued.

Blenheim: Blenheim Township, Oxford County. This congregation was organized in 1839, and continued until 1974 or 1975 when they joined the Biehn congregation and formed the Nith Valley Mennonite Church. The meetinghouse was located on the Wilmot-Blenheim Township line about one and a half miles southwest of New Dundee. The brick building erected in 1902 is now used as a Retreat and Bible Study Centre.

Böhm: Clarence Township, Erie County, New York. Included from 1848-1852, at which time "Clarence" was included, and it is evidently the same meetinghouse. The Conference Mennonites still have a church at Clarence Centre. Preacher Howard Bauman of Elmira served there for a while.

Brant: Brant Township, Bruce County. This was a residence appointment which first appeared as "Haase" in 1868. From 1874-1876 it was listed as Schwartz, Reier, Wryer, or Berge. It was then changed to Brant in 1877, and then to Hanover in 1882. It is not known when it was discontinued.

Cayuga: South Cayuga Township, Haldimand County. This appointment was included in 1848, but its name was changed to "South Cayuga" in 1891. The Old Order Mennonites discontinued it in 1931. The Markham-Waterloo Conference held services here until 1941. John E. Sherk was the last Old Order minister at Cayuga.

Cedargrove: Markham Township, York County. This congregation was included in the calendar of 1867. The Old Order Mennonites discontinued it in 1891, although the Conference Mennonites continue to worship there. In 1986 the Steele's Ave. congregation (the former Reesor's group that left the Markham-Waterloo Mennonites) joined the Cedargrove congregation and formed Rouge Valley Mennonites.

Clarence: Clarence Township, Erie County, New York. Clarence was included in 1853. At that time Böhm was discontinued. It lost the Old Order connections in 1905. Today Clarence Centre-Akron is part of the New York Mennonite conference.

Clemens: Grey Township, Huron County. This residence was included in 1878. The appointments were once every eight weeks. It was served by the ministers of Waterloo and discontinued in 1879.

Conestogo: Woolwich Township, Waterloo County near the Three Bridges. The land was purchased in 1844, and a log schoolhouse was built and worship services were held there. The original schoolhouse was on the west side of the road. The exact location and when it was torn down are not known. A meetinghouse was built in 1851 or 1852. After the division of 1889, the Old Order Mennonites surrendered the site in 1893 and then built a new meetinghouse in 1894, half a mile to the south where stands the present Old Order Mennonite Meetinghouse. Conference Mennonites used the old meetinghouse until 1915 when they built a church in St. Jacobs. The original cemetery is still used by the St. Jacobs Mennonites. During the 1940s the Old Orders enlarged their meetinghouse, and fifty years later the original structure was torn down and the meetinghouse rebuilt.

Culross: Culross Township, Bruce County. The ministers from Waterloo held services in this residence from 1884-1890, once every four weeks. Dr. Joe Good moved to Formosa about 1880, and some of his family were baptized at Culross.

Dettweiler: North Dumfries Township, Waterloo County, near Roseville. A log meetinghouse was built in 1830 or 1840 [I. G. Martin records both]. This congregation was not yet included in 1837. A stone meetinghouse was built in 1855, and used until 1965. The building was restored and dedication services held in September 1999.

Elmira: Markham Township, York County. This appointment was included in 1861, and then changed to "Almira." See Almira.

Elmira: Woolwich Township, Waterloo County. When the Markham-Waterloo Conference was organized in 1939, they called the formerly known "West Woolwich" Meetinghouse "Elmira." The Old Order Mennonites also adapted "Elmira" in 1975 (see also West Woolwich).

Eby, Benjamin: Waterloo Township, Waterloo County. The first Mennonite Meetinghouse was built in Waterloo County. It was constructed of logs on Bishop Benjamin Eby's farm in 1813. A white frame building was erected on the same site in 1834, which was used until 1902 when a brick church was built on the same site. It is now known as the "First Mennonite" Church.

Eby, Christian: Christian Eby was the son of Bishop Benjamin Eby who also succeeded his father in the ministry and on the home farm. In 1855, "Benjamin Ebys" was changed to "Christian Ebys," later known as First Mennonite.

Eby, David: Waterloo Township, Waterloo County. This appointment appears in the 1837 calendar, but services were probably held there earlier. David Eby gave the land for the cemetery and meetinghouse at the corner of Hallman Road and Erb Street in Waterloo. In 1902, the old building was torn down and a new church erected on Erb Street West in Waterloo. The congregation, known as Erb Street Mennonite, has continued to use the old cemetery on the original site.

Elmwood: Brant Township, Bruce County. It was only included in 1890.

Fall: Niagara Township, Niagara County, New York. This appointment was located about twelve miles east from the falls. It was included in the calendar from 1857-1885.

Geiger: Wilmot Township, Waterloo County south of Baden on the David Geiger farm off Bleams Road. It was included in 1837. It is currently known as the Wilmot Mennonite Church. The name was changed when the congregation was amalgamated with the Baden Mennonite Church in 1977. The newly-formed congregation then erected a new building on the old Geiger site.

Haase: Brant Township, Bruce County. See "Brant" for further information.

Hanover: Township line between Brant and Bentinck Townships, Bruce and Gray Counties. This appointment was first included in 1882 and was connected with the "Brant" appointments. The ministers from Waterloo preached there every eight weeks in the residences until 1890. (See also "Brant")

Hallman: North Dumfries Township, Waterloo County. This congregation was included in 1837. The cemetery had been in use since 1831. The appointments were discontinued in 1869, and then were again included from 1872-1874. It again appeared from 1884-1890, when it was discontinued. The meetinghouse has been removed for some time. The appointment was close to Dettweilers meetinghouse.

Hay: Hay Township, Huron County, south of Zurich. The Waterloo ministry served this community as early as 1837. In that year Minister Henry

Schuh died at Hay while on a preaching trip. Although there are ordination records of a minister and deacon being ordained in 1861, this congregation was not included in the calendar until 1866. At times there was disunity in this community and that may have been the reason why it was not included before. The Old Order Mennonites held services until 1890. The Conference Mennonites continued to have services at Zurich after 1908 and are known as the Zurich Mennonite Church.

Hagey (Hegy): Waterloo Township, Waterloo County. This meetinghouse was also known as "Union." The Mennonites and Tunkers both used this meetinghouse during the early years. The Hagey deacon book describes this place as "Union" in 1824, and so does the 1837 Calendar of Appointments; however, there was another union meetinghouse and school near Hespeler where the Mennonites and Tunkers also shared a building. Samuel Bechtel had donated the land, and the appointment in 1837 was given as "Samuel Bechtel." See also "Samuel Bechtel." After the meetinghouse had been twice damaged by fire [in 1950 and 1953] a church was built in Preston. The congregation was then known as the Preston Mennonite church. This congregation is the oldest in Waterloo, even though it did not have the first meetinghouse. There is also reference to an old Mennonite Meetinghouse that was located somewhere at the present highway 401 and 8 interchange. John Erb, the miller at Preston, had built that meetinghouse to appease the Mennonites because he, as Justice of the Peace, had been instrumental in pressing the Mennonites into army transport service in the 1812-14 War. This meetinghouse was also used by other denominations because at that time in Ontario a church was to be free for all dissenters. Before 1842 it was not possible for the Mennonites to hold legal title to a church. For some reason the Mennonites relinquished the first meetinghouse, and then they moved to the present Hageys cemetery-location in about 1842.

Hembling: Woolwich Township, Waterloo County, north of Floradale. It was included in 1857; the appointment was named after Deacon William Hembling. Meetings were first held in a log schoolhouse. Services were then held in an old frame church just north of the old school. In 1872 a new location was chosen about one-quarter mile north and a meetinghouse built. When Deacon Hembling separated and joined the Mennonite Brethren Church movement, the meetinghouse was called "North Woolwich."

Huber: Whitchurch Township, York County. It was probably a residence that was included in 1852. It was discontinued in 1861 when "Elmira" was added. According to Clarence Smith's records, Martin Hoover (1760-1849) served this community in their homes. This would have been before 1837 because Hoover moved to Ohio on Sept. 22, 1837.

Jordan: Clinton Township, Lincoln County. It was included in 1848 and discontinued in 1850, though it was possible that meetings were held there much earlier. After the Daniel Hoch split in 1849, this group used the meetinghouse. The Jordan Historical Museum Complex is on the site today.

Cressman: Waterloo Township, Waterloo County, at Breslau. This appointment was included in 1837 and very likely meetings were held there earlier. It was built on the John Cressman farm and evidently named after him. It is now known as the Breslau Mennonite Church.

Latschar: Wilmot Township, Waterloo County about half a mile west of Mannheim. The Latschar congregation was organized in 1835, when a log meetinghouse was built. It was named after Isaac Latschaw and is still in use. In 1853 the log meetinghouse was replaced by a stone building. The present brick structure was built in 1908 and is still in use. The congregation is known as the Mannheim Mennonite Church

Lehmann: Ellice Township, Perth County. This appointment was held at the residence of Jacob Lehmann. Here the ministers of Waterloo held services once every eight weeks from 1852-1881.

Martins: Waterloo Township, on the Waterloo-Woolwich township-line at King Street, Waterloo. The cemetery was started in 1830 or earlier. It was built on the Henry Martin farm some time between 1831-34 and services have continually been held at the site. An old copy of the New Testament is still preserved in the pulpit of the Martin's Meetinghouse in which was inscribed the date April 1, 1831, by the first deacon Peter Burkhart. The Martins meetinghouse has seen several renovations, but it was never completely torn down. Isaac Martin recorded in his diary on May 27, 1900, that he was at the first service after the meetinghouse had been enlarged. Before World War I there had been chains strung along the road to tie up the horses. During the war those chains along the road were stolen, but not those on the church property. During the summer of 1993 the Old Order Mennonites decided to discontinue to use the Martins meetinghouse because of heavy traffic on the highway. The last service was held in January 1994, but the Markham group continues to use the meetinghouse.

Maryboro: Maryborough Township, Wellington County, on the fifth concession probably at the Wyandot School. It was a small congregation included in 1872 and then discontinued in 1890. The Mennonite Brethren Church group at one time had a church on the fourth line of Maryborough, but it is doubtful if the Mennonites used that location.

Meyer: Clinton Township, Lincoln County, at Vineland. This was the first congregation organized in Canada in 1801. The Old Order Mennonites discontinued services here in 1928, but the Conference Mennonites still have a congregation there. The present church is located on the east side of the cemetery; however the Old Order meetinghouse stood on the northwest side. The present congregation is known as the First Mennonite Church, Vineland. The present building was erected in 1962.

Mosa: Mosa Township, Middlesex County. This meetinghouse was across the Thames River from Aldboro. See also "Aldboro." The Old Order Mennonites discontinued using it in 1890.

Port Elgin: Saugeen Township, Bruce County, at Lake Huron. In 1858, Solomon Eby was ordained as a minister and his father Martin Eby as deacon. They went with the Mennonite Brethren Church movement in the 1870s and Port Elgin was first included in the calendar of appointments in 1879. Services were held there every four weeks until 1890 when the Old Order Mennonites discontinued holding services at Port Elgin.

Rainham: Rainham Township, Haldimand County, beside Lake Erie. The Old Order Cemetery is right beside the lake where the first meetinghouse also stood. The present Rainham Church is about one mile north of the old cemetery. This appointment was first included in 1860; however, meetings must have been held there much earlier. The Markham-Waterloo Conference Church held the occasional services there until 1955.

Reist, Daniel: Waterloo Township, about two miles east of Breslau. It was held at residences between Breslau and Shantz Station. It was included in 1857 when the "I. J. Shantz" was discontinued. It was discontinued in 1871.

Reesor [Risser]: Markham Township, York County. It was included in 1848 and remained Old Order after the 1889 division but in 1929 or 1930 the Old Order Mennonites withdrew and the Markham-Waterloo Conference Church continued services. The Steele's Ave congregation also used it until 1986. It is possible that services were held before 1836 in the area but there are no records. In 1836, Bishop Benjamin Eby ordained Jacob Grove minister. Indications are that he also ordained John E. Reesor, Adam Wideman, and Deacon Daniel Hoover at the same time. On Nov. 18,1836 we have record of a stove being bought for a *Schulhouse*. This log schoolhouse was on Lot 1 Con. 11 and was located on the farm of John E. Reesor, where the Reesors Meetinghouse stands. In 1857 the first burial was made at Reesors. Land was transferred for a meetinghouse in 1858, and in 1878 half an acre was added to the plot and the meetinghouse was moved to the north side of the lot. After the division the Conference Mennonites discontinued to use Reesors. The Markham group used the Meetinghouse until October 1994.

Schmitt: Vaughan Township, York County, near Edgley. The appointments were included in 1848, but meetings were probably held there earlier. An old log meetinghouse was used until 1890. The log meetinghouse stood about a quarter mile north of Edgley on a sideroad off of highway 7. This meetinghouse is now located at the Black Creek Pioneer Village.

Schneider: Waterloo Township, Waterloo County, northwest of Bloomingdale. This meetinghouse was named after Deacon Jacob (Joch) Schneider who gave the land in 1806. It was included in 1837, but a meetinghouse of logs or frame was evidently built earlier. The Mennonite appointments discontinue in 1874 when the Mennonite Brethren Church Church took possession of the meetinghouse and then built a brick church. The Mennonites again gained possession and the Conference Mennonites continue to use the building. It is currently known as the Bloomingdale Mennonite Church. After 1888 the Old Order Mennonites discontinued it in their calendar.

Shantz: Wilmot Township, Waterloo County, north of Baden. It was named after David Y. Shantz, the owner of the land. The congregation was organized in 1845, and the first meetinghouse built in 1849. The congregation at present exists as the Shantz Mennonite Church

Shantz, I.Y.: Waterloo Township, near Shantz Station. Meetings were held at the home of Isaac Y. Shantz from 1851-1857 when "Reist" was included. (See "Reist, Daniel")

South Peel: Peel Township, Wellington County, west of Wallenstein. An Old Order Mennonite congregation was formed there in 1901, and services have continued. From April 1963 to December 1965 the Markham-Waterloo Mennonites used the Peel Meetinghouse on a varied schedule of once every six to eight weeks. In 19— the building was razed and rebuilt farther north on the same lot. The appointment is now known as "Peel."

Stanley: Stanley Township, Huron County. Meetings were held at the Steckle residence, which were included in 1887. The Old Order Mennonite ministers held services at this home until 1954 once every eight weeks. In 1955 the Markham-Waterloo Conference held services there once every four weeks until 1966.

Stauffer: Blenheim Township, Oxford County. It was held at the residence of Jacob G. Stauffer that was included from 1837-1863 when it was discontinued.

Stecklin: Whitchurch Township, York County. It was probably a home that was included in 1856. It was discontinued with "Huber" when "Elmira" was founded in 1861. There is an old Stecklin cemetery in that area but the fieldstone marks are no longer readable. (See also "Huber")

Union: Waterloo Township, Waterloo County, north of the 401 highway on Regional Road 17. This meetinghouse was later known as "Hagey" (See "Hagey" for further information).

Wanner: Waterloo Township, Waterloo County, northwest of Hespeler. This was an early place of worship and was included in 1837. The Wanner Congregation has continued until the present at the original site and a large cemetery adjoins the church.

Wambold: Blenheim Township, Oxford County. It was at the residence of Abraham Wambold near the Blandford Township line. The appointment was discontinued with "George Bechtel" in 1849 when "Blandford" was included.

Wallace: Wallace Township, Perth County. The appointment was included in 1865. A meetinghouse was also built in 1871; however, in about 1875, the Mennonite Brethren Church congregation laid claim to the first meetinghouse that was located on the sixth line of Wallace Township at the present Brotherston Mennonite Meetinghouse. In 1882 the Mennonites built another meetinghouse on the fourth line of Wallace

Township at Kurtsville. After the 1889 division the Old Order Mennonites discontinued services at Wallace. The Kurtsville meetinghouse was later sold to the Evangelical Church in 1902. About ninety years later the Conservative Mennonites purchased this site.

Weber: Waterloo Township, Waterloo County, near Strasburg. It was evidently named after David Weber, an old settler. Cassel's history says a school was used for worship services until 1842 when a meetinghouse was built. This congregation was organized some time before 1848. This is now known as Strasburg Mennonite Church. In 1972 the name was changed to Pioneer Park Christian Fellowship-Mennonite.

Wellesley: Wellesley Township, Waterloo County, second side road west of St. Clements. This appointment was held in an old schoolhouse beginning in 1860. A cemetery was started at the site; however, the congregation failed and in 1885 the appointment for services was discontinued and in 1904 the unused part of the cemetery was sold back to the farm and the cemetery abandoned.

Weidman or Wideman: Markham Township, York County. This was an early congregation founded around 1816. In 1929 the Conference Mennonites built a new church which is still being used. The Old Order Mennonites discontinued services at Wideman church after it was rebuilt. By 1930 the Old Orders withdrew and no longer held fellowship with the Markham group.

West Woolwich: Woolwich Township, Waterloo County, west of Elmira. Christian Schneider of Bloomingdale donated the land for this meetinghouse. He had purchased a large tract of land west of Elmira for his sons. The first deed for this church property was made to Deacon David Good in 1854; however, this appointment first appeared in 1853, and a meetinghouse was also built at that time. About 1880 an addition was built on the east end. Another addition was added in 1908, which brought the dimensions to thirty-five by seventy feet. It was again enlarged in 19—. Services were first held once every eight weeks, but in 1856 it was changed to once every four weeks. West Woolwich or "Elmira" as it is now known has been a strong congregation and has continued.

North Woolwich: Woolwich Township, Waterloo County. This congregation was begun in 1857. [See "Hembling" for more information.]

Appendix B

Conference Reports

Printed conference reports are not common within Old Order Mennonite circles. The Markham-Waterloo conference has printed several over the years. I have on file reports for the following years but do not know if the list is complete: 1930s, 1955, 1970, 1973, 1988, 1996, and 2000. There are minor variations over the years, but we will only include three of these reports.

Markham Conference Report

(This report is not dated, but a fair assumption is made that it was written in the 1930s, before Waterloo was united with Markham.)

Office of Bishops, Ministers and Deacons: Refer to booklet on Confession of Faith of the Mennonites and translation of Church Regulations published by Benjamin Eby, Berlin, Ontario on August 30, 1841.

Insurance: Life insurance is unconditionally forbidden. For such who desire the protection of fire insurance, the Mennonite Aid Union is recommended. Liability insurance on automobiles and trucks is left to individual choice.

Dress: The advice of Conference is that the nearer we keep ourselves alike the stronger we can be in the sight of God. In showing our non-conformity to the world in this manner we believe that we can retain the respect of the powers that be with apparel that shows a desire not to make the world and the church into one.

Musical Instruments: Our principle of non-conformity to the world excludes the use of musical instruments and radios in our homes.

Pensions and Allowances: As non-resistants it is felt that it would be inconsistent with this faith to accept pensions, allowances, or relief, as these are meant for the state and not the church.

General: Conference members are recommended not to vote. The attitude towards cars and homes should be spiritually inclined and not to follow too much the inclination of the world. Fairs, exhibitions and shows should not be attended. Buying on Sundays, where it can be avoided, is discouraged. Parents are admonished to bring up their children in the fear and admonition of the Lord. Excessive use of intoxicating liquors is not tolerated and the use of cigarettes is considered a thing of the world.

Markham-Waterloo Mennonite Conference Statement—1955

(Based on the May 29, 1955, meeting of the conference and former conferences.)

Bishops, ministers, and deacons are the official conference members.

Duties of the bishops: To preach the Word of God, to baptize and receive new converts into the church fellowship, to have charge of communion as well as feet-washing. Also to solemnize marriages, to excommunicate disobedient and sinning members, and to administer the anointing with oil, when requested.

Duties of ministers: To preach the Word, cry aloud, warn sinners, comfort saints, and stand by the church wherever needed. In case of emergency, they may, with the consent of the bishop, perform marriage or baptism.

Duties of deacons: Read the text at church services; help the bishops at communion and baptismal services; take care of the poor and needy in the church; endeavour, by God's grace, to settle all disputes in a peaceful way. Consult also the "Confession of Faith" for duties enjoined upon conference members.

Duties of members: Members should consider it not only their duty, but have an earnest desire to observe the instructions and decisions of the conference, and live faithfully and consistent Christian lives in testimony of the faith of Jesus Christ. Romans 6:16; Heb 13:17; 1 Peter 3:15.

The following are unconditionally forbidden: Fornication: (1 Cor. 5:9-11; 1 Cor. 6:9-10; 1 Cor. 6:13-16; 1 Cor. 7:2); Adultery: (Matt. 5:27-28; Luke 16:18; Luke 18:20; Gal. 5:19-21); Oaths: (Matt. 5:34-37; James 5:12); and Drunkenness: (Gal. 5:20-21; Romans 13:13-14; Luke 12:45-46; 1 Cor. 6:10). Non-resistance is admonished: (Matt. 5:39-44; Romans 12:14-21; 1 Peter 3:9; Matt. 7:13; Luke 6:31; Is. 2:4; Matt. 10:23). Anyone joining the military forfeits his or her membership.

Life insurance is not accepted: (Ps. 118:8; Matt. 6:31-34). To those who wish a systematic way in helping one another in time of loss on buildings and contents, the Mennonite Aid Union is recommended (Gal. 6:2). Insurance for public liability and property damage to others has been granted for those who wish it.

Non-conformity: (1 Tim. 2:9-10; 1 Peter 9:3-4; 2 Cor. 6:17; Heb. 7:26). Dress: It should be plain and uniform. The more nearly we keep to one pattern, the stronger will be our witness. Clothing cannot take one to heaven, but it is possible that clothing can take one to hell. The reason we believe in, and have, a pattern different from the rest of the world is because the Word tells us to come out from the world "and be ye separate," and again if we wear it in earnest, it signifies what we represent.

Head Covering: 1 Cor 11:1-16. A scriptural teaching for the sisters. We truly advise that ribbons (strings) be kept on the coverings. As man is the head of the house, he should surely do his part, so that the upholding of the doctrine does not fall too heavily on the weaker vessel. We feel that the necktie could be done without. The wearing of jewellery, we believe, belongs to the world. It is possible that a wolf wear sheep's clothing, but rarely would a sheep wear wolf's clothing.

Homes should also conform with our non-conformity principle.

Musical instruments, radio, and television: We do not need them and they bring more harm than can be overcome with the little good they have (1 John 2:15-16) .

Pensions and Allowances: We feel it the duty of the church to take care of our own, and not to be burdensome to the powers that be, and by so doing we show our appreciation for the privileges that have been granted us as non-resistant people. (1 Tim. 5:8; Gal. 6:2)

Conference members are expected to refrain from voting and serving on jury. We recommend that cars should be so kept as to not weaken our non-conformity principle. We recommend one colour—black. Fairs, exhibitions and shows should not be attended, nor should we seek or take anything given as a prize for what we have done or grown. Avoid buying on Sunday if at all possible.

Be careful that our trips are not altogether for pleasure. We believe that to go and see some of the wonders of God's creation is not wrong, but if we enjoy going to the beaches where the world gathers, we are out of place. The bathing suit surely does not become us. We would rather admonish to visit the brethren during our journeys.

May God help us by His grace to bring up our children in the nurture and admonition of the Lord (Eph. 6:4). Regarding smoking: We discourage smoking on the ground that it is very popular and up-to-date in worldly circles and if never started, is never missed; that in the future we may be clean of the habit (Romans 4:14-15; 1 Cor. 8:13; 2 Cor. 6:17; 2 Cor. 7:1).

Under normal conditions anyone staying away from communion for two years forfeits his or her good standing in the church. Anyone changing membership from one congregation to another should ask for a church letter of recommending them to the congregation to which they are going, and the approval of the home congregation will be asked for before giving such letter. In case of sickness, we would upon request have services in the home. Any form of public meetings without consent or support of conference are not authorized.

Author's comments: At the April 1970 conference the following decision was made: "Conference decision is that all members are asked to free themselves and their family from the use of tobacco. A limited time for this preparation is suggested." Three years later the September 1973 conference report reads: "The act of using tobacco is not accepted for members." At this time a number of members left the conference and joined fellowship with the Conference Mennonites. Some of the old members at Markham also found this recommendation a challenge. A number of years later the Old Order Mennonites followed suit and also, after a period of patience, made the use of tobacco a test of membership.

The above statement on receiving a recommendation of approval when changing membership, I would suggest, refers to the switching from one conference to another, not moving within the same bishop district.

General Recommendations of the Markham Waterloo Mennonite Conference—2000

Statement of Faith: We support and teach the Apostolic Confession of Faith, the Eighteen Articles of Faith and the Ordinance of the Holy Kiss (Romans 16:16; 1 Peter 5:14; 1 Tess. 5:26).

Leadership of the church: The church leadership consists of bishops, ministers, and deacons. Ministers and deacons are chosen from among the church members, but the bishops from among the ministers (Acts 1:15-26; Acts 6:1-6). All nominees are to be scripturally qualified (Acts 6:3; 1 Tim. 3:1-13; 2 Tim. 2:2; Titus 1:5-9) . When there are two or more nominees the choice is made by use of the lot (Acts 1:24-26).

The offices of leadership have their various duties: The bishops are to preach the Word in its purity, visit the sick, comfort the saints, admonish the sinners, baptize and receive into the church those who have come to true repentance and faith. They administer Holy communion, solemnize marriages and, when requested, apply anointing with oil (James 5:14-15; Mark 6:13). Their duty includes expelling disobedient members and receiving them into church membership again if they prove to be repentant.

The ministers are to preach the Word in its purity, warn the sinners, comfort the saints, visit the sick, stand by the bishops and the church to solemnize marriages, and baptize when a bishop so requests.

The deacons' duties are to read the Scripture at worship services, assist the bishop at communion and baptismal services, and prepare and supply that which is needed at these services. They shall ask alms of the church which shall be used according to the best of their abilities to help the poor. Their part includes visiting the sick and comforting the saints. They will try, if possible, to preserve and restore peace among members.

Membership Standards: The members (which includes the ministry) are expected to live a life of holiness, and respect and be obedient to the decisions of the Conference as given in the conference report (Hebrews 13:7, 17), and be examples to their children and raise them in the nurture and admonition of the Lord. The Lord's Day is to be kept holy, not spent in pleasure seeking, nor buying or selling. Social drinking or indulging in strong drink is forbidden (Gal. 5:21; Eph. 5:18). The use of tobacco by members is not acceptable.

Non-resistance and Financial Concerns: It is required that the doctrine of non-resistance be observed throughout the church in peacetime as well as in time of conflict (Matt. 5:39-44; Romans 12:14-21; 1 Peter 3:9; Luke 3:14). [In the early 1960s the Markham church held several special non-resistant services on a Sunday afternoon. On one such occasion the ministry handed out a tract "Nonresistance VS Political Pacifism." These occasional special services were well attended, but the conference later decided to select a certain Sunday once a year when non-resistance is the topic throughout all the churches.] Business dealings and the fulfilling of obligations must be done honestly. All investments should be deeply considered before being made, lest they connect with life insurance or otherwise cause conflict with Christian faith. Life insurance is not tolerated.

Government grants are strongly advised against. All members are encouraged to help one another with financial needs (Gal. 6:2). Old Age Pension and Child Tax benefit are not to be accepted (1 Tim. 6:8). Voting is discouraged because of the belief that church and state are separate (Psalms 118:8).

Places of employment where labour union membership is required are to be avoided. Be careful about places of employment where one is asked to conform to a uniform which is immodest and would show identity to the World rather than to the Church. Parents should help children choose occupations that will promote spiritual growth rather than hinder it.

Non-conformity to the World: In respect of the doctrine of non-conformity members are expected to adhere to and support the conference report as faithful Christians and live a simple life. The wearing of gold rings and jewellery is forbidden.

Plain suits and long sleeved shirts are recommended for brethren. They are also asked to wear a decent black hat for formal attire. Modest hats or caps without logos are accepted otherwise. Fashionable hairstyles are inconsistent whether long or short. Sideburns are not accepted.

Sisters are to wear plain cape dresses which come well below the knees and have modest necklines and sleeves (1 Peter 3:3-4; 1 Tim. 2:4). Black hosiery and decent shoes are recommended to be worn. Sisters are expected to show that they accept the headship of man by wearing a plain and good-sized head covering which has strings attached (1 Cor. 11:1-15). Clothes having fur collars, bright colours or large patterns are immodest. Sisters are expected to wear the bonnet when out in public and wear a suitable and modest headgear when outside around home.

The conference expects all parents to dress their children modestly, which is in harmony with the Word (Prov. 22:6).

The radio, CB radio, television, video-cassette recorder, tape recorder and player and other such items are not tolerated. All other musical instruments are strongly advised against.

Cars are to be black with no trimmings. Sport models and unnecessary accessories are discouraged. Tractor and truck pulls are discouraged.

Mixed swimming is not accepted.

It is not accepted of married people or youth to be engaged in industrial or other league hockey or baseball; likewise married people and youth are discouraged from organizing and playing sports among themselves (2 Tim. 3:4). Everyone's support and acceptance is needed for the non-use of the arena. The act of disobedience will require visitation and Church discipline.

In order to stay free from worldly and ungodly influences, the use of the computer on the Internet system is forbidden, as are similar on-line services. The conference body has a great concern that the computer be used for practical purposes only and not for entertainment and games.

Public liability and property damage are suggested coverage for cars and trucks, but not collision insurance.

These recommendations should be taught and testified by all the ministry. "Be perfect, be of good comfort, be of one mind, live in peace; and the God of love and peace shall be with you" (2 Cor 13:11).

Appendix C

Waterloo County Ministry

The Mennonite Ministry of Waterloo County at the time of the division, in the year 1889. Those marked with an X remained with the Old Order.

Bishops:

X Abraham W. Martin	St. Jacobs
Amos Cressman	New Hamburg
Elias Weber	Breslau

Ministers:

X Peter Martin	Elmira
Moses Bauman	Mannheim
Moses Erb	Berlin
Menno Cressman	New Hamburg
Jacob Woolner	Kossuth
X Joseph Gingrich	Elmira
X Elias Snider	Waterloo
Tobias Bauman	St. Agatha
X Daniel Brubacher	St. Jacobs
Noah Stauffer	Strasburg
Samuel Bauman	Berlin
Joseph Nahrgang	Haysville
Jacob Gingrich	Preston
Solomon Gehman	Blair
Isaac Weber	Howick Twp.

Isaac Hallman	Wallace Twp.
Henry Dettweiler	Stanley Twp.
Deacons:	
Jacob Hagey	Preston
Aaron Biehn	Strasburg
John Z. Dettweiler	Blair
John Cressman	Washington
X David Martin	Waterloo
X Menno S. Shantz	Waterloo
David Eschelman	New Dundee
John Shantz	Baden
John Nahrgang	New Hamburg
X David Cressman	Mannheim
X Levi P. Martin	St. Jacobs
X Peter Bowman	Floradale
Jacob Z. Kolb	Berlin
Peter Reist	Kossuth
Henry Baer	Mannheim
X John Schiedel	Kossuth
X Daniel Steckle	Stanley Twp.

John Nahrgang of Wilmot Twp. moved to Woolwich Twp. 1899. He joined the Old Order group and served at South Peel.

Appendix D

Ministry of the David Martin Church

Bauman, Enoch (19—) Ordained minister.

Bauman, Isaac M. (19—) Ordained deacon.

Bauman, Simeon M. (19—) Ordained minister on November 10, 1985.

Bearinger, Amos (18—19—) Ordained minister in October 25, 1923 for Wellesley. He was excommunicated May 4, 1924, and he then returned to the Old Order church.

Brubacher, Daniel M. (1840-1921) Ordained minister in 1876 for Conestogo by the Conference Mennonites. In 1889 he stood with the Old Order movement. In 1909 Bishop Paul Martin put him out of the church. He then held meetings in his residence until he was invited to join the David Martin group in 1917. In the spring of 1918 he was chosen by lot as bishop for the David Martin group. In the fall of 1920 he separated from the David Martin group and stood alone until his death.

Brubacher, Menno (1873-1953) Ordained minister in October 1918 for the Woolwich meetinghouse. Later he stood alone. Candidates were Deacon David W. Martin and Tilman Martin. Because of the flu this ordination was postponed for several weeks. He served until the fall of 1920 when he and his father Daniel again worshipped in their home. His father Daniel ordained him bishop in 1921. Menno stood alone until his death.

Frey, Abraham Ordained minister in May 1956. He was ordained bishop in August 1958 and excommunicated on September 8, 1985.

Frey, Manassah Ordained minister on October 7, 1952.

Frey, Martin Ordained minister for Wellesley on June 9, 1925.
Frey, Noah B. Ordained deacon for Badjeros in 2001.
Hoover, Tilman (1937-) Ordained deacon on October 5, 1974 for the Hoover group. When the Hoover group broke up in 1986, he chose to join the David Martin church and was appointed deacon with David Martin in 1987.
Horst, Enoch Ordained minister in September 1918 for Wellesley. In March 1921 he was ordained bishop and served until he was banned on May 4 1924. He then moved to Mornington Township where he worshipped alone.
Houser, Franklin (1859-1933) Old Order Mennonite, then David Martin. Ordained deacon in March 1889 for Cayuga. He moved to Waterloo in 1913 and served at North Woolwich until 1929 when he joined the David Martin church. He was buried in the Wellesley cemetery.
Martin, Aaron B.M. (19—) Ordained minister on January 17, 1988.
Martin, Abraham David Martin Ordained deacon in March 1957.
Martin, Alvin S. (19—) Ordained minister on January 17, 1988.
Martin, David B. (1838-1920) Old Order Mennonite then David Martin. Ordained minister in November 1890 for Elmira. He was transferred to South Peel in 1901. In 1917 he separated and began the David Martin group.
Martin, David W. (1873- 1959) Ordained deacon on June 14, 1913 for South Peel. In 1917 he with his father David B. Martin began the David Martin church. In January 1921 he was ordained minister and then in 1925 he became bishop of the David Martin group. Candidates: Henry Horst, Amos Gingrich, Menno S. Bauman
Martin, Edwin B. (19—) Ordained minister on November 10, 1985.

Appendix E

Ministry of the Orthodox Mennonites

Bauman, Jesse H. (1951-) Hoover then Orthodox. Ordained minister on October 27, 1981. When the Hoover group broke up in 1986, he united with the Orthodox Mennonites.

Bowman, Henry M. (1932-) Ordained minister on December 15, 1959.

Brubacher, Menno W. (1951-) Ordained minister on March 7, 1978. He was ordained bishop in 2002.

Brubacher, Noah (19 —) Stood alone then united with the Orthodox. He was ordained by John Dan Wenger of Virginia. On April 2, 1967, he united with the Orthodox Mennonites.

Hoover, Anson (1920) Ordained minister October 12, 1965. In March 1974 he left the Orthodox and began the Hoover group. On March 28, 1976, he was excommunicated and he then left the fellowship and united with the Conservative Mennonites.

Horst, Noah (1960) Ordained minister December 12, 2000, for the Kinloss group.

Horst, Samuel David Martin then Orthodox, ordained deacon on May 29,1941. Banned in December 1956.

Martin, Elam S. David Martin then Orthodox, ordained minister on October 23,1934. On March 11, 1956 he was excommunicated on the question of the ban. On January 1, 1957, he began to hold services on his own and founded the Elam Martin group, who later adopted Orthodox as their official name.

Martin, Edward G. (1903) Ordained minister on June 11, 1940 for West Woolwich (Elmira) Old Order Mennonite. He left the Old Order Mennonites and joined the Orthodox Mennonites. On June 14, 1970 the Orthodox Mennonites accepted him as a minister. He was excommunicated on May 24, 1984, because he had returned to the Old Orders where he had no official charge as a minister.
Martin, Mervin W. (1954-) Ordained deacon on November 8, 1994.
Sherk, Amos (1947-) Ordained minister on April 29, 1975, for the Hoover group. On October 3, 1976, he was advanced to bishop by church council. When the Hoover group broke up in 1986, he took the remaining followers with him and united with the Orthodox Mennonites, but he at that time laid aside his bishop's office.
Sherk, John (1939-) Ordained minister on May 9, 1978. He was ordained bishop on October 14, 1980.
Wideman, Amos (1975-) Ordained on August 27, 2002 for the Kinloss group.
Weber, Alvin (1956-) Ordained on August 27, 2002 for the Kinloss group.
Weber, Amos B. (1960-) Ordained deacon on May 23, 2000.
Weber, Ephraim (1921-) Ordained deacon on November 19, 1985.

Appendix F

Part II Confession of Faith

Drawn up at Dordrecht, at a certain Peace Convention on the 21st day of April, 1632. Entitled, "Declaration of the Chief Articles of our General Christian Faith."[1]

Article One: Of God And The Creation Of All Things

Whereas, it is declared, that "without faith it is impossible to please God," (Heb. 2:6), and that "he that cometh to God must believe that he is, and that he is a rewarder of them that diligently seek him." Therefore we confess with the mouth, and believe with the heart, together with all the pious, according to Holy Scripture, in one eternal, Almighty, and incomprehensible God - Father, Son and Holy Ghost, and none more and none other; before Whom no God existed, nor will exist after Him. For from Him, through Him, and in Him are all things. To Him be blessing, praise, and honour, for ever and ever. Gen. 17:1. Deut. 6:4. Isaiah 46:9. 1 John 5:7. Romans 11:36.

In this one God, who "worketh all in all," we believe. Him we confess as the Creator of all things, visible and invisible; who in six days created and prepared "heaven and the sea, and things that are therein." And we further believe, that this God still governs and preserves the same, together with all His works, through His wisdom, His might, and the "word of his power." Gen. 5:1,2. Acts 14:15. 1 Cor. 12:6.

Now when He had finished His works, and had, according to His good pleasure, ordained and prepared each of them, right and well, according to its nature, being and quality, He next created the first man Adam, the father of all of us, gave him a body formed "of the dust of the ground, and breathed into his nostrils the breath of life;" so that he "became a living soul; created by God in his own image and likeness," in "righteousness and true holiness" unto eternal life. Further He regarded him also in particular above all other creatures, and adorned him with many high and excellent gifts; put him into the Garden of Eden, and gave him a commandment and interdiction. Thereupon He took a rib from the said Adam, made a woman out of it, brought her to him, and gave her to him as a help meet and housewife. Consequently He has also caused, that from this first man, Adam, all men who "dwell on all the face of the earth," have been begotten and have descended. Gen. 1:27. Gen. 2:7,15,17,22. Gen. 5:1. Acts 17:26.

Article Two: Of The Fall Of Man

We believe and confess, that according to the content of Holy Scripture, these our first parents, Adam and Eve, did not long remain in the happy state in which they were created; but did—after being seduced by the deceit and "subtilty" of the serpent, and envy of the devil—violate the high commandment of God, and became disobedient to their Creator; through which disobedience "sin entered into the world, and death by sin;" so that "death passed upon all men for that all have sinned," and thereby incurred the wrath of God and condemnation. For which reason our first parents were also driven by God out of Paradise, to cultivate the earth, to maintain themselves thereon in sorrow, and to "eat their bread in the sweat of their face," until they "returned to the ground, out of which they were taken." And that they did, therefore, through this one sin, so far apostatize, depart, and estrange themselves from God, that they could neither help themselves, nor be helped, by any of their descendants, nor by angels, nor by any other creature in heaven or on earth; nor be redeemed or reconciled to God; but would have had to be lost forever, had not God, (who pitied His creatures), in mercy made provision for their fall, and interposed in their behalf. Gen. 3:6, 23. Rom. 5:12-19. Ps. 49:6-9. Rev. 5:3. John 3:16.

Article Three: Of The Restoration Of Man Through The Promise Of The Advent Of Christ

As it regards the restoration of the first of mankind and their descendants, we believe and confess that God, notwithstanding their fall, transgression, and sin, and although they had no power to help themselves, did nevertheless not wish to cast them off entirely, or permit them to be eternally lost but that He again called them unto Him, comforted them, and showed them that there were yet means with Him for their reconciliation—the immaculate Lamb, the Son of God; who "was foreordained" for the purpose aforesaid "before the foundation of the world," and who was promised to them and all their descendants, while they (the former) were yet in Paradise, for their comfort, redemption, and salvation; yea, who was given to them thenceforward, through faith, as their own, after which all the pious patriarchs, to whom this promise was often renewed, longed and searched, seeing it at a distance through faith and expecting its fulfilments—expecting that He (the Son of God) would at His advent, again redeem and deliver the fallen race of man from their sins, their guilt, and unrighteousness. John 1:29. John 11:27. 1 Pet. 1:18-19. Gen. 3:15. 1 John 2:1-2. 1 John 3:8. Gal. 4:4-5. Heb. 11:13-39.

Article Four: Of The Advent Of Christ Into This World, And The Reason Thereof

We believe and confess further that "when the fulness of the time was come," after which all the pious patriarchs so ardently longed, and which they so anxiously awaited—the previously promised Messiah, Redeemer, and Saviour, proceeded from God, being sent by Him, and, according to the prediction of the prophets and the testimony of the evangelists, came into the world, yea, into the flesh, so that the Word itself thus became flesh and man; and that He was conceived by the Virgin Mary, (who was espoused to a man named Joseph, of the house of David,) and that she bare Him as her first-born son at Bethlehem, "wrapped him in swaddling clothes, and laid him in a manger." John 4:25; John 16:28; 1 Tim. 3:16; Matt. 1:21; John 1:14; Luke 2:7. Further we believe and confess, that this is the same One, "whose goings forth have been from of old, everlasting;" who has "neither beginning of days, nor end of life." Of whom it is testified, that He is "Alpha and Omega, the beginning and the end, the first and the last." That this is also He—and none other—who was chosen, promised and sent; who came into the world; and who is God's only, first, and proper Son; who was before John the Baptist, before Abraham, before the world; yea, who was David's Lord, and who is God of the "whole earth, the first-born of every creature;" who was sent into the world, and Himself delivered up the body prepared for Him, as "an offering and a sacrifice to God for a sweet smelling savour;" yea, for the comfort, redemption, and salvation of all- of the whole human race. Micah 5:2; Heb. 7:3; Rev. I:8; John 3:16; Rom. 8:32; Col. 1:15; Heb. 10:5.

But how, or in what manner, this worthy body was prepared, or how the Word became flesh—man itself—as to that, we content ourselves with the declaration which the worthy evangelists have given and left in their description thereof; according to which we confess with all the saints, that He is the Son of the living God; in whom consists all our hope, comfort, redemption, and salvation; and which we are to seek in no one else. Luke 1:31-35; John 20:31.

Further, we believe and confess by authority of Scripture, that when He had ended His course, and "finished" the work for which He was sent into the world, He was by the providence of God delivered into the hands of the unrighteous; suffered under the judge Pontius Pilate, was crucified, died, was buried, rose again from the dead on the third day, and ascended into heaven; where He now sits on the right hand of the Majesty of God on high," whence He will again come to judge the living and the dead. Luke 23:1,33,53; Luke 24:5,6,51.

And that thus the Son of God died, "tasted death for every man," shed His precious blood, and thereby "bruised the head of the serpent," destroyed the works of the devil, "blotted out the hand-writing," and purchased redemption for the whole human race; and has thus become the cause of the eternal salvation of all these who from the time of Adam to the end of the world shall have believed in Him, and obeyed Him. Gen. 3:15; 1 John 3:8; Col. 2:14; Rom. 5:18.

Article Five: Of The Law Of Christ, Which Is The Holy Gospel Or The New Testament

We also believe and confess, that Christ before His ascension, established and instituted His New Testament, and left it to His followers, to be and remain an everlasting testament; which He confirmed and sealed with His own precious blood; and with which He has also so strictly charged them, that it may not be altered either by men or angels; nor any thing taken there from or added thereto. Jer. 31:31; Heb. 9:15-17; Matt. 26:28; Gal. 1:8; 1 Tim. 6:3; Rev. 22:18,19; Matt. 5:18; Luke 21:33. And that He has caused this testament (in which the whole counsel and will of His heavenly Father, insofar as these are necessary to the salvation of man, are comprehended) to be proclaimed, in His name, through His beloved apostles, messengers, and servants, (whom He chose and sent into all the world for this purpose)—to all nations, people, and tongues; these apostles preaching repentance and remission of sins. And that He consequently caused to be declared in said testament, all men, without distinction, as His children and rightful heirs, insofar as they, as obedient children, through faith, follow, fulfil and live according to the precepts of the same; having thus excluded none from the precious inheritance of eternal salvation, except the unbelieving and disobedient, the headstrong and unconverted; who despise such salvation and thus by their own actions incur guilt by refusing the same, and "judge themselves unworthy of everlasting life." Mark 16:15; Luke 24:46, 47; Rom. 8:17; Acts 13:46.

Article Six: Of Repentance And Amendment Of Life

We believe and confess, that, as the "imagination of man's heart is evil from his youth," and consequently inclined to all unrighteousness, sin and wickedness, therefore, the first doctrine of the precious New Testament of the Son of God, is repentance and amendment of life. (Gen. 8:21. Mark 1:15.) Therefore those who have ears to hear, and hearts to understand, must "bring forth fruits meet for repentance," amend their lives, believe the gospel, "depart from evil, and do good," desist from wrong, leave off sinning, "put off the old man with his deeds, and put on the new man, which after God is created in righteousness and true holiness." For neither baptism, sacrament, nor communion, nor any other external ceremony, can, without faith and the new birth, a change or renewal of life, help us—can so qualify us, that we may please God, or receive any consolation or promise of salvation from Him. (Luke 3:8; Eph. 4:22-24; Col. 3:9,10.) No. But on the contrary, we must go to God "with a true heart, in full assurance of faith," and believe in Jesus Christ, as the Scriptures speak and testify of Him. Through which faith we obtain the pardon of our sins, become sanctified, justified, and children of God; partakers of His mind, nature, and image; as we are born again of God through His incorruptible seed from above. (Heb. 10:21,22. John 7:38;2 Pet. 1:4.)

Article Seven: Of Holy Baptism

As it regards baptism, we confess that all penitent believers, who through faith, the new birth, and renewal of the Holy Ghost, have become united to God, and whose names are recorded in heaven, must, on such scriptural confession of their faith, and renewal of life according to the command and doctrine of Christ, and the examples and usage of the apostles, be baptized with water in the reverential name of the Father, the Son, and the Holy Ghost, to the burying of their sins, and thus become incorporated with the communion of saints whereupon they must learn to "observe all things" whatever the Son of God taught, left on record, and commanded His followers to do. (Matt. 3:15; Matt. 28:I9-20; Mark 16:15,16; Acts 2:38; Acts 8:12,38; Acts 9:1; Acts 10:47,48; Acts 16:33; Rom. 6:3,4; Col. 2:12.)

Article Eight: Of The Church Of Christ

We believe in and confess, a visible Church of God consisting of those, who, as before remarked, have truly repented, rightly believe, are rightly baptized, are united with God in heaven, and incorporated with the communion of the saints on earth. (1 Cor. 12:13.) And these, we confess, are a "chosen generation, a royal priesthood, an holy nation;" who have the testimony, that they are the "bride" of Christ; yea, that they are "children and heirs of eternal life," a "habitation of God through the spirit " built on the foundation of the apostles and prophets, of which "Christ himself is the chief cornerstone"—the foundation on which His church is built. (John 3:29; Matt. 16:18; Eph. 2:19-21; Tit. 3:7; 1 Pet. 1:18,19; 1 Pet. 2:9.) This church of the living God, which He has purchased and redeemed through His own precious blood and with which He will be—according to His own promise—for its comfort and protection, "always, even unto the end of the world," yea, "dwell among them, and walk among them" also preserve them, that no "winds" nor "floods," yea, not even the "gates of hell shall prevail against it,"—may be known by its scriptural faith, doctrine, love, and "godly conversation;" as also by its useful career and its practice and observance of the true ordinances of Christ, which He has strictly enjoined on His followers. (Matt. 7:25; Matt. 16:18; Matt. 28:20; 2 Cor. 6:16.)

Article Nine: Of The Office Of Teachers And Ministers—Male And Female—In The Church

As it regards the offices, and election of persons to the same in the church, we believe and confess that, as the church cannot exist and prosper nor continue in its structure, without offices and regulations, that therefore the Lord Jesus has Himself, (as a Father in His house), appointed and prescribed His offices and ordinances, and has given commandments concerning the same, as to how each one should walk therein, give heed to his own work and calling and do as it becomes him to do. (Eph. 4:11-12) For He Himself, as the faithful and great shepherd, and bishop of our souls, was sent into the world, not to wound, to break, or destroy the souls of men; but to heal them, to seek that which is lost, to pull down the hedges and partition wall, so as to make out of many, one; thus collecting out of Jews and heathen, yea out of all nations, a church in His name; for which—so that no one might go wrong or be lost—He left His own life, and thus procured for them salvation, freed and redeemed them; to which blessing no one could help them, or be of service in obtaining it. (1 Pet. 2:25; Matt. 18:11; Eph. 2:13,14; John 10:9,11,15.)

And that He, besides this, left His church before His departure provided with faithful ministers, apostles, evangelists, pastors, and teachers, whom He had chosen by prayer and supplication through the Holy Spirit, so that they might govern the church, feed His flock, watch over and superintend the same; yea, do in all things as He left them an example, taught them, did Himself, and commanded them to do; and to teach the church to observe all things which He commanded them to do. (Eph. 4:11,12; Luke 6:12,13; Luke 10:1; Matt. 28:20.)

Also that the apostles were afterwards, as faithful followers of Christ and leaders of the church, diligent in these matters, namely, in choosing through prayer and supplication to God, brethren who were to provide all the churches in cities and on circuits, with bishops, pastors, and leaders, and to ordain to these offices such men as took "heed unto themselves and unto the doctrine" and flock, who were sound in the faith, pious in their life and conversation, and who had—as well within the church as "without"—a good reputation and good report; so that they might be a light and example in all godliness and good works, might worthily administer the Lord's ordinances—baptism and the sacrament—and that they (the brethren sent by the apostles) might also, at all places (where such were to be had) appoint faithful men as elders, who were able to teach others, confirm them in the name of the Lord "with the laying on of hands," and who (the elders) were to take care of all things of which the church stood in need; so that they as faithful servants, might well "occupy" their Lord's money, gain thereby, and thus "save themselves and those who hear them." (1 Tim. 3:1; 1 Tim. 4:14-16; Acts 1:23,24; Tit. 1:5; Luke 19:13.)

That they should also take good care, (particularly each one of the charge over which he had the oversight) that all the circuits should be well provided with almoners (deacons), who should have the care and oversight of the poor, and who were to receive gifts and alms, and again faithfully to distribute—them amongst the poor saints who were in need; and this in all honesty, as is becoming. (Acts 6:3-6.)

That we should also choose honourable old widows as servants; who, besides the deacons, are to visit, comfort, and take care of the poor, the weak, the afflicted, and the needy; as also to visit, comfort, and take care of widows and orphans; and further to assist in taking care of any matters in the church that properly come within their sphere, according to their best ability. (1 Tim.5:9, 10; Rom. 16:1,2.)

And as it further regards the deacons, that they (particularly if they are fit persons, and chosen and ordained thereto by the church) may also in aid and relief of the bishops, exhort the church (being, as already remarked, chosen thereto) and thus assist in word and doctrine; so that each one may serve the other from love, with the gift which he has received from the Lord; so that through the common service and assistance of each member, according to his ability, the body of Christ may be edified, and the Lord's vineyard and church be preserved in its growth and structure. 2 Tim.2:2.

Article Ten: Of The Lord's Supper

We also believe in and observe the breaking of bread or the Lord's Supper, as the Lord Jesus instituted the same (with bread and wine) before His sufferings, and also observed and ate it with the apostles; also commanded it to be observed to His memory; as the apostles did also consequently teach and observe the same in the church and commanded it to be observed by believers in memory of the death and sufferings of the Lord—the breaking of His worthy body and the shedding of His precious blood—for the whole human race. So is the observance of this sacrament also to remind us of the benefit of the said death and sufferings of Christ, namely, the redemption and eternal salvation which He purchased thereby, and the great love thus shown to sinful man; whereby we are strongly exhorted also to love one another—to love our neighbour—to forgive and absolve him—even as Christ has done unto us—and also to endeavour to maintain and keep alive the union and communion which we have with God, and amongst one another; which is thus shown and represented to us by the aforesaid breaking of bread.(Matt. 26:26; Mark 14:22; Luke 22:19,20; Acts 2:42,46; 1 Cor. 10:16; 1 Cor. 11:23-26.)

Article Eleven: Of The Washing Of The Feet Of The Saints

We also confess a washing of the feet of the saints, as the Lord Jesus did not only institute and command the same, but did also Himself wash the feet of the apostles, although He was their Lord and Master; thereby giving an example that they should also wash one another's feet, and thus do to one another as He did to them; which they also consequently taught believers to observe; and all this as a sign of true humility; but yet more particularly as a sign to remind us of the true washing—of the washing and purification of the soul in the blood of Christ. (John 13:4-17; 1 Tim. 5:9,10.)

Article Twelve: Of Matrimony

We also confess that there is in the church of God an "honourable" state of matrimony between two believers of the different sexes; as God first instituted the same in paradise between Adam and Eve, and as the Lord Jesus reformed it by removing all abuses which had crept into it, and restoring it to its first order. (Gen. I:27; Gen. 2:18, 22, 24.)

In this manner the apostle Paul also taught and permitted matrimony in the church, leaving it to each one's own choice to enter into matrimony with any person who would unite with him in such state, provided that it was done "in the Lord," according to the primitive order; the words "in the Lord," to be understood, according to our opinion, that just as the patriarchs had to marry amongst their own kindred or generation; so there is also no other liberty allowed to believers under the New Testament dispensation, than to marry amongst the "chosen generation," or the spiritual kindred of Christ; that is, to such—and none others—as are already—previous to their marriage—united to the church in heart and soul, have received the same baptism, belong to the same church, are of the same faith and doctrine, and lead the same course of life, with themselves. (1 Cor. 7:1-40. 1 Cor. 9:5. Gen. 24:4. Gen. 28:6,7. Num. 36:6-9.) Such are then, as already remarked, united by God and the church according to the primitive order; and this is then called: "Marrying in the Lord." 1 Cor. 7:39.

Article Thirteen: Of The Office Of Civil Government

We also believe and confess, that God has instituted civil government; and this for the punishment of the bad, and the protection of the pious; as also further, for the purpose of governing the world—governing countries and cities; as also again to preserve its subjects in good order and under good regulations. Wherefore we are not permitted to despise, blaspheme, or resist the same; but are to acknowledge it as a minister of God, be subject and obedient to it; particularly in such matters as do not militate against the law, will and commandments of God; yea, "to be ready to do every good work," also faithful to pay it custom, tax, and tribute: thus giving it what is its due; as Jesus Christ taught, did Himself, and commanded His followers to do. We are also to pray to the Lord earnestly for the government and its welfare, and in behalf of our country; so that we may live under its protection, maintain ourselves, and "lead a quiet and peaceable life in all godliness and honesty." And further, that the Lord would recompense it here and hereafter in eternity, for all the benefits, liberties, and favours which we enjoy under its laudable administration. (Rom. 13:1-7; Titus 3:1, 2; 1 Pet. 2:17; Matt. 17:27; Matt. 22:19-21; 1 Tim. 2:1, 2.)

Article Fourteen: Of Defence By Force

As it regards revenge, whereby we resist our enemies with the sword, we believe and confess, that the Lord Jesus has forbidden His disciples and followers all revenge and resistance, and has thereby commanded them not to "return evil for evil, nor railing for railing," but to "put up the sword into the sheath," or (as the prophets foretold) "beat them into ploughshares." (Matt. 5:39, 44; Rom. 12:14; 1 Pet. 3, 9; Isa. 2:4; Micah 4:3.)

From this we see, that according to the example, life, and doctrine of Christ, we are not to do wrong or occasion grief or vexation to anyone; but to seek the welfare and salvation of all men; also, if necessity should require it, to flee, for the Lord's sake, from one city or country to another, and suffer the "spoiling of our goods," rather than give occasion of grief to anyone; and if we are struck on our "right cheek, rather turn the other also," than revenge ourselves, or return the blow. (Matt. 5:39; Matt. 10:23; Rom. 12:19.) We are, besides this, also to pray for our enemies, comfort and feed them when they are hungry or thirsty, and thus convince them by well-doing. (Rom. 12:20, 21.) Finally, that we are to do good in all respects, "commending ourselves to every man's conscience in the sight of God," and according to the law of Christ, do nothing to others that we would not wish them to do unto us. (2 Cor. 4:2; Matt. 7:12; Luke 6:31.)

Article Fifteen: Of The Swearing Of Oaths

As it regards the swearing of oaths, we believe and confess, that the Lord Jesus has dissuaded His followers from and forbidden them the same; that is, that He commanded them to "swear not at all;" but that their "yea" should be "yea," and their "nay," "nay." From which we perceive that all oaths, high and low, are forbidden; and that instead of them we are to confirm all our promises and covenants, declarations and testimonies of all matters, merely with yes that is yes, and no that is no, and that we are to perform and fulfil at all times, and in all things, to every one, whatsoever about which we thus affirm, as faithfully as if we had confirmed it by the most solemn oath. And if we do thus, it is our conviction, that no one—not even government, itself—has a right in justice, to require more of us. (Matt. 5:34- 37; James 5:12; 2 Cor. 1:17.)

Article Sixteen: Of Excommunication Or Expulsion From The Church

We also believe in, and confess, a state of excommunication—a separation from—of spiritual punishment by the church, for the amendment, and not for the destruction, of offenders; so that what is pure may be separated from what is impure. That is, if a person after having been enlightened, has received the knowledge of the truth, and has been received into the communion of saints, and does wilfully, or out of presumption, sin against God, or commit some other "sin unto death," thereby falling into such unfruitful works of darkness, that he becomes separated from God, and debarred from His kingdom; that such an one—when his works are become manifest, and sufficiently known to the church cannot remain in the "congregation of the righteous," but must, as an offensive member and notorious sinner, be excluded from the church, "rebuked before all, and purged out as a leaven;" and thus remain until his amendment, as an example and terror to others; as also that the church may be kept pure from such "spots and blemishes;" so that not for the want of this, the name of the Lord be blasphemed, the church be dishonoured, and a stumbling block be thrown in the way of those "without." Finally, that the offender may not be damned with the world, but may be convinced of the error of his ways, and again brought to repentance and amendment of life. (Isa. 59:2; 1 Cor. 5:5, 6, 12; 1 Tim. 5:20; 2 Cor. 13:10.)

As it further regards brotherly admonition, as also the instruction of the erring, we are to "give all diligence" to watch over them, and exhort them in all meekness to the amendment of their ways (James 5:19, 20), and in case any should remain obstinate and unconverted, to reprove them as the case may require. In short, the church must "put away from among itself him that is wicked," whether it be in doctrine or life.

Article Seventeen: Of The Shunning Of Those Who Are Expelled

As it regards the withdrawing from, or the shunning of those who are expelled, we believe and confess, that if any one—whether it be through a wicked life or perverse doctrine—is so far fallen as to be separated from God, and consequently rebuked by, and expelled from, the church; he must also, according to the doctrine of Christ and His apostles, be shunned and avoided by all the members of the church, (particularly by those to whom his misdeeds are known), whether it be in eating or drinking, or other such like social matters. In short we are to have nothing to do with him, so that we may not become defiled by involvement with him, and be partakers of his sins; but that he may be made ashamed, be effected in his mind, convinced in his conscience, and thereby induced to amend his way. (1Cor. 5:9-11; Rom. 16:17; 2 Thess. 3:14; Tit. 3:10, 11.)

That nevertheless—as well in shunning as in reproving such an offender- such moderation and Christian discretion be used, that such shunning and reproof may not be conducive to his ruin, but be serviceable to his amendment. For should he be in need, hungry, thirsty, naked, sick or visited by some other affliction, we are duty bound, according to the doctrine and practice of Christ and His apostles, to render him aid and assistance, as necessity may require; otherwise the shunning of him might be rather conducive to his ruin than to his amendment. (1 Thess. 5:14.)

Therefore we must not treat such offenders as enemies, but exhort them as brethren, in order thereby to bring them to a knowledge of their sins and to repentance; so that they may again become reconciled to God and the church, and be received and admitted into the same—thus exercising love towards them as is becoming. (2 Thess. 3:15.)

Article Eighteen: Of The Resurrection Of The Dead And The Last Judgment

As it regards the resurrection of the dead, we confess with the mouth, and believe with the heart, that according to Scripture all men who shall have died, or "fallen asleep," will—through the incomprehensible power of God—at the day of judgment, be "raised up" and made alive; and that these, together with all those who then remain alive, and who shall be "changed in a moment, in the twinkling of an eye, at the last trump," shall "appear before the judgment seat of Christ," where the good shall be separated from the bad, and where "every one shall receive the things done in his body, according to that he hath done, whether it be good or bad;" and that the good or pious shall then further, as the blessed of their Father, be received by Christ into eternal life; where they shall receive that joy which "eye hath not seen, nor ear heard, nor hath entered into the heart of man." Yea, where they shall reign and triumph with Christ forever and ever. (Matt. 22:30-32; Matt. 25:31; Dan. 12:2; Job 19:25, 26; John 5:28, 29; 1 Cor. 15:1-58; 2 Cor. 5:10; 1 Thes. 4:13; Rev. 11:12.)

And that, on the contrary, the wicked or impious, shall, as the accursed of God, be cast into "outer darkness;" yea, into eternal, hellish torments; "where their worm dieth not, and the fire is not quenched;" and where—according to Holy Scripture—they can expect no comfort nor redemption throughout eternity. (Isa. 66:24; Matt. 25:46; Mark 9:46; Rev. 14:10,11.) May the Lord through His grace make us all fit and worthy; that no such calamity may befall any of us; but that we may be "diligent, and so take heed to ourselves, that we may be found of him in peace, without spot, and blameless." Amen.

Notes

[1] Benjamin Eby, *The Origin and Doctrine of the Mennonites* (Waterloo: Markham-Waterloo Mennonite Conference, 1999), 106-20.

Appendix G

Constitution for Mennonite Christian Schools

The Old Order Mennonite school constitutions are similar in content. I have included the Markham Waterloo School Constitution and the Appendix from the Old Order constitution that lists the various committees. These committees have members from both Old Order and Markham churches.

CONSTITUTION and BY -LAWS
for
MENNONITE CHRISTIAN
SCHOOLS
of the
MARKHAM-WATERLOO
CONFERENCE
March 1973
Reprinted Jan. 1992

1. Aim

(a) To co-operate with those brethren who pioneered Christian schools in our communities.
(b) To provide facilities to educate children in regions where schools are requested by parents (conference members) where no suitable or comparable accommodation is available.

2. Purpose

Whereas God's Word places responsibility upon parents to teach their children, these schools shall assist the parents and the church by providing a setting where children may receive their education in an environment favourable to develop Christian character and inspire a faith in God.

(a) To educate children to enable them to provide for themselves and guide them to Biblical truths.

(b) To shield them from the erring teachings of evolution and false science theories.

(c) To protect them from ungodly practices and teachings such as family planning which creates disrespect for life and God's creation.

3. Administration

(a) The school shall be under the jurisdiction of the Conference ministry.

(b) A school board of three brethren as trustees (not restricted to conference members) shall be elected by the brotherhood in the immediate area or district for each school.

(c) Trustees shall be persons whose life, conduct and faith can be approved by the conference.

(d) The board shall consist of chairman, assistant chairman and secretary-treasurer, serving for three-year terms. First term to be for three years, two years and one year, to alternate expiry date, with terms to expire at year-end.

(e) The board members shall not be subject for immediate re-election except secretary-treasurers whose office may be extended at the discretion of the board but not to exceed two terms.

(f) Board offices shall be filled by board members elected from the board.

(g) The chairman shall call and preside at an Annual meeting and all other meetings as required or practised.

(h) The secretary-treasurer shall keep records of all activities and meetings of the board, serve as correspondent, keep accurate records of all finances and present a financial report and budget to the local deacon immediately after the calendar year-end.

4. Supervision

The board shall supervise all school operations in conjunction with conference ministry.
(a) Hire teachers, caretaker and purchase necessary supplies.
(b) Purchase text books and other literature and prepare a curriculum acceptable and agreeable with teachers and other schools operated within the conference with special emphasis on singing and usage of the English language in classroom and playground.
(c) In the event of discipline or other problems the board shall assist teachers in finding a scriptural solution suggesting actions to parents where deemed necessary .
(d) Board members of all schools operated by conference, teachers, and conference ministry should conduct an annual mid-term session for sharing problems and experiences.

5. Qualifications Of Teachers

Teachers shall be sound in faith and doctrines, apt to teach, be an example of Christian life of separation from the world in plain and modest attire, attempt to maintain proper discipline using the Word of God to comply with the standards of the church.

6. Qualifications Of Pupils

(a) Pupils shall be dressed modestly and sensibly, having their bodies properly covered.
(b) Short skirts, slacks, jeans and cut hair are not permitted for girls.
(c) Boys shall dress modestly and decently: sleeveless shirts, tight body-fitting clothes, cowboy type hats, etc. are not permitted. Filthy and immoral language shall not be allowed.
(d) Pupils are expected to develop obedience and respect toward the teacher, other students and the general public.
(e) Any students conforming to these standards are welcome and acceptable at these schools as space is available.

7. Duties Of Teachers

(a) Teach curriculum provided by the board.

(b) Keep records as the Department of Education or other authorities may require.
(c) Have daily devotions with pupils involved, with guidance from the ministry.
(d) Encourage each student to study for his or her own personal benefit.
(e) Guard against the spirit of pride in pupils, by incentives used to encourage concentration on lessons with special emphasis to encourage those who are not able to attain the highest rewards, thereby creating a spirit of preferring one another in love.
(f) In the event that discipline becomes a problem, after informing parents, shall have the full right to report the matter to the board.

8. Responsibilities Of Parents

(a) See that children meet qualifications as set out above.
(b) Support the school programme through prayer, moral and financial support and attendance at school meetings, etc.
(c) The transportation of pupils is the full responsibility of parents thereby encouraging attendance at local schools.
(d) In event of discipline or other problem, the parents shall pledge their full support to the teacher before considering the complaint of the child.

9. Ministering Brethren

Ministering Brethren should occasionally visit schools to give encouragement to teachers and pupils.

10. Finances

(a) The original cost of schools shall be borne by church through offerings.
(b) The cost of running our school system is paid through free-will church offerings sponsored by the deacons who will reimburse the various boards for the same.
(c) The cost of having non-conference pupils in our schools shall be adjusted in all fairness to the ones involved.
Note! Section 10 may be revised according to need and experience after three years.

11. School Properties

Shall be the property of Markham-Waterloo Conference. In case of loss or damage by fire or storm the Mennonite Aid Ordinance shall cover damages.

12. Amendments

To this constitution may be made when deemed necessary only with a quorum (two-thirds of Conference ministry) approving.

13. Other Decisions

Also need at least a two-thirds majority of members present, excepting board member elections which need only a simple majority.

14. Teaching Encouragement

It is agreed that we should encourage our people to teach at these schools, if such persons display the necessary abilities, ambition and interest. We encourage our youth, as well as older people, that this is an opportunity to use your talent in the service and work of the church, and its future welfare.

Various committees and other appointments are made from time to time as the needs arise. Valuable support and assistance is provided through the following:

(i) Book Committee—This nine-member committee is responsible for the provision of schoolbooks and curriculum materials.

(ii) Summer School Committee—These seven experienced teachers plan and organize the agenda for the annual two week teachers' classes. They also arrange student teaching for beginning teachers and assist in setting up teacher teams.

(iii) Teacher Teams—Teachers with ten years or more experience are teamed up with those with less experience. These senior partners are responsible to provide moral and academic support for their junior partners. The senior partner is expected to make several classroom visits in a school term.

(iv) Standardized Test Team—Three appointed people with previous teaching experience administer standardized tests throughout all schools once a year. Most of these tests were prepared as a standardized test of basic skills for elementary schools across Canada. These tests help to objectively measure our pupils' and teachers' performance.

(v) Teachers' Meeting Committee—A committee of five teachers plan and organize teachers' meetings and appoint another committee for the next teachers' meeting.

(vi) Travelling Library Committee—This committee is responsible for the maintenance of the travelling libraries which rotate among the schools.

Glossary

Brotherhood: In the traditional German, *Gemeinde* means brotherhood. One meaning of the English word church is synonymous to the German word *Kirche* which the Old Orders identify as the place of worship of the mainline churches, and they refer to the people as *Kirchelied.* Because of this, the second English definition of church, meaning the congregation, has mixed connotations for the Old Order people. To them brotherhood connotes more the traditional German *Gemeinde.*

Call: At the time of baptism every Old Order man acknowledges the ninth article of their confession and promises to accept the "call" of serving the church in the ministry if in years to come he should be chosen. At the time of their baptism, the women are asked to promise to support their future husbands if they are called into the ministry. There is little space for one to decline. To the Old Order the "call" is from God, not man.

Erntefest: German for the Old Order Harvest Meeting, which is their official Thanksgiving Day.

Frema Geisht: The teaching of eternal security generated an audacious air amongst its adherents, which rankled the traditional Old Order thought of humility. Boldness in Christ was strange to them, as were the teachings of dispensationalism and modern premillennialism. These different doctrines were labelled as the *Frema Geisht.* This new teaching in the Old Orders' minds had little in common with their traditional Gelassenheit.

Gelassenheit: Gelassenheit is a word for which there is no English equivalent. It refers to an attitude that is ready to yield, abandon, or surrender personal desires before God and the community. Not only does Gelassenheit shape the Old Order understanding of salvation, it shapes everyday life in the community.

Inquiry: The inquiry is an assembly of the ordained body and those who are nominated for the expected ordination. At the inquiry the candidates (those who are nominated) are questioned if they are willing to submit to the order of the brotherhood, Gelassenheit, and accept the "call." On rare occasions individuals have withdrawn their names, but this is not an acceptable practice.

Lot: It is a very solemn and binding ordinance, based on Acts 1:24-26, which is used to select the person to be ordained. The Old Order consider it wrong to question the results of the lot because for them the lot is God's.

Ordnung: The word Ordnung was introduced into the Old Order community via Amish and historical writings. The Waterloo Old Orders traditionally used the word "order." The German meaning of Ordnung evades a simple English definition. In broad terms, Ordnung means a set of rules and orders of the church that are covered with a sacred shroud. Not that the Mennonites would consider the Ordnung sacred, yet a violation against the Ordnung brings upon the offender similar repercussions as a transgression against the Word. An Old Order Amish bishop wrote, "The Ordnung is God's example of the universe—nobody doubts the time of sunrise or sunset, nobody argues the timing of the moon."[1] In other words: God is a God of order, therefore there is need of an Ordnung to avoid confusion among the members and also to give a consistent example to the world. To an outsider Ordnung appears to be bondage or the law of the Old Testament, but to those who have learned to love and respect the Ordnung, it presents more freedom, more privileges, and more peace than can be obtained outside the brotherhood.

Peace Churches: Mennonites, Amish, Tunkers, and all churches professing non-resistance.

Penn's Holy Experiment: Penn's "holy experiment" was the Quaker administration under which the Quakers tried to govern the state (Pennsylvania) by Biblical values and tried to avoid the use of the militia. This was the first state to advocate religious freedom to other denominations.

Scotch-Irish: The Scotch-Irish were a group of people who came from Ireland but were of Scottish descent and settled more in the back woods.
Testimony: Giving testimony means to acknowledge that one is in agreement with what was said, and to make further brief comments regarding the messages spoken by both speakers at a worship service.
Time: The Old Order "time" was the Sunday night youth gathering. The youth sang hymns at first but later spent some time playing ring games, and there were simple forms of dancing. This dancing should not be compared with a public dance where alcoholic beverages are the norm. Although the "wild" boys may have had a few drinks, the girls did not. The "times," although questionable, were in general a sober social event. After World War II these youth gathering became known as "singings."
Umfrag: German for council meeting. This is a very important function of the Old Order Mennonite circles. It is the congregation's opportunity to have church input.

Notes

[1] Theron F. Schlabach, *Peace, Faith, Nation* (Scottdale, PA: Herald Press, 1988), 210.

BIBLIOGRAPHY

Abbreviations

AS—Alternative Service
CGUC—Conrad Grebel University College
CHPC—Conference of Historic Peace Churches
CO—Conscientious Objector
MBC—Mennonite Brethren in Christ
ME—Mennonite Encyclopaedia
MHS—Mennonite Historical Society of Ontario
MQR—Mennonite Quarterly Review
OHS—Ontario Historical Society
NRMA—National Resources Mobilizations Act
SS—Selective Service
WHS—Waterloo County Historical Society
WB—World book Encyclopaedia

Bauman, Angus. Diary, 1933-1954. Leonard Freeman collection. Elmira, Ontario.

Bauman, Brent. *Forged Anew.* Floradale, Ontario: Floradale Mennonite Church, 1996.

Bauman, James. *Journal of the Center for Pennsylvania German Studies.* Millersville University. 7 no. 4: 5.

Bean, Isaac. "Three Generations Tell of Bethel Church." Kitchener, Ontario: Waterloo Historical Society, 1983.

Bearinger, Noah. "No Spears of Iron." *Family Life* (June and July 1986): 29-32.

Bearinger Noah M. Letter to Thomas Reesor, December 5, 1918. Leonard Freeman personal collection.

Bechtel, Ken. *Three Score Years.* Elmira, Ontario: Bauman Printing, 1984.

Bergy, Lorna. Conversation with Author, 1998.

Bible, King James Version.

Bloomfield, Elizabeth. *Waterloo Township Through two Centuries.* Kitchener, Ontario: Waterloo Historical Society, 1995.

Boehm, M.S. *History of the Boehm Family.* Kitchener, Ontario: Waterloo Historical Society, 1936.

Boettner, Loraine. *The Millennium.* Philadelphia, PA.: The Presbyterian and Reformed Publishing Company, 1957.

Bricker, I.C. *The History of Waterloo Township up to 1825.* Kitchener: Waterloo Historical Society, 1934.

Brubacher, Abner. Monthly Newsletter. Eagle Wings Discipleship Ministries, Aug. 2001.

Brubacher, Barbara. Autobiography. N.p, n.d. Author's collection.

Brubacher, Glenn. "The Frema Geisht." Unpublished college essay, n.d. Author's collection.

Brubacher, Emanuel. Conversation with Author, 1995.

Burkholder, L. J. *A Brief History of the Mennonites in Ontario.* Altona Manitoba: Friesen Printers, 1986.

Clarke, Adam. *Clarke's Commentary.* New York: Abingdon Press, no date.

Conference Reports. "Discussions of the Preachers and Deacons of the Mennonite Parishes in the County of Waterloo containing the Resolutions Passed at the Semi-Annual Conference." Compiled and translated by Isaac Horst. Conference held in Berlin (Kitchener), Ontario, 1842-1890. Author's collection.

Cressman, Kenneth, "The Development of the Conservative Mennonite Church of Ontario." Unpublished college essay, no date. Manuscript #70113845 at CGUC.

Cronk, Sandra. "Gelassenheit : The Rites of the Redemptive Progress in Old Order Amish and Old Order Mennonite Communities." MQR (1981): 5-44.

Driver, John. *Radical Faith: An Alternative History of the Christian Church.* Kitchener, Ontario: Pandora Press, 1999.

Dyck, Cornelius J. *An Introduction to Mennonite History.* Scottdale, PA: Herald Press, 1981.

Dyck, Peter & Elfrieda. *Up From The Rubble.* Scottdale, PA: Herald Press, 1991.

Eby, Benjamin. *Origin and Doctrine of the Mennonites.* Markham-Waterloo Mennonite Conference, 1999.

Eby, Elias. Diary 1872-78. Isaac Horst trans., CGUC.

Enns, Gerhard. *Waterloo North and Conscription 1917.* Kitchener: Waterloo Historical Society, 1963.

Enns, Herb. Conversation with Author. Waterloo, Ontario, 1985.

Epp, Frank H. *Mennonites in Canada* I. Toronto: Macmillan of Canada, 1974.

———. *Mennonites in Canada* II. Toronto: Macmillan Canada, 1982.

Fast, Gilbert, Galen A. Peters, and Joe A. Springer. *Biblical Concordance of the Swiss Brethren, 1540.* Kitchener, Ontario: Pandora Press, 2001.

Fletcher, George B. "The Millennium What it is NOT and What it IS." Pamphlet, Berachah Baptist Church, Hampton, VA, no date.

Friedmann, Robert. *Mennonite Piety Through the Centuries Its Genius and Its Literature.* Scottdale, PA: Herald Press, 1980.

Freeman, Leonard. Papers, Elmira.

Fretz, J. C. "The Early History of the Mennonites in Welland County ON." MQR (January 1953): 55-75.

Fretz, W.M. "The First Mennonite Church Vineland 1801-2001 Bicentennial." Vineland: N.p., n.d.

Fretz, Winfield J. *The Waterloo Mennonites: A Community in Paradox.* Waterloo, Ontario: Wilfrid Laurier University Press, 1989.

Funk, Henry. *Restitution or an Explanation of Several Principal Points of the Law,* English translation. Elkhart, Indiana: Mennonite Publishing Counpany, 1980.

Gingerich, Melvin. *Service for Peace.* Scottdale, PA: Herald Press, 1949.

Good, Abner. Letter to Frank Epp, Apr. 23, 1975. CGUC Archives.

Good, Milton, R. *Folklore of Waterloo County.* Waterloo, ON: Waterloo Historical Society, 1981.

Good, Reginald E. *Frontier Community to Urban Congregation: First Mennonite Church, Kitchener 1813-1988.* Kitchener: First Mennonite Church, 1988. (The 1889 division account is well illustrated in this book.)

Guillet, Edwin C. *Early Life in Upper Canada.* Toronto: University of Toronto Press, 1963.

Haldane, Elizabeth Anna. *The Historical Geography of Waterloo Township, 1800-1835.* M.A. Thesis, McMaster University, 1963.

Hansard Records: "Health, Welfare and Social Affairs." October 18, 1973.

Heick, W.H. *The Lutherans of Waterloo County During World War I.* Kitchener: Waterloo Historical Society, 1962.

Heise, D.W. Letter to S.F. Coffman, July 5, 1918. CGUC Archives.

Hershberger, Guy F. *War, Peace & Nonresistance.* Scottdale, PA: Herald Press, 1981.

Hoover, Amos B. *The Jonas Martin Era.* Denver, PA: Muddy Creek Library, 1982.

Hoover, Anson. Conversation with Author. Carthage, Ontario, 1990.

Horst, Isaac R. "Mennogespräch." *MHS of Ontario* 6: 2 (1988).

———. *Close Ups of the Great Awakening.* Mount Forest, Ontario: Isaac R. Horst, 1985.

———. Conference records compiled and published by Isaac R. Horst. Author's collection.

——— trans. "Persecution Against Daniel Hoch." Author's collection, CGUC, 1984.

Janzen, William and Frances Greaser. *Sam Martin Went to Prison: A Story of Conscientious Objection in Canada and Military Service.* Winnipeg, Manitoba: Kindred Press, 1990.

Janzen, William. *Limits on Liberty.* Toronto: University of Toronto Press, 1990.

Juhnke, James C. *Vision, Doctrine, War.* Scottdale, PA: Herald Press, 1989.

Kauffman, Daniel. *Doctrines of the Bible.* Scottdale, PA: Herald Press, 1928.

Keith, Fern. "More Pioneer Hamlets of York." *Canadian-German Folklore* 9 (1985).

Klaassen, Walter. *Anabaptism: Neither Catholic nor Protestant.* Waterloo, Ontario: Conrad Press, 1973.

MacMaster, Horst, and Ulle. *Conscience in Crisis.* Scottdale, PA: Herald Press, 1979.

MacMaster, Richard K. *Land, Piety, Peoplehood.* Scottdale, PA: Herald Press, 1985.

Martin Abraham. Unpublished manuscript, no title. Author's collection, CGUC, ca. 1998.

Martin, Charlotte. "My Relatives, Ultra-Conservative Mennonites." *Ontario Mennonite History* XVI, 1998, 1-7.

Martin, David M. *Wallenstein Bible Chapel.* Wallenstein, Ontario: Wallenstein Bible Chapel, 1968.

Martin, Elizabeth. Diary. Waterloo, 1935-1937. Author's collection.

Martin, Ezra. "Mennonite Settlement 1887-1915 May City, Iowa." Waterloo, Ontario, Author's collection, 1983.

Martin, Isaac. Diary. Waterloo, Ontario, 1936-40, CGUC.

———. Letters, conference reports and diary extracts. Translated from the German, Author's collection, 1962.

———. "Origin of the Mennonites." Unpublished manuscript. Waterloo, Ontario: Author's collection, 1960.

Martin, Jason. "Christian and Ells Martin: Immigrant Patriarch and Matriarch." *Pennsylvania Mennonite Heritage* (July 1987).

Martin, John. Telephone Conversation with Author. Tavistock, Ontario, 1999.

Martin, Levi P. Deacon records 1873-1915. CGUC Mennonite Archives.

Martin, Noah. Conversations with Author, 1990.

Martin, Urias. Family papers, 1910-1950. Alma, Ontario, Aaron Martin collection.

McLaughlin, Kenneth. *Cows and Town Life: Berlin in the 1870s* Kitchener: Waterloo Historical Society, 1987.

MCC files. Letters and legal documents, 1966-1977. Box CCP, Kitchener, ON.

Mennonite Encyclopaedia. Scottdale, PA: The Mennonite Publishing House, 1955.

Moyer, Carson. *The Mountain Church at Campden.* Kitchener: Mennonite Historical Society, March 1986.

Newswanger, Rachel. *Undaunted Venture from Ontario to Michigan.* Kutztown, PA: Rod and Staff Publishers Inc., 2000.

Nigh, Harold. *The Lost Tribes of the Niagara Plain Folk.* Kitchener: MHS, Sept 1986.

Noonan, Gerald. *The Local Mentality: A History beyond Words.* Kitchener: Waterloo Historical Society, 1980.

Orthodox Mennonite Church Directory. Third Edition, 2001. 43067 Howich-Turnberry Rd. ON. N0G 2X0.

Panabaker, D.N. *Statement of Losses, Block 2 Residents , War of 1812.* Kitchener: Waterloo Historical Society, 1928.

———. *Historical Sketch of the Clemens Family.* Kitchener: Waterloo Historical Society, 1921.

———. *Glimpses of the Industrial Activities of Waterloo County About Fifty Years Ago.* Kitchener: Waterloo Historical Society, 1933.

Regehr, T. D. *Mennonites in Canada 1939-1970: A People Transformed.* Toronto: University of Toronto Press, 1996.

Preston, Richard A., Sydney F. Wise, and Herman O. Werner. *Men in Arms.* New York, Washington: Frederick A. Praeger, Publishers, 1962.

Reaman, G. Elmore. *The Trail of the Black Walnut.* Scottdale, PA: Herald Press, 1957.

Rudy, Elizabeth. "History of the Brubacher Church." Author's collection, N.p., 1958.

Ruth, John L. *Conrad Grebel Son of Zurich.* Scottdale, PA: Herald Press, 1975.

———. *Maintaining the Right Fellowship.* Scottdale, PA: Herald Press, 1984.

———. *The Earth is the Lord's.* Scottdale, PA: Herald Press, 2001.

———. *Twas Seeding Time.* Scottdale, PA: Herald Press, 1976.

Schlabach, Theron F. *Gospel Versus Gospel.* Scottdale, PA: Herald Press, 1980.

———. *Peace, Faith, Nation.* Scottdale, PA: Herald Press, 1988.

———. "Reveille For Die Stillen Im Lande: A Stir Among Mennonites In The Late Nineteenth Century." MQR (1977): 213-25.

Schweitzer, Vera, Wilfrid and Olive. *Canadian-German Folklore* 5. Kitchener: Pennsylvania Folklore Society, 1975.

Scott F.S Letter to Coffman S.F. Conrad Grebel University College Archives, June 25, 1918.

Shantz, Ervin. Conversations with Author and records from parochial schools.

Shantz, Menno. "Adventures in Colonization." Unpublished manuscript written by J.Y. Shantz's son. Grace Schmidt Local History Room of the Kitchener Public Library, Kitchener, Ontario.

Sherk, A.B. *Recollections of Early Waterloo*. Kitchener: Waterloo Historical Society, 1915.

Sherk, Amos. Conversations with Author, 1990s.

Sherk, Abraham. *Excerpts of Letters from Abraham Sherk*. Kitchener Public Library, Waterloo Historical Society, 1959.

Shirk, Peter. *Family History of Peter Shirk*. N.p., 1984.

Shirk, Peter. Letters to Jacob Mensch in Skippack, PA, 1893-1904. Author's collection.

Simons, Menno. *The Complete Writings of Menno Simons*. Scottdale, PA: Herald Press, 1966.

Smith, Clarence. Letter. Waterloo, Ontario, ca. 1990. Author's collection.

Steiner, Samuel J. *Vicarious Pioneer: The Life of Jacob Y. Shantz*. Winnipeg, MB: Hyperion Press Limited, 1988.

———. "Effects of the 1870s New Mennonite Division on Bloomingdale Mennonite Church" MHS, XV vol 1 (Apr. 1997).

Swalm, E. J. *Non-resistance Under Test*. Nappanee, IN: E.V. Publishing House, 1938.

———. Conversation with Author. Collingwood, Ontario, ca. 1985.

Toews, J. A. *Alternative Service in Canada during World War II*. Winnipeg, MB: Christian Press Ltd., 1959.

Unruh, Heinrich. "Autobiography of our father and Grandfather Heinrich Unruh Teacher, Preacher and Elder of the Halbstaedter Mennonite Church (congregation) South Russia" Author's collection, 1917.

Van Braght, Thielman J. *Martyrs Mirror: The Story of Seventeen Centuries of Christian Martyrdom, From the Time of Christ to A.D. 1660*. Joseph F. Strohm trans. Scottdale, PA: Herald Press, 1950.

Weaver, John. English translation of a letter dated Dec. 5, 1871.

Weber, Eldon D. *A Historical History of Waterloo Township by Ezra E. Eby*. Kitchener Public Library: Eldon D. Weber, 1984.

Weber, Samuel. English translation of Weber's letters. Waterloo, Ontario, 1965. Author's collection.

Weiler, Lloyd M. "An Introduction to Old Order Mennonite Origins in Lancaster County, Pennsylvania: 1893 to 1993." *Pennsylvania Mennonite Heritage* (Oct. 1993).

Williams, Neville. *Milestones of History.* New York: Newsweek Books, 1974.

Wilson, Lesslie C. Letter to L. J. Burkholder. Conrad Grebel University College Archives, July 5, 1918.

Wenger, J. C. "Documents on the Daniel Brenneman Division." MQR (January, 1960): 48-60.

Woolwich Township Archives. Municipal drain No. 1, 1907 to present.

Woolwich Township Archives. Township minutes 1900-1914.

World Book Encyclopaedia. World book Inc., 1985

Index

About Pandora Press

Pandora Press is a small, independently owned press dedicated to making available modestly priced books that deal with Anabaptist, Mennonite, and Believers Church topics, both historical and theological. We welcome comments from our readers.

Visit our full-service online Bookstore:
www.pandorapress.com

Karl Koop. *Anabaptist-Mennonite Confessions of Faith: the Development of a Tradition*. (forthcoming 2003)
Softcover. ISBN 1-894710-32-0

Mary A. Schiedel. *Pioneers in Ministry: Women Pastors in Ontario Mennonite Churches, 1973-2003*. (2003)
Softcover, 204 pp. ISBN 1-894710-35-5

Harry Loewen, ed. *Shepherds, Servants and Prophets*. (2003)
Softcover, 446 pp. ISBN 1-894710-31-2

Robert A. Riall, trans., Galen A. Peters, ed. *The Earliest Hymns of the* Ausbund*: Some Beautiful Christian Songs Composed and Sung in the Prison at Passau, Published in 1564*. (2003)
Softcover, 473 pp., bibliography, index. ISBN 1-894710-34-7

John A. Harder. *From Kleefeld With Love*. (2003)
Softcover, 198 pp. ISBN 1-894710-28-2

John F. Peters. *The Plain People: A Glimpse at Life Among the Old Order Mennonites of Ontario*. (2003)
Softcover, 54 pp. ISBN 1-894710-26-6

Robert S. Kreider. *My Early Years: An Autobiography*. (2002)
Softcover, 600 pp., index. ISBN 1-894710-23-1

Helen Martens. *Hutterite Songs*. (2002)
Softcover, xxii, 328 pp. ISBN 1-894710-24-X

Stuart Murray. *Biblical Interpretation in the Anabaptist Tradition.* (2000)
Softcover, 310 pp. ISBN 0-9685543-3-4

Loren L. Johns, ed. *Apocalypticism and Millennialism.* (2000)
Softcover, 419 pp., indices. ISBN 0-9683462-9-4

Later Writings by Pilgram Marpeck and his Circle. Volume 1: The Exposé, A Dialogue and Marpeck's Response to Caspar Schwenckfeld. Trans. by Walter Klaassen, Werner Packull, John Rempel. (2000)
Softcover, 157 pp. ISBN 0-9683462-6-X

John Driver. *Radical Faith. An Alternative History of the Christian Church.* Carrie Snyder, ed. (1999)
Softcover, 334 pp. ISBN 0-9683462-8-6

C. Arnold Snyder. *From Anabaptist Seed. The Historical Core of Anabaptist-Related Identity.* (1999)
Softcover, 53 pp., discussion questions. ISBN 0-9685543-0-X
Also available in Spanish translation: *De Semilla Anabautista,* from Pandora Press only.

John D. Thiesen. *Mennonite and Nazi? Attitudes Among Mennonite Colonists in Latin America, 1933-1945.* (1999)
Softcover, 330 pp., 2 maps, 24 b/w illustrations, bibliography, index. ISBN 0-9683462-5-1

Lifting the Veil, a translation of *Aus meinem Leben: Erinnerungen von J.H. Janzen.* Leonard Friesen, ed.; trans. by Walter Klaassen. (1998)
Softcover, 128 pp., 4 pp. of illustrations. ISBN 0-9683462-1-9

Leonard Gross. *The Golden Years of the Hutterites,* rev. ed. (1998)
Softcover, 280 pp., index. ISBN 0-9683462-3-5

William H. Brackney, ed. *The Believers Church: A Voluntary Church.* (1998)
Softcover, viii, 237 pp., index. ISBN 0-9683462-0-0

An Annotated Hutterite Bibliography. Compiled by Maria H. Krisztinkovich; Peter C. Erb, ed. (1998)
(Ca. 2,700 entries) 312 pp., cerlox bound, electronic, or both. ISBN (paper) 0-9698762-8-9/(disc) 0-9698762-9-7

Jacobus ten Doornkaat Koolman. *Dirk Philips. Friend and Colleague of Menno Simons*. Trans. by W. E. Keeney; C. A. Snyder, ed. (1998)
Softcover, xviii, 236 pp., index. ISBN: 0-9698762-3-8

Sarah Dyck, ed. & trans. *The Silence Echoes: Memoirs of Trauma & Tears*. (1997)
Softcover, xii, 236pp., 2 maps. ISBN: 0-9698762-7-0

Wes Harrison. *Andreas Ehrenpreis and Hutterite Faith and Practice.* (1997)
Softcover, xxiv, 274 pp., 2 maps, index. ISBN 0-9698762-6-2

C. Arnold Snyder. *Anabaptist History and Theology: Revised Student Edition*. (1997)
Softcover, xiv, 466 pp., 7 maps, 28 illustrations, index, bibliography. ISBN 0-9698762-5-4

Nancey Murphy. *Reconciling Theology and Science: A Radical Reformation Perspective.* (1997)
Softcover, x, 103 pp., index. ISBN 0-9698762-4-6

C. Arnold Snyder and Linda A. Huebert Hecht, eds. *Profiles of Anabaptist Women: Sixteenth Century Reforming Pioneers*. (1996)
(Waterloo, ON: Wilfrid Laurier University Press, 1996).
Softcover, xxii, 442 pp. ISBN: 0-88920-277-X

The Limits of Perfection: A Conversation with J. Lawrence Burkholder 2nd ed., with a new epilogue by J. Lawrence Burkholder; Rodney Sawatsky and Scott Holland, eds. (1996)
Softcover, x, 154 pp. ISBN 0-9698762-2-X

C. Arnold Snyder. *Anabaptist History and Theology: An Introduction*. (1995)
Softcover, x, 434 pp., 6 maps, 29 illustrations, index, bibliography. ISBN 0-9698762-0-3

James C. Juhnke and Carol M. Hunter. *The Missing Peace: The Search for Nonviolent Alternatives in United States History*. (2001)
Softcover, 321 pp., index. ISBN 1-894710-13-4

Ruth Elizabeth Mooney. *Manual Para Crear Materiales de Educación Cristiana.* (2001)
Softcover, 206 pp. ISBN 1-894710-12-6

Esther and Malcolm Wenger, poetry by Ann Wenger. *Healing the Wounds*. (2001)
Softcover, 210 pp. ISBN 1-894710-09-6

Pedro A. Sandín Fremaint. *Cuentos y Encuentros: Hacia una Educación Transformadora.* (2001)
Softcover 163 pp ISBN 1-894710-08-8

A. James Reimer. *Mennonites and Classical Theology: Dogmatic Foundations for Christian Ethics*. (2001)
Softcover, 650 pp., index. ISBN 0-9685543-7-7

Walter Klaassen. *Anabaptism: Neither Catholic nor Protestant,* 3rd ed. (2001)
Softcover, 122 pp. ISBN 1-894710-01-0

Dale Schrag & James Juhnke, eds. *Anabaptist Visions for the new Millennium: A search for identity*. (2000)
Softcover, 242 pp. ISBN 1-894710-00-2

Harry Loewen, ed. *Road to Freedom: Mennonites Escape the Land of Suffering*. (2001)
Hardcover, large format, 302 pp. ISBN 0-9685543-5-0

Alan Kreider and Stuart Murray, eds. *Coming Home: Stories of Anabaptists in Britain and Ireland.* (2001)
Softcover, 220 pp. ISBN 0-9685543-6-9

Edna Schroeder Thiessen and Angela Showalter. *A Life Displaced: A Mennonite Woman's Flight from War-Torn Poland.* (2001)
Softcover, xii, 218 pp. ISBN 0-9685543-2-6

C. Arnold Snyder and Galen A. Peters, eds. *Reading the Anabaptist Bible: Reflections for Every Day of the Year.* Introduction by Arthur Paul Boers. (2002)
Softcover, 415 pp. ISBN 1-894710-25-8

C. Arnold Snyder, ed. *Commoners and Community. Essays in Honour of Werner O. Packull.* (2002)
Softcover, 324 pp. ISBN 1-894710-27-4

James O. Lehman. *Mennonite Tent Revivals: Howard Hammer and Myron Augsburger, 1952-1962.* (2002)
Softcover, xxiv, 318 pp., index. ISBN 1-894710-22-3

Lawrence Klippenstein and Jacob Dick. *Mennonite Alternative Service in Russia.* (2002)
Softcover, viii, 163 pp. ISBN 1-894710-21-5

Nancey Murphy. *Religion and Science.* (2002)
Softcover, 126 pp. ISBN 1-894710-20-7

Biblical Concordance of the Swiss Brethren, 1540. Trans. by Gilbert Fast and Galen Peters; introduction by Joe Springer; C. Arnold Snyder, ed. (2001)
Softcover, lv, 227 pp., index. ISBN 1-894710-16-9

Orland Gingerich. *The Amish of Canada.* (2001)
Softcover, 244 pp., index. ISBN 1-894710-19-3

M. Darrol Bryant. *Religion in a New Key.* (2001)
Softcover, 136 pp., bibliography. ISBN 1-894710-18-5

Sources of South German/Austrian Anabaptism. Trans. by Walter Klaassen, Frank Friesen, Werner O. Packull; C. Arnold Snyder, ed. (2001)
Softcover, 430 pp., indices. ISBN 1-894710-15-0

Pedro A. Sandín Fremaint y Pablo A. Jimémez. *Palabras Duras: Homilías.* (2001)
Softcover, 121 pp. ISBN 1-894710-17-7

Pandora Press
33 Kent Avenue
Kitchener, ON
Canada N2G 3R2
Tel./Fax: (519) 578-2381
E-mail:
info@pandorapress.com
Web site:
www.pandorapress.com

Herald Press
616 Walnut Avenue
Scottdale, PA
U.S.A. 15683
Orders: (800) 245-7894
E-mail:
hp@mph.org
Web site:
www.mph.org